OUT WEST ON THE OVERLAND TRAIN

OUT WEST

O

ON THE VERLAND TRAIN

Across-the-Continent Excursion with Leslie's Magazine in 1877 and the Overland Trip in 1967

by Richard Reinhardt

THE AMERICAN WEST
PUBLISHING COMPANY
Palo Alto, California

A Word of Thanks

The author and publisher are indebted to the San Francisco Public Library and to Mr. C. A. Harvey, of Sunnyvale, California, for making available the original editions of Frank Leslie's Illustrated Newspaper *from which the pictures in this book were reproduced.*

In editing and footnoting the Leslie articles, we have drawn on the resources of the Joslyn Museum of Omaha, the Chicago Historical Society, the Cheyenne County (Nebraska) Historical Society, the Library of the University of California at Berkeley, the Southern Pacific Railroad, the Union Pacific Railroad, the Nevada State Museum, the Denver Public Library, the Chicago Sun-Times, *the Chicago* Daily News, *the Virginia City* Territorial Enterprise, *and the Sidney (Nebraska)* Telegraph. *We owe much of the biographical information on the Leslies to Madeleine B. Stern's unique biography of Mrs. Frank Leslie (*Purple Passage, *Norman, Oklahoma, 1953).*

Among the many persons who made essential contributions to this volume were Roger Olmsted, who conceived the idea; Tom Watkins, who gathered the scattered materials; John Beyer, who designed the book; and Helen Hosmer, who typed the manuscript. They left little for the authors, 1877 and 1967, to do except ride the overland train, enjoy the scenery, and jot down occasional comments on the quality of the cooking.

R.W.R.

For Eloise Rathbone Reinhardt

Before Climbing Aboard ...

THIS IS THE STORY of three journeys to the West. The first began on an April evening in 1877 with the pop of champagne corks and the crackle of fireworks. It lasted five months, cost a fortune, and generated an outburst of illustrated articles that ran for almost two years in one of the country's leading weeklies. Although transcontinental railroad travel was something of a novelty at the time, this Grand Tour would never be surpassed: the classic first encounter between the elegant snobs of Fifth Avenue and the western wilderness of the overland route.

The second was a quiet trip in the dead of winter in 1967. It was a wistful, rather furtive journey, undertaken at a time when economists and engineers were saying that railroad passenger travel was an outgrown style of transportation that could not survive another decade. As an historic event, it neither attracted publicity nor established precedent, but it did prove that the trains are still running, whatever you may have heard.

The third, which can be found only between the lines, is the journey of the overland train through the history of the American West. If the economists and engineers are right, the story is almost over, and chapters 1877 and 1967 stand near the beginning and the end.

In 1877, when Frank Leslie made his splashy railroad excursion from New York to the Pacific Coast, the United States was just a year past its hundredth anniversary, and the transcontinental track had been open for less than a decade. The western railroads were luring landless immigrants from Central Europe. The state of Nebraska was only ten years old; Colorado, only one. The Dakotas, Arizona, New Mexico, Wyoming, and Utah had not yet been admitted to the Union. The gold rush to the Black Hills, which had occasioned the final uprising of the Sioux, was still underway, and California, now a mature state thirty years old, was trembling at the brink of its second great real estate boom — the Southern California bubble of the early eighties.

Leslie, a practical man, put his trip to a number of uses. As he told reporters along the way, he hoped to combine business with pleasure and enjoy the vacation in California while sending back pictures and articles to New York. To this end he had brought along not only his wife and her Skye terrier, Follette, but also two close friends and half a dozen staff writers and artists from *Frank Leslie's Illustrated Newspaper*. He was quite at the service of the railroads: advising emigration to Nebraska, plugging tourism, helping to restore the confidence of travelers who had been frightened by a disastrous wreck the previous December on the Michigan Southern Railroad at Ashtabula, Ohio. And the railroads undoubtedly repaid his services with transportation and hotel accommodations.

But the transcontinental excursion was more than a nineteenth century publicity junket. It was good copy. Although the West had been described abundantly to magazine readers in the East, it remained of compelling interest. Seen from the window of a train, every shanty and snowshed on the old Overland Trail had new significance. *This* West was no longer a distant region that one could reach only at risk of death, but a new national plaything to be enjoyed on a summer vacation. The Grand Tour to the Pacific obviously was feasible. Could it also be comfortable?

The Leslies took on the job of scouting the route. Sipping oyster soup in their private Pullman Palace Car, scattering handouts to Indian squaws on the station platforms, gossiping with San Francisco millionaires at the Palace Hotel, they blazed a trail for thousands of later tourists.

Few others would travel in such magnificence. But for Leslie and his decorative, vivacious wife, conspicuous consumption and personal publicity were natural functions. Leslie, a robust, heavily bearded man with a peppery temper and a salty tongue, was the founder and publisher of a chain of popular magazines, most of which carried his name in the title. Not all of them were respectable, and some were so short-lived they hardly could be called periodicals; but the best of them had paid him richly in prestige as well as money. Like many publishers, he had become a newsmaker as well as a news reporter.

Born in Ipswich, England, on March 29, 1821, Leslie was the son of a prosperous glove manufacturer, and had been marked for a career in business. He was more interested in art, however, and developed a precocious talent for wood engraving. To hide his work from his father, who disapproved of such frivolity, he used a pen-name instead of his real name, Henry Carter. As "Frank Leslie," he finally deserted the family glove counter in 1841, married a young woman named Sarah Ann Welham, and went to work as an engraver for a newly established, excitingly different newspaper — the *Illustrated London News*.

The *Illustrated London News* was the first paper of its kind in the world. After working for a while in the engraving department, Leslie took charge of all picture production. For six years he explored the new field of illustrated journalism, then as uncharted as television reporting would be a century later. In 1848, having mastered the fundamentals of magazine graphics, he emigrated to the United States with his wife and three sons and set up shop as an engraver in New York. He prepared engravings for *Gleason's Pictorial Drawing-Room Companion* (a Boston monthly), illustrated elaborate programs for Jenny Lind's American tour under the sponsorship of P. T. Barnum, and turned out cuts for Barnum's short-lived (New York) *Illustrated News*.

In January, 1854, Leslie started the first of his own publishing ventures — *Leslie's Ladies' Gazette of Fashion*, a pictorial encyclopedia of the "fancy work" that women stitched prodigiously in the years just before the Civil War. A year later, he brought out the *New York Journal of Romance*; in December, 1855, came the *Illustrated Newspaper*; and in 1859, the *Budget of Fun*.

Leslie's acknowledged ambition was to produce "mental pabulum" for all classes of society. He aimed publications at every level of age and interest. There was *Frank Leslie's Chimney Corner*, his *Lady's Magazine*, his *Lady's Journal*, his *Boy's and Girl's Weekly*, his *Sunday Magazine*, his *Chatterbox*, his *Pleasant Hours*, his *Boys of America*, his *Jolly Joker*, his *Illustrated Almanac*, and his *Comic Almanac*. In addition, he produced a number of other magazines to which, for one reason or another, he did not affix his name.

The most successful of all was the *Illustrated Newspaper*, which is still esteemed among collectors for the technical and artistic excellence of its engravings. At its best, the *Illustrated Newspaper* compared favorably with the publications of Leslie's great rivals, the Harper brothers. Well printed, stylishly written, and carefully edited, it is readable to this day. Text was used primarily to support pictures of sensational events. Leslie had devised a method to speed up the slow process of engraving by dividing large wood blocks into twenty or thirty small sections and assigning each piece to a separate engraver. Two dozen engravers could complete overnight a double-page illustration that would have taken a single engraver weeks. Thus, murders, executions, prize fights, political debates, and natural disasters could be recorded pictorially almost as fast as they were verbally.

Just before the outbreak of the Civil War, Leslie hired a distinguished archeologist named Ephraim George Squier to do a series of articles on Central America, which Squier knew first-hand as a diplomat and explorer. Squier soon became editor of the *Illustrated Newspaper*. At about the same time, Leslie separated from his wife, Sarah Ann, and moved in with Squier and his gray-eyed, golden-haired, 25-year-old wife, Miriam.

The Squier house on East 10th Street, Manhattan, was a strange menage, and its occupants, according to slanderous reports, were an unholy trinity. But for several years it was a rewarding residence for a lonely publisher. And beautiful Mrs. Squier found a place for herself as editress of *Frank Leslie's Chimney Corner* and *Frank Leslie's Lady's Magazine*.

The chaotic sixties, tragic for the nation, were years of triumph for the Leslie magazines. Leslie's on-the-spot coverage of the Civil War was a significant advance in pictorial journalism. During the Reconstruction period, his six major magazines waxed fat. Single editions sometimes ran as large as 500,000 copies. New magazines appeared every year. Even Leslie's domestic arrangements improved. He succeeded in 1872 in obtaining a divorce from Sarah Ann Welham Leslie, and two years later he married Mrs. Squier.

Miriam Folline Peacock Squier had been born in New Orleans around 1836. She apparently was of Creole ancestry; but the neglect of her father and mother, Charles and Susan Danforth Follin(e), to get legally married cast a shade of ambiguity on her origins. As Mrs. Frank Leslie, she was rumored to be the illegitimate daughter of the King of Belgium, of a New York parlor-house madame, of a circus rider, or of a Negro slave. She had grown up in the old French Quarter of New Orleans, and her father had coached her in the foreign languages that she later flung around with high éclat. At 17 she had a brief marriage, apparently of the shotgun variety, to a jeweler's clerk named David Peacock, and after that union had been annulled, she toured for a time with Lola Montez as "Minnie Montez, Lola's little sister." She married Squier, who was making a name as a railroad entrepreneur in Central America, in 1857.

The Squire-Leslie wedding took place in the fashionable St. Thomas Church on Fifth Avenue. The bride wore a diamond solitaire as large as her knuckle. She was 38, coppery-haired, and regarded herself as "a mere child." Leslie was 53, ruddy, white-bearded, and stout, but manifestly an adequate match for her. A month after the ceremony, the new Mrs. Leslie gave testimony that was instrumental in committing her brilliant and versatile former husband, Squier, to an insane asylum on Long Island—one of the very institutions that Leslie had denounced in the *Illustrated News* as extralegal lockups for innocent persons who had caused annoyance to rich relatives.

The national centennial in 1876 came at the peak of Leslie's fortunes. His publishing business occupied a five-story building on Pearl Street in lower Manhattan. He had three or four hundred employees and the supply of postage stamps on hand often totaled $300,000. Still, both Leslie and his wife found time to take over collateral social arrangements for the Exposition in Philadelphia. Leslie was New York State commissioner, and his fellow commissioners from other states elected him president. He constructed a Frank Leslie Pavilion and stocked it with bound copies of all his periodicals for the entertainment of visitors. When Dom Pedro II, the Emperor of Brazil, came to the United States to see the fair, the Leslies entertained him at their town quarters on Fifth Avenue and at their baroque summerhouse, "Interlaken," at Saratoga.

The "Frank Leslie Excursion to the Pacific Coast" was to mark a still higher pinnacle in their social and journalistic eminence. Although they had come late to the task of exploring the West, they could bring to it a flamboyance that would have impressed even Captain Frémont. More than a hundred friends gathered at Grand Central Depot to see them off. Porters loaded hampers of fruit and champagne into a Wagner Drawing-Room Car that had been renamed for the occasion "The Frank Leslie." Torpedoes exploded under the wheels; Follette, the Skye terrier, yelped; and whistles sounded along the New York Central track as the great transcontinental journey began.

Frank Leslie's Illustrated Newspaper carried long dispatches on the trip from July, 1877, until late 1878, when the series trickled out in a dribble of vignettes from Southern California. The engravings were cut from drawings by two young artists, Walter R. Yeager and Harry Ogden, and photographs by W. B. Austin. Leslie and his wife wrote some of the articles; the rest were by Bracebridge Hemyng, the star reporter on Leslie's juvenile magazines. Although none of the essays was signed, it is easy to recognize Hemyng's strong, poetic descriptions of prairie and mountain scenery, Leslie's hyperbolic humor, and Mrs. Leslie's self-conscious xenologisms.

Mrs. Leslie prepared, in addition to her articles, a book called *California: A Pleasure Trip from Gotham to the Golden Gate.* Published in 1877 by G. W. Carleton & Co. of New York, it is decorated with many of the sketches that also appeared in the *Illustrated Newspaper*. The book gives a reasonably savory taste of American life in the "Tragic Era," although it is strongly flavored with Mrs. Leslie's violet essence. At least one of her friends liked it enough to claim the honor of having been its ghostwriter.

The excursionists were away from New York for almost five months. After crossing the Plains with leisurely stopovers in Chicago, Cheyenne, Denver, and Salt Lake City, they spent a summer among the railroad magnates and mining speculators of San Francisco. On their return trip, they inspected the sweltering mines of the Comstock Lode and interviewed Brigham Young a few weeks before his death.

They got home to find a pack of creditors baying for Leslie's luxuriant pelt. His publications were yielding $60,000 to $100,000 a year, but his expenditures had been prodigal. The transcontinental tour had cost $15,000 above and beyond the free lodging and transportation Leslie had cadged from hotels and railroads. To satisfy his creditors, he had to put his publishing business under the supervision of a referee, impose strict limits on his personal expenses, and promise to pay off all debts within three years. He was allowed to continue as manager of the publishing house.

The following July, the Leslies suffered an even worse blow. Rollin F. Daggett, a talented and vituperative newspaper editor in Virginia City, brought out a special edition of his *Territorial Enterprise*, accusing Mrs. Leslie of being, among other things, an adventuress, a bastard, a fornicatrix, and a snob. Infuriated by her gratuitous and widely published comments about the moral atmosphere of Virginia City, Daggett had determined to take revenge on behalf of the proud little mining town. He aired the unsanctified relationship of Mrs. Leslie's parents, the details of her quickly annulled marriage to David Charles Peacock, her stage career as the putative sister of Lola Montez, her extramural liaison with a Congressman from Tennessee, her premarital affair with Leslie, and the sordid elements of Leslie's divorce from Sarah Ann Welham. Reprinted as a pamphlet, the diatribe was circulated in New York, where its racy tidbits amazed the readers of Leslie's homey periodicals. From the nature of the disclosures, Mrs. Leslie's biographers have concluded that Daggett's informant must have been the ill-used archeologist, Ephraim G. Squier.

Plagued by debts and scandal, Leslie fell sick with a fatal illness. On January 10, 1880, he died, aged 58, of cancer of the throat. With characteristic pictorial enterprise, the *Illustrated Newspaper* ran a wood engraving of his empty office, decorated with crepe and sheaves of wheat.

The office was empty only briefly. Then Miriam Leslie took over. She borrowed money to refinance the business and repaid the loan before it had run its term. She trimmed costs, suspended unsuccessful publications, and bettered Leslie's speed in covering news events, notably the assassination of President Garfield. Eventually, she had her name legally changed to Frank Leslie to protect the publications from competition and claims by Leslie's sons.

Except for her short, sterile marriage to Oscar Wilde's impotent brother, Willie, the remainder of her life was relatively orderly. In her old age, she made a diligent search of her genealogy, which convinced her she was of titled French ancestry; and thereafter she called herself the Baroness de Bazus. She was a patroness of the woman suffrage movement, and, at her death in 1914, left two million dollars to Carrie Chapman Catt for the suffragist cause. The last of the Leslie periodicals, *Leslie's Weekly*, survived until 1922, when it was merged with the now-defunct magazine, *Judge*.

When the Leslies made their journey, the train from Chicago to San Francisco took seven days, with station stops for dinner and supper, slowdowns to shoo importunate cattle off the tracks, and scenic interludes at Thousand Mile Tree, Echo Canyon, and the gorge of the American River. One had ample opportunity to observe the scenery. Still, the account that appeared in *Leslie's Illustrated Newspaper* was based on impressions from both the westbound and eastbound trips, and the same is true of the notes on modern travel that accompany each chapter.

To see the Plains by daylight nowadays, a train traveler has to create his own schedule of supper stops. The *City of San Francisco* is the only through train that follows the route taken by the Leslie excursion, and it is a swift, nocturnal traveler. It reaches Chicago at 6 P.M. daily in the charge of the Milwaukee Road; reaches Omaha, where the Union Pacific Railroad takes over, at about 3 A.M.; crosses Wyoming by day and passes into the control of the Southern Pacific at Ogden that evening; traverses Nevada and the Sierra by night; and gets to San Francisco around noon. By hopping on and off half a dozen times and taking feeder buses here and there, you can stop in all the important towns. It is an awkward way to travel, but I viewed my itinerary as a masterpiece of logistical planning. The round trip took about two weeks.

Much of the time, I sat in observation domes, roomettes, and smoking rooms with a stack of enlarged photocopies of Leslie magazine articles at my elbow, reading, deliberating, and occasionally gouging at Mrs. L.'s Queen Ann prose with a sharp, black pencil. The experience convinced me that there was no use in trying to reenact or comment upon the Leslies' journey. Following the track of historic expeditions is a literary device that works reasonably well on the route of Marco Polo, St. Paul, or Lewis and Clark; but the Leslie transcontinental excursion was not an historic expedition — it was an interlude of American social life in a style that has disappeared. The modern equivalent would not be a commemorative train trip but a luxurious vacation on a chartered jet.

Hence, my notes are related to the Leslies' story only as the *City of San Francisco* is related to the Pullman Palace Car of 1877: they follow the same track. I have had the advantage, however, of editing the Leslies' report and, to this extent, putting my own stamp upon their work. I admit to having treated their copy with more consideration for the reader than for the writers. If you object to deletions and corrections, you would do better to wade through the original in a library. I have made peremptory changes in punctuation and spelling, have grouped articles into chapters and sentences into paragraphs, have trimmed adjectival clauses by the thousands, and have weeded out a considerable number of typos, misspellings, and plain mistakes of the sort that crept into magazines of the 1870's as they do, alas, into magazines (and books) of today. I have not the slightest doubt it reads more smoothly than it did before.

As for outrageous, offensive opinions on Indians, Chinese, Mormons, Irish servants, and San Francisco dowagers, I have let the Leslies have their say. Nor have I tried to fill in their omissions.

It does seem incredible that observant journalists could have visited San Francisco in the summer of 1877, when sandlot orators were inciting anti-Chinese mobs to riot in the streets, and have reported instead upon the furnishings of Senator Sharon's veranda and the dimensions of Mrs. Stanford's dining room; but the world, obviously, consists of many worlds. One might wish that Mrs. Leslie, interviewing Brigham Young a few weeks before his death, had been less concerned with the domestic intrigues of polygamous marriage and more interested in the ultimate goals of the radical religious utopia in the Salt Lake Valley; that Frank Leslie, touring the Comstock mines, had paid less attention to the stamp mills and more to the Cornish miners; and that the entire excursion party, sight-seeing among the tragic remnants of the Plains Indians, had looked at the lives of the Cheyenne and Shoshone instead of their vermilion cosmetics. But one is grateful for the abundance and precision of the observations that *are* included.

Having recounted their overland adventures with candor and gusto, the Leslies deserve to be judged on what they wrote, not what they left out; and I humbly beg the same consideration. ☐

CONTENTS

Before Climbing Aboard 5

Chapter I THE HUDSON ROUTE—OVERNIGHT PASSAGE TO THE WEST

    1877: Poetry of Motion in a Wagner Car 12
    1967: Some Romantic Notions Left in Slowly Passing 19

Chapter II THE UNCEASING MARVEL OF CHICAGO

    1877: A Crib Gets Rid of Minnows in the Milk 20
    1967: A Great Place to Live If You're a Chevrolet 26

Chapter III WEST IN A PULLMAN HOTEL CAR

    1877: Dyspepsia Is Obsolete in a Palace on Paper Wheels 28
    1967: Take a Good Look 35

Chapter IV OMAHA—FRONTIER AT MID-CONTINENT

    1877: Six-Shooters, Bogus Lockets, and Farms for $40 Down Payment 37
    1967: The Night-Life of Ahamo 42

Chapter V THE FABULOUS, FEATURELESS VALLEY OF THE PLATTE

    1877: Tripods and Linen Dusters Astound the Westerners 44
    1967: What Became of Plum Creek? 54

Chapter VI THE HARD PLACES OF THE PLAINS

    1877: Indians and Emigrants—and Bitter Memories of War 56
    1967: Smile, You Are in Sidney 62

Chapter VII CHEYENNE—"HELL ON WHEELS"

    1877: Promiscuous Shooting and Cutting Is Becoming Quite Rare 64
    1967: Magic Fingers in the Old Corral 70

Chapter VIII THE DRAWING ROOMS OF DENVER

    1877: A Hole in the Liquor Laws Pops Open at Colorado Springs 72

Chapter IX THE LARAMIE PLAINS

    1877: A Lonely Land of Army Posts, Coal Mines, and Soda Lakes 75
    1967: The (Solid) Wasteland 88

Chapter X THE CANYONS OF THE WASATCH

    1877: New England Villages and Mountains like Petrified Sponges 90
    1967: This Is Ford Country 94

Chapter XI A PROMISED LAND AT GREAT SALT LAKE

    *1877: Brigham Young Explains the Peculiar Matrimonial
    Customs of the Latter-Day Saints* 96
    1967: A Revolution in Deseret 109

Chapter XII NEVADA—HIGH, DRY, AND ABORIGINAL

    1877: A Dash Across the Desert at Twenty Miles per Hour 111
    1967: Some Vanishing Americans on the Ogden-Carlin Run 122

Chapter XIII   THE GRACIOUS LIFE OF THE PALACE CAR TRAVELER

    1877: Oyster Soup by Lamplight 124
    1967: The Creme of the Automatic Buffet 126

Chapter XIV   FELLOW TRAVELERS

    1877: Newspaper Editors, Railroad Tramps, and a Parlor Organ in the Van . . 128
    1967: India-Rubber Men and Tattooed Ladies 133

Chapter XV   TO CARSON AND VIRGINIA

    1877: Fresh Milk and Boston Brown Bread 134
    1967: The Mystic Allure of the Bell, Plum, and Cherry 140

Chapter XVI   COMSTOCK SILVER

    1877: English Noblemen and Busted Millionaires Pick Paydirt 1,500 Feet Down 142
    1967: Getting By on False Coin 160

Chapter XVII   OVER THE SIERRA

    1877: Fresh Strawberries for the Passengers and Silver Bullion for the Mint . 162
    1967: A Non-Passenger Train for the Convenience of Non-Passengers 170

Chapter XVIII   EXTRAVAGANT SAN FRANCISCO

    1877: Haphazard Social Standards and a Hotel Bursting Out with Bird Cages . 172
    1967: Will the Real San Francisco Please Stand Up? 180

Chapter XIX   NIGHT IN CHINATOWN

    1877: Dark Alleys, Opium Dens, and Dancing Acrobats with Horns 182
    1967: Some Discordant Notes on the Flower Drum 188

Chapter XX   BARONS AND BOUNDERS

    1877: Stanford, Sharon, and "Lucky" Baldwin—and Accessible
    Ladies with Names on Their Doors 190
    1967: From SFO to LAX—by Escalator, Conveyor Belt,
    and Butterscotch Velocipede 196

Footnotes 199

Index 206

FRANK LESLIE'S ILLUSTRATED NEWSPAPER

Entered according to the Act of Congress, in the year 1877, by Frank Leslie, in the Office of the Librarian of Congress at Washington.

No. 1,136—Vol. XLIV.]   NEW YORK, JULY 7, 1877.   [Price, with Supplement, 10 Cents. $4.00 Yearly. 13 Weeks, $1.00.

CHAPTER I

The Hudson Route –
Overnight Passage to the West

1877: Poetry of Motion in a Wagner Car

WHEN THE LAST SPIKE was driven home on the 10th of May, 1869, uniting the two branches of the great iron highway across the Continent, a new era dawned on the history of travel. Space was no longer an obstacle. Time was, to a certain extent, controlled, and the attention of thinking men was directed to the comfort of the traveler. A trip across the Continent could never become popular until the tedium of the journey had been neutralized and the saloon of a passenger coach made to resemble a person's own parlor. The efforts of rival companies have at length brought palace cars as near perfection as our present knowledge of railroading will permit. It was, therefore, with feelings of unalloyed pleasure that our little party assembled at the Grand Central Depot, New York, on the 10th of April, for the purpose of making the transcontinental tour.

We are seated in our luxurious Wagner drawing room and sleeping car,[1] surrounded by every possible comfort. Here are our chairs, sofas, divans, mirrors, tables; in fact, our drawing room, as it is rightly named, and there are the means for changing it, by the hands of experienced servants, into a series of sleeping apartments with baths and dressing rooms belonging to them. No disturbing conductor is to shout at night, "Passengers, change cars!"

Our Chief looks around with an air of satisfaction,

and he cannot but be gratified when he reads his own name emblazoned upon his new home; for Mr. Wagner has christened it the "Frank Leslie."

Mr. Leslie intends on this journey to combine the *utile* and the *dulce*. Mrs. Leslie is all-observant, intending on her return to New York to record her experiences in a book. The two young ladies who accompany her are bent on pleasure alone; the scientific gentlemen of the group will doubtless find satisfaction in meteorological experiments, metallurgy, bugs, and fishes; while the photographers and artists will everywhere meet objects to engage their attention. There are twelve of us according to the muster roll: Mr. and Mrs. Frank Leslie; their friends, Mr. and Mrs. C. B. Hackley; Mr. Bracebridge Hemyng, the star juvenile writer of the Leslie magazines; Mr. Edwin A. Curley, historian of the excursion; Miss G. A. Davis, Mr. Walter R. Yeager, and Mr. Harry Ogden, the young artists; Mr. W. B. Austin, the staff photographer; Mr. Hamilton S. Wicks, the business manager; and Mr. W. K. Rice, son of Governor Rice of Massachusetts. We have also Mrs. Leslie's Skye terrier, Follette.

We leave punctually at 8:30 in the evening. The first startling incident is a terrific explosion under our wheels, caused by the train passing over some torpedoes laid upon the track, by which we are made to fire our own salute as we depart. The gentlemen take

BOARDING THE TRAIN AT GRAND CENTRAL DEPOT, NEW YORK CITY.

it as a compliment, for which it was intended; the ladies regard it as a preliminary catastrophe; but the nerves of all are soon quieted, and they sink into pleasant slumbers. And thus by night we pass along the banks of the Hudson, so often viewed in its beauty and grandeur by day — so often indeed, that frequency has robbed it of the charm it has for those less accustomed to its scenery.

We were due at Rochester soon after ten o'clock and,

having made our toilets at leisure, were induced to leave our home for half an hour to breakfast at the Burnett House, on shore, where we found an abundant meal provided for all the travelers excepting those whose early morning appetites had been satisfied with a more hasty meal at Syracuse.

Upon reaching Rochester we found an engine under steam in readiness to convey our Wagner car to Niagara, where it had been arranged that we might spend

THE CHAIN OF LOCKS AT LOCKPORT, N.Y.—AS PHOTOGRAPHED

a day. Afterward, we would join at Buffalo a train that left New York ten hours later than ourselves. While we were at breakfast, our conductor had our car attached to the Niagara train, and when the meal was over we found ourselves being rapidly whirled in the direction of the Falls.

Lockport is the last stopping place before we arrive at Niagara. The locks of the Erie Canal,[2] at the time of their construction, were considered to be the triumph of engineering skill, and they cannot be surveyed even now without admiration. Unwieldy barges with hundreds of tons of cargo are raised in a few moments from the lower stream to a plane ninety feet above it.

THE TRAIN LEAVING ROCHESTER.

The town itself is a busy place, full of factories and workshops, but our attention was most attracted to the locks — artificial basins, mounting like watery stairs where the railroad bridge crosses the canal. The train was here stopped so that our photographers might reproduce the wonderful effect for our readers.

And now we catch our first glimpse of the broad lake with the blue sky,

Like the horizon's fair deceit
Where earth and heaven but seem,
alas, to meet,

and then, rolling onwards, we approach the great cataract, throbbing like a mighty artery as it pours the floods of the Erie into the bosom of the Ontario.

The first impressions of Niagara depend much upon the approach. Crossing the high Suspension Bridge of the railroad, a few miles below, the traveler experiences a feeling of disappointment; the height of the fall is diminished by the perspective. But when he comes to view it from a lower level, this disappointment is overcome by surprise at the sudden growth of the gigantic torrent.

As we came towards it, we first saw a narrow strip of lazy, smooth, slow water of the deepest blue, just flecked here and there with streaks of foam, slipping away between steep gray walls of rock, not unlike the palisades of the Hudson; a light bridge is then seen spanning the straight, clean-cut groove; now we catch the first sight of white pouring water, solid and immense, and a cloud of dense white steam hanging over the narrow blue river at what seems to be its source.

We are here between seasons. Winter is the season

NIAGARA FALLS AS SEEN FROM PROSPECT POINT — FROM A SKETCH BY HENRY OGDEN.

DESCENDING THE INCLINED RAILWAY AT NIAGARA FALLS.

EXTERIOR OF THE INCLINED RAILWAY.

for Niagara — summer for visitors. But Niagara at all seasons is indescribably magnificent. Viewed in solitude, when the empty halls and corridors of the great hotels appear to re-echo the ghostly merriment of departed visitors, it causes a feeling akin to religion to creep over the soul. Companionship and the whirl of busy life are not always the most appropriate accompaniments when contemplating the wonders of nature.

There are numerous localities where splendid views of the cataract may be obtained, but Prospect Point afforded the best effect of color. The intense blue-green of the stream below the Falls; the snow-white foam and mist and flying spray; and the clear, deep beryl tint of the Fall itself, are beautifully contrasted. Leaning on the parapet, we stared down into the chaos of white mist that shrouded the crash of the waters and saw a bit of rainbow tangled in it. At the right of the Fall, and at its foot, there was piled up a great rounded hill of ice, an accumulation of the winter's frozen spray.

We now entered a little open car which carried us on the incline railway to the base of the cataract, through a long tunnel, dark and damp, at an angle of thirty-three degrees. We emerged into the open air on a strip of sodden snow and ice at the water's edge, by the foot of the slippery hill, which several of our party, including an adventurous young lady, climbed that we might obtain a better view. Here we looked up at one hundred and sixty feet of massive waters, poured, as it were, out

PAINTING THE BRIDGE AT NIAGARA FALLS.

A SNOWBALLING FROLIC BENEATH THE FALLS.

of the hollow of the blue sky, and scanned the steep precipice, where quaint figures fashioned of icy stalactites were lodged in the niches or hanging from the projections of the rocks. We clearly understand the incapacity of all painters to put Niagara Falls upon canvas. They show you the width and height, but they cannot convey the slightest idea of its thunder or of the grand poetry of its majestic motion.

As we turn to re-pass the bridge on our way to occupy our movable home again, we behold three men like flies suspended upon the wires of the bridge, which they are painting. Our draughtsman seized the opportunity to take their portraits — for which they obligingly gave him a hanging.

We left Niagara at a late hour in the afternoon. We had had enough of exercise for one day, and the poetry of motion, at least in a Wagner Drawing-room Car, was never more fully appreciated.

Next morning the sun's rays were reflected into our windows from the polished surface of Lake Erie. Our way lay along its shores, on the road appropriately called "Lake Shore," which is a continuation of the New York Central and is controlled by William H. Vanderbilt. It is in splendid condition, and as it has the advantage of immense local traffic, will undoubtedly overcome all competition. The lake was always on our right, while on our left were wooded prairies and cultivated farms, interspersed frequently with large towns.

A LADY ON THE ICE.

THE GRAIN ELEVATOR AT TOLEDO.

THE RAILROAD DEPOT AT TOLEDO.

BAGGAGE-CHECK WAGON IN TOLEDO.

The first approaches to Toledo would indicate a city of sawmills and grain elevators. At the "Island House" a substantial breakfast had been prepared for those of us who had the leisure to partake of it, while our artists, who had already broken their fast, were busily occupied in sketching the hotel and in photographing an enormous elevator which has a capacity of 1,500,000 bushels.

Some of us strolled through the city. The streets are wide and many of the buildings are splendid. Toledo is an evidence of the marvelous growth of Western towns. They spring up, like Jonah's gourd, in a night, and extend their branches in all directions.

Toledo today has extensive railroad connections: the Lake Shore and Michigan Southern; Toledo, Wabash, and Western; Dayton and Michigan; Detroit and Toledo; Flint and Pere Marquette; Canada Southern; Columbus and Toledo; Toledo and Mannell; Toledo and Sylvania; and Toledo, Tiflin, and Eastern. All these railroads concentrate at an immense union depot. The chief items of trade are grain and flour. Besides these two commodities, a large business is transacted in general provisions, livestock, whiskey, iron, tobacco, wool, hides, cotton, and lumber.

Mr. Leslie and party met with a cordial reception from the editorial fraternity, and in the office of the *Toledo Blade* were shown a blade of Toledo presented to the proprietor by the Spanish Commissioners at the recent Centennial Exhibition [in Philadelphia, 1876]. Like its American namesake, it is sharp and trenchant, but here the similarity ends, for it is heavy and unwieldy and would prove a dangerous weapon in the hands of an awkward man — to himself. □

1967: Some Romantic Notions Left in Slowly Passing

IN THE WINTER OF 1967, I boarded a transcontinental passenger train for what I hoped would not be the last time. My itinerary was simple: San Francisco to Chicago; three days in Chicago; then back to San Francisco. The trip would approximate Frank Leslie's excursion of ninety years ago, less a wife, seven employees, a Skye terrier, a private railroad car, and a bundle of firecrackers under the wheels. Unlike the Leslies, I would not occupy the same car straight across the country. In order to cross the great plains by daylight, I would have to change trains several times and travel for a day and a night in the coach of the Union Pacific mail train. All in all, I did not anticipate a restful journey, but I looked forward to momentous experiences that would make up for any temporary discomforts.

Like many Americans, I feel a strong romantic attraction to passenger trains. Although I seldom travel by rail, no one can top me for righteous indignation when some board of directors decides to scrap a fine old train that is losing money by the fistful. I attribute this sentiment to a childhood misspent reading murder mysteries by Agatha Christie and listening to a radio program called *Grand Central Station* ("Crossroads of a million lives...").

In those days, certain railroad expeditions ranked with climbing Mount Everest or exploring the headwaters of the Amazon. All you needed was a ticket on the Orient Express, the Trans-Siberian Railroad, or the Blue Train, and you were practically guaranteed several days of hair-raising adventure. Sinister figures slipped aboard at stations in the swamps; rioting mobs broke through the barricades as the train gathered speed; and the clatter of wheels drowned out a terrified shriek from Upper 13. Lately, the spy-infested, cadaver-laden Orient Express has become a pastoral tourist haul; the Trans-Siberian is a unit in a five-year plan; and the Blue Train is a forty-and-eight for sunburned Parisian clerks coming home from the August holiday. Only the overland route across North America retains the irresistible, nomadic lure.

The overland train never was notorious for inexplicable disappearances or strangulations in the vestibule. Its only mystery was the imponderable complexity and vastness of the American landscape. Its spell was that concatenation of imperishable stations with the taste of coal-dust and ice water, chilled cantaloupe and maple syrup: Clinton, Council Bluffs, and Omaha; Laramie, Green River, and Ogden; Winnemucca, Sparks, and Sacramento; and its wayside marvels were corncribs on the sidings, yellow clapboard houses, piles of apples, and tiny canoes in the station at Cheyenne.

The other day I read in the paper that a research institute employed by the Southern Pacific Railroad had concluded that there is no future for intercity passenger travel by rail. "The generations of Americans most accustomed to train travel are slowly passing," the research institute said, "and few in the younger generations have any interest in this mode."

I can't dispute this, much as I dislike being classed with a group of old fuddies who are disappearing into the ether like crystals of naphthalene. But I am filled with pity for these "younger generations" who have never seen a sign that says, "Please Do Not Flush When Train Is Standing In Station"; have never written a dinner order with the sharpest imaginable pencil upon the smallest imaginable carbon paper tablet; have never stood on the shuddering metal plates above the couplings, waiting for the porter to throw open the door and put down the yellow footstool; have never bought Aplets from a candy butcher; have never come upon a sign that said, "Dining Car in Opposite Direction"; and what is more, *have no interest.*

The slowly passing crowd that I sport around with was intensely interested—perhaps I should say astonished—to hear that I was planning to cross the continent by rail.

"You're actually taking the *train*?" they said. "I'd love to do it myself if I had the time. What's it like nowadays?"

In the notes that follow each episode of the Leslies' journey, I have tried to answer that question. □

THE LAKE SHORE RAILROAD DEPOT AT CHICAGO.

CHAPTER II

The Unceasing Marvel of Chicago

1877: A Crib Gets Rid of Minnows in the Milk

CHICAGO, "THE CITY ON THE LAKE," will never cease to be a marvel to the present generation. Her wonderful development in forty years from a small aggregation of balloon-shaped log cabins to a city of 450,000 will not strike the average visitor as forcibly as will the extraordinary obstacles encountered and overcome.[1] Quicksands are not favorable locations for houses; but here they have been made to pay tribute to the energy of a great people. The disadvantages of a sluggish stream in the heart of the city may be seen at a glance; but, bridged above and tunneled below, with wide, lighted avenues for horseman or pedestrian, it becomes a serpentine for the pleasure-seeker, a never-failing anchorage of commerce, and a monument of the scientific skill of the nineteenth century. Water saturated with the accumulated abominations of a large city and fragrant with the odor of stale fish is not seductive; but here it served to direct the minds of the citizens into other channels, and the result was the tapping of a great inland sea and a superabundant supply of pure, fresh, cool water.

Fire scourged Chicago in 1871; but this wonderful people lost no time in vain repinings.[2] A few days were sufficient for organization, a few months for courageous efforts, and the city sprang anew from its ashes, like the fabulous phoenix, grander, more beautiful, more durable than of old. The destructive fury of the elements has but ministered to Chicago's growth and prosperity.

Some twenty years ago we visited Chicago for the first time. It was then the chief town of the far Northwest, but it is now an Eastern city with its own vessels plying directly to the ports of Europe. It then claimed some eighty thousand inhabitants. Report says that these included the hotel arrivals of the year and the frogs that croaked in the vacant lots. It now claims, with more solid reason, half a million people.

The Grand Pacific Hotel³ looms up in magnificent proportions only a block from the Lake Shore terminus. Entering, we find a magnificent hall, one of the finest we have seen in the United States; and we are soon located in elegant apartments. We have the comfort and seclusion of home while we are regaled with whitefish from the lakes, shad from the Eastern rivers, green peas from New Orleans, and asparagus from Memphis. Each guest on an average uses more than a dozen dishes for his dinner.

A special steam engine operates the roasting jack by which our meats are done to a turn. The store rooms; the fruit room, with its uniform temperature of forty degrees; the butcher's shop; and all the offices of the establishment strike us as singularly complete.

Among items in the purveyor's department that interest us, we find that in the last season 25,527 dozens of eggs, 31,488 pounds of butter, 25,350 birds, and 10,220 boxes of berries were consumed.

The materials and mode of construction are intended to render the immense structure absolutely fireproof. All parts of the building are kept free from the common fumes of hotel atmosphere by ventilating passages connecting with a large smokestack that excites an ample circulation.

Chicago undoubtedly surpasses in the safety, elegance, and general excellence of her hotel accommodation. The prices are also less, in proportion to quality, than in any other place with which we are acquainted; and in this important matter it is necessary that Eastern cities look to their laurels if they do not wish to lose them.

Prices Are Less in Proportion to Quality

SCENE IN THE VESTIBULE AND OFFICE OF THE GRAND PACIFIC HOTEL.

STATE STREET, LOOKING SOUTH.

CLARK STREET, LOOKING SOUTH FROM RANDOLPH STREET.

Twenty years ago, the wet and springy prairie sod gave way under one's feet in many public streets; now, the streets are paved with wooden blocks, and the wide walks are covered with massive tables of granite and limestone. Chicago's wooden pavements have become famous in New York and other American cities, and they have been tried in Europe. (Nevertheless, these "parallelopipedons" are scarcely a success, even here. They are dirty and repulsive, like the fat fisherwoman who received this name from a ponderous wit, and they are prone to decay.)

When we visited the city before, they were raising the grade of the streets out of the mud-swamp. The old Tremont House was standing upon a unique foundation of jackscrews. To every jackscrew there was a man-jack, and to the sound of a gong he gave one turn of the screw. Thus the huge brick structure was lifted to the required position, while the guests came and departed and business proceeded as usual.[4] Now the huge hotels of Chicago need no such enginery of elevation. Their foundations are well laid, with no swamps around them.

Then, the stores were chiefly wooden shanties. Now, the news vendor, cigar dealer, and barber are ensconced between heavy brick walls, with plate glass fronts and lofty ceilings, and each has his strong room where he can deposit his "stamps" or coin in safety from thieves or fire.

Then, the stocks of the merchants were comparatively poor in quality and insignificant in amount; now, in the magnificent establishments on State, Madison, Clark, and some other streets and avenues, the display of goods will compare very well with Broadway and the chief business streets of New York.

Then, Chicago received in a year less than fifty thousand cattle, while she now receives over a million. Then, she received less than two hundred thousand hogs a year; now, she receives over four million.

Chicago now claims to have not only the largest livestock market in the world, but the most perfectly arranged stockyards. An almost infinite variety of arrangements is required for the comfort and good condition of so many animals. Yet the whole of this vast work is done by one organization — the Union Stockyards Company — and its yards and buildings cover 370 acres.[5] The yards contain 475 cattle yards, 675 covered hog and sheep pens, 375 chutes and pens, 15 corncribs, 10 hay barns, several miles of macadamized streets and alleys, and a network of sewers and water pipes. Twenty-four miles of railroad tracks connecting with the yards are also owned by the company.

These stockyards and the packing industries which they feed employ more than one-sixth of the male adult population of the city. Fortunately their management has been so admirable as to provoke little controversy. They are very popular with the people, and every citizen of Chicago is proud of the unique suburb where enterprising industry gathers cattle from the Upper Mississippi and Missouri; Kansas and Nebraska; Dakota, Wyoming, Montana, and far-off Idaho; Colorado, New Mexico, and the distant Texas plains of the Rio Grande.

We visit the waterworks of Chicago and examine them with especial care. Within the last ten years the city was still being supplied with water from wells, cisterns and pumping works on the shore of the Lake, near the odorous mouth of the river. Some of the water was contaminated with foul matter. Some of it, purer than the rest, was filled with minute and innumerable fish. The finny tribe became ingredients in the dishes and beverages of every repast. Even the cows were noted for the vast number of minnows in their milk, and honest dairymen were in despair at the bad name given them by visitors who did not fully understand the circumstances of the city. Fish-spawn floated in the air. It got into casks and barrels and bottles, in spite of all possible precautions. The fish hatched out in the strongest old whiskies and drank so much as to impair both quality and strength. If an Eastern guest ordered Veuve Cliquot with his dinner, landlord and waiters were in mortal dread lest a frog should jump out as the cork was extracted.

Then somebody conceived the happy idea of making a tunnel under the Lake, to the cold, deep waters where minnows and frogs would trouble no more. It was begun where the main waterworks now stand on the shore of the Lake.

"The Crib," a huge triple-walled cofferdam, was built, floated two miles out, and sunk. Then a shaft and tunnel from "The Crib" met a tunnel from the shore. A lofty tower and huge steam pumps were erected at the shore end.[6] The water, lifted by the pumps to the tower, thence by hydrostatic pressure, found its way through all the service pipes of the city.

A second tunnel has lately been added, and another tower built in a distant part of the city. Water rents not only pay interest and expenses, but they support the fire department and otherwise aid the finances of the city.

The crooked little Chicago River gives some important and curious features to the city. It has been dredged and dug out until it now affords a frontage for shipping of thirty-eight miles. It formerly flowed into the Lake, but by an immense outlay of time and money it has been connected with the Illinois River and its headwaters deepened until it now flows with a steady current from the Lake into that river, and thence through the Mississippi to the Gulf. This is the first authentic instance of reversing the current of a river on a scale of such magnitude.

The windings of the Chicago render many bridges necessary. These are all provided with draws and are occasionally closed for vehicles and pedestrians alike. But the go-ahead people of Chicago did not like these delays. Encouraged by the success of their "big bore" under the Lake, they constructed two tunnels under the river bed. Each has two lanes for vehicles and one for pedestrians. These tunnels are dry and cool in summer and warm in winter, and they are so great a success that they will eventually be multiplied in number.

The majority of Chicago's business blocks are concentrated within one-half mile commencing one street west of the Lake and a little south of the main Chicago River. Wabash Avenue, State, Dearborn, and Clark Streets, and Fifth Avenue run parallel with the lakefront. Lake, Randolph, Washington, Madison, Monroe, and Adams Streets run east and west. On the whole, Clark Street is the finest of them all. Here are the publishing houses of Jansen, McClurg & Co. and of

THE WILSON SEWING-MACHINE BUILDING ON STATE STREET.

Kelme, Cooke & Co., and some fine art galleries. Close by, in Randolph Street, is the Western News Company, through which our Western readers are supplied with the numerous periodicals emanating from the publishing house of Frank Leslie. Thus we find that Chicago is devoted to literature and art as well as to fashion and money-getting. The Wilson Sewing Machine Company may be cited as an example. From the Chicago headquarters Wilson does business in every State in the Union and has numerous branch offices in this country and in Europe.

As we drive along the boulevards, we are surprised at the number and magnificence of the mansions of Chicago. They, like the business portion of the city, have been built almost exclusively since the fire. The architects and their patrons have been bold innovators, indeed, each trying some pet theory of his own as to style, methods, and materials of construction. Their experiments have been more successful than we should have expected. Comfort has seldom been sacrificed, but almost every residence has some peculiarity that renders it quite unique. Among them we noticed especially those of Mr. Perry Smith[7] and G. M. Pullman of "Pullman Car" fame.[8] The house, conservatories, and grounds of the latter occupy a large block.

Among the public institutions of Chicago, perhaps no other is so important as the Board of Trade.[9] It dates from 1848, but for the first few years had about as much as it could accomplish in maintaining a precarious and not very useful existence. Since 1857 it has exercised an increasing supervision over the trade of the whole Northwest and a great influence upon that of the whole country. The splendid building which it now occupies was erected in 1872 to replace a large and handsome structure destroyed by the fire. It has a frontage of 93 feet on Washington Street and 181½ on La Salle Street. Exchange and Calhoun Places separate it from all adjacent buildings.

The ground floor is occupied chiefly by banks and insurance companies and the first floor by offices. The great Exchange Hall above is 142 feet long, 87 wide, and 45 high. The roof is thrown over in a single span without the obstruction of pillars, and the ceiling and walls are elaborately frescoed. On the south is a gallery whence visitors may watch the struggles between bulls and bears and note the success or disaster attending "corners" in corn, wheat, beef, cattle, or pork. On the north is an elaborate rostrum for the president, with a large allegorical painting on either side of it. On the right the destroying devil is sticking his torch into every combustible corner to give the people of Chicago a roasting. On the left a strapping big angel is towing some sort of heavenly craft, laden with contributions for the needy, while below are the tottering and smoking ruins. In each corner of the hall are telegraph stands. At intervals on the floor are small oblong platforms, three steps high, to be mounted by those operators who have offers to make. The dealers in each line of business—wheat or pork, for instance—have platforms assigned to them alone, and this prevents much confusion.

Throughout the building the furniture is elegant, the wood finish being walnut and ash. All the principal doors are of glass, with costly and ornate arabesques and devices. The staircases are solid mahogany, with massive newel posts of fancy woods surmounted with bronze figures.

The day before the great fire, the Board of Trade

A SESSION OF THE CHICAGO BOARD OF TRADE IN THE CHAMBER OF COMMERCE BUILDING.

had completed the heaviest week of wheat receipts ever known. At the first meeting after the fire, they passed a special rule settling all of these contracts at the prices current at the time the fire broke out. By this proceeding, many operators gave up chances of realizing large sums through violent fluctuations of the market; but they settled, on a just and sensible basis, a condition which would otherwise have overwhelmed many with disaster and inflicted an additional blow on the credit of the city. This was energetic and wise, generous and just, and it has helped much to strengthen the bonds which unite the members of this body, as well as to increase the admiration and respect of the general public. □

25

1967: A Great Place to Live If You're a Chevrolet

THE DAY I ARRIVED IN CHICAGO, all the local papers were carrying long reviews of a new book called *Division Street, America*, which a popular radio performer had put together out of interviews with representative Chicagoans. Prostitutes, police inspectors, dope fiends, and other typical citizens described their life in the city, and their gamier doings made *Studs Lonigan* seem like romantic whimsy. My favorite in the Home Town Booster category was a man who said: "Chicago is a great place to live if you're a Chevrolet."

That remark, sarcastic as it was, seemed to sum up all the gibes Chicago has endured for almost half a century, ever since it stopped being the wonder city of the world and turned into the world's largest disappointment. For there is no denying that Chicago, in spite of its grandeur, wealth, and power, is an unpopular city. All over the world it is known primarily as the habitat of *gang-stairs* and other social abominations; and among the practitioners of city planning, political science, and sociology, it is regarded almost universally as an overgrown, ill-governed, urban monstrosity.

Its immense Negro slums, which once represented the first step toward independence for black farmers from the South, now epitomize our failure to grant Negroes the full riches of American citizenship. Its splendid lakefront buildings, which once symbolized the maturity of the Middle West, now seem to be a facade, masking the discomfort, ugliness, indifference, and inequity of the vast city behind them.

All the same, there are poets and politicians who call Chicago muscular, creative, and exciting, and I must say its first impression on me was favorable. The weather was pleasantly mild for January; a bluish sun was floating in the turbid air; and everybody wore an amiable face. I promised myself to keep an open mind and show proper respect for world records, which Chicago, like New York, holds dear. My guidebook urged me to visit the World's Largest Commodity Market, the World's Tallest Marble-faced Commercial Structure, the World's Busiest Corner, and the World's Largest Fountain. Also included were instructions on how to find the World's Largest Post Office Under One Roof, the World's Largest Exchange Dealing in Perishable Commodities, the World's Largest Aquarium for Living Specimens, the World's Tallest Church, and the Former Site of the World's Tallest Building Ever to Be Torn Down. (From the window of a bus on the Near North Side, I spotted the World's Largest Tuxedo Rental Service, which the guidebook did not even mention.)

Naturally, I stayed at the World's Largest Hotel, the Conrad Hilton. It is the sort of place the Leslies would have been crazy about: two thousand employees, world records galore, and so many bedrooms (around three thousand, give or take a few suites and display rooms) that you could sleep in a different room every night for eight years. (This would cost roughly sixty thousand dollars, not counting meals, tips, valet service, and outside telephone calls at twenty-five cents each, and no one, so far as I know, has been tempted to try it.)

The hotel gives each patron a brochure chock-full of impressive statistics about such utilities as the elevators, the kitchen, and the telephone switchboard. The elevators, for example, have traveled a distance equal to ten round trips to the moon since 1927, and the catering department serves more than two and one-half million meals a year. (This type of information always fazes me. How far away *is* the moon? What would two and one-half million meals *look* like, laid end to end?) As for the switchboard, it has enough sockets to serve a town of forty thousand, which the main lobby certainly resembles during hours of peak traffic.

For all its enormity, the Conrad Hilton advertises itself as one of the world's *friendliest* hotels. In evidence of its good will toward men, it prints the house telephone directory in French, German, Spanish, Italian, and Chinese; and when you check out, the bellhops and chambermaids gather round and gaze ardently into your eyes and say in voices choked with emotion: "You hurry back, now."

I've never considered friendliness to be an essential attribute of hotels, especially places with two or three thousand chums in residence; but comradely behavior is much esteemed in Chicago. One day I went into a large Woolworth store in the Loop to buy some thread and immediately was befriended by a motherly clerk in Main Floor Notions.

"A loose button?" she said. "Don't you need somebody to sew it on for you, dear?"

I told her my wife was in California. The good woman clucked in sympathy and patted the back of my hand. She had been out to San Francisco for a whole month herself, she told me: felt a damp chill the entire time, and the whole place smelled constantly of burning peanuts.

"You get your sweet wife back home before they wreck her health," she advised, giving me such a clubby smile that I hadn't the heart to tell her I have lived in San Francisco all my life.

Chicago's friendly attitude showed up even at the Board of Trade, an institution that I would have rated hostile, or at best aloof. Years ago, when I first peered down on the Board of Trade from the visitors' gallery, wild-eyed men in cotton jackets were striding up and down, raising their hands in strange gestures and shouting at the top of their voices. It shook me up, because I thought I was seeing fortunes lost and men ruined before my very eyes. This time, I went down to the commodity market on a Friday afternoon, after the trading pits had closed for the week. The day's quotations for choice steers, rapeseed, sorghum, oats, and so on were chalked on bulletin boards, and the floor was knee-deep with shreds of colored paper, old newspapers, coffee cups, cigarette butts, and candy wrappers. A few janitors and teletype operators were wandering around, chewing gum and whistling. It looked more like the aftermath of a New Year's Eve party than a scene from the works of Upton Sinclair or Frank Norris.

The concierge of the observatory on the forty-fifth floor of the building was particularly solicitous and followed me around the platform, pointing out tall buildings that I ought to notice. I asked if any of them was the world's largest this or that.

"Well, you won't find anything like Marina City in Peoria," she said, somewhat defensively. I quickly agreed. Marina City is a pair of cylindrical 60-story towers that invariably remind visitors of stacks of plates with scalloped edges. My hostess told me, without supporting evidence, that they are the World's Most Photographed Buildings.

The World's Most Visited Police Department also is located in Chicago; and it, too, has a matey atmosphere. The cops hold perpetual open house, advertised in all the entertainment guides: Come in, folks, and see the World's Most Modern Police Communication System. In the main lobby they have a picture gallery of convivial Chicago police chiefs down the years; and up on the second floor, in a dimly lighted, glass-enclosed chamber, are twenty-six dispatchers watching illuminated maps of Chicago, keeping track of 1500 patrol cars. By picking up a telephone outside the glass panel, you can hear a recorded lecture from the superintendent, who tells you gamely, without a hint of recrimination, that the Chicago police department gets a million and a half complaints a year. (This puts the department in a class with the PBX board at the Conrad Hilton, which it rivals also for sheer friendliness.) Down the corridor, you can look in at a battery of computers that registers 13,000 traffic citations, 30,000 arrests, and 150,000 radio dispatches a month.

Chicago's reputation for haphazard local government also is belied by a new City-County Office Center, completed in 1965, in the northern part of the Loop. This no-nonsense skyscraper was designed by Mies van der Rohe and has in its main lobby a series of plaques illustrating various aspects of a comprehensive plan for Chicago — "Development of High Accessibility Corridors," "Principles for Metropolitan Structure," and the like. Neither the building nor its decoration shows the numbing influence of gangster rule.

Chicago always has been bold in architectural innovation, and the Office Center is characteristically novel. It has an external skeleton of vertical steel beams, within which the floors are set like trays in a rack. As the risers age, they are expected to ripen to a rich, reddish brown. So far, they have simply rusted, to the consternation of a number of Chicagoans who think the spread looks slightly unfinished.

Although Chicago fails to live up (or down) to its ill-repute in the field of civic nonfeasance, I fully expected its nightlife to be a model of depravity, and I was almost disappointed to find that the "Old Town" section resembled the entertainment districts of other, less notorious cities — *many* others, in fact, including Tokyo, San Francisco, Amsterdam, London, Hollywood, and Hamburg. I went to a theater-restaurant that showed a satirical revue on the main floor and old Laurel and Hardy movies in the basement. Intense, white-lipped girls in turtleneck sweaters, miniskirts, and mesh stockings served Irish coffee, *gluhwein*, mead, *himbeersaft*, and black coffee laced with the intoxicants of all nations. Afterward, I walked along North Wells Street, past blazing galleries of souvenir shops: draught beer, homemade fudge, Toulouse-Lautrec lithographs, red lacquered boxes. There were Tiffany glass lamps in the pizzerias, bullfight posters in the hot sake bars, stained glass windows in the shish kebab parlors. Rock 'n' roll drifted on the winter air, and young men whose hair lay lank and long on the shoulders of their peacoats were squinting eagerly through slits in the windows of the cantinas. I squinted, too, and saw to my joy the incarnated spirit of Chicago: an enormous Negro woman playing, on a trombone, "Hello, Central, Give Me Doctor Jazz. . . ."

I felt a rush of affection for Good Old Chi. Why should everybody sneer at Good Old Chi? Is this a reaction to Chicago's childish boasting? Is it a spite campaign by insular New Yorkers? Is it all a mistake?

Friendless, grimy, touseled by the wind, Chicago comforts itself with world records — an infantile habit, like thumb-sucking. But in spite of its records, its rust-colored Civic Center, its hospitable police station, its gregarious three-thousand-room hotel, Chicago is not loved. It simply is not a very comfortable place for human beings to live; and that, when you get down to it, is the heart of the complaint.

A number of other American cities are on their way to being twice as uncomfortable, but most of the go-ahead people who are building them will not be around to enjoy the murky megalopolises of the future. They should be great places to live if you're a helicopter. A rich, white helicopter with a gas mask. □

DEPOT OF THE CHICAGO AND NORTH WESTERN RAILROAD.

CHAPTER III

West in a Pullman Hotel Car

1877: Dyspepsia is Obsolete in a Palace on Paper Wheels

WE LEFT CHICAGO ON APRIL 16TH. At ten o'clock in the morning a special stage of Parmelee's[1] with four horses drives up to the private entrance and we leave for the depot of the Chicago and North Western Railway. This celebrated road is the shortest route between Chicago and Omaha, a great advantage for travelers to whom time is important. It was the pioneer line in the overland route between the Atlantic and the Pacific, forming a junction with the Union Pacific several months in advance of all its competitors. The line is almost wholly made of steel rails. It is also the only road on which the luxury of Pullman hotel cars can be enjoyed between Chicago and Omaha. Its enterprise is something amazing even in these days of vigorous railroad competition: it has thirty-one agencies in Australia, China, Japan, New Zealand, and the Sandwich Islands, and thirty-three in Great Britain. If you are going from the East to Japan, or to St. Paul, or to any part of Wisconsin or Minnesota, the Chicago and North Western Railway[2] is the route you must adopt in the interest of dispatch and comfort.

From Chicago our trip was continued in a Pullman hotel car — the "President." This elegant conveyance was on exhibition at the Philadelphia Centennial last year, and it was also the car in which Dom Pedro[3] made his rapid journey across the continent.

While our party was viewing the exterior of the vehicle, Mr. George Pullman himself strolled up. Pointing to the wheels, he made the somewhat alarming announcement that they were made of paper! In proportion to its weight, he said, good paper, properly prepared, is one of the strongest substances in the world. It offers equal resistance to fracture in all directions. While the toughest woods are sometimes liable to crack and split under severe trial, and ordinary iron becomes brittle from the constant jarring on the smoothest of steel rails, paper possesses a certain amount of elasticity very desirable in a car wheel. Paper wheels, he said, were subjected to an enormous hydraulic pressure and, when surrounded with a flange of steel, were the most perfect wheels yet invented.

Stocking the car with provisions is a matter of some

moment. The company has large storerooms in Chicago, where provisions of every description, bought at wholesale, are placed. The conductor of the car, acting as steward, receipts for the stores for his trip and makes his return to the storekeeper at the expiration of his voyage. Everything for the commissariat, except fresh meat and vegetables, is stowed away in closets beneath the car at the beginning of the journey; and even these perishable foods can be preserved sweet and fresh in ice closets throughout the entire trip.

The excursionists were ushered into the interior of the "President," where every comfort is provided. A spacious saloon, through the magic of a drop curtain, can be made sitting room, smoking room, drawing room, and retiring room at pleasure. Whatever one longs for in his own house is procurable. The kitchen is a gem of its kind, with every convenience from a mammoth roaster to a charcoal broiler. Pots, kettles, pans, and knives are ranged around the apartment in perfect order. It is located in the rear of the car, and two large tanks suspended from the roof are supplied with water from the outside by means of a hose. Our cook was an artist in his line, and dyspepsia and indigestion were obsolete terms on board the "President."

MAKING UP THE BERTHS.

MR. PULLMAN EXPLAINING THE PAPER WHEELS.

STOCKING THE CAR FOR A JOURNEY.

THE COOK IN HIS WELL-EQUIPPED KITCHEN AT THE REAR OF THE CAR.

INSPECTING THE LINEN-CLOSET.

Adjoining the kitchen is the linen closet, whence are obtained the unlimited supply of snow-white sheets, napkins, and cloths that adorn our beds and tables every day. The appropriate station of the conductor-steward, when he is not otherwise engaged, is in the wine closet, from which he ministers to the parched palates of his guests.

There are two other servants on the car, one of whom, when meals are served, takes position in the pantry, adjoining the kitchen. Dishes are handed him by the cook through a small window. These are passed to the other servant and come to the table piping hot. The services of plate, glass, and china are costly and elegant, and few hotels can boast of a handsomer or more appetizing display.

The washroom is not large, but ample for the necessities of a greater number than were gathered together on the "President."

It will thus be seen how few are the vexations of modern traveling. Should a passenger become unwell he has but to order what he wishes from the kitchen. Should he desire his meals at unusual hours, he has but to give his order to find his every whim gratified.

THE WINE-CLOSET.

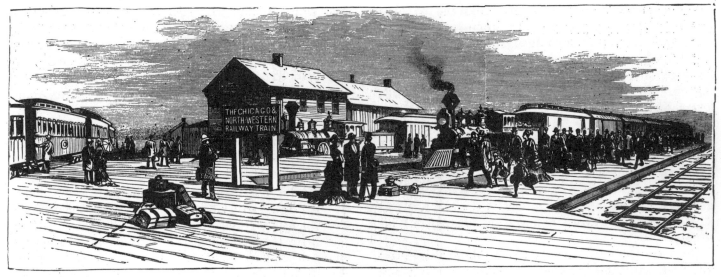

ARRIVAL AT COUNCIL BLUFFS.

Bottoms" — wide, almost level land of surpassing fertility, at one time overflowed by the Missouri River. They are often swampy and subject to malarious influences. The lakes and sluggish streams abound in game, and the nimrods of our party emptied the contents of their revolvers from the platform to the amusement of the passengers and astonishment of the wildfowl who, if they noticed it at all, probably imagined that the train had adopted some new form of amusement for the passengers.

The next place of importance is Council Bluffs, a town of ten thousand inhabitants and the western terminus of the Chicago and North Western Railway. The town is concealed by bluffs and makes but little show from the depot, but an inspection revealed a number of substantial brick hotels and some blocks of large and well-filled stores. The place derives its name from a council ground of the Indians, but it was formerly Kanesville, a settlement of Latter-Day Saints. Some five or six railways converge here to connect with the Union Pacific Railroad over the great iron bridge which spans the Missouri.

The bridge is about half a mile long and constructed to defy the ravages of the seasons. The difference between high and low water marks at this point is some twenty-seven feet, so that the bridge is sometimes required to withstand an immense pressure of ice, water, and refuse. The columns are eight feet in diameter and filled with concrete, and the whole structure presents an appearance of stability which only time is powerful enough to change.[7] □

34

1967: Take a Good Look

I HAD INTENDED WHILE IN CHICAGO to increase my limited knowledge of railroad terminology, and at the same time whet my appetite for transcontinental travel by visiting the Pullman Company maintenance shops at Calumet, an industrial suburb on the south side of the city. In anticipation of a day among peek-a-boo beds and folding lavatories, I had been reading in the way of historical background a description of American railroad cars written in 1877 by a member of the British Parliament, H. Hussey Vivian. I thought it would be instructive to compare Mr. Vivian's impressions with my own, since he obviously considered American passenger cars abnormal and exotic and likely to astonish English readers from Cornwall to Simla, or wherever Britain was holding dominion that year.

"Imagine a very minute church with nave and lean-to aisle (without pillars) on wheels," Mr. Vivian suggested, "and you have a fair section of an American Pullman car."

I found this ecclesiastical simile so recherché that I did not hope to equal it, partly because I think the modern Pullman car resembles a maximum security prison. Yet Mr. Vivian's meticulous care in describing what was, to me, merely an old-style American sleeping car impressed me with the evanescence of devices that we take for granted, and it inspired me to make my own descriptions equally precise and circumstantial, lest they should be read some day by a person who has never seen a passenger train.

"Close to the aisle window," Mr. Vivian explained, sticking to the basilical image, "are the pews or seats, and a passage passes down the centre; the seats are *meant* to hold two in width, and face each other; at night they slide down, meet, and make a capital bed, far better than any berth on board ship, in fact all a traveler could desire. Our car conductor tells me that at the time of the 'Centennial' they used to have a queer lot of 'outwesters,' and that as many as six have slept in one of these beds. Upon my expressing incredulity, he explained that they consisted of 'an old man and his wife and four children.' He declared that three were quite 'commonly' packed into one that crowded time — two one way and one the other. It might be possible, but not pleasant."

After making a note to remind myself to inquire about the occupancy record for a modern roomette, I telephoned the Pullman Company and asked permission to visit a representative passenger car, preferably one in the throes of construction or repair. The man I talked to sounded rather startled. The Pullman Company, he informed me, had not built any new passenger cars since 1947, when it was ordered by a Federal court to shuck its construction business and limit itself to operation and repair. Pullman still launders thousands of acres of bed linen and vacuum-cleans hundreds of miles of carpets for the fifty or so railroads that jointly own the company; and lately it has remodeled a number of sleeping cars, knocking out bedrooms here and there and installing little kitchens to save the railroads the cost of carrying separate diners. But there is nothing going on at the Calumet yards, the Pullman attaché assured me, that could not be seen just as well on board a train.

As for Pullman Standard, the corporation that inherited the car-building side of the business, it is busy making freight cars, automobile carriers, and piggyback flatcars for toting trucks; it has not built a passenger car for several years. In fact, passenger cars are so expensive to build that my informant doubted any more would *ever* be manufactured, at least in this country.

From the tone of voice over at Pullman, I concluded that an afternoon in Calumet would be fairly gloomy, and I decided to postpone my passenger car inspection until after I boarded the Domeliner *City of San Francisco/City of Los Angeles*, which leaves Union Station in Chicago for the Pacific Coast at six o'clock every evening.

This train bears the names of two notoriously incompatible cities because it is, in theory, two trains. They run simultaneously, and hooked together, as far as Ogden, Utah, where the *City of San Francisco* falls under the ascetic rule of the Southern Pacific Railroad and the *Los Angeles* veers south in custody of the Union Pacific. "Domeliner" means that several of the cars have domelike glass penthouses from which you get an unobstructed view of the right-of-way. This term apparently is a refinement of "streamliner," a word that enjoyed high vogue in the 1930's, when it was applied to almost every object with rounded edges.

Getting onto a train for a 48-hour ride to California is a considerably less elaborate process than checking in for a one-hour airline hop. A couple of conductors at a table in the lobby look at your ticket, and one of them mutters: "Track 28." Nobody weighs your baggage, asks whether you would like to rent a car at your destination, or offers to sell you a life insurance policy; and there is none of the ritual grinning and bonvoyagerie that airline employees use to distract your mind from the certainty that the plane is going to crash. The Union Station, built in the olden days of the ubiquitous baggage porter, has no moving stairways, moving sidewalks, or conveyor belts. With luck you can find a Self Service Luggage-Kart for Travelers' Convenience, which looks like a wire grocery basket and has a sign on it that says: "Please Do Not Leave Child Unattended in Upper Compartment."

My car was the last in the train — a red and orange Union Pacific sleeper labeled "Pacific Island." It was divided into half a dozen bedrooms, which were closed up tight, like isolation chambers in the contagious wing of a hospital, and eleven one-passenger roomettes. In two or three of the roomettes, passengers were sitting with their hands folded, but most of the spaces seemed to be empty.

By the time I had stowed my suitcase under the seat, washed my hands at a metal washbasin that unfolded from the wall, and walked back three cars to the Dome Diner, the train was sneaking quietly out of the station. It moved so furtively that two bosomy women, absorbed in eating veal sauté, looked up and cried out in delighted surprise when an electric sign flicked past the window; and by then we had almost reached the Bensenville Freight Yards.

Today, the overland train takes the track of the Milwaukee Road instead of the Chicago and North Western; but the route is practically the same. For almost an hour you are in Chicago, or what amounts to Chicago: first a sooty, grayish welter of machine shops and storage lofts; then the World's Largest Automobile Dealer, blushing under a huge canopy of pink neon tubing; and then miles and miles of red brick houses, drive-in restaurants, swollen creeks, and tennis courts covered with snow. After the train breaks out of the suburbs, it avoids large towns and makes only three regular stops between Chicago and Omaha, almost five hundred miles west. I was able to apply myself without distraction to dinner (charcoal broiled spring lamb chops, mint jelly, $4.50) and car-inspecting.

The Dome Diner had cheerful pink tablecloths, plaques of stylized Western scenes bolted to the walls, and dark blue window curtains. In the rear were half a dozen tables, at one of which a young man and woman in new-looking clothes sat in silence, staring at their plates. When they had finished staring, the steward escorted them out and came back rubbing his hands together.

"Great occasion," he said, addressing the whole car. "If I'd of got married every time I was in love, I'd of been married a hundred times. As it is, I only been married three times."

I took the opportunity to ask whether I might look at some of the domestic arrangements of the train — say, the commissary.

"Take a good look," the steward said, suddenly gloomy. "Who knows? Next year, the year after . . . maybe we'll be carrying dry rations."

He led me to the galley, which was in a sort of dip below the main floor and seemed to consist entirely of stainless steel cabinets. Then we went up a flight of steps into the dome section above. The lights were out, and you could see stars and dark pastures and a frozen river glittering with streaks of moonlight.

"Nice in the daytime," the steward said. "You can have breakfast up here tomorrow."

But this reminded me that I would be leaving the train early in the morning. I said goodnight and went back to my roomette.

Except for its decadent profusion of mirrors, the most notable features of this little chamber were its built-in toilet, artfully concealed under a small, leatherette bench, and its abundance of instructional markers — Lower Basin, Waste Cups, Hook Bed Here, and so on. The bed, neatly made up with heavy muslin sheets and brown woolen blankets, literally *was* one of the walls; when it was lowered to a horizontal position, it filled the entire space, like a cot in a closet. This put the toilet out of reach, but I found I could regain access by climbing out of bed and into the corridor, raising the bed into the wall, and then coming back into the roomette. Afterward, of course, one has to go into the corridor again to lower the bed.

The tick was good — as good, I am sure, as any Mr. Vivian ever slept on. But it would not be pleasant for three, even laid head to toe, especially if any of them happened to make frequent use of the toilet. As for its accommodating an old man, his wife, and four children, I will have to say they could not be *my* wife and *my* children. □

THE TERMINAL AT COUNCIL BLUFFS, WITH OMAHA IN THE DISTANCE.

CHAPTER IV

Omaha–
Frontier at Mid-Continent

1877: Six-Shooters, Bogus Lockets, and Farms for $40 Down Payment

OMAHA, THE GREAT COMMERCIAL EMPORIUM of Nebraska, is beautifully located, partly in the broad valley of the Mississippi River and partly on the high bluffs beyond. It has an industrious and enterprising population of twenty thousand. There are many public buildings of imposing exterior, among which are the United States Post Office and Court House[1] and the Omaha High School. Other indications of prosperity and progress are the number and excellence of the newspapers in Omaha and the comfort and elegance of the hotels.

Mrs. Leslie writes: We took a carriage and set forth to view the town. We found it big, lazy, and apathetic; the streets dirty and ill-paved; the clocks without hands to point out the useless time; the shops, whose signs mostly bore German names, deserted of customers, while managers and clerks lounged in the doorways, listless and idle. This depressing state of affairs is, presumably, temporary, for we were told that two years ago Omaha was one of the most thriving and busy cities of the West. Its position at the terminus of three great Eastern roads and the beginning of one great Western one would naturally entitle it to that preeminence.

When the present hard times are over, Omaha doubt-less will shake off the lethargy depressing her and rise to the position her citizens fondly claim for her. We saw some tasteful private residences, with conservatories and stables; the High School building, which might justly be called a palace of learning; the military headquarters, and barracks of the armory of the state; the Grand Central Hotel, a large and imposing edifice, admirably conducted; and also the less imposing but more remarkable Cozzens House, erected in 1867 by the brilliant and erratic George Francis Train,[2] who, arriving at Omaha one day, was told there was no accommodation for his party.

"No rooms to be had? Then I'll build me a hotel!" —and he did, within six weeks.

Returning to the station, we found the platform crowded with the strangest and most motley people it has ever been our fortune to encounter. Men in alligator boots and loose overcoats made of blankets and wagon rugs, with wild, unkempt hair and beards and bright, resolute eyes, almost all well-looking, but strange as denizens of another world.

The women looked tired and sad and were queerly dressed in gowns that must have been old on their grandmothers, and with handkerchiefs tied over their heads in place of hats; the children were bundled up in

LUNCH BASKETS
FILLED
FOR 25 CENTS
TAKE NOTICE
BLACK HILLERS

A CHARACTER SCENE IN THE EMIGRANT WAITING ROOM OF THE UNION PACIFIC DEPOT AT OMAHA.

BRIDGE OVER THE MISSOURI RIVER AT OMAHA.

garments of nondescript purpose and size, but they were generally chubby, neat, and gay as they frolicked in and out among the boxes, baskets, bundles, bedding, and babies' chairs piled waist high on the platform.

We found that these were emigrants bound for the Black Hills — by rail to Cheyenne and Sioux City, and after that by wagon trains. A French family attracted attention by the air of innate refinement which seems to attach to every grade of society in France, and we chatted with them for some moments. A great many families were German; and Ireland, England, and Scotland also were represented.

We passed on to visit the emigrant lodging house and outfitting shop adjoining the station. The shop, although large, was crowded, and the air insufferably close; long counters ran across the room, and upon them, and upon lines stretched above, lay or hung every variety of equipment desirable for pioneer life — clothes, blankets, mats, tins, hats, shoes, babies' rattles, impartially mixed and exhibited, while some attention to the aesthetic needs of humanity was shown in various stuffed heads of moose and deer with quails perched upon their antlers.

In the eating room a good, substantial, homely dinner is neatly served at twenty-five cents a plate, and a placard informs the guests that children occupying seats at table will be charged full price; a precautionary measure not unreasonable, it seemed to us, in view of the swarms of innocents. Lodging is the same price as dinner, and the superintendent triumphantly informed us that the sheets were changed every night.

Leslie's Newspaper continues: This unpretending though sufficiently commodious "Emigrant House" is provided by the Union Pacific Railroad Company to save strangers, and especially emigrants, who cannot afford the luxury of a first-rate hotel, from extortion and fraud.

Women, children, aged grandfathers, border ruffians, dogs, gambling sharps, peripatetic vendors, soldiers, thieves, and pickpockets are jumbled together in a heterogeneous mass. A confused babel of sounds and the clinking of glasses denotes the ever-present proximity of the drinking bar and its deluded votaries. While a mother dandles a child in her arms, two ferocious-looking loungers within a couple of feet of her are dilating upon the merits of their six-shooters; and within a yard, a railroad sharp has pinned a grizzle-haired miner to the wall with the enraptured sight of his bogus chains and lockets. The eager, questioning anxiety of some who have invested their all in the present venture, and the devil-may-care air of others who have nothing to invest are contrasted with the self-satisfied demeanor of the seasoned backwoodsman as he chuckles to himself over the struggles that are just beginning.

The emigrant department is fitted up with kitchen, sleeping apartments, washing and dressing rooms. Luncheon baskets filled here can be replenished from supplies carried on the trains. All these arrangements are under the supervision of persons responsible to the railroad company, an especial duty of whose agents is to give information and assistance and to see that settlers and emigrants are protected from imposition.

Such inducements have their weight at this juncture, when factories are idle, business at a standstill, and thousands aimlessly wandering about the streets and begging their bread. Mr. Greeley's motto[3] was never more appropriate. Were these unemployed people on free homesteads in the West, food and lodging would be assured; and it would be difficult to produce more than could profitably be sold to the markets of the East, the starving populations of Europe, or the miners in Nebraska, Wyoming, and Colorado. Many a poor fellow has worn out three times the energy in begging for work that would be necessary to take him from New York to Nebraska.

Go West! Go cheaply, before your clothing is worn out and all of your earnings are expended for food. A little money on your arrival will secure you a home where there is no rent to pay and no fear for the morrow! Your prairie farm will be a savings bank with an added feature — the more you take out of it, the more thoroughly you till it, the greater will be the amount

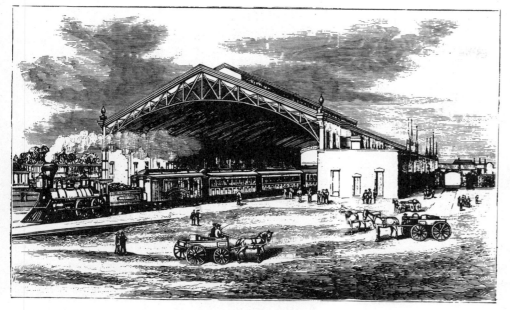

EXTERIOR OF THE OMAHA DEPOT.

deposited to your credit. These inducements appeal with tenfold force to men with families.

Nebraska is in that central portion of the United States which has grown most rapidly in population and wealth. Through the entire length of the state, along the wide and fertile valley of the Platte, the Union Pacific Railroad extends ample facilities to the farmer. The eastern part of Nebraska is the most desirable for farmers. Here the railway company has millions of acres of splendid land in the Platte bottoms and on the contiguous uplands, while at a distance from the railroad there are large tracts still open for settlement under the Homestead and Preemption laws. The soil of the Platte bottom is chiefly a dark, rich, sandy loam, quick and light and exceedingly productive. The adjacent upland consists almost entirely of the famous lacustory or lake deposit, often to the depth of from fifty to a hundred feet. It is nearly identical with dried Missouri River mud. No intelligent farmer need fear drought. Plow deep enough and sufficient moisture can always be obtained. Fruits thrive well. The soil is identical with that whence comes the Rhine wine of Germany. The fall of snow and rain in winter is trifling, though the free sweep of the winds frequently causes deep and extensive snow drifts. The autumn months are dry, while those of spring and early summer are favored with abundant rains which are absorbed by the soil with wonderful rapidity. This gives a dry atmosphere which carries on an average one-half the amount of moisture necessary to produce rain. This is conducive to health and hence the freedom this section enjoys from malarious diseases so often generated in new countries.

In the Platte bottom excellent water is everywhere obtained at the door of the settler by the simple and useful contrivance called a "Drive Well." It consists of an iron tube, perforated with many fine holes and shod at the end with a sharp conical point. This is driven to a depth of fourteen or fifteen feet, according to the elevation above low-water mark in the Platte. An ordinary pump is then attached to the upper end and the water is never-failing.

Terms of payment for land vary much with the circumstances of buyer and seller. The Union Pacific Railroad Company has definite rules for its sales. Better terms are offered to colonists than to single purchasers. The company sells for cash at a discount of ten per cent on its published prices, but to colonists and actual settlers only it grants a credit of ten years at six per cent.

The total payments of principal and interest for 80 acres of land at $5 per acre are $529. In other words, a man pays an average rental per year of $52.90 for 80 acres of good land, and at the end of that time the land is *his own*, with the natural increase in value and all the improvements he may have made.

The first year he will have vegetables for his family and sufficient corn and fodder for his two horses, two cows, and two pigs. He will sell some butter and eggs and have one pig to put in the barrel and one to keep over.

To do this comfortably with a wife and small family, he should be able to start with about $800, distributed as follows:

For his two first payments on his land	$ 61.60
For his family	100.00
For a rude cabin and furniture	150.00
For horses and wagon	250.00
For plow and implements	100.00
For two cows and pigs	100.00
Incidentals	38.40
Total	$800.00

Many have done the first year with a sod house, which with all its furniture has not cost $50. But with less than $500 it would not be reasonable for a man to undertake a farm of his own. Everything that is commenced with a small capital involves both energy and self-sacrifice in its first stages, but the poor young farmer who will select wisely 80 acres of good prairie will not long have to deny himself and family the solid comforts of life. □

1967: Night-Life in Ahamo

A FRIEND OF OURS whose business takes him occasionally to Nebraska told me that he had visited Omaha three times before he caught on to the anagrammatic meaning of Ak-Sar-Ben, the huge civic organization that entertains the city the year round with theatricals, rodeos, concerts, and horseraces.

"I thought it was one of those Arabic things, like the Shriners," he recalled. "Then I realized — backwards! And I said to myself, 'Well, isn't that just like Omaha?'"

I counted this as a trifling slander on a sturdy, if unspectacular, American city, because, as cities go, Omaha certainly is not backward. On the contrary, it is rather forward, continually advertising itself as the Strategic Center of the Nation, the Marketing Hub of America, and the GO City. (GO stands for "Greater Omaha.") Its soul is orderly and prudent: a city of packing houses and ubiquitous insurance companies, of Cudahys, Joslyns, Peter Kiewit & Sons, and Father Flanagan's Boys Town.

But there is no denying Omaha has a certain peculiarity of outlook — not exactly backward-looking, but Janus-like. It seems to be constantly glancing behind itself, over its shoulder, toward the East, while at the same time gazing fondly westward at its own unique empire on the prairie, the new world of late immigrants from Eastern Europe and Scandinavia, of Willa Cather, Mari Sandoz, and William Jennings Bryan.

A century ago, Omaha was the dividing point between the "West" and the "Far West." It is still a border town: the most easterly city of the West — or, perhaps, the most westerly city of the East. Crouched on the western bluff of the Missouri at the beginning of the open plains, Omaha seems to have one toe hooked back over the river, onto the shore of Iowa, the established land.

Getting down from the train on a January night, I thought I could detect this tender balance, this ambivalence of soul. Every vehicle within the great division yards appeared to be in flux. Engines were shunting to and fro, cars coupled and uncoupled, back and forth over the river bridges, with the dark, divisive water swirling down below: decisions for the East, options for the West, then everything rushing outward in the grip of an irresistible centrifugal force.

No passengers, of course: the enormous waiting room was as empty as the temple of a dead religion. The huge chandeliers illuminated rows and rows of vacant benches, closed wickets, and deserted aisles. A couple of redcaps, whispering in a corner, eyed me as if I were a piece of food. I escaped them by hiding my suitcase in a locker and ducking into a phone booth. There I called an acquaintance and asked him what he'd do on a night in Omaha.

"This is the wrong time of year to be in Omaha," he said gloomily. "Omaha stays home at this time of year."

It occurred to me to ask what Omaha was doing at home, but I was afraid that might lay me open to an invitation to make a fourth at bridge; so I wished my friend a comfortable winter and took a cab out to the Joslyn Museum to see whether it afforded any clues to Omaha's geographic fixation.

The Joslyn is a well-organized, splendidly housed institution that displays, among other things, a fine collection of paintings of the American West. I marked this as evidence of a westering tendency. While I was examining a collection of Nebraska plowshares, however, I was accosted by an elderly lady swathed in black furs who told me, after learning I was from California, that she was very fond of San Francisco and had last been there for the Exposition of 1915. This, I felt, was a definitely Midwestern confession.

When the museum closed at nine o'clock, I walked downtown, past a night college that had just released several hundred students in loden coats and levis into the parking lot. (Western influence? They certainly looked more like the students of UCLA than those of Harvard.) Behind the school some boys were playing basketball in the dark. (Midwestern. Such devotion to basketball scarcely is known west of Indiana.) On Nineteenth Street I passed a couple of Shriners in the fezzes of Tangier Temple. (Midwest again.)

In the business district, East met West with an impact worthy of a *National Geographic* article about Beirut. At the Circle C Bar (Western) near the new Federal Building (Eastern boilerplate), several men were drinking Michelob beer (Midwestern) and listening to Sarah Vaughan (Eastern) sing a popular song adapted from a minuet by J. S. Bach (Mittel-European).

Thoroughly confused, I went into a restaurant that had been recommended by my hibernating Omaha acquaintance and ordered a Nebraska-fed steak, which I was sure would be indigenous. The restaurant had the Far-Western atmosphere considered appropriate by operators of steak houses everywhere. There was a photographic mural of badlands on the back wall, and a cook in a white cap and neckerchief stood at a copper-plated counter and handed large platters of beef to the waitresses. I recognized the touches of Pacific Coast hospitality: the mixed green salad was accompanied by a lazy Susan holding three kinds of dressing — French, Roquefort, and Thousand Island — and the waitress spooned sour cream and chopped shallots onto my baked potato, which was steaming sullenly in a damp wrapper of aluminum foil. In fact, the only way you could tell you were not in California was by looking at the wine list. Under "Red Dinner Wines," the management listed Mogen David Concord Grape, Gallo Ruby Port, and a carbonated rosé. I ordered milk, and the waitress nodded in approval.

"Are there some nightclubs in town?" I asked. "I mean, where's the action?"

"You mean The Strip?" the waitress said, collecting my saucer of olive pits.

"Is there a Strip?" (That had to be a point for the West.)

"Motel strip," she said. "That's where the nightclubs . . . you got a car?"

I said I was traveling through on the great transcontinental railroad. The waitress, a pretty but rather sulky girl, looked at me suspiciously.

"There's Mickey's downtown," she said. She went and got an entertainment newspaper that had a full-page advertisement for Mickey's Continuous Entertainment: "The first bevy of lovely a-go-goers start at noon, just in time for lunch a-go-go! Day and night it swings! The magical hour in the evening is 7:00, when another flock of tempting go-go beauties move in."

I believe we are indebted to the French for the term "a-go-go," but its use in the context of Mickey's ad suggested a West Coast influence that might settle the question of Omaha's cultural orientation. Although I had missed the magical hour, I finished my coffee in a hurry and headed down Farnam Street toward Mickey's, passing on the way a viaduct that straddles the street like a Bridge of Sighs and a crowd of women in evening gowns and pink camellias. The viaduct turned out to be an overhead parking garage, and the women were helpmeets of the National Turkey Federation, which was convened at the Sheraton-Fontenelle Hotel.

The main room at Mickey's was crowded, and you could see down into a basement area where some figures were bobbing around in almost total darkness. I found a place at the bar, which was tended by a young, blonde woman dressed in a pink turtleneck sweater and navy blue slacks. (Female bartenders, I think, are Eastern. At any rate, they are not Western.)

Over in a corner of the room, under a bluish spotlight, a girl was making exaggerated swimming movements with her arms and legs, roughly in time to a Beatles record. She was dressed entirely, and quite

modestly, in row upon row of glistening, silver fringe. The lights struck sparks of cold fire from the swirling fringe; the girl smiled vaguely toward the ceiling; and the men at all the crowded tables panted like a pack of basset hounds.

I felt that at last I had stumbled onto a significant clue to the Omaha mentality. As the dancing girls of New York, Chicago, San Francisco, and Los Angeles are stripping away the last vestiges of clothing, their counterparts in Omaha are *covering up!* This tempting go-go beauty was clothed more fully than many a girl on a public beach; yet the audience gave responsive growls at every movement of her fringe-encrusted torso.

To my delight, one of the dancers plunked down at the next barstool and gave me a cautious smile. She was a slender girl, not much over twenty, with her hair combed into a tall, champagne-colored mound—a great, inverted teardrop that looked like a spindle full of waxy filaments balanced on her head.

"Hey, Donna," she said to the barmaid. "What became of my stuff? Right here—a pack of Salems and a vodka gimlet on the rocks?"

While Donna was searching the back counter, the girl introduced herself as Mink—*the* Mink of a dancing trio called Twink, Wink, and Mink. (Mink, I have learned, is a very important word in this part of the country. It signifies an annual music competition among school children from Missouri, Indiana, Nebraska, and Kansas.) I asked her how Mickey's Continuous Entertainment was a-going over.

"You see any empty seats?"

I admitted I did not. Then plunging right in, I suggested: "It's probably something about Omaha that makes them go for that . . . fringe."

"*Om*aha?" Mink said, very indignant. "*I* invented that fringe, mister. and *I'm* from Chi*cago*."

"It's a very nice fringe," I said humbly.

"I got pregnant," Mink explained. "And I didn't want to stop dancing, see? So I went down to this dime store and got yards and yards of this fringe. All the girls liked it and before you know it they all started wearing it. That's the way things get started in show business."

And, with a swish of fringe, she left me. It was, I saw in a few moments, her number. □

FREMONT STATION, AT THE JUNCTION OF THE PLATTE AND ELKHORN VALLEYS.

CHAPTER V

The Fabulous, Featureless Valley of the Platte

1877: Tripods and Linen Dusters Astound the Westerners

WITH OMAHA WE LEAVE BEHIND the last suggestions of life in the States and drink in the first breath of the grandeur and savage freedom of the Plains. Our road lies due west on the straight single track of the Union Pacific; and the train, relaxing its headlong speed to the easier rate of twenty miles an hour, runs smoothly and steadily, describing no more oscillating curves and subject to no erratic jolts and jars. The cozy little tables are put up, the portfolios and sketchbooks spread out, and in half an hour the industrious workers of the party are plying pencils and pens as comfortably as though seated at their own desks at home.

We have entered the Valley of the Platte, whose monotonous level forms the first section, so to speak, of the Plains. It is a desolate, shadeless, featureless land whose only trace of civilization is found in patches of plowed earth, rich and black, alternating with unfenced fields of young grain, and in a few lonely settlements of half a dozen houses with thatched outbuildings which dot the naked landscape at long intervals. Trees there are almost none, except in occasional clumps for which we thank the labor of the settlers and not Nature's liberality. Throughout Nebraska a certain day is yearly set apart for the universal planting of trees upon these desolate ranches, otherwise so exposed to the tremendous sweep of the winds. "Arbor Day"[1] is as familiar a household word in these Western homes as "Thanksgiving" along the Atlantic slope.

To the south we catch sight of the silvery Platte, running due west between its steep, dark bluffs. For some five hundred miles it keeps to this point of the compass, flowing among wide sandy shallows and low islands, fringed with willow and cottonwood and green with swampy meadows; but farther on it winds and doubles in every direction among the Wyoming and Colorado mountains, counting eleven hundred miles, more or less, since surveyors have been unable to trace its remote sources. Sometimes the gleam of water flashes white in the sunshine; sometimes it disappears altogether; but we can always trace its course by the dark line of bluffs and the far-off, feathery fringe of cottonwoods and willows, the only trees that seem to take kindly to the soil of the Plains.

The cottonwood is a characteristic feature of the country west of the Missouri. Slender-stemmed, with smooth, light-yellowish bark and delicate foliage, it blossoms out in June with the downy, fluffy, white flakes to which it owes its name. Its bark is the only winter forage of the Indian herds and frequently an acceptable morsel to our cavalry horses on a Winter campaign. The borders of the Platte are fringed with its soft, grayish masses, mixing with the willows; and farther on we shall see it nursed and watered in the otherwise shadeless "Cities of the Plain" in Colorado and Utah.

At Waterloo Station we cross the Elkhorn River

44

where salmon flourish, having been introduced to those waters by chance and a railway accident. A carload of fish fry en route for California was emptied into the river during a freshet; the young ones grew and multiplied, in spite of theories which confine their existence to streams having access to the sea; and at present the inhabitants of Waterloo have the pleasure of hooking eight-pound salmon. We take a flying glimpse of this little settlement and station, speeding smoothly on to Fremont,[2] where thirty minutes are allowed for dinner.

Fremont is flourishing, as Far Western towns go, with substantial buildings sprinkled among the exceedingly temporary-looking frame structures, and a population of three thousand. Spread before us on the platform are grand specimens of the genuine Westerner, big-bearded and loose-limbed, overlooking with serene contempt the "green Down-Easters," who carry an incongruous atmosphere of Broadway and Beacon Street. There are tired-faced, lean women, in obsolete gowns and bonnets, from the backwoods of Wisconsin and Iowa; flax-headed, sunburnt children, stretching their legs and their lungs; linen-dustered tourists in blue spectacles, exhibiting every stage of disorder and general limpness; and here and there a gaunt old backwoods-

man, as gnarled and brown as some thousand-ringed forest tree. Here come three bouncing Western beauties, arm in arm, who inform the world and the traveling public generally that they have "been out to New York, and glad to git home agin — wouldn't live East thar for nothing in the world!" There, jostled by them as they march up and down, creeps a pale-faced, wasted girl clinging to her mother's arm. No need to tell us *her* errand to the Far West! The mother "has heerd that the air's good for lung troubles up in Virginia City; *he* (supposedly the husband and father) has got a sister thar, and they've wrote out for Carrie to come and try it." And so they are going; but not even the air of Virginia City, be it ever so healing, will bring the color of life back into "Carrie's" sharpened face again.

"All aboard!" The thirty minutes are up. There is a wild charge from the dining room, and mothers chase their broods down the platform and whisk them with nervous haste into the cars again. The girls scramble up the high steps, making considerable gymnastic display by the way; and, last of all, our artist, pocketing his sketchbook, swings himself leisurely up on the rear platform as the long train smoothly and silently rolls on.

OUR FIRST VIEW OF FREMONT AND THE PLATTE RIVER VALLEY.

The chief beauty and interest of the Plains is borrowed from their relation to the sky. The Platte Valley, with its absence of marked features and strong lights and shadows, is something like an expressionless human face to which, on this windy April afternoon, the rolling cloud shadows lend life and change and incessant variety. Great masses of white cumuli pile up in the blue, trooping westward like ourselves before a strong, driving wind; the sun wakes hot on the tawny brown mat of last year's grass; and, as far as eye can reach, there is no shade and no motion in the landscape, except from these hurrying clouds.

The long, parallel lines of smooth, shining rail and the diminishing ranks of telegraph posts, stretching away as we sit on the rear platform, are wonderfully important and suggestive features in the scene. Watching all day, you will scarcely see a curve in that long "iron trail"; only now and then, for a few miles, a sidetrack travels with us and unites at some little station or roundhouse.

Near North Bend, somebody on the back platform raises a shout of "Indians!" Everybody rushes for the first sight. We are rewarded by a cluster of lodges, or, as they are better known, tepees, pointing their white cones within a stone's throw of the track. They are composed of freshly dressed skins and have a picturesque and holiday aspect. We are prepared for meanness and squalor, and are agreeably surprised by a general decency and dignity which savors quite strongly of Cooper braves. We see only a group of tall, motionless figures, bareheaded and blanketed, with long black braids framing each furrowed and stern face; some chubby children, blanketed likewise, standing over a campfire; and two or three squaws, with their swathed-up and mummified papooses. "Why, they are really handsome!" cries the enthusiastic young woman of the party, who has never seen an Indian before.

The tepees have disappeared while we are talking of them. Lounging on our easy seats we discuss Indians and the Indian question, the march of civilization and the chances of buffalo along our route, and learn, to the disgust of some of the party, that we may expect to meet with nothing wilder than the great herds of cattle which have begun to dot the plains. Within the last three years the buffalo have entirely disappeared from the belt of land traversed by the Union Pacific, and only their bones lie bleaching where the trails used to run due north and south.[3] The antelope are fast following, having already retreated west of the Rocky Mountains, and the principal targets for pistol practice on the platform will be prairie dogs and ground owls.

VIEW ON THE PLATTE VALLEY PLAINS, NEAR COLUMBUS,
NEBRASKA, AS SEEN FROM THE UNION PACIFIC RAILROAD.

Trains That Pass

EASTWARD AND WESTWARD BOUND TRAINS PASSING ON THE PRAIRIE.

Soon after Fremont, we find vast excitement in the approach on one of these switches of a train bound east, every window full of heads and arms.

Our photographer, diving into the curtained section which has been set apart for the storage of bags, hampers, and instruments, rummages wildly for his plates and chemicals. Our artist, constituting himself assistant, snatches the camera and disappears; and presently there is diffused over the easy, lounging group of dusty passengers, brakemen in shirtsleeves, and trim, gold-buttoned conductors a universal and frigid atmosphere of "sitting for their pictures."

Everybody strikes a hasty attitude and composes his features; the engineer reclines gracefully against his cowcatcher, and all the hands, with one instinctive impulse, seek sheltering pockets, while artist and photographer shift their tripod from spot to spot, hit the happy point of sight at last, and fix the picture.

Then there is a scramble for the platforms again. The engines puff and wheeze. In another minute there is only a trail of brown smoke hanging over the plain beside us, and we are once more alone on the great empty waste.

THE SCHUYLER STATION: DEPARTURE OF AN EASTWARD TRAIN.

Schuyler,[4] grandly denominated "the county seat of Colfax County," is the next station of consequence, and here again our photographer is on the alert with his instruments. There is a fair sprinkling of neat houses and a show of white paint; and here by the station is that universal feature in a Western landscape, the tank house and tall skeleton windmill, whirring briskly in the strong wind. The "population of eight hundred" is thinly represented by masculine stragglers on the platform: brown-bearded men, with pantaloons tucked in their big cowhide boots, and not a woman in sight, if we except two specimens of three feet high, who take prominent positions on the railroad ties as soon as the camera is mounted. We frequently wonder where in these sparse settlements, which the guidebook respectfully designates "thriving towns," the women manage to secrete themselves, for we never catch sight of a skirt or a bonnet.

48

A stretch of barren prairie again, grazing cattle far away, and the eternal dance of the cloud shadows. Here and there, we pass a solitary ranch or a low "dugout" that gravelike mound of earth thrown up with its boarded front and rough door, crowned, perhaps, with a pair of spreading ox horns. In the Indian skirmishes of a few years back, these molelike burrows, with their roofing of solid earth and stout rawhide, did good service in protecting the beleaguered settlers; now they serve a more peaceful end and are used chiefly as storehouses, standing by the mud-and-thatch stable and large corral of some lonely ranches.

The afternoon is wearing on as we reach Columbus.[5] This "county" is a neat, thrifty-seeming little settlement, too utterly unlike an Eastern town or village to be designated by either name. Our brief pause gives us the general impression of broad, shadeless streets, neat stores, and a smart brick building or two, with a glaring white hotel fronting the track. There is so strong a family likeness among all these baby cities that the traveler turns in despair to his guidebook to learn the characteristic points and the difference in population. Columbus is a very twin of Schuyler, just passed; but it overtops that small rival by twelve hundred souls and gains in dignity accordingly—on paper.

Our artists availed themselves of every opportunity on the route to take flying sketches of the characteristic human oddities of the country. Now, it would be an independent, female member of the Order of Mennonites, regaling herself with a pipe on the platform of a passing train. Then the pencils would be brought into play to depict a party of Pawnee scouts, or a group of children standing ankle-deep in a pool by the track, saluting our train with cheers and waving hats.

Vendors of prairie dogs were occasionally encountered, with their living prey carefully boxed up after the Washington Market fashion. The villages of these quaint little animals are seen on every side for many miles. The animals, always fat, are about sixteen inches long and of a grayish-red color. The Indians eat them, professing to prefer them to squirrels. They live underground in extensive communities of slanting burrows, terminating, after a descent of six or eight feet, in wide chambers. These they sagaciously excavate at a little higher point than the bottom of the passages, so that the larger apartments, which they sometimes share with rattlesnakes and owls, are not flooded by rainstorms. The little fellows squat like rabbits on their plump haunches at the entrances to their burrows, peering inquisitively about. At the approach of an intruder they give a quick, sharp yelp, not loud enough to be called a bark, and disappear headforemost into the earth. But their curiosity is more powerful than their timidity, and in a short time their little noses are seen emerging from the holes.

The rise in the grade from Omaha has been so gradual and continuous that one is at first surprised to discover himself nearly fifteen hundred feet above the sea. And yet, although the whole surrounding landscape seems low and level, there is a curious sense of elevation in the purity of the air and the strong sweep of the

OUR ARRIVAL AT COLUMBUS, AT THE JUNCTION OF THE LOUP FORK AND PLATTE RIVERS.

49

PAWNEE SCOUTS OFF DUTY.

AN INDEPENDENT MENNONITE.

CHILDREN SALUTING EXCURSION TRAIN AT CLARKS.

Scenes on the

AN INHABITED TELEGRAPH POLE,
CLARKS, NEBRASKA.

Prairie

SELLING PRAIRIE DOGS.

A VILLAGE OF PRAIRIE DOGS DIVING INTO THEIR BURROWS.

winds. By feeling, rather than sight, one is conscious of being nearer cloudland.

We are now one hundred-odd miles from Omaha and just south of the extreme corner of the Pawnee Reservation, a tract of land said to be one of the finest in the state, which now lies wholly unoccupied, this particular body of the Government's "wards" having turned their backs upon it and gone into the Indian Territory. The tribe has dwindled to a mere handful since the days, not far distant, when they lorded it over the Platte Valley, fought the Sioux, massacred the settlers and dotted

with their lodges all the willowy surface of the Plains. Not far from Silver Creek we are given a flying glimpse of this savage life in the shape of a band traveling eastward. We have no means of ascertaining the tribe, but it is a picturesque and not unpleasing sight—the string of shaggy Indian ponies ridden by grim, blanketed "bucks," trailing their lodge-poles behind them; the papoose-laden squaws; and the brown children, driving a stray pony or two in the rear. They pass close by the track, and as we rush past them all their faces, hideously shining with red paint, are turned up to our windows and seen for an instant before we leave them far behind.

Before we reach the supper station at Grand Island, sunset overtakes us. Not such a sunset as we have seen in the East, but a marvel of cloud scenery, a solemn, splendid pageant, the likeness of which is unrolled nowhere but above these great plains. All the little, fleecy, flying clouds and all the great snowy banks that drifted and piled in the sky today have gathered together and massed themselves in the west, "Pelion on Ossa," rising to the very zenith in stormy blue-black domes and ragged peaks whose bases burn with long lines of gold and fire. We never have known before the height and depth and vastness of the sky or seen more than a little strip, a tiny acre or two. Here the lower world is lost and forgotten in the wonder overhead. The earth is a vague, dusky unreality, and the heavens are islanded with solid hills, darkened with mountain chains and grim, black ramparts, and aflame as with the light of a thousand conflagrations.

All the glory has departed when we reach Grand Island. We have passed four thriving "towns"—Clark's, Lone Tree, Chapman's, and Lockwood—which boast two or three stores apiece and where, according to the guidebook, trade is "lively"; and now, as the twilight gathers, we approach the ever-welcome supper station. Grand Island, so called after a large and well-settled island in the Platte River, is a place of consequence, and its recently built hotel, fronting close on the track, has the reputation of furnishing the best meals along the route. The large, white building looms up quite imposingly in the dusk, with cheerful light in its many windows and a vista of crowded tables within, round which waitresses flit while the traveling public engages in a terrific attack upon the dishes. Outside, there is a fair proportion of mere lookers-on, like ourselves—parties who have come provisioned for the trip, and to whom dinner and supper stations merely afford chances for a constitutional on the platform. Quite a long promenade is built out on either side of the hotel, enclosing a grassy square in front where a tiny fountain plays refreshingly; and a real treat is the short, rapid walk there in the fresh wind, with the starlight brightening overhead.

Here we saw the first tufts of buffalo grass—that richest and most nutritious of all the varieties for which Nebraska is famous, formerly the uniform carpeting of the whole Platte Valley. It grows in thick, short bunches, never exceeding two or three inches in height, with curiously crimpled blades, matted so as to give it an elastic spring to the tread. Dry and withered as it looks, it is wonderfully sweet and rich and furnishes a perpetual forage to the herds that rove in its

A CITY ON THE PLAINS: KEARNEY JUNCTION, ON THE PLATTE RIVER.

neighborhood. Like the buffalo which it fed, however it is gradually disappearing under the foot of the settler, and it is rarely that a bunch can be found so near the line of the wayside stations.

Darkness gathers, but an illumination is prepared for us farther on: a bright, hot patch of flame away to the south of us. Hardly have we flocked on the platform to look at this than another is discovered in the north, and gradually the whole night is dotted with these far-away conflagrations, round which we can here and there see dark figures moving as the settlers gather to fight the terrible foe.

We are fast gaining that section of the country where vegetation dwindles down to a mere stubble; even the cottonwood is thinning out, and only along the borders of the river we see its dusky fringe in the distance. Patches of alkali crop out occasionally, like a thin coating of hoarfrost between the rapidly increasing tufts of buffalo grass. It is a weird, wild-looking world, between the moonlight and firelight, from which all familiar features seem stricken out.

The lights of Alda twinkle through the dark, and we thunder over its iron bridge, spanning the tiny stream known ambitiously as Wood River. In the days of '59 and '60 when Alda was a frontier settlement, this stream was thickly fringed with timber, and hence its name; but the building of the Union Pacific road rapidly swallowed it up for fuel and other needs. Some of the first log houses are still to be seen in this vicinity —venerable ruins of seventeen years' standing.

Kearney,[6] once a flourishing point for the shipment of cattle and a rendezvous for stockmen and herders, is now almost deserted, and the ruins of its old "corral" can be seen from the car window. Kearney Junction, four miles beyond, is a rapid, five-year-old town with a population of one thousand and a goodly show of brick and mortar and neat frame buildings. Here, for the first time, the westward-going tourist will look upon a town literally without a tree; not a patch of shade or a cluster of friendly green — not even an apology in the shape of a shrub—appears to variegate the tawny brown stretch upon which these little white houses are dotted, like a child's toy village set up at random on the nursery floor. The crops raised here are said to be excellent, and the grazing lands are fine; but one cannot help thinking that the sun-baked dwellers at Kearney Junction must be willing to barter some of these advantages for a handsbreadth of foliage.

The Burlington and Missouri Railroad here connects with the Union Pacific, and the little town is an outgrowth of this junction. Besides its ordinary, active flow of life, it is occasionally enlivened by a raid from Texan herdsmen, whose cattle are driven up now and then to graze in the vicinity; these visits are usually productive of a murder or two, or a row at the least. Colin with the pipe and the crook is obsolete; your guardian of the flocks today sweeps the country like a centaur, with jangling spurs, flashing bowie knives in his boots, a ready revolver or two and, in place of amorous ditties, a round fire of unique oaths, always ready on the shortest notice and in the most unlimited quantity. □

1967: What Became of Plum Creek?

IN HER INTRODUCTION TO *My Antonia*, Willa Cather describes a trip across the prairie with an old friend from the Nebraska town where she grew up.

"While the train flashed through never-ending miles of ripe wheat, by country towns and bright-flowered pastures and oak groves wilting in the sun, we sat in the observation car, where the woodwork was hot to the touch and red dust lay deep over everything. The dust and heat, the burning wind, reminded us of many things. We were talking about what it is like to spend one's childhood in little towns like these, buried in wheat and corn, under stimulating extremes of climate: burning summers when the world lies green and billowy beneath a brilliant sky, when one is fairly stifled in vegetation, in the color and smell of strong weeds and heavy harvest; blustery winters with little snow, when the whole country is stripped bare and grey as sheet-iron. We agreed that no one who had not grown up in a little prairie town could know anything about it. It was a kind of freemasonry, we said."

My own prairie town was in Iowa, not in Nebraska; and I did not grow up in it but only passed some summers there, battening in the tall corn as a visitor from the Pacific Coast, a region that Iowans of my grandparents' generation vaguely distrusted, apparently on moral grounds.

Still, in spite of these deficiencies of breeding, I recognized familiar scenes in all the small Nebraska towns along the railroad line: a pool of melting snow, reflecting Ma's Café and Dr. Siefert's dental office on the second floor; the overbearing pediment of a Masonic Temple in Grand Island; a waiting room with white-tiled floor, glazed crullers, pyramids of apples, and a painting of the Grand Canyon over the door; a hotel with its name spelled out in yellow bricks embedded in the red brick wall.

It was this brick mosaic-work that plunged me into a particularly funky, moist nostalgia. Brick mosaic, whatever its demerits, is undeniably a lost art, related to the sacred inlays of Constantinople and Ravenna and the enormous aggregates of pastel glass and pyrites that mask the faces of savings and loan offices on Wilshire Boulevard. It survives in its archaic purity in only a few places such as the walls of the City Artificial Ice Plant, the Light and Power Plant, and the Wheatgrowers Hotel in Kimball, Nebraska. All afternoon I looked for brick mosaics, and each one I saw afforded me a twinge of pleasure, pity, and self-recognition.

But as the hours went past and the brick mosaics accumulated, I began to suspect that my sentimental reaction was not the result of a real affinity for prairie towns but of a literary heritage common to most Americans who lived between the two world wars.

In those days, small-town life was an inescapable experience to everyone who opened a book or a magazine or turned on the radio. American writers were obsessed with small-town attitudes, not only on the Nebraska plains but in Winesburg, Ohio, Spoon River, Massachusetts, and Pine Ridge, Arkansas. Fitzgerald's flappers and Hemingway's expatriates were in reckless flight from the small town. Sinclair Lewis's Carol Kennicott was trapped in it. Zona Gale, Ruth Suckow, Thornton Wilder, Booth Tarkington, Eugene O'Neill, Glenway Wescott, and Oxydol's own Ma Perkins played variations on it — praising it, protesting it, regretting it, bidding it goodbye forever.

Then, rather suddenly, the small town vanished from our archetypal literature. Plum Creek and Grundy Center slipped our minds, along with the overland railroad trains, their red plush seats and dusty mahogany paneling. My generation, raised in the Great Depression on John Dewey principles, Big-Little books, and after-school jobs peddling *Liberty* and *Country Gentleman*, may be the last to read with sympathy about the suffocating social life, the ennui, the convoluted sexuality, the stifling heat and blinding cold of the Great Plains. The freemasonry of the prairie has died or moved to Arizona; and writers like Willa Cather and Sinclair Lewis will be read in the future, if at all, not as sensitive artificers of well-remembered scenes, but as chroniclers of quaint times and places as remote as Hawthorne's New England, James's New York, or Twain's Missouri. Nowadays, our reading matter has to do with international conspiracies, slums, the Sunset Strip, New England universities, Big Sur, Connecticut, Las Vegas, Pennsylvania, the psychiatric ward, the pillbox, and the moon. None has the scent of Western soil about it: no corncobs, no chicken feathers, no weather — in fact, scarcely any landscape at all, except what is man-made — and certainly no small towns.

The reasons are clear enough. We are an urban people now, and urban people never see the country at less than panoramic distance. We fly over this great midland in jet airplanes, leaping from New York to Los Angeles, from Washington to San Francisco. When could we find time to look at the in-between? Even from an automobile freeway, the village streets are hidden by hedges of oleander.

In any case, the small towns have changed. The wilderness is sown with trailer parks, oil wells, rocket-launching pads, and television pylons that look like miniature Eiffel towers. Frozen strawberries, Cornish hens, and spinach soufflés go thundering nonstop across the Great American Desert in the diesel rigs of the Pacific Intermountain Express and Consolidated Freightways. The prairie is just like Everywhere Else. It is hard to remember why we once were so concerned about its *influence*, and impossible to imagine how the fate of Plum Creek could interest a man passing over it in a jet.

Viewed close-up, Platte Valley towns are as alike as the red bricks they are made of. A gray station house and an empty platform flash past the windows of the train; a tank of anhydrous ammonia, a granary, a John Deere warehouse; then the frozen earth spreads out again, burned black along the tracks, but gray and sallow in the distance. The yellow stubble fields are striped with dingy snow. Black cattle tug at bales of hay. There are piglets in the leafless woods and sheep in the naked fields, and the pale sun glows like a luminous thumbprint on the blank, gray surface of the winter sky.

In the late afternoon—way out on the western prairie, gray-brown, tawny and bare, with puffs of tumbleweed caught in the barbed wire fences — we stopped in one of those old cattle-shipping towns that has a tank-farm and some loading chutes and a grove of willows by the creek. A man in a brown tweed overcoat and a teal-green hat came out of the station and took a bag of mail from the train. Our brakeman leaned down from the platform between the cars and said: "Hey, how come you don't have no passengers for us when we make this nice stop for you?"

The stationmaster laughed.

"Nobody left, I guess."

"What's it gonna do, rain?" the brakeman asked.

"Five per cent chance," said the stationmaster. "Guess that's it, huh? Highball, Gene? Highball?"

As we pulled away, a brown dog was loping right down the center of Main Street, past the apple-green facade of Bergen's Department Store. I felt that I had seen it all a hundred thousand times, and I saw myself again as a freemason of the prairie towns, with Willa Cather and her friend Jim Burden and their Antonia: last of a doomed tribe, like the handful of passengers on the train from Omaha. □

CHANGING MAILS ON THE UNION PACIFIC RAILWAY AT RIVERSIDE, NEBRASKA — FROM A SKETCH BY WALTER YEAGER.

CHAPTER VI

The Hard Places of the Plains

1877: Indians and Emigrants— and Bitter Memories of War

THE FIRST NIGHT ON THE PLAINS is probably passed by every curious and enthusiastic traveler in spasmodic efforts to keep awake and see as much as the darkness will reveal to him from his section windows. If there be a moon, the temptation is irresistible; and, drawing back the curtains, he will lie, as we did, dozing, waking, and staring lazily out, conjuring up fantastic shadows in the moonlight of distant tepees, herds of grazing buffalo (which, by the prosaic sunshine, would turn out mere barnyard cows), howling coyotes and dark unknown shapes that traverse the plain with flying leaps and disappear into mystery. Then a warm red star twinkles out near the track, and we come upon some little wayside station, with glowing windows, wide open door, and a wakeful lounger or two on the platform, seen for a second and gone again.

So, in our first night ride we pass a host of little towns and "side tracks"—Stevenson, Elm Creek, Overton, Josselyn, and then Plum Creek, a place with a history—such a history as most frontier towns can tell, repeating each other with painful fidelity through details that would put a dime novelist to the blush.[1]

The Overland Stage Company had formerly a station at Plum Creek, and the Indians and settlers met in sharp conflicts more than once. In 1867 a band of Cheyennes commanded by a chief euphoniously known as Turkey Leg succeeded in wrecking a train on a small culvert near the creek, firing the cars, and capturing all the merchandise. In the moment of their triumph, while reveling among the spoils, the marauders were discovered by a detachment of Pawnee scouts belonging to the command of Major Frank North,[2] and there ensued a brisk fight between Turkey Leg's Cheyennes and the forty-eight Pawnees under Uncle Sam that ended in the utter rout of the hostiles.

A few miles beyond Gannett our train goes roaring over a pile bridge spanning the North Platte near its junction with the main river. The North Platte rises in Colorado, near the Medicine Bow Mountains, and its waters are fed by countless streams and springs in the rugged hills through which it passes. A few years ago it formed the southern boundary of the Sioux Reservation, now shifted farther north. Fort Fetterman, the scene of the terrible Fetterman massacre of 1868, is built on this stream.[3]

The stations are growing smaller and fewer as we travel west. North Platte is notable for its dairy manufactory, an enterprise, like the town, still in its infancy. Nichols, O'Fallon's, Dexter, and Alkali are mere sidetracks. In Alkali we find a reminiscence of Bret Harte, who has given us an almost photographic glimpse of the station, with its "sagebrush, sand and alkali" stretching east and west; of the stationmaster; and of Cicely and Polly. Between this point and Ogallala, nine miles beyond, another Indian fight is recorded. It is well that these battles leave no scars behind them or the whole surface of this lonely land would be darkened with ugly reminders of bloodshed.

Julesburg, one of the "hard" places on the route, took its name from Jules Reni, a Frenchman notorious on the frontier, who was killed by the still more notorious desperado, Jack Slade.[4] The feud between these worthies had run long and high when Slade at last captured his victim. He bound Beni to a post and devoted an hour or two to pistol practice on the animated and helpless target, stolidly ignoring the prayers for death and only taking final aim when the living body was riddled with wounds. The list of murders charged to Slade is a fearful one, and the stories one hears of him testify to his savage cruelty and savage courage; but this cool daredevil, who had braved any odds in a free fight, turned utter coward in the hands of a vigilance committee with the noose at his throat.

Those of us who are watchful through the small hours find food for speculation in the sudden stopping of the train between Julesburg and Chappell. Nobody is sufficiently awake to ask the reason, but as the gray morning breaks — a rainy and desperately dark morning, too — we are told that a freight train a few miles ahead has been wrecked, and we will be stationary until the track has been cleared of debris.

"If the rain would only stop!" cries everyone, panting for a run over the Plains; but it pours on relentlessly, and we stare out at the desolate scenery through a steady and almost blinding storm.

Some of us are not sorry for a glimpse of the Plains in this new phase — a vast brown ocean of low hills, poetically called "divides," rolling away, wave beyond wave, into the distance; the broad Platte close by us, marked by its dark line of willows and cottonwood; the leaden-gray sky overhead; the white sheets of slanting rain; and the wind — such a wind! — shrieking round the cars and converting the telegraph wires into the chords of a ghostly harp. Nobody knows what the wind can do and say save those who have felt its fierce buffets on the Plains. The romantic young woman of the party, emerging upon the platform with the intent of poking for trophies among a pile of buffalo bones close to the track, is instantly knocked flat by these roving breezes and soaked with a gust of rain which cures her of all desire to walk abroad; the men, nevertheless, brave the elements and, getting well to the lee of the train, take a short turn on the sodden ground. North of the track, just under one of the steep divides, is a solitary ranch[5] with a corral and thatched stables and a stockyard; and we watch two roughriders in shiny India rubber who are busy turning out herds of cattle and horses to pasture.

Then, back in the cars, the sketchbooks come into play, and the pens also; the rain drips in, and we dodge its encroachments from table to table; and the wind runs its wild gamut of sobs and cries for two, three, *five* mortal hours, while we sit writing.

The signal is given at last, and we start. Only a short distance on, we pass the wrecks of the train which came to grief in consequence of cows. The cars and engine are smashed, and the six unhappy beasts who chose to disport themselves on the track at so critical a moment are involved in the ruins; but no human lives have been lost or even endangered.

And now we run close to the riverside, so that from the windows we can look down on the sandy shallows and into the brown rippling water. The land is growing more hilly, and the ever-changing lines of the divides are perpetual curves of beauty. As the river recedes again, we are met by the old wagon road or emigrant trail passing close to the track, its deep ruts worn by wheels, and many a little heap of bleached bones marking the spot "where the slow-footed cattle lay down to die" in some hungry march long ago. Near Lodge Pole we pass our first emigrant "Ship of the Plains" — the great canvas top wagon so familiar in pictures of Western life, the team of horses turned loose to graze, an ox browsing near them, and another huge brute lying on its side with a rough group of wet and dejected men standing over him. He has dragged his last load, poor fellow! and next year *his* bones will make another little white landmark in the long, weary journey.

"Arbor Day" in Nebraska

A pleasant feature of the scenery since we left Omaha has been the constant succession of pretty groves of trees, giving to the prairie frequently the appearance of a noble park. This is due to the wise foresight of the settlers. The Nebraskans celebrate a holiday in which the entire population joins in tree planting. This is called "Arbor Day." The tree most popular is the cottonwood, which grows very easily and is quite luxuriant in foliage; however, it is valuable for shelter and stove wood only, not for manufactures. There are trees planted as cuttings in the Platte Valley that have in thirteen years measured twenty-two inches in diameter. Little boys are tempted by large premiums from their parents to test their capacity of tree planting on Arbor Day. Astonishing rapidity has occasionally been known, one farmer having planted from sunrise to sundown 14,000 trees, and in the course of one spring season, over 200,000. Settlers, as fast as they arrive, aim to accomplish two things: first, to break the sod for a cornfield; next, to plant timber shelter. The winds which blow from the west are very constant, often fierce, and a shelter is of immense value to stock and fruit trees. Hedges of white willow several miles in length have been laid, which, at five years from cuttings, have made a perfect fence fifteen feet high; one farm alone has four miles of such continuous fence.

The rain ceases, but the wind has no mind to abate its wrath. Increasing our speed to make up for lost time, we rush past Lodge Pole and Colton. We have entered the region of buffalo grass, and its little tufted cushions cover the whole land, mixing now with dry bunches of cactus whose green, prickly pads show scarcely two inches above the ground. As we near Sidney[6] the divides grow steeper and bolder, taking the form of overhanging bluffs in whose shelter, just south of the track, we soon discern a little cluster of white tents, a bare, square barracks, and then the straggling outskirts of the town.

Sidney is another "hard" place, notable for this attribute and as the nearest railroad point to the Black Hills; the starting point of the weekly stage line to the Spotted Tail agency; and the chief outfitting post, next to Cheyenne, for emigrants to the gold regions. A military post (Fort Sidney) also gives life to the place.[7] The white tents we saw were an encampment of Pawnee scouts bound for the Powder River country.[8] Some of these dark warriors present themselves on the platform, buried in blue army coats three sizes too large, with their long, shaggy hair blowing about their faces. Stiff officers with gold straps and buttons are stirring among the long-booted and slouch-hatted civilians. There is a knot of men about the depot—a little excitement, but not too much, for the cause is only a murder. A gambler has been shot just over the way and was carried into the depot; but that was fully an hour ago, and public interest has died out.

Buttoning overcoats tightly and grasping our hats with a firm hand, we dismount from the cars. Twenty minutes are allowed here for dinner, and these twenty minutes we take for investigations—not at first in the town proper, on the plank sidewalks and among the shops and saloons and outfitting stores, but on the bare slope at the foot of the bluffs lying northwest, where a queer little village of dugouts is nestled to the hillside.

We cross a wide patch of bare, baked earth, hard as iron and covered with an abundant crop of cinders, bones, old iron, broken crockery, broken bottles, and decayed boots, and stop beside a group of emigrant wagons drawn up together, the unharnessed horses staring blankly about them in search of a stray blade to nibble and the shaggy drivers, blue with cold, bustling about among their stores. Two men have put up a little tent and lit a fire inside, and there they sit, cooking some mess in a black kettle, while the ragged canvas flaps and the tent pole creaks dismally in the wind. There are three or four such tents, scarcely high enough for a big man to stand upright in them. Higher up toward the bluffs, the sod-roofed dugouts are seen, each bristling with a rusty stovepipe in lieu of chimney and some boasting a roughly glazed window beside the low doorway. There is a goodly show of clotheslines up among these simple habitations, with flapping linen dancing about in the wind; a horse or two tethered along the bluff, rubbing his nose on the sterile soil; a wandering cow; and, of course, children; but here, as elsewhere, we are obliged to take the female population on trust, for not a solitary representative do we see.

The female members of our party brave the savage winds on the platform and stare wildly about in search of desperadoes. Every man, being a possible murderer and a *most* probable gambler, is invested with a dark and awful interest, albeit most of them

A STREET OF "DUG-OUTS" ON THE HILLSIDE IN SIDNEY, NEBRASKA.

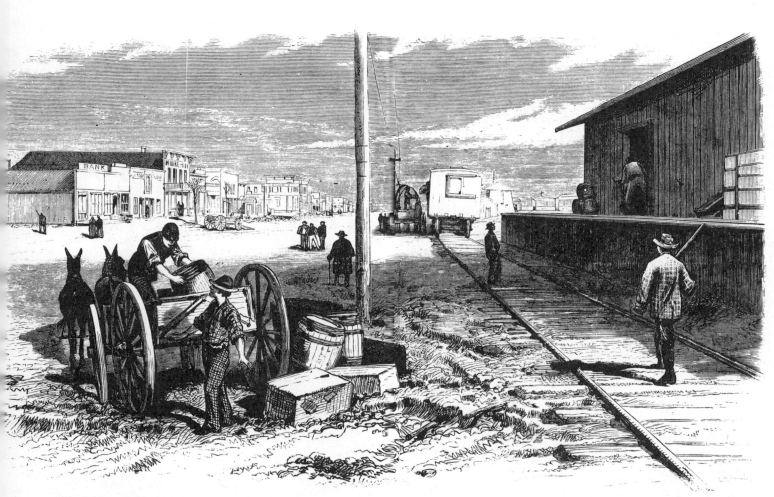

VIEW OF THE TOWN OF SIDNEY, THE NEAREST RAILROAD
STATION TO THE BLACK HILLS.

are sober, quiet-looking citizens, a little given to excess hair, eccentric as to hats, and utterly rejecting "biled shirts," but by no means villainous in physiognomy, and with no visible instruments of offense or defense about them.

One of the ladies, thirsting for information, struggles in the teeth of the wind as far as a little cabin, midway between the depot and the bluffs, and interviews a sociable-looking colored woman, seated on the threshold, as to the morals of Sidney.

"Oh, it's quiet enough roun' yer; nobody troubles me none," she replies with a broad grin.

"No fighting, or anything of that sort?" (in great surprise and faint disappointment).

"Law, no! I don't never hear nothin'. Over yonder —" (indicating with an easy sweep of her hand the

59

A SIDNEY FITTING-OUT STORE FOR BLACK HILLS EMIGRANTS.

opposite side of the railroad track) "—they gambles and fights most all the time, and they kills somebody among 'emselves every now'n' then. But *I* hain't never seen anything of it. There's a lot over there in the buryin' ground[9] that was stabbed or shot or somethin'."

Amply satisfied, the interviewer withdraws. In the meantime our artists have found a mine of interest among the outfitting shops. The word "outfit" is peculiarly a Far Westernism, applied indiscriminately to the movable belongings of a party and to the party itself: any body of people, whether it be a military command or a religious convocation, an exploring party or a sewing circle, comes easily under that head. In the present instance the outfits are almost exclusively of emigrants to the gold region, and the outfitting shops, of which there are several,[10] supply every possible need. Rifles, guns, revolvers — firearms of every description and every patent; knives as numerous and in equal variety; ammunition, cartridge belts, and boxes; buckskin pouches and powder horns are crowded side by side with tins and ironmongery, forks, spoons, flatirons, teakettles, mining implements, and bedding. There is a store of canned meats and vegetables; rolls of flannel, woolen checks, calicos, and hosiery. Everything, almost, for domestic service, from a looking glass to a rolling pin, is jumbled together in this long, low, dark shop and turned over and appraised by a crowd as heterogeneous as the stock itself. A strong, energetic-looking set of men are these Black Hills emigrants,

fresh from the farm lands of Wisconsin, Iowa, Kansas, or the farther Eastern states, where the gold fever has laid hold of them. Whether they will be as successful as the Argonauts of '49 is still a question; but one pities the women who cast their lot with them — tired, desponding-looking women, young and old, carrying heavy babies and herding offspring of larger growth — whom one sees wearily sitting about the outfitting shops or among shabby boxes and bundles outside.

Some huge, heavy emigrant wagons with white canvas covers are loaded and ready to start. A string of these — five or six — are hitched together and drawn by a "team" of ten to sixteen mules in double harness. It is an interesting and exciting business to see the starting-out, the plunging, backing, rearing, and kicking of the mules, and to hear the fluent adjurations of the driver punctuated with incessant cracks of his huge rawhide whip.

As we turn away, a fresh-looking emigrant touches the shoulder of a member of our party, who is carrying Follette, the pet Skye terrier under his arm.

"Say, d'you want to sell your dorg?"

"Well, I hadn't thought of it before."

This vague reply the would-be buyer evidently takes favorably. He proceeds to offer as high as five dollars for the animal, inasmuch as he "wants a good barkin' pup to scare the Injines away nights!"

As at other stations along the route, we hear "Injun" stories at Sidney. The town dates its existence only so far back as the building of the railroad, whose progress was fiercely opposed at this point, as at others, by the neighboring tribes; and the crumbling remains of breastworks formerly raised in preparation for their raids can be seen. Now, nothing more alarming than a Pawnee scout is to be seen. Glancing at one of these warriors, it is difficult to imagine them akin in race to the strong, fierce foes of eight years ago. But, however civilization may have tamed or degraded an Indian — and the terms seem to be synonymous — he keeps to the very end a gleam of the devil in his eyes, a covert snaky glitter that suggests all the horrors one ever heard and sends a curious little chill down one's back.

Our time is up — too soon for the artists and note-takers of the party — who come running wildly from all directions at the shout of "All aboard!" The hideous shrieks of departing engines are rarely heard on Western roads; the trains start smoothly and silently, a custom which is grateful to the senses of the traveler but is occasionally attended with embarrassing results, as in the case of that stray member of our party who was counted among the missing at Chicago in consequence of one of these ghostly departures.

Scrambling on board, we take our places at the windows again as the sharp, high lines of distant bluffs begin to draw nearer to the track and take new shapes. Long breastworks, as of smoothly hewn stone, cut sharp against the horizon, sometimes broken into abrupt notches, cropping out into square towers, or

ridged with massive buttresses. Walls of ragged, calcareous rock, ochery yellow or warm brown, sweep upward from the plain, their steep fronts eaten out into niches and deep holes from which it is not hard to fancy a wild face or two peering out. Sometimes they sink into the level of the plain and disappear, and then another furlong will bring us to some great monumental shape starting up alone and isolated from the dead flat or cresting the ridge of a divide. They have taken the place of trees in the landscape. No other shapes now come between the brown plains and the low, gray sky.

The next stations after leaving Sidney — Berwison, Potter, Bennett, and Antelope — are merely incidental dots along the plain that rather add to than detract from its vast loneliness. Adams and Bushnell follow, and then Pine Bluffs, so-called from a few low, scrubby pines that fringe the bluffs. An Indian trail crosses here, traveled yearly by tribes passing to and fro between the buffalo grounds on the Republican River and Horse Creek and the North Platte.

Tracy is the last station of Nebraska, and here we are 5149 feet above sea level. The sun is going down as we pass the little side track, and the heavy storm clouds are shot through with lines of flame. The crumbling, yellow bluffs have a coppery light upon them against the sky; and they look more weird and wild than ever as we slide past them, chasing the last gleam of sunset into the remote gray shadows of twilight. □

1967: Smile, You Are in Sidney

SIX HOURS WEST OF OMAHA, the *City of San Francisco* makes a one-minute stop at the notorious hellhole of western Nebraska, where Union Pacific conductors used to warn passengers not to get off if they valued their lives.

It is 7:33 in the morning, a cloudless, translucent morning, as pale and cold as pewter, and the wind is staging a protest in some naked hackberry trees on the slope north of the tracks. Up at the top of the bluff, the winter sun is glittering feebly on a silver water tank with SIDNEY painted on the side.

A ticket agent has come down to the end of the platform in a blue Plymouth sedan to say hello. He offers me a ride to the station, 100 yards away, and I decide to risk it. Luckily, there is not much cause for alarm about the character of the ticket agent, and even less about the moral atmosphere of the station. Some trainmen of luminous countenance are sitting on the enameled wooden benches, rubbing their knuckles together and staring at the floor, and a man in blue denim coveralls and a cap with woolen earflaps is reading the comic page of a Denver newspaper. Fourteen churches list themselves on a bulletin board that bids you welcome.

The ticket agent shows me a cupboard where I can store my suitcase under his close supervision. On the wall is a drawing, printed on pink paper, of a beaming masculine face with the admonition: "Smile You Are in Sidney." Adjusting my face accordingly, I thanked the ticket agent and headed downtown to look for some breakfast.

Few people were outdoors, but now and then a pickup truck or a large, sober-colored Buick would go past, scraping on the reddish grit that the public works department sprinkles around when the pavement gets icy. Red dust whirled up in miniature tornadoes, and you could feel the sandy particles between your teeth. Just as I was passing Greenlee's Clothiers, a chunk of tumbleweed the size of a basketball came rolling down the center of the street, past the Western Auto Supply, Mode o' Day, and Fine's Ready-to-Wear, and stopped in the center of the intersection at Tenth and Illinois Streets, just opposite the Rexall Drug Store. While I was standing there, wondering whether the tumbleweed would be permitted to loll around all day in the heart of downtown Sidney, it suddenly spun like a dervish, gathered up a retinue of gum wrappers and other minor litter, and danced away in the direction it had come from.

A few blocks farther on, I stopped in at the Fort Sidney Motor Hotel and ordered some pancakes and a cup of coffee. The swimming pool out in the yard was covered with a sheet of black plastic weighted down at the edges by concrete blocks. Occasionally, a gust of wind would catch inside and billow the fabric into a huge mound like the back of a water monster rearing up from the pool, and there would be a murmur of apprehension around the coffee shop.

"It's supposed to keep the dirt out of the water," my waitress told me, "but it's just like a sail. Life of its own. Whipped butter on your pancakes?"

I told her I could visualize the inflated plastic sheet carrying off the Fort Sidney Motor Hotel like Dorothy's house in the *Wizard of Oz*, but my waitress shook her head.

"Air's too heavy," she said authoritatively. "This wind has got mud in it."

After breakfast I examined some black-and-white lithographs decorating the walls of the coffee shop. They showed a row of outfitting stores, a wagon with "Black Hills or Bust" painted on its canvas top, and what appeared to be a view of Sidney from the bluff north of the depot, with Indian tepees and a roundhouse near the tracks, and an Army post, surrounded by a wooden palisade, over on the east side of town.

These reminders of Sidney's exuberant past sharpened my appetite to see more of the landmarks. I bundled up again and walked south, past a square where they were digging foundations for a new Cheyenne County Courthouse, and all the way down to the American Legion Park. The park, like the streets, was deserted except for a few brown squirrels in thick winter coats. I looked at the empty swimming pool, the softball field, the headquarters building of the National Guard, and the skating pond on Lodge Pole Creek. From time to time, someone would drive past in a dark Buick or a pickup truck and peer at me. Finally, I decided I had seen enough landmarks and should now visit the outfitting shops, where it was likely to be warmer and less gritty.

At the Town and Country One-Stop Market there was a dazzling abundance of low-calorie, sugarless beverages, potato chips, scrubbed carrots in plastic bags, honey in squeeze-bottles shaped like little girls, and breakfast cereals flavored with caramel, chocolate, honey, fruit acids, spices, and herbs, and decorated with benevolent, toothless, anthropomorphic tigers.

I can report in full confidence, as did the Sidney *Telegraph* ninety years ago, that no one traveling by way of Sidney need provision himself first in Chicago, Omaha, or other cities. Lee's Department Store, across from the S&H Green Stamp Redemption Center on Illinois Street, is surely the exact modern equivalent of the historic Black Hills outfitter. Lee's was having its January Sale of Sales. Paint-on-Velvet Sets, regularly $11, were selling for $5. You could buy plastic Batmobiles for $2.99. The 13-ounce Aquanet Soft Hair Spray was 57¢, and Teflon-lined, Hi-Dome Buffet Electric Skillets were knocked down to $15.88.

It was midmorning when I finished inspecting landmarks and outfitting shops, and by that time I had begun to feel the need of some economic and political information. Sidney seemed to be unusually subdued, not only in contrast to its days as a "hard" place on the Plains, but also compared to many small towns on the East and West coasts. I wondered whether this quiescence was merely a temporary result of harsh winter climate or a permanent evidence of stagnation. Figuring that the town clerk or business manager would be a reliable informant, I asked directions to the City Hall, which proved to be a one-story brick structure three or four blocks from the business district. The building is only five years old and quite innocent of decoration, and it has a look about it of nonpartisan municipal efficiency. On the walls of the lobby are several of the pink posters advising you to smile in Sidney.

The city manager, an amiable, gray-haired Californian named George Felsch, agreed to answer whatever questions he could, but confessed he was weak on local history. He had been in Sidney for only about a year, and before that had been administrator in Helena, Montana, and some other, small, Western cities. I did not ask him how Sidney stacked up against his other professional posts, but I got the impression that he likes it as well as any Californian can like a place that has cold winters. He told me Sidney has grown from about one thousand population around the turn-of-the-century to more than eight thousand, has a community television cable, an excellent twice-weekly newspaper, and an AM radio station called KSID that used to broadcast midmorning interviews with visiting celebrities at the Fort Sidney Motor Hotel until the girl who did the interviewing moved to Denver.

Shortly after the outbreak of World War II, the Government established the Sioux Army Depot not far from the northern city limits. At its peak of activity the Depot employed nearly three thousand persons, but it has been gradually dismantled since the end of the war. At last count, the staff was down to a few hundred to keep inventory and guard the remaining buildings.

Naturally, this loss of customers has hurt the merchants of Sidney, and accounts for some of the vacant stores one sees on the side streets of the business district. Other developments, fortunately, have helped to heal the wounds. In 1949, oil was discovered in commercially usable quantity in the Nebraska Panhandle and since then many prolific wells have gushed up in Sidney's neighborhood. A few years ago there were 357 oil wells and 30 gas wells in production in the county. Altogether, they contributed about two and one-half million dollars a year in wages and royalties to the people of Sidney.

All the same, it is not what real estate men call a boom town. The local industrialists limit themselves to making draperies, refining petroleum, rendering vegetable oils, and building tractor cabs. Minute Man missile installations are scattered nearby; but Sidney hears

rumors that these, like the Depot, are being "phased out." The Sidney Chamber of Commerce tried last year to talk the Atomic Energy Commission into building its latest linear accelerator project at the old Army Depot; when that project went to Illinois, the Chamber was relieved to secure instead a State technical school that has installed two thousand relatively unaffluent students in the abandoned Sioux barracks. It is a rare vehicle in Sidney that does not carry on its bumper a red and blue sticker reading: "Sidney, Nebraska, Home of Western Nebraska's Vocational Technical School."

After loading me with maps and leaflets, Mr. Felsch took me out by car to see the municipal corporation yard, which stands on the spot where the stages used to start for Deadwood, Dakota Territory. Then we drove up onto the bluff to look at the view and admire the jack pines and cypresses the schoolchildren had planted during their vacation from classes last Arbor Day.

"Some people say there are too darned many trees in Sidney," Felsch confided. "Chinese and American elms, mostly, and they break in the autumn when the wind gets started. But when you're in Nebraska, planting trees is almost sacred."

Last year the children of Sidney planted 10,000 seedlings from State nurseries. Some high school boys who were caught scribbling obscenities on the water tank were sentenced to water the trees on the bluff, and the rate of survival, at least for the trees, has been unusually high. We followed a line of flourishing evergreens along the east division road all the way to the nine-hole municipal golf course at the south end of town. Our tour ended with a rather wistful visit to some flat, brown pastures, optimistically zoned for light industrial development, along the Union Pacific tracks.

In the afternoon, Felsch turned me over to a strapping, blond young man named Ken McMillen, who is president of the Cheyenne County Historical Society.

"It's not easy to learn the history of Sidney," McMillen told me. "Not much of it got written down."

I admitted I found it difficult to imagine Sidney as a "hell-on-wheels" in the 1870's. The only places of nocturnal resort that I had seen were the Log Cabin Cafe (Dancing Fri. & Sat. Night) and the Fox Theatre (Home of Hits), which was showing Gregory Peck in *The Guns of Navarone.*

"Well, there's a certain, wide-open tradition," McMillen said. "For example, this is one of the few towns in Nebraska where you can buy hard liquor by the drink. We've got sixteen or seventeen bars."

"More than one for every church," I suggested.

"Lots more," McMillen said cheerfully. He drew my attention to a collection of mean-looking sidearms in the museum the Society has established in the Chamber of Commerce building. "You know why so little has been written about Sidney?" he went on. "It's because most of it was just plain unprintable."

The idea seemed to give him satisfaction. □

making from one thousand to twelve hundred persons en route to the Hills in that short distance. At the depot were two carloads of machinery for one mining firm, just unloading for the Hills, and a large quantity of miscellaneous freight for various parties. From May 1st the daily stage is limited by its mail contract to three days for the whole distance and expects to make it in sixty hours. When we consider that one of the Leslie party passed seven weeks in the Black Hills last year without being able to obtain any communication with the outer world, this seems to mark an astounding advance in communication and shows that the value of the new gold regions is no longer open to question.

A flying visit to the Black Hills by an advance member of our party reveals that Deadwood is a city of a single street, and a most singular street it is. The buildings which grace its sides are a curiosity in modern architecture, and their light construction is a standing insult to every wind that blows. Paint is a luxury only indulged in by the aristocracy.

The business street of Deadwood runs along the mountain stream, Whitewood, which flows between two lofty adjacent mountains. South Deadwood and Gayville each have their single street, which are offshoots from the Deadwood thoroughfare at the union of the Whitewood and Deadwood Gulches.

Wells are dug in the middle of the streets, all sorts of building material occupies them and every manner of filth is thrown into them. The city is honeycombed by shafts run down into the bowels of the earth from every

A PARTY OF GOLD MINERS STARTING FOR THE BLACK HILLS.

yard. A keen-eyed, money-grabbing set of men makes up the population, but they are far from the blood-thirsty scoundrels the average newspaper correspondent would make them out to be. Shooting is not frequent; fighting is only occasional; and property is perfectly secure. Our flying representative parted with only $3 for hotel fare during his one day's visit and could have obtained board for from $12 to $18 per week. On his return he expressed himself so well satisfied with the diggings that he may be said to have caught the "Yellow Fever."

For two or three blocks the main street of Cheyenne keeps up a character of solid respectability, with neat brick buildings, a large hotel, and an attractive show of shop windows; but it soon drops such mimicry of the "effete East" and relapses into a bold disregard of architectural forms and proprieties. The oddest examples of this are in the two theaters, owned and run by an enterprising citizen who also keeps one of the largest gambling establishments in town. The larger of the theaters — "variety shows" in the fullest sense of the term — connects with the gambling rooms and bar in a long, low, brick building which hangs out numerous flaming red signs under the moonlight.

Entering the barroom, the curious visitor is confronted by a glittering show of chandeliers, fresh paint, cheap gilding, mirrors, and some extraordinary frescoes, supposably of Yosemite views, which blaze in every conceivable gradation of color over the bar itself. Turning to the right, we enter a passage leading to the

THE WESTERN DRAMA — A VARIETY ENTERTAINMENT IN CHEYENNE.

"OLD ZIP COON."

Cheyenne has many noted characters. Some are noted for their shooting, others for their gambling, and some few for their liberality and public spirit. Cherokee Bob, an old Plainsman whose clothes hang loosely about his attenuated form, tied together with strings, wears a well-ventilated hat and often appears on the street with a single boot on. He is famous for his stories and the amount of liquor he can "stow away." Old Zip Coon is known and appreciated in every convivial circle in the Territory. He is an artist on the violin, which he manipulates to accompany the vocal melodies with which his brain is abundantly stored. We were favored with some of his choicest rhymes, which he delivered in a loud, hitching voice that blended excruciatingly with the high, squeaking notes of his fiddle. The bland smile of his expressive features is finely portrayed in our sketch.

parquette, or pit, of the theater. A narrow flight of stairs passes up to what in the East would be the dress circle, but which in the Cheyenne house is a single tier of small boxes. At the head of the stairs is another and smaller bar, from which the waitresses procure strong drinks to be served in the aforesaid boxes; and over the staircase is posted a gentle hint, couched in the words: "GENTS, BE LIBERAL."

From these little boxes, gay with tawdry paintings and lace hangings, we look down upon as odd a scene as ever met New York eyes. The auditorium is shaped rather like a funnel, expanding at the mouth to the width of the stage. It is so narrow that leaning out of one box we could almost shake hands with our opposite neighbors. The trapezes, through which the wonderful Mlle. Somebody is flying and frisking like a bird, are all swung from the stage to the back of the house, so that her silken tights and spangles whisk past within a handsbreadth of the admiring audience, who can exchange civilities, or even confidences, with her in her aerial flight.

The floor below is dotted with round tables and darkened with a sea of hats; a dense fog of cigar smoke floats above them; and the clink of glasses rings a cheerful accompaniment to the orchestra as the admiring patrons quaff brandy and "slings," and cheer on the performers. The house, for all its cheap finery of decoration, its barbaric red and yellow splashes of paint, and its bizarre Venuses and Psyches posing on the walls, is marvelously clean; the audience, wholly masculine, is unconventional (let us put it courteously), but not riotous. As for the performance, it is by no means bad, and the trapeze feats are indeed exceptionally startling and well executed. The hours of the entertainment are from 8 P.M. until 2 A.M., while the doors of the connecting gambling saloon are never closed.

So three-quarters of the town are up and stirring until the stars fade. By daylight it looks more commonplace but has its peculiar interest still. We snatch what time we can to hurry through the dusty, wooden-paved streets and among the shabby, loose-jointed looking shops. The streets are full this morning, for an emigrant train starts at noon, and there are four or five families camping in tents around the railroad depot. We look in at them in passing — men, women, children, and household stuff crowded together inside the flapping canvas, with a very few old battered trunks tied round with rope and a queer assortment of movables. One family we notice, in a very new, white tent, has a little pile of ancient brown books, much bethumbed, laid away on a packing box; but this evidence of literary taste is exceptional.

Strolling among the shops of Cheyenne, we pass a good half-hour at Josselyn & Park's, the "old established" jeweler's firm. We look at moon agates, tastefully set, and heavy chains wrought of gold straight from the Black Hills, which might have come out of Tiffany's workshops. The feminine curiosity hunters pull over a box full of unpolished agates, petrifications, and arrow-

heads from the Plains and secure the richest at a nominal price; and then we turn to an ammunition dealer's; admire his arsenal of knives and firearms; combat a strong inclination on the part of the romantic young woman to purchase a fringed leather game pouch which would be "so convenient for carrying specimens and things"; and so by slow degrees get back to the railway station again.

How loath we are to leave these stirring, crowded streets! Look at that rich dash of color in the dusty street — a Mexican rider on a fierce, little mustang, his great, white sombrero rolled up at the side, his long, wild hair blown back, his scarlet cravat flying and the wind whirling out his great, blue cloak, showing the purple jacket underneath, the silver-buckled belt, the stamped leather stirrups, the flashing silver spurs, and the gleam of a pistol at his side — there! he has gone, with a clatter of hoofs and a cloud of dust; and no one turns to look after him except us "down-Easters!"

And there comes a real Adonis of scouts: a tall, brown, broad-shouldered hero with a dash of the dandy about him in his weather-stained buckskin suit, fringed and beaded at the seams, the bright necktie knotted low at his handsome throat, the sealskin cap tossed to one side on the long, wavy hair, and an aristocratically small foot fitted to an exquisite nicety in his cavalry boots. Our female scribblers announce that small feet and right boots are essentials in the makeup of a real hero of the West; they are equally enthusiastic over the good breeding of a Cheyenne crowd, wherein the veriest rough springs aside to let a woman go by. Could we boldly assert the same of a Sunday afternoon promenade on The Avenue? □

SCENE IN FRONT OF THE INTER-OCEAN HOTEL, CHEYENNE.

1967: Magic Fingers in the Old Corral

WHEN A WRANGLER RIDES into Cheyenne, Wyoming, he can tell right away that this is a town that sticks to its traditions — bronco busting, cow punching, drilling for oil, and fighting off Indians.

The depot shows a comforting resistance to innovations. Alongside the tracks they keep an Overland Stage Coach that made its last trip in 1866. It should be handy if transportation gadgets like the supersonic jet don't pan out. In the waiting room a station agent with elastic bands around his shirt sleeves is chalking arrivals and departures on a blackboard, and you can hear the telegraph clicking frantically, no doubt reporting Hostiles on the warpath somewhere down the line. The empty wooden benches look as though they should be occupied by green troops on their way to the Little Big Horn.

But it is at the motels and restaurants of Cheyenne that you find the true spirit of the Old West. You can bed down at the Ramada, the Frontier, the Long Horn, the Home Ranch, the Apache, the Buck Horn, the Big Horn, the Pioneer, the Plains, or the Western Sky, and you follow the grub line to the Lariat Cafe, the Bonanza Sirloin Pit, the Town Pump, the Bunk House, or the Wild Horse Cafe. There is a Western House of Pizza, a Westward Ho Malt Shop, and even a dog kennel called the K-9 Corral.

The boss layout is the Hitching Post Motor Hotel out west of town. It has 135 rooms, a year-round swimming pool, a sauna bath, and a 24-Hour Coffee Shop. All the top hands gather there to sing songs and swap stories when the coyotes are howling and there's silver on the sage.

As soon as I had checked my suitcase at a bunkhouse downtown, I cut out for the Hitching Post in a maverick taxicab. I could tell it was a maverick because the driver was smoking a tailormade cigarette. It turned out he was an Easterner, from Illinois.

The saloon at the Hitching Post looked a trifle citified. Some dudes with coats and neckties on were standing at the bar, and a three-piece band was playing "La Vie en Rose." But the bartenders wore red-and-black-striped vests. (The vest is a notoriously Western garment.) And the ceiling was beamed with what appeared to be rough-hewn timbers that were on fire. To my disappointment, the timbers proved to be long, narrow boxes made of plywood. Each box covered a line of pipes and electrical conduits, and the reddish glow came from neon tubes shining through slits in the wood. The bartenders, however, were bartenders. I asked one of them for a shot of snake juice.

"Name your brand," the bartender said. "Old Crow ... Grand-dad ... Fitzgerald ... Scotch? White Horse, Walker's, Cutty Sark...."

I laid a dollar bill on the counter and silently pointed at one of the bottles.

"Chivas Regal?" the bartender said.

I nodded, hoping no wranglers had heard.

About that time, a young woman in riding breeches and a red-and-black vest like the bartender's rushed up to the service counter and read off a small pad of paper: "Two vodka martinis on the stem, a V.O. and soda and a liebfraumilch over ice ... she says."

I figured the order must be for some east-of-the-Hudson parlor floozies, and I peered around furtively, expecting to see the tell-tale swaying of red plush curtains at the door to the back room. Instead, I met the eye of a gray-haired woman who was making a complex readjustment to the shoulder strap of her underclothes. She returned my stare with noticeable indignation.

Did I mention that the Legislature was in session? So it was, and the Hitching Post was crowded with settlers from all parts of the Territory, who had come in to protect their water and minerals, parcel out the tax revenues, and shoot the lid off the town. Right next to me, an evil-looking hombre with a pockmarked face and squinty eyes was saying out of the corner of his mouth: "The trouble with the one-man, one-vote rule is it's fine in theory but when you try to apply it ...." And his sidekick, a mean little cayuse who kept snuffing at a Vick's inhaler, was shaking his head and muttering: "All right, Joe, but given the electoral imbalance that already existed between those two districts ...."

Down at the end of the room, a weather-beaten woman pounded her fist on the bar and cried out savagely: "All I care about is a return to fiscal responsibility!"

I've heard that sort of talk in the East, too, and I've never known it to lead to anything but trouble. The ornery little varmint behind me braced himself with a snort of his Vick's inhaler, hooked his thumbs in the pockets of his vest, and started edging along the bar toward the weather-beaten woman. At once she was surrounded by a group of eagle-eyed defenders with American flags on their lapels. It looked as if things were heating up.

Not hankering for lead poisoning, I tossed off my coffin varnish and vamoosed down the hall to the 24-Hour Coffee Shop, where they were playing *Hawaiian Dreams* on the hi-fi stereo and conditions looked momentarily peaceful.

Of course, you never can tell what will happen next in these wide-open Western towns. The waitresses, always alert to trouble, were huddled near the cash register, keeping a close eye on the Schrafft's mints, and the hostess directed me to a table where I could keep my back to the wall. Unwrapping a cellophane packet of Kitchen-Rich Party Toasts, I coolly pretended to read the menu. It led off with Eggs Foo Yong and Reuben Sandwich.

Before long, one of the waitresses ventured away

from the corner and timidly approached my table. In a calm voice, I asked her what was cooking out in the chuckwagon.

"The petite dinner steak is nice," she murmured. "Comes with a baked potato with sour cream and chives and the green salad with French, Roquefort, or Thousand."

"*Petite* dinner steak?" I said, wondering what had become of the substantial grub they used to serve on the Old Chisholm Trail. I told her I'd have the Cattleman's Special, and I saw a flicker of admiration in her deep blue eyes.

"You want it on the dinner?" she asked. "With the baked potato, sour cream, and chives?"

Nodding laconically, I ripped open another packet of Kitchen-Rich Party Toasts. I was itching to get downtown to the Old Mayflower Dance Hall. When the waitress brought my baked potato, I asked her whether she would advise me to steer clear of the Mayflower tonight.

"The Mayflower? No, how come? They've got a real nice combo. Tommy Strange. Plays at one of the big casinos in Las Vegas."

I knew she could tell from the set of my jaw as I spooned out sour cream and chives that neither hell nor high water would keep me out of the Mayflower Dance Hall.

The Mayflower was crowded with settlers — barefoot and shaggy-haired, most of them, with only black, turtleneck jerseys and wide-wale corduroy pants to cover their nakedness. I elbowed my way to the bar, put my back to the mirror, and scrutinized the couples sashaying around the dance floor to the twang of an electric guitar. A young Indian brave in a Beethoven sweatshirt was moving solemnly from table to table, asking the women to dance. Each time he was refused, he would perform a solitary war dance, holding a can of beer above his head and muttering, "Yeah, yeah, yeah."

I gave the barmaid my tight-lipped smile and said I guessed this was the sort of place where you did not ask what anybody did for a living.

"These kids?" she said. "They're mostly stationed out at the missile base. Biggest in the world."

"*Missile* base?" I said. To think of that unfenced prairie scattered with ICBM sites! Staring at the bartender's ten-gallon hat, at the stuffed moose head over

the door, at the saddle slung over the split-rail fence surrounding the bandstand, at the cattle brands burned onto the walls, I felt cruelly cheated. Cheyenne had been taken over by homesteaders — nesters and drift fencers — and the Old West was as dead as Camelot.

"How about the redskin?" I said at last.

"Yeah," said the barmaid. "How *about* him! I guess I'll have to run him outa here. He's getting stoned, and he's bugging people."

I looked at her with growing interest. It was not that I held anything against the Indian; but I needed a talisman to prove that this was not a foggy dream of the Old West. Measuring out my words, I said:

"You'd never throw anyone out. Not from the *missile* base."

The barmaid cracked a toothpick between her teeth, delivered two creme de menthe frappés, a Drambuie, and a Black Russian, and then walked over to the Indian, who was dancing alone with his eyes closed, a beatific expression on his face, and beer slopping onto his Beethoven sweatshirt. The top of her head reached his chin. I could not hear what she was saying, but it must have been one of those mystic frontier words like "Git!" The Indian opened his eyes, looked down in astonishment, and a moment later, put down his can of beer and shuffled out the door.

Now, I gazed at the barmaid in admiration, feeling the presence of a reincarnated Calamity Jane. My disillusion, like the Beatle melodies they were playing at the Old Mayflower Dance Hall, evaporated in the starry night. Walking back to my motel, I whistled "Home on the Range." I curled my lip at the young man who was sitting at the desk, reading a paperback by Kurt Vonnegut, Jr., and barked out my orders: the keys to my bunkhouse and a pack of coffin nails — *pronto*.

"The machine's over by the elevator," the kid said. "Right next to the ice cube machine. You need any ice cubes?"

"Nope," I said. "I reckon I'll just turn in."

"All the beds are equipped with Magic Fingers," the kid said helpfully. "Put a quarter in the box and it vibrates for half an hour. Very relaxing."

Up in my room I turned down the heater-air conditioner a couple of degrees, put two bits in the Magic Fingers, and hit the trail to dreamland. □

CHAPTER VIII

The Drawing Rooms of Denver

1877: A Hole in the Liquor Laws Pops Open at Colorado Springs

Mrs. Leslie writes:

GOING TO SLEEP IN CHEYENNE we awoke in Denver, our car having been attached during the night to a train upon the Denver Pacific R.R. Denver lies broadly and generously upon a great plain sloping toward the South Platte, with the grand sweep of the Rocky Mountain chain almost surrounding it. A large number of handsome houses have been built on the western side of the city, facing the mountain view; and one foresees that when Denver is forty instead of twenty years old, this will be the fashionable and charming quarter.

By the way, can anyone explain why the western side of so many cities is the aristocratic one? In London, New York, Boston, there are no Rocky Mountains — but this subject is too wide for further handling just here; so we return to the rows upon rows of cottonwood trees, transplanted from their native groves to the streets of Denver and kept alive by irrigating ditches beside the street. The streets themselves are as fine as the drives in Central Park — solid, hard, and never muddy, the soil being an apparently indigenous macadam. The style of building is different from that of the East. It is the fashion here to construct bed, dressing and bathrooms on the ground floor, as well as parlor, library, and dining room; verandas are popular, and nearly every house has a little garden in front.

We spent the evening pleasantly at the residence of a member of the Colorado Legislature — a prominent citizen of Denver — who had invited a number of the dignitaries of the state to meet us. These gentlemen, almost without exception, impressed us not only as men of strength, purpose, and ability, but conspicuous for that heartiness of manner and gentle kindness of feeling which make the Western gentleman a new and charming type.

The following morning we started with our hosts of the previous evening for a visit to Colorado Springs and its adjacent wonders.

We took passage upon the narrow-gauge railway called the Denver and Rio Grande, running south from the city, and immediately began the steady upward grade by which it climbs the "divide" between the South Platte and Arkansas Rivers. At the highest point lies Summit Lake, in the shadow of a great sugarloaf mountain, with a background of purple foothills and the snows of Pikes Peak. The waters of this little lake run impartially north and south, and in descending we bade goodbye to the snow and welcomed the buffalo grass and cactus plants telling of a higher temperature. We saw ourselves surrounded on every side by weird, fantastic buttes — turrets, winged castles, needle-like shafts that might have been the home of ghoul or sprite of the desert, and detached columns of red sandstone of every height and proportion from a toadstool to a Corinthian pillar.

Colorado Springs, presumably so called because the springs are five miles away, is not without attractions. There are five roads leading away from it; Pikes Peak looks condescendingly down on it. The air is said to be excellent for asthmatics, who therefore abound here; and its morals are guarded by the sternest of liquor laws. At Colorado and Manitou Springs are the cottages of two of our most cherished American female authors, Helen Hunt [Jackson][2] and Grace Greenwood.[3] Helen Hunt's cottage is cozy and attractive, with a huge bay window brilliant with flowers. Grace Greenwood's home is also characteristic and tasteful, with some branching antlers above the door, as in a forester's house in Tyrol. At some little distance from here, we heard, the daughter and sons of the late Canon Kingsley make a home in the heart of the wilderness, finding a piquant delight in the vivid contrast between the most artificial grade of English life and the utter naturalness of the American desert, which may yet be taught to blossom like the rose.

There are some fine hotels at Manitou and several mineral springs of varying degrees of unsavoriness, as at Saratoga. The one near Grace Greenwood's cottage flows into a stone basin and bubbles joyously over with a musical invitation to the thirsty visitor not justified by the flavor of its alkaline waters.

From here we drive up the Ute Pass, a canyon popular with those peaceful savages, perhaps for its beauty,

72

Nothing is impossible to those who are in earnest. Close to the depot is a hostelry, yclept the Pike's Peak House, where an announcement in English and German informs the wayfarer that meals can be had for the moderate sum of forty cents.

Entering the house, one finds an empty room. A door in a wooden partition admits into an inner apartment where four Hoosiers are playing the interesting game of "Devil Amongst the Tailors."[1] Presently, a German approaches and inquires what is wanted, and being informed that there exists a laudable desire for lager beer, he replies:

"Shust put a quarter in dot hole, and de beer gomes up quick!"

Accordingly, the tourist approaches a wooden wall and perceives a slit in the board, dirty from use. He drops in a twenty-five cent piece and says, addressing no one in particular and speaking in a very sepulchral tone: "A quart of beer."

With magic celerity, a sliding panel is revealed, which goes up; and on a bracket there appears a jug of foaming beverage. Subsequently, the traveler is informed that anything in any quantity in the drinking line can be obtained in the same mysterious manner at this oasis in the Temperance Desert.

On the 18th, President Barnard of Columbia College, the Rev. Dr. Armitage, and a number of other gentlemen left New York City for a trip to the Rocky Mountains, stopping at Denver and Colorado Springs. This information will be valuable to them in case they should require any stimulants, as it will enable them to satisfy their thirst promptly and without embarrassing inquiries; for even their distinction will not secure them exemption from the Territorial liquor laws.

Leslie's Illustrated Newspaper, July 7, 1877

more probably for its directness. The narrow roadway climbs up between high walls of red sandstone, zig-zagging beneath stupendous cliffs, with a lovely little stream foaming far below, leaping down into two lovely cascades whose voice is the only sound in these eternal solitudes. Clumps of dark evergreen are fringed with the tender green of budding willows. The tourist might look for hours at mountain torrent, waterfall, foliage —the oppressive grandeur of the heaven-piercing crags above and the dizzy abyss below.

No more impressive scene is to be found among Alps or Andes; and so, by-and-by, the restless world will know, and the Ute Pass will grow as vulgar as Chamonix.

Returning to Manitou, we branch off to visit the Garden of the Gods, whose happy, if not especially appropriate, name has lured us on through days of expectation. The hard, red road along which our fleet little horses spatter so gaily winds suddenly into a wooded hollow, and we pause before a stupendous gateway formed of two great, parallel masses of sandstone —smooth, shining, and glowing in the sun. These colossal gates rise three hundred and fifty feet and leave an entrance two hundred feet wide, through which some gorgeous Pharaonic procession may be imagined passing, with chariots and horsemen and barbaric fanfare. Gazing through the gateway, we see Pikes Peak in the far distance, its crest like burnished silver against the sky, and close at hand the sharp spires and minarets of the "Cathedral Rocks." A little farther on sits the "Nun," who has strayed out for some open-air devotions. The garden contains about fifty acres of land, its floor of finely disintegrated red sandstone partially covered with thickly tufted buffalo grass and silvery-gray sagebrush, while the slopes and rises are dotted with evergreen trees whose somber green adds the shadow needed to sustain this riot of color. Surely never was sky so blue as that which bent above the Garden of the Gods, never was sunshine so yellow, never were snow-clad peaks and quartz cliffs so dazzlingly white, never red sandstone so richly red and glowing.

Our guide, well up in the office, glibly catalogued this and that formation: this was the "Seal" and that the "Scotch Giant," the "Camel," the "Frog," the "Lion"; but having meekly received as much information as our shallow brain would contain, we drew back within ourselves to gaze in silent, ignorant delight at these petrified forms of wonder.

From dreams like these we are recalled by the Chief's cheerful voice. Again we pass the beautiful gate and enter once more the cold, gray landscape of the Plains, where even the sky is less blue and the sunshine less golden. Twisting our necks for one last glimpse, we photograph on our brain the grand gateway sharply drawn against the vivid blue, the great, snow-clad peak in the far distance, and the hooded Nun, who seems to look after us as we are reluctantly borne away.

Our next point is Glen Eyrie, a formation similar to, but much less wonderful than, the Garden of the Gods. It, too, is entered between two gigantic portals—garnet, green, crimson, and purple upon the outer face, while the inner displays every shade of a warm yellow-green. Inside are some grand, red sandstone buttes, a wilderness of cottonwood and fir, a pretty stream, and fine distant views of the snow-clad mountains and purple-tinted foothills. This glen is the property of General Palmer, and in its midst stands the handsome villa built to welcome his young bride, under whose direction the house was pulled to pieces several times before it became the ideal home of which every bride dreams but very few possess.[4]

The chill and exhaustion of the return ride after a morning of such excitement proved too much for flesh too weak to obey the willing spirit. By the time we reached the Crawford House, the writer was seriously ill and spent a bad half hour while the others dined. Yet, this experience is among the most precious of all our Western tour, for it gave us a treasure rarer than gold—it gave us a friend.

Having already admired our hostess of the preceding evening, and quietly noted in her beautiful house the selection of pictures, engravings, books, and *objets d'art* that proclaimed their mistress a person of high literary culture, artistic taste, and extended travel; the fine manners, the tone of the best society, the ease, cordiality, and aplomb which made every one of her guests the object of special attention, while never neglecting the rest; now, beneath the touchstone of sickness and suffering, we saw traits of tenderness, unselfishness, wisdom, and gentleness befitting a Sister of Mercy rather than a woman of society; and as her gentle touch, kindly eyes, and assuring voice smoothed away the pain and terror and weariness, a sentiment sprang into being whose life will only end with our own, and all the rest of life will be stronger and better for that hour in which an angel stirred the waters and love rose from their depths.

And now the dinner is concluded; the invalid is on her feet again; and we are at the station. But the wind is so high that it is not deemed prudent to start the train upon this narrow-gauge road. We pass an hour and a half in great anxiety, as we have calculated our day's excursion to return just in time to connect with the outward-bound train at Denver; but presently arrives a telegram with the cheering assurance that the train shall be detained until our arrival, not too greatly to the discomfiture, let us charitably hope, of the punctual passengers already on the ground—another exemplification, by the way, of the adage we heard quoted at Toledo: "Served the bird right for being out so early." □

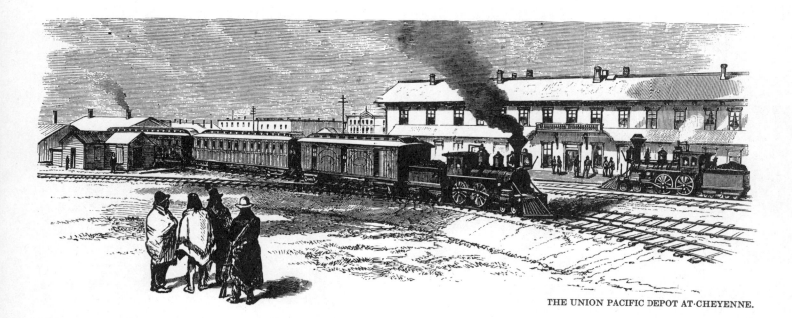

THE UNION PACIFIC DEPOT AT·CHEYENNE.

CHAPTER IX

The Laramie Plains

1877: A Lonely Land of Army Posts, Coal Mines, and Soda Lakes

WESTWARD ONCE MORE: a new world of red granite buttes crowded down to the track; short, steep canyons, where we toil upgrade behind two panting engines; stunted pine trees clinging along the tawny ridges; sharp, pale-blue peaks of the Black Hills — the Wyoming Hills, not the gold mountains of Montana; and, far away to the south, a single glittering white cone, like frosted silver, which they tell us is Long's Peak.

The Turin Mountains show their heads, peeping clear-cut above the northern horizon, and we hear how that notable terror of the frontier, Jack Slade, once had his lair in their vicinity. Heavier still grows the grade, yet we are scarcely conscious that it is so rapid, for the horizon line sweeps level as ever. But here we are at Sherman, 8242 feet above the sea. If we doubted it while seated in our car, we can doubt no longer on emerging. Such winds as these never run riot on a lower level, and though we are informed that it is "only a fresh breeze," it appears so like a cool tornado that nobody cares to extend his walk very far. How the people of Sherman manage to live in a perpetual high gale is more than the average traveler can conceive; but here we see scattered about a dozen or so wooden homes, a little brick hotel, and the inevitable saloons that start up like mushrooms along the line of the frontier. No wilder or more grandly lonely landscape has yet unfolded itself before us than this vast, billowy sweep of low hills, tawny with the little withered knots

of buffalo grass and gray with tiny bunches of sage; the scattered boulders of rough, red-gray granite; the long line of rocky buttes against the northern horizon, bristling with stunted black pines; and, stooping down to meet it all, the flawless blue of an intense, noonday sky barren of a single cloud.

The down grade commences, and we descend to the great Laramie Plains. Grotesque rock masses are heaped near the track and painted against the gray horizon, where certain ominous low clouds are gathering. Midway between Sherman and Dale Creek we come upon Skull Rocks, huge rounded boulders of pale, reddish-gray granite, worn smooth by some prehistoric chiseling process and heaped in a great pile, through whose interstices bristle gnarled and stunted pines. Eyes that love color are never weary on these plains: every hour brings a new study, as now, when the warm tawny rocks, the olive-black pines, and the faint, cool, silvery-gray-green of the sagebrush create a sober harmony of color that fits well with the great sweep of outline. The sagebrush has rapidly increased since we left Cheyenne, disputing every inch of ground with the buffalo grass. Its little bunches, not exceeding six inches in height, are a tough, tenacious growth whose soft foliage has a peculiar pungent odor, accounted by most noses intensely disagreeable. No other root will live among the alkali patches; but even on the dreary Humboldt Desert we shall see these little gray-green tufts dotting the powdery white soil.

THE TOWN OF SHERMAN, WYOMING TERRITORY, 8,242 FEET ABOVE THE LEVEL OF THE SEA — HIGHEST POINT ON THE UNION PACIFIC.

A Marvel of Iron Trestle Work

Dale Creek Bridge[1] comes into sight. There is a rush to the platform to enjoy the sensation of crossing on a spider's web. Seen from a distance, this marvel of iron trestle work spanning the deep, rocky bed of the stream has the airiest and most gossamer-like effect; but it is a substantial structure over which our long train goes roaring in safety, though not without a few shrieks from those on the platforms who are averse to seeing a hundred and thirty feet of empty space yawning below them. It is very far down to those great, ruddy boulders, far enough to give one a dizzy qualm as he leans over the unsteady railing and stares into the chaos of rock and sand and stunted pine under his feet and catches a fleeting glimpse of the few tiny cabins that perch among the boulders.

THE EXCURSION TRAIN CROSSING THE DALE CREEK IRON VIADUCT NEAR SHERMAN.

VIEW OF LARAMIE CITY, WYOMING TERRITORY, AS SEEN FROM THE U.P.R.R.

From the Black Hills to the Medicine Bow range, the Laramie Plains stretch away their endless, ragged buttes — forty miles in width, one hundred in length. Away to the southwest the Medicine Bow Mountains rise in sight, and the Diamond Peaks prick up sharp and clear, painted in dusky blue against the chilly sky. Still farther is a line of shining peaks that are always white and cold, even in August when the blazing sun bakes the dry soil and the air is stinging with alkali dust. The level valley of the Platte, which we thought so grandly desolate yesterday, becomes monotonous and tame in our memory, measured with this wild, stern waste.

Hour by hour the buttes take wilder and more fantastic shapes; there are the strangest arabesques cut deep in their tawny surfaces, weird intaglios, like the "picture-writing" of some past age; uncouth figures hewn out like Egyptian gods; long rows of rugged columns, pyramids, and crumbling turrets. We are descending the slope of the Black Hills, the first range of the Rockies, and are still nearly eight thousand feet above the ocean, higher than Mount Washington — think of it, ye among us who have boasted of climbing those six thousand and odd feet! — and still above us and beyond us new peaks are rising, lonely and unattainable in the distance. As we pass Tie Siding, a telegraph station with a sparse scattering of cabins and a saloon or two, the western horizon is barred across with a solid blue rampart of mountains.

Fort Sanders[3] is the next station — a military post established here in 1866, and probably not destined for long occupation by the United States troops. Its clustered log houses and barracks, inside a high stockade, crowd close to the track. We catch a glimpse of a private or two off duty and of the corral full of government horses, pricking up their ears at the long train shooting by. The post is directly on the old military road that crosses the Black Hills through Cheyenne Pass to old Fort Walbach and to Forts Carlin and Russell,[4] near Cheyenne.

The little tables are being hooked into place at every window and the fresh, white table linen handed out, which means that the afternoon wears late and we are nearing the supper station — Laramie, a thriving town, with its three thousand inhabitants, its brick and stone "blocks" and public buildings, and its boastful title, "Gem City of the Mountains." Compared with Cheyenne, its aspect from the railroad is imposing, but it lacks the dash and picturesqueness of the other town. It is a busy place and will become more so as the great mineral resources of its neighborhood are developed — soda lakes; mines of cinnabar, plumbago, iron, and a dozen other ores; and rich beds of clay and limestone, whose extent is as yet only partially estimated.

Taking our constitutional on the long platform, we have a view just west of the track of the Wyoming Penitentiary. The laws of the land are evidently respected in Laramie — nowadays, at least; its infancy eight years ago was as stormy as any period in the histories of Cheyenne, Sidney, or Julesburg. But those days of tents, saloons, dugouts, and gambling dens are to a certain extent past, and we are told that churches

ARRIVAL AT LARAMIE STATION, "GEM CITY OF THE MOUNTAINS."

ROCK CREEK HOUSE, THE NUCLEUS OF A SETTLEMENT.

are now patronized and the play of cards and dice (ostensibly) suspended on the first day of the week. Brawls and murders are no longer incidents of daily occurrence, and judges and juries have done away with the wholesale practice of lynch law, a change of administration which, it is to be feared, does not meet with the whole-souled approval of some of the oldest inhabitants. A grizzly old frontiersman, browner than an autumn leaf, gave us his view on this subject as we paced the platform.

"Thar *was* a time," he remarked, with a stern shake of the head, "when it was mighty onsafe to kill a man out yer; but it's gettin' to be easier nowadays. Murder's done with *im*-punity now. I tell you, young fellers, there never was but *one* judge that made no mistakes, and that was Judge Lynch, and we didn't gain much by gettin' red of him!"

At the end of the platform an interested group is collected around a Fairbanks scales,[5] where almost every woman in the train will have her turn before the engine starts. Weights will be compared and guessed at with as much eagerness as if the same process had not been gone through — and the same results announced — at least twice during the preceding twenty-four hours. Our fair fellow voyagers let no opportunity slip for ascertaining their exact avoirdupois and chronicling the pounds gained since they shook the dust of New York from their small button-boots; and here they are, as usual, anxiously inspecting the scales and crying out that they certainly aren't true, because, according to *this*, somebody has actually *lost* two pounds and a half since day before yesterday!

Laramie City, seen as we glide away, has somewhat the appearance of a manufacturing town, with the tall chimneys of its rolling mills, the great machine and repair shops, and the large roundhouse. As such, it is less interesting to us than the small centers of half-barbaric life that we have lately passed. Decidedly, Laramie is not half "hard" enough to please our *exigeant* seekers after excitement and novelty.

The clouds are lowering grimly as we speed on, and fine, sifting snowflakes begin to waver on the gusts of the north wind. Our trail lies over desolate divides, utterly given up to sagebrush and greasewood—a little, low shrub not unlike the sage, with the same gray-green foliage and an intensified unpleasantness of odor. By

sunlight it might be less dreary; but now in the cold, colorless twilight, with the fast-thickening snow drawing its pale film over the distances, it is a picture of lifeless desolation. The far-off mountain ranges appear only as ghosts of hills: the Wind River range, away to the north, and south of us the Medicine Bows, gray and spectral through the storm. This range is rich in undeveloped mines, most of which still await the prospector, and it yields no inconsiderable wealth in timber; almost all the railroad ties, posts, fences, and corral poles used on the Laramie Plains are supplied from these mountains.

WEIGHING THE LADIES AT LARAMIE.

Crossing Laramie River on a wooden bridge, we pass Howell, a little side track and station which, with its suggestion of human life, varies for an instant the bleak emptiness of the landscape. Never on earth was there such utter loneliness. The ground is whitened already, and through the snow prick little tufts of sagebrush, dotting it with black bunches as far as the eye can reach; there is nothing astir but the north wind, which soughs over the divides in its own ghostly fashion.

No, stay — for myriads of jackrabbits are frisking in the snow, nibbling the sagebrush, flirting with the flying flakes, and pricking their ears as the noisy mon-

TEN MINUTES AT CARBON, WYOMING TERRITORY.

ster of a train roars past them. Somehow, they only make the stillness more still, the loneliness a shade lonelier, by their feeble little presence. Lying luxuriously among the pillows of our sofa, it is fascinating to stare away into the dimness of the strange, wintry world, to watch the hovering flakes, to follow the scurrying rabbits, and to trace far back in the white mist the weird shapes of solitary buttes or the long, heaving swells of the divides, rolling away, north, south, east, and west, utterly without limit or boundary now as the horizon line is blotted out by the storm.

And now comes Howells, with his little stepladder in one hand and a match in the other, and climbs up to light the lamps in their reflectors, violently harassed by Follette, who yelps at his first appearance. The tables come out, and the notebooks, or a pack of cards perhaps; but we who are wiser keep our places at the window, flatten our noses against the glass, and stare out as long as there is a glimmer of light.

The country is rugged and broken and scarred with deep cuts where the iron trail runs through, and such view as we might have is constantly shut off by the snowsheds through which we plunge noisily. These long, wooden shelters are built wherever the slope of the land catches the winter winds most strongly and the snow drifts pile deepest. Doubtless a blessing to the winter tourist, they are a torment to all others, shutting out, as they do so frequently, the very most interesting and ardently desired points of the scenery,

and sometimes darkening our flight for nearly half a mile with their stout planking and pillars.

Rock Creek[6] is another little sidetrack, with a smart, new-looking white house and a whirring windmill. The creek that gives its name to this infant settlement crosses our road just at this point on its way from the Medicine Bow Mountains to the Medicine Bow River. Here we are on the eastern border of the great coal basin that underlies the center of our continent.

Passing Wilcox,[7] we are confronted by Como, with the lake of that name in the distance. This little sheet of water is fed by warm springs which breathe out a dense white vapor in chilly weather, and it has no visible outlet. Among its other attractions are yearly visitations of wild ducks and the constant presence of an agreeable species of lizard, ranging from six to eighteen inches in length, which supplies the chief diet of the ducks.

Medicine Bow Station[8] follows, a place from which military supplies are shipped to neighboring posts. It has a large government freight depot; a few stores, saloons, and dwelling houses; and a roundhouse where relays of extra engines are kept for use on the steep grade between this point and Carbon, the next station. A wagon road leads north to Fort Fetterman,[9] a distance of ninety miles, and there is also a short and direct route open to the gold regions in the Dakota Black Hills. Indian raids were reported here as recently as 1875 — bloodless ones, however; the Otoes at that

A TROOP OF U.S. CAVALRY DRILLING NEAR FORT STEELE.

A Decent Little Town

RAWLINS, WYOMING, A COMMUNITY OF RAILROAD EMPLOYEES.

Rawlins presents to the curious eye severely utilitarian frame houses, devoid of flowers, turf, or shrub, or even an inclosure where such might be nourished; the invariable fresh paint of the saloons; and the brawny loungers with a bevy of huge, lumbering Newfoundlands, gaunt hounds, and overgrown curs to bark at the train.

Rawlins is not an exciting place — not even a wicked one. It is simply a decent little town of six hundred souls — chiefly railroad employees — full of talk about mining interests, prospecting, and untold wealth that is going to roll in from its sulphur springs and beds of soda when some enterprising party "takes them in hand."

date merely stampeded some three or four hundred horses grazing the plains and retired with them to the Red Cloud and Spotted Tail agencies, without personal molestation of the "pale-faces."

Down we rush to Carbon,[10] a brisk little mining town where a shaft has been sunk by the railroad company and about a hundred and fifty men are employed underground. Their homes are queer little adobe cabins — or log huts filled in with adobe — with mud roofs; loose-boarded shanties, looking as if a brisk breeze would blow them down; and dugouts of the true primitive pattern. There are some decent houses and a sprinkling of stores; the "Wyoming House and Billiard Saloon," bare, square, and glaringly white; a few tall, black, factory chimneys; and an atmosphere of coal dust. Of all this we take a windy view during the ten minutes' stoppage, seeing half and guessing at part by the bright lights at windows and doors and the swinging lanterns of friendly brakemen.

The wild, rugged Plains keep up their savage character, and the road winds and twists around the steep bluffs and plunges through narrow cuts in the crumbling walls of limestone until it enters the valley of the North Platte. And then comes Fort Steele,[11] with its big wooden barracks, log houses, and corral. The soldiers' quarters are rather cast into the shade by the imposing height of the great stone hospital, built by the government in 1875; but at least the log houses are picturesque — which the stone one is not. However uncomfortable they may be as homes, they look thoroughly in keeping with the lonely waste sweeping all around them. There is no resemblance between this valley of the North Platte and the larger Platte Valley east of the Black Hills; the broad, low bottom lands of the one and the sage desert of the other, with its abrupt red bluffs and sharply outlined divides, are as far removed as the opposing elements of east and west. On our return through Fort Steele a few weeks later, we were entertained with a drill of a troop of cavalry.

Three miles west of Creston, an insignificant little telegraph station, there was once a flagstaff planted to mark the summit — not the highest point, but the central one—of the Rocky Mountains. From the long, gently rolling ridge of this divide you may look for a moment, east and west, over the undulations of two great slopes. Then the train rushes downgrade, and the eastern slope drops out of sight, carrying the Black Hills peaks and the domes of the Medicine Bows with it. It is a breezy point in the road, and the sentinel flagstaff was blown down some time ago. Storms are frequent and fierce over this section of the "backbone," even when all the surrounding country is sunshiny and clear, and the snowdrifts pile higher and deeper than at almost any other point. Here, in 1872, was the greatest snow blockade that ever impeded travel on the Union Pacific, when the trains took an enforced rest of seventeen days; and here, for many a mile, the snowsheds follow closely on each other, and the snow fences wind beside the track, their long timbers sloping inward at an acute angle.

As we roll down the steep grade, the Wind River Mountains rise up in the north, shining white with snows, and far away, down on the western slope, Pilot Butte pricks up its rugged head from the plains. It is a barren land of low, gray sage and crusted alkali, red buttes and red, sandy soil. The alkali sifts through the air, whitens the dust that is blown through the train, and flavors, with its strong, bitter taste, every drop of water in the artesian wells. These wells are sunk at every station, and great tanks and windmills mark their presence; but the water thus brought to the surface is disagreeable and even nauseating to the taste, and dangerous to use in engines and boilers on account of its thick deposits.

The stations along the route slip away and leave no other impression behind than of a brown dot in the vast space. We rush through a narrow, rocky ravine into the Bitter Creek Valley, passing the little stream

THE BUTTES OF THE GREEN RIVER VALLEY.

that winds through it, brackish and undrinkable as Dead Sea water. Then come mile after mile of bluffs, sharp curves, and long ranks of buttes, thick with grotesque carvings and delicate tracery; solitary lights in lonely little telegraph houses; tall, columnlike boulders at Point of Rocks and a few scattered houses, remnants of what was once a fast little town before it gave up the ghost. As the sun rises for the fourth time since we left Omaha, we roll, rejoicing, into the Green River Valley.

"There's mighty pretty sceneries through yere, ladies," we hear Howells remarking, as he shuffles down the aisles between the double row of green curtains. The ladies emerge, eager and smiling, from their toilet mysteries, and we all meet in the hastily arranged sections where Howells and his coadjutor are whisking their feather dusters. The snow lies white and deep in every hollow, but the sun is out dazzlingly, and a cry goes up for smoked glass, blue spectacles, anything in the way of protection for the eyes; one weird-looking pair of wire goggles, flouted and derided at an earlier stage of the journey, is now at a premium. In the midst of a contest over the possession of these treasures, somebody rushes in with a thrilling announcement.

"Here's a scalped man! A conductor—but don't look at him because he doesn't like it!"

Everybody cranes his neck to stare.

"Tommy Cahoon," as well known on the Union Pacific Road as the buttes themselves, has just come on our train, and has been collared, so to speak, on his first appearance. It is just possible that he "doesn't like" our catechizing; but he is courteous and civil-spoken and tells his story for the nine hundred and ninety-ninth time.

He was fishing in the creek near Cheyenne in '69, so he says, when the Indians pounced on him, took the prized scalp lock, and left seven of their arrows in his body. Contrary to the rule in such cases, Tommy Cahoon revived and was strong enough to crawl three

Knobs and Excrescences

The buttes around Green River are wonderful in size, shape, color, and variety; there are towers, castles, and cathedrals, bulbous knobs and excrescences, colossal mushrooms, "giant's clubs" and "giant's teapots," forts, temples, tombs, and shapes of things unknown, possibly, in the heavens above and certainly in the earth beneath; all carved out of rich red and brown and cream-colored limestone, strata upon strata of varying color. The river sweeps in great curves, washing a white, sandy beach with its clear, emerald-green waters — the brightest, richest green that ever flashed in sunlight, caught from the color of the shale over which it runs. Every foot of ground for miles about is rich with fossil flowers, ferns, fishes, and even insects, buried in every layer of shale, waiting for the treasure-seeker's hammer.

THE DEPOT AT GREEN RIVER STATION, WYOMING TERRITORY,
SHOWING THE PECULIAR TOWER-LIKE FORMATION OF THE
GREEN RIVER BUTTES, EXTRAORDINARY FEATURES OF THIS REGION.

TWENTY MINUTES FOR REFRESHMENT AT GREEN RIVER STATION,
WHERE PASSENGERS MAY VISIT THE CALIFORNIA LIONS AND
VIEW OTHER "ROCKY MOUNTAIN CURIOSITIES."

miles back to Cheyenne, where good care and nursing soon sent him out as well as ever, with a ghastly scar to carry to the grave. And then Tommy, on solicitation, doffs his hat and shows an oval depression seven inches long in the back part of his skull.

"Wouldn't you like to have *your* way with those fellows just once?" somebody asks.

"Well, *my* way would be to give 'em a pretty wide berth, gentlemen," says Mr. Cahoon, with a shake of the head; and so goes on down the car, glad to get rid of us.

Reaching Green River station, we make a bound for the bar, where a choice assortment of "Rocky Mountain Curiosities" is advertised. We find the neatest and prettiest of rooms, in which fossils and petrifactions jostle mixed drinks and brandy straight. There are whole logs of petrified wood, broken down the middle to show sparkling quartz crystals bedded in their hollows; slabs two feet long, with delicate dark tracery of fishes, ferns, or water plants; moss agates of every shade; milky-white, dark gray, and purple amethysts; and California diamonds—clear, sparkling crystals, colorless as water. These an inquisitive old gentleman is inspecting, and he holds the largest up in derision.

"Now, who do you suppose could be gulled into thinking this a real diamond, my friend?" he demands of a long-bearded plainsman behind the bar.

"Nobody but some derned fool of a Down-Easter," replies the "friend."

The old gentleman lays down the crystal and smiles feebly.

Certain fierce snarling sounds and catlike hisses have been mysteriously proceeding from the end of the platform ever since we alighted. Shrieks of ecstasy from the small boys announce "wild cats." Approaching the iron cage around the corner of the station, we find two magnificent specimens of the California or mountain lion romping behind the bars.

They are splendid creatures, tawny yellow, like the lion, but maneless, and as large as the common panther which they very closely resemble. Of their temper and disposition, they are giving ample evidence just now. Goaded by paper pellets and taunts from the masculine bystanders, they are snapping, growling, and flinging their lithe bodies against the bars with yells of impotent fury. Now and then, a long arm with white, hooked claws darts out unexpectedly, and there is a wild stampede and a few feminine shrieks; but no harm is done and not even a coattail captured.

The twenty minutes slip away, and we are hurried back to the cars to whirl along the palisades of the Green River. The early sunlight blazes on the snow, the deep rich red of the rocks, and the rippling green water, and overhead the sky is blue—such a blue! Every man longs to be a painter, but what painter could copy all this upon which the sun shines every day?

Piedmont is reached by a heavy upgrade. The track crawls, winding, around the spurs of the Uintah Mountains, whose range we have begun to cross at an elevation of 7540 feet. White crests crowd the southern horizon. It is a wild, windy region where winter storms rage as no dweller in the lowlands can ever picture, and the yearly snow drifts are mountains in themselves. Snowsheds and drift fences follow the

A Good Camping-Ground

The buttes crowd thick for many miles around the river banks, and the rock cuts are frequent and abrupt. Soon the Uintah Mountains heave in sight, looking but a short five miles' walk to the south of us. The clear atmosphere creates endless deceptions, for these sharp, clean-cut cones are nearly eighty miles away. From their pointed peaks run long, wavy ridges cutting through the snow in streaks of deep, dark purple. We are passing up the Black's Fork Valley, and we presently cross the little stream and keep closely beside its winding trail for the next twenty or thirty miles. On its opposite banks the long, solid lines of buttes rise, in form something like truncated cones, brown and tawny yellow, streaked with lines of snow. A few low cottonwoods make a scattered fringe along the water's edge, and their sparse clusters tower to our eyes like the wildest luxuriance of vegetation after the recent miles of sagebrush.

This neighborhood is a good camping-ground for emigrant trains, and eastward-going trains passing this point as the twilight comes down may be almost sure of seeing the heavy, canvas-topped wagons drawn up together, the grazing horses tethered about, and the thin, blue column of smoke lazily rolling up from a flickering red campfire. Little danger hovers over these travelers nowadays, but it gives one a shiver round the roots of his hair to think of the possibilities attendant upon such a party ten years ago. One would think that the campers-out would scarce sleep under their canvas covers for dreaming of ghostly predecessors, wandering forever, driven by the night winds and the rain in this howling wilderness where their bones are buried.

CHURCH BUTTES, IN THE "BAD LANDS" OF WYOMING TERRITORY.

The Architecture of Nature

At Church Buttes we see some of the grandest freaks of the desert architect. The great pile which gives the station its name stands ten miles south of the track and seems but a stone's throw from us. Why "Church" buttes it is hard to say, as they certainly resemble no ecclesiastical architecture of any age or type; but a commodity of good names was wanting when these Western wonders were christened, and the sponsors plainly lacked imagination. Church Buttes is a curious range of steeply sloping mounds and domes built up with evenly laid strata of varying shades, propped with quaintly carved buttresses and columns ranging one above the other like slender pyramids. Between these shafts the face of the brown sandstone is hewn into deep niches and crowded full of fantastic altorelievos;

the fluted pyramids themselves are rough with traceries and carvings, which at a distance take on the likenesses of all human and brute creation. Toward the end of the buttes, the columns vary in pattern. When the sunlight strikes aslant them, they are like grim rows of Egyptian gods, facing north in the fixedness of eternal contemplation. It is a part of the "badlands" — this weirdly beautiful pile — and, coming down to geological facts, is no palace of desert genii but only "a deposit of sedimentary sandstones and marly clay."

It is good hunting land, stocked with deer, elk, bears, wolves, and the detested coyotes. Sulphur and soda springs abound also; and from Carter a government road is shortly to be opened into Montana and the Yellowstone Park.

SNOW-SHED AND DRIFT FENCE NEAR PIEDMONT.

84

track almost continuously, and at the summit of the divide comes the longest shed of the Union Pacific road — 2700 feet of arched timbers — through which we go thundering in a semi-darkness, crossed by bars and pencils of light that strike through the long chinks and wrapped in the heavy, black smoke clouds from our engine. The station itself is but an apology for a "place," and its most interesting edifice is the "general merchandise" store close to the track — a long, low hut of hewn logs filled in with adobe, with a mud roof and a mighty, white signboard crowned with a pair of storm-bleached antlers stolen from the front of some giant elk. We have a glimpse of a woman and a baby in the doorway, a few great-coated, slouch-hatted men on the stoop, and some contemplative pigs in the mud below — and this we carry away with us as a picture of life in Piedmont.

Long, low bluffs heave wildly all around Aspen,[12] a lonely little dot of a settlement, and every bluff is crossed and intersected with drift fences, hinting strongly of what winter life must be. Think of a December night out here in the desolate heart of Wyoming Territory, when you and the fire inside and the shrieking, savage wind without seem to be the only things alive in a great, black, starless, snowy world! But there are homes here, and men and women work and love and sorrow and rejoice, and children are born, and old folks die, and life runs in much the same grooves, after all, and repeats the same old story as it tells down in the crowded marts of a fuller civilization.

Some five hundred feet below Aspen is Hilliard Station, a new place even for the Plains. It is only about three years old and owes its being chiefly to the Hilliard Flume and Lumber Company, which has extensive works close to the depot. The little brown station and the few buildings near the track seem doubly insignificant here, for the charcoal kilns form a crowded village in themselves — great white cones like exaggerated beehives ranged in solid ranks at the foot of the long, low bluffs. There are twenty-nine, both large and small, the larger pits burning forty cords of wood at a filling and the lesser, twenty-six. Some of the little ones are open as we pass, and the glow of heat inside burns the ruddier for contrast with the snow, which makes the whitewashed cones look like dirty blots against its spotlessness. Beside the kilns there is the timber flume, whose trestles span the track and carry down loads of pine wood from the Uintah Mountains, twenty-four miles away — cordwood for the coal pits, lumber, sawlogs, and railroad ties.

A queer, long, low shanty of logs filled in with adobe stands just east of the station, upholding a huge signboard having thereon, "Wo Lee, Washing and Ironing." It is the first indication we have seen of "Chinese cheap labor," and there comes Mrs. Wo Lee herself, stamping out in the snow on her odd little wooden pattens and covering half her olive face with a paper handkerchief. She is clad in five dark blue bags, one bag apiece for each limb, and a wider but equally short one for the body; and her shining black hair is dressed butterfly-wise, two great wings projecting above each ear — a structure whose elaboration amply makes up for the excess of simplicity in the rest of her toilet. A dreary home has Mrs. Wo Lee, but the Chinese household gods

A CHINESE LAUNDRY AT HILLIARD.

are few and humble. The snow is banked up against the door and lies deep on the mud roof, but from the crooked stovepipe there is a cheery puff of smoke, and we imagine Mr. Wo Lee plying the flatiron inside or sprinkling the fine linen and the "boiled shirts" of the dwellers in Hilliard after his own peculiar fashion. "Lee," by the way, is clearly the Chinese equivalent of Smith. Every second Chinaman whom you meet on the Pacific Slope has it tacked somewhere to his personal cognomen, and you are stared in the face by Hop Lees, Sing Lees, Sam Lees, and Lee Yips at every turn through the Chinese quarters.

We are winding now through the Bear River Valley,[13] said to be one of the most fertile in all the range of the Rockies; but we, in this month of April, are greeted with nothing but snow and a sad, withered remnant of vegetation cropping out through the shallow drifts. The low hills and bluffs harbor hordes of game — jackrabbits, sagehens, and coyotes mingling with the California or mountain lion, the lynx and elk, catamounts, bears, and dainty antelopes.

A MERCHANDISE STORE AT PIEDMONT.

FOUR MILES EAST OF THE UTAH LINE — EVANSTON, ON THE BEAR RIVER.

Less than two miles west of Hilliard is the empty site of a departed railway town that once enjoyed the worst of reputations under the name of Bear River City. It was laid out in 1868 and at first promised well, for the population speedily rose to two thousand. Speculation in lots ran high. But the desperado element was strong and murder and sudden death so alarmingly frequent as to render the advent of Judge Lynch imperative. There were three prompt executions, as promptly followed by a fierce fight between the outraged friends of the deceased and the peaceful citizens; and after this battle — neither short nor bloodless — Bear River City died a lingering death. Now there is nothing to mark its site but two or three weather-stained headboards, planted at the graves of as many rioters who once made it "red hot" in Bear River City.

Over Bear River on a trestle bridge and into Evanston we pass at an early hour of the afternoon. The brakeman tells us that by four o'clock we shall run into Echo Canyon, and everybody is afire with impatience for this wonder of all wonders on the Union Pacific road.

Dinner is ready in Evanston at the Mountain Front Hotel, hard by the track; and, though we have dined already, we follow the crowd inside, lured on by the apparition of a pigtail at one of the windows. We have reached the point where the Irish element drops out of sight and is replaced by a delectable atmosphere of the Orient. Celestial laborers along the road, Celestial waiters at the hotels, serene moonfaces, and almond eyes greet us everywhere in place of the unshorn, unwashed, unsavory Celtic countenance.

There are several Chinamen on the platform, shuffling up and down in their corksoled shoes, with their long, thin pigtails swinging halfway to their heels and their hands thrust under the loose folds of the dark blue blouse into the dark blue trousers pockets. Their bland, smooth, yellow faces, all youthful and innocent and utterly inscrutable of expression, turn toward us with a sweet smile, while probably they jeer us in their native tongue for each other's delectation. Groups are working along the railroad track, bare-legged and barefooted, with huge platters of braided straw on their heads, secured by a strap under the chin, and with their pigtails coiled up neatly out of the way. We can hear them jabbering to each other in shrill, falsetto voices.

In the little hotel — a gem, in its way, for neatness and order — we find the dining room given over to their presiding influence, and nothing can be more soothing to the traveler's nerves than such a silent, soft-stepping, light-handed attendant, gliding behind one's chair like a shadow, handling plates like eggshells, always ready, always smiling, and always deferential. We settle the Chinese labor question — from an aesthetic point of

TIMBER-FLUME AND CHARCOAL FURNACE AT HILLIARD.

THE ARRIVAL AT EVANSTON STATION.

THE ALMA MINES, IN PIEDMONT.

view—on the spot; and contrasting these comely figures in baggy, blue trousers, dainty, white shirts and trim little gold buttons, with their smooth-shorn pates wreathed with serpentine coils of blue-black braids—contrasting these charms with the frowsy figures of heavy-handed, red-armed Irish maids and slovenly, ill-mannered Irishmen who haunt the dining rooms of the land—we sigh for a little taste of Chinese cheap labor on the Atlantic as well as on the Pacific slope. They giggle and chatter like children over a scrap of a sketch on the back of an old letter, which one of our artists has taken on the spot from the comeliest of the waiters. "Heap smart! Heap smart!" is the verdict, and our party goes forth covered with glory.

In the little office of the hotel there is a good deal of decoration—Chinese and Japanese pictures, stuffed heads of buffalo and lesser game, and a large dish of fresh-caught trout on ice, which adorns one of the windows. The hills are full of game; the principal trout streams of the Rocky Mountains are close at hand and easily accessible to fishing parties; and guides and outfits can be procured in the town at reasonable terms.

Evanston is more picturesquely situated than most of its sister towns along the route. The windings of the Bear River on one side and the steep divides on the other lend life and variety to the picture. We take a hurried glance at the railroad repair shops and the little "Chinatown" north of the track, where unpainted shanties crowd together, each one labeled with long strips of red paper about the doorposts, and all as dirty as it is possible for anything to be—short of an Indian tepee. How the Chinese, specklessly clean in their persons, can manage to maintain such filth in their dwellings is a mystery passing Caucasian comprehension. We carry it into our car for consideration, the thirty minutes being up and the last straggler already scrambling into the "Pullman Hotel."

A few miles north of Evanston is the coalminers' town, Alma, where the Rocky Mountain Coal Company owns and works three large mines and supplies the Central Pacific road with coal. The tall furnaces and hoisting works can be seen from the car windows, each thin, black chimney plumed with a long trail of smoke. Under those hills there is a steady fire eating out the coal veins—a fire that cannot be quenched and is only increased by the action of water upon the veins of fireclay which help to feed it. Workmen have walled it in with rock, sand, lime, and airtight chambers, and unconcernedly go about their business in another part of the mine; but it breaks out now and again in a fresh place, and the flames travel in spite of them and probably will while the supply of fuel lasts. There is a force of watchmen always on duty, and every precaution is taken against the insidious march of the fire—but think of watching, as it were, next door to a furnace a thousand feet under ground! □

THE SNOW-PLOWS OF THE UNION PACIFIC AT EVANSTON.

1967: The (Solid) Wasteland

HALF AN HOUR WEST of Cheyenne, a disarmingly mousy-looking woman showed interest in some books I had piled up next to my seat in the Dome Car. I told her that I was reading Frank Leslie's story of a journey across the country ninety years ago, and that I found it difficult to recognize the landmarks that had impressed railroad travelers in 1877.

"Why, of course," the woman said, obviously appalled by my stupidity. "Things have changed." And she eyed me scornfully for a moment. "Tell me, which places have changed the most?"

"It would be easier to say which places have changed the *least*," I said. "This part around here, for instance."

At the time, we were out in the open country between Cheyenne and Laramie, on a nonstop, 56-mile run that takes an hour and 19 minutes. The plains were as tempting in color as a freshly baked cake, golden-brown and lightly powdered with confectioner's sugar; the sky was a hard, bright blue; and a fierce wind was lifting the scattered snow and swirling it into a thin, capricious mist that occasionally blotted out the view. Every tuft of sagebrush had a parabolic drift of snow behind it, like the jet stream of an airplane; and dunelike drifts had formed against the rocks and fences. The fields were quite deserted — no people, no cows, no horses, no barns. It might have been the territory of the Sioux, except for a few lines of power poles marching along the right-of-way and some large signboards facing the transcontinental highway.

"Billboards? Highways? Power poles?" the woman said in an accusing tone. "It seems to me this part has changed a lot."

But I argued that the red plains of Wyoming were relatively durable, at least compared to the trans-figured cities on the route. Look at the permutations wrought by the electric lamp, the automobile, and the airplane on the landscape of Chicago, Omaha, or even Cheyenne: skyscrapers glittering with lights, a rush of freeways, and monumental parking garages, taller than the Tower of Pisa. In the cities, all our social problems were in view — the poisons polluting our air and water, the monotony of mass-produced goods, the congestion of people and machines, the deterioration of old buildings, the inequality of races, the ugliness of our fabulous technology. Out here, one could see only the rawness of a new civilization; it was still the frontier land of America.

Laramie seemed to confirm my thesis. All at once, there it was — cattle cars, sawdust kilns, and a sprawl of little, square, wooden houses that almost shone with newness, rawness, and impermanence. From the station we could see a row of honky-tonk saloons — the Cowboy Bar, the Music Box — and a spot of park that looked as if someone had laid it out in honor of a visiting senator. It was impossible to believe that Laramie would be a century old next year — unshod, ungelded, bristling with rough edges, and dewy with great expectations.

"Well, it doesn't appeal to me," the woman said as we were pulling out. "I'm from Madison, Wisconsin. Going out to San Francisco to visit my children. My daughter and her husband and their children." She had lost interest in the argument rather abruptly, it seemed to me. In a moment she announced she was off to join her husband for a before-lunch stimulant.

I stayed in the Dome, keeping track of the signs of permanence and change. The walls of glass on either side permitted me to absorb far more scenery than I could have seen from an ordinary train window; and I could observe the sort of minutiae the Leslies saw as they clattered along at twenty miles per hour. There were jackrabbits bobbing in the sage, range ponies standing with their tails to the wind, and tiny, gray clapboard houses huddling beside the tracks. In Rawlins it was all petroleum tanks and tract houses of pastel stucco — pistachio, pink, and peach — but the most prominent buildings were still the Union Pacific roundhouse and the State Penitentiary.

It was 1877 reenacted: the Great Plains, the harsh towns, the passenger pressing his nose against the pane while the alien West lurched past in exotic pageant. We even carried a conductor who was the cynosure of all the tourists. He was an authenticated jinx. Last time he was aboard (and it was several months ago, you can be sure) a thirty-one-year-old woman had tried to kill herself by swallowing barbiturate pills, and an older woman had slipped on the steps and broken her leg. (I had all this from our porter.) This time, the conductor had caused a woman in the car ahead of ours to develop excruciating chest pains. Five minutes out of Green River, the accursed conductor could be seen in a vestibule, taking his hat off from time to time and wiping his forehead, poised to rush out and summon a doctor for the passenger he had hoodooed. Those of us who knew him for what he was glared at his back and kept our distance.

Green River is still a major stop on the Union Pacific line. It is an old-fashioned, hard-bitten town, brick-red, gray, and sepia, sulking among splendid, thronelike buttes at the edge of a frozen river — a tiny glacier that gnaws the base of Castle Rock. The passengers stormed the waiting room and plundered the cigar stand of magazines, candy bars, Ritz crackers, and ham salad sandwiches, while the conductor, hat in hand, went scrambling away on a putative mission of mercy. Down the platform in the direction of the Green Gander Bar and the Isis Theatre, three children, momentarily released from one of the coach cars, were running circles on the icy, brown lawn.

Wyoming was the same as it had always been, if you

discounted a few billboards, paved roads, and power poles, and kept your eyes on the eroded sandstone bluffs, the sagebrush, and the rivers. Unfortunately, the more attention I gave to bluffs, sagebrush, and rivers from my omniscient perch in the Dome, the more I noticed billboards and power poles. After a while, I began to suspect that the woman from Madison was right — this part *had* changed a lot. I recalled that every town we had seen along the way nestled in a nimbus of hard wreckage: abandoned railroad cars, windowless concrete sheds, used-car lots, lumberyards, and junk heaps. On the west end of Rock Springs, I even had noticed an immense advertisement created from a Quonset hut. The entire building was painted white, with red, yellow, and blue polka-dots and "Wonder Bread" in large letters on each side.

Could it be that the changeless red plains were filling up with rubbish? There seemed to be scarcely a barn-yard that did not have a few morsels of "solid waste," as the urban planners call it. The rusty chassis had replaced the windmill as the mark of man upon the vast horizon.

I remembered an article I had read in the *Daily News* as we were leaving Chicago, and I went back to my roomette to get it. The article reported that automobiles are being scrapped at a rate of five to six million a year. By 1975, the number would reach eight million a year. In Chicago alone, 21,212 cars were *abandoned* in 1965.

The last figure hinted at a horrible dilemma. It is becoming more difficult — in Chicago, at least — to get rid of a dead car than to hide an unexplained corpse. The corpse, with know-how, can be reduced to about a quart of fine mineral ash and old dental fillings; whereas the defunct automobile, stripped of its upholstery, seat belts, and other burnable padding, is a grossly distended lump of metal that is not particularly desirable

even to a steel mill. The only solution is to export one's old jalopy to the lone prairie, where plenty of parking space is available (for the next few years), and where one is not likely to be caught and punished for littering.

Walking back to the Dome Car, I pondered this odd pattern of trade and wondered what Wyoming was exporting in return — slaves? rum? indigo? Then I realized it was a simple barter: Wyoming is getting the old automobile carcasses and giving, in return, its land.

Evidently, this is considered a keen transaction in Wyoming. Out in what used to be called the Wide Open Spaces, auto bodies are regarded as a decoration, sharing the attention of the tourist with beer signs, wind-blown trailer parks, and chemical plants along the route to Yellowstone and the Grand Tetons. If your old clunk will not make it to Wyoming on its own power, you can turn it over to some dealer who, for a small charge, will agree to transport it to the cow country and add it to some breathtaking, twentieth century construct of bashed metal and smoldering upholstery that is building, Chartres-like, year by year, on the edge of Rawlins or Hanna.

In Evanston, a cozy little town at the foot of Bear River Valley, I saw a unique retirement yard for old railroad baggage wagons. Hundreds of them, all painted dark green, stood along the tracks in the gathering twilight. Some day they may be going back into service in Ogden or Grand Island; but I suspect that, sooner or later, they will return and end up with the rest of the solid waste, out where the coyotes howl and the wind blows free.

I meant to point out this novel reliquary to the woman from Madison as amendatory evidence of how things have, indeed, changed in ninety years. But she was down in the bar section again, arguing with some friends from St. Paul about the political aspirations of Richard M. Nixon. □

SNOW-FENCES IN THE ROCKY MOUNTAINS.

CHAPTER X

The Canyons of the Wasatch

1877: New England Villages and Mountains like Petrified Sponges

THE DIVIDES GROW HIGHER and steeper. There is a dash of warm red now in the rock, and as we pass Wahsatch we catch a little fichu of green tinting the slope of the plain. How bright and springlike it looks after the shivering white snowdrifts around Green River this morning! Four miles from Wahsatch[1] is a signpost that makes the dividing line between Wyoming and Utah. We dash past it and in the twinkling of an eye are in the land of the Latter-Day Saints.

Round capelike projections and through steep walls of red sandstone our train goes winding, swinging from side to side like a ship among the waves. At the very gateway of Echo Canyon, on the crest of a great hill north of the track, is a weatherworn ruin all built in crumbling red stone. They call it "Castle Rock." Its doorway is the mouth of a cave one hundred and fifty feet deep, and its columns are the work of no meaner architects than Nature and Time themselves. But nothing we have seen along the way is more suggestive of man's planning and execution than this "Castle Rock," crowning the summit of a steep divide, overlooking the long descent of the canyon and the winding road crawling through it .

And then follow wonders as fast as the minutes chase each other. No one can see them all, far less describe them; there is left on the mind a confusion of huge outlines, colossal bulk, glowing color, and unimaginable shapes. There are needle-like spires, red and gray, carved and fretted like chessmen as tall as houses; roughly squared columns, mighty domes, and boulders like headless birds, spreading huge wings for a flight that is never taken; sheer walls of sandstone eaten into holes and niches till they look like mountains of petrified sponge; rocks that are gray, rocks that are ruddy as if washed in a perpetual sunset, rocks of tawny or creamy yellow, belted with orange and dashed with white; and layers upon layers of stratified sandstone.

The ground is covered with loose, broken rock from which you may pick up curious pieces perforated like honeycombs, crusted with white and yellow crystals, and flecked with every imaginable color; and you may carry home, as a priceless paperweight, a bit of Echo Canyon, painted in pale green and rich ochery red, with a grain of garnet color shot through.

The north fork of Echo Canyon crosses our road, and the sides of the gorge draw closer together. Through these "narrows," as they call them, General Johnston's[2] men marched in '57, when an invasion of Salt Lake City was threatened; and the Saints came down in force to fortify Echo Canyon. Upon these steep bluffs they piled breastworks of rocks and heaps of boulders to roll down on the heads of the marching men, and there we see them today, dwarfed by the great height to the size of a child's marbles. Passing the site of the Mormon camp, where the "Nauvoo Legion" under General Daniel H. Wells[3] prepared to receive the Gentile invasion, we come to "Steamboat Rocks," a most belittling name for the colossi of the canyon. We can measure these towers of sandstone by two or three Trinity steeples piled one upon the other. They are like the prows of a vessel, hewn out in brilliant red sandstone and seamed across with belts of tilted strata; in their shadow the long train shrinks into a child's toy. The train has stopped, and we have all hurried out to stray up and down, pick up stones and bits of sagebrush and cedar, and stare until the eyes ache. Ten minutes are gone like a second.

"Sentinal Rock" comes next, a roughly squared column; then "Bromley's Cathedral" and "Pulpit Rock," the one a mile-long mountain of rock, with pinnacles and domes and slender, needle-like spires, the other a turret, sixty feet above the track, that looks as much like a high-shouldered owl as a pulpit. Here, through a sudden gap, the Weber River[4] comes pouring in, joining its clear, green waters with those of Echo Creek.

We pass out of Echo through a narrowing gorge, past a tiny Mormon settlement whose chief building is its "Bishop's Palace," a by no means palatial structure of brick. The fantastic rock formations disappear, and nature shows only rugged grandeur: precipitous hillsides draped with a film of green and, away up on the heights, the fine needle-like shafts of pine trees drawn black against the sky. All the warm, rich, sunset colors of Echo Canyon have faded out, and there is only the gray rock, the faint, tawny green of the sod, and the deeper green of the little river at the base of the bluff. Here and there, a wall of craggy limestone rises sheer

Among a Peculiar People

OUR ENTRANCE INTO UTAH: ECHO CITY, ON THE WEBER RIVER.

Right in the bosom of the canyon lies Echo City, where one could wish to live and die, so beautiful does it look, walled in by those giant ramparts of sandstone, and peeping at itself forever in the mirror of the Weber River. The trees are in their first delicate leafage, and among the green are dashes of white — freshly painted houses, a church spire, and a fence or two. We at once recognize that we are out of the land of the Gentiles and among a peculiar people. Painted fences, white houses, and green blinds were left behind on the farther side of the Missouri; but we take them up again in Utah, looking as fresh and familiar as ever we saw them in New England.

THE ROCK FORMATIONS OF ECHO CANYON.

A CAMP AMONG THE ROCKS, ECHO CANYON.

A Spellbound Region

The highest and most picturesque formations of Echo Canyon are all on its northern side, a spellbound region, wherein every living creature has been stricken into stone and left rooted in grim silence forever. There is always more or less a suggestion of life in rocks, but these seem half-human. The rude cones of the Battlement Rocks, hewn out of warm, red sandstone, look like so many cowled monks leaning together; the "Witches," perched high up on a ledge, are thin, fantastic caricatures dressed in red and gray with belts of yellow — you can almost see them turning their long necks and whispering as you whirl by; and Monument Rock is a hooded giant, measuring two hundred and fifty feet from the apex of his conical cap to the sagebrush carpet on which he stands.

Glancing up, we catch sight of something stirring. Are the pillars of stone waking up? No, it is only a tiny human figure standing on a ledge.

There are two or three more behind him, a flicker of fire among the loose stones, and a puff of blue smoke floating above them.

"That's a hunter's camp," says the brakeman, who sits swinging his long legs on the railing of the rear platform. "That thar place looks as if 'twas made a-purpose for 'em, don't it?"

They have camped on a broad shelf that juts out in front of a deep cranny in the bluff. This miniature cave may be ten or twelve feet deep and high enough inside for a man to stand upright. With a handful of straw spread on the stony floor and the campfire fed by the crackling, resinous cedars and dry sagebrush piled across its mouth, there could be no more delicious resting place.

against the sky, honeycombed with deep, ragged holes like irregularly hewn windows. In the niches there are hundreds of eagles' nests, high up out of reach of all but winged creatures; lower down, the swallows build, and the great, sun-warmed rock is as full of life as an anthill.

"Thousand Mile Tree's just ahead," sings out the brakeman. He is a socially disposed fellow who keeps us company on the platform, furnishing useful information to the female inquisitors and jumping off at every stopping place to snatch up stones and specimens for them. The said specimens accumulate along the passages at the end of the car and gradually form stone quarries under every seat until Howells spirits them away under pretense of "jes' layin' 'em to one side for the ladies."

We stop at the landmark. It is nothing very remarkable, only a big cedar, right on the bank of the noisy little river. To one of its lower limbs is fastened a great signboard. One thousand miles from Omaha and the Missouri — that dividing line of the Continent, cutting off "the States" from "the frontier" — and nearly as far from that civilization of the West that concentrates at San Francisco. It gives one a vaguely regretful feeling to be reminded that more than half our journey is over — and that only forty-eight hours lie between us and the end of our iron trail.

But we pick up stones with the rest of the travelers and duly pose for our pictures. In the sudden silence of the canyon, now that the train is silent, we can hear the foaming ripple of the Weber River as it runs past between the high bluffs, can feel the stillness and the loneliness close around us, and guess at what they were before we came and will be in a minute hence, when we are gone.

The fat cook seizes this opportunity to drop from the platform and dive into his icebox under the car, an object of wild curiosity to half a dozen small boys who eagerly watch the bringing forth of an antelope steak. *We* have forgotten that it is nearly dinner time; but William probably has been thinking of nothing else all the way through Echo Canyon, and the stern necessities of mushroom sauces and meringue puddings and lobster salads have crowded out of his brain such trivial accidents of Nature as bluffs and buttes and outdoor galleries of rock sculpture.

Off we go again, to the deep relief of the brakeman who chafes at all our delays, yet cannot resist pointing out every hundred yards or so something that "*had* ought to be photographed if anything was."

He has evidently an appreciative eye for scenery and accepts our raptures with the coolness of one who has a sort of personal proprietorship therein. He is "going to run over to the States in the fall," he informs us. He was raised there, but he "ain't goin' to stay, *you bet!* No, sir, there ain't elber-room over thar for a man that has once lived on the Plains.

"It's a queer thing," he adds, "that all the women that come out yer' want to stay, and the men are mostly ready to run back again. Now, how d'ye account for that?"

We follow the Weber River down the somber canyon, with great, green bluffs and gray rock ribs on either side. The bluffs are channeled through by deep cuts, like miniature canyons opening to let in a glimpse of the wider world beyond. A few miles from the signal tree a steep, green hillside sweeps up to the south of us, rising sheer from the margin of the narrow stream and scored from crest to base by two parallel ledges of slate gray granite, fourteen feet apart, fifty feet high, and eight hundred feet in length. Two strongly built, massive and weather-worn old stone walls they seem, these upturned ledges of strata that somebody has so inanely christened the "Devil's Slide." There are no similar formations near the two isolated ridges, which cut through a smooth, grassy sod with no rocks or boulders in their neighborhood. But only a few miles beyond, the hillside is full of outcropping ledges, tilted up at the same angle as Devil's Slide and quite as peculiar, though less regular and uniform. Every here and there, a bare rib pushes through, grim and gray and cold-looking in the warm sunshine.

A SETTLER'S HUT IN THE CANYON.

THE ONE-THOUSAND-MILE TREE, DIVIDING LINE OF THE CONTINENT.

IN THE WEBER CANYON — DEVIL'S GATE.

"Tunnel No. 3," a mouse hole at the base of a green rampart, takes us through the mountains. We emerge, blinded by the dazzle, upon an open valley crossed by the foaming, noisy little river and shut in by strangely terraced ranges of hills, through which we have yet one more gloomy passage to make — "Tunnel No. 4," giving into Round Valley. And now the Wasatch Mountains are fairly crossed. To the left, their great white peaks burst into view, springing high into the blue air, upborne by buttresses of purple rock. Then come strange vistas of green fields — real fields where seed is sown and harvest gathered — and budding orchard trees and new plowed land and the little homes of Morgan City.

Morgan City is known to the Gentiles[6] chiefly by its telegraph station, Weber; but we are interested not in the Gentile element but in the Saintly one. Over a big, square, white store not far from the track is a square sign, bearing the legend, so mysterious to the uninitiated — "Z.C.M.I."[7] This is the Morgan branch of the Zion Cooperative Mercantile Institution, which flourishes throughout Utah. Here, under the immediate shelter of the Church and the patronage of its Saints, are dispensed calicoes and coffee, boots and shoes, flour and straw hats, thimbles and rake handles, tape and ironmongery. Nearly opposite this valuable institution and the cluster of adjacent houses, a great white lime-kiln lies under the brow of the bluffs, its two circular, black doorways looking like eyeholes in a dry, bleached skull.

These refreshing bits of pastoral landscape — the acres of "garden stuffs" and the tender young wheat — are soon left behind, and we dash past the frowning heights of a great snow-capped mountain into the "Devil's Gap." The Enemy of Mankind appears to stand to the average intellect as a synonym for all grandeur, sublimity, and wonder in nature. In passing over a hundred miles or so in any given direction in this country, one may feel certain of finding at least three of Satan's bargains in real estate; and with characteristic greed he has invariably fastened on the choicest bits of scenery for his slides, castles, and gateways.

The "Gate" in this instance is one of the most curious as well as beautiful spots on the line of the two roads. The Weber River, dashing between its frowning walls, describes a loop like a great letter "U" around a huge mass of towering granite spanned by a high trestle bridge. Around the outer rim of the river rises a vertical wall of granite nearly a thousand feet in height and scarred deep with grooves and seams — old glacier marks perhaps, scratched when the earth was like clay in the potter's hand. The huge boulder in the middle of the loop shuts off part of this magnificent wall, and we look beyond it into the amphitheater that the river has cut for itself, and up at the towering heights of the cold, gray wall. The curve faces south, and no ray of afternoon sunlight can strike into its hollow. There is a chilly twilight even now hovering over the deep gorge.

Our train stops midway on the trestle bridge, and a few passengers descend to stride along the ties in a spider-like and precarious manner, following the photographer, who is hurrying to get his camera into position. Our friend, the brakeman, seating himself with a heavy sigh on the edge of the bridge, puts up fervent prayers that "the next party travelin' special will get a special en-gine along with their car." ☐

1967: This is Ford Country

ALL AFTERNOON I SAT in the green glass bubble of the Dome Car, skimming over the sagebrush in company with several elderly couples, who muttered to one another out of the corners of their mouths, and four regal old ladies with tortoise-shell combs in their hair and knitting bags on their knees. The old ladies never stopped knitting and talking and passing a box of candy to and fro until 4:30 P.M., when a steward stuck his head up the steps and said, "First call for dinner." At this signal they instantly closed their box of chocolates and their knitting bags and trooped off, followed by the muttering couples, leaving the Dome to darkness and to me.

It was lightly snowing, and the empty cattle pens and motionless windmills looked utterly forlorn. I watched for evidences of the Mormon hand upon the landscape, until I remembered that the familiar token of Mormon colonization, the groves of Fremont poplar trees, would be unrecognizably naked at this season. The canyons west of Evanston are barren and sparsely populated; the track descends in great, sweeping curves; and one can imagine he is all alone on a vast toboggan run.

My toboggan was joined at 4:35 P.M. by Sonny and Cher, Simon and Garfunkel, Paul Revere and the Raiders, and the Turtles, whose recorded voices reached us through a four-inch long transistor radio brought into the Dome by a robust and prosperous-looking man, about sixty-five, who cuddled the receiver against his plump cheek like a toothache pack. He dropped into the seat behind me and turned up the volume. When I peered around at him, he nodded and smiled. I nodded and did not smile.

At 4:45, when I could no longer stand "Snoopy and the Red Baron," I gathered up my papers and left, casting back what I hoped was a withering glare. The owner of the radio, it appeared, was sound asleep, with his head back and his mouth open, while a voice from Evanston invited him to come in and open an account.

Down in the lounge section under the floor of the Dome, I found the bartender engaged in conversation with, or by, a woman of grandmotherly age in a lavender dress and persimmon-colored hair. On the table in front of her was a glass that contained either a remarkably strong highball or a generous serving of apple cider. I was about to walk in when I heard the woman say: "If we're going sout' why is it getting colder?"

The tail end of the question was aimed in my direction and caught me as I was backing out. I murmured that I supposed it had to do with the altitude; but before I could complete my getaway, the persimmon-haired woman cried out in anguish: "You t'ink we're going *nort'?"*

Without really knowing which way we were going, I felt I had better go in and render aid to the bartender, who was rolling his eyes upward like an El Greco saint and seemed about to collapse. I got out a map from my briefcase and seated myself. The bartender ungratefully slipped past us and fled without even taking my order.

My companion flipped her spectacles onto her nose and scrutinized the map. I should explain that she wore the sort of glasses that have slender safety chains attached to the earpieces; but instead of letting the glasses fall forward like a necklace when they were out of service, she kept them pushed up on her forehead. This gave her a curiously vigilant look and allowed her to bring the lenses into working position with a single flick of her hand. Long before I had located our position on the railroad chart, she was reading aloud the stations of the line, working westward from Chicago, in a tone of growing indignation. Each town seemed to confirm her suspicion that the climate had been getting colder as we traveled south, although I never figured out whether she blamed this on the railroad, the weather bureau, or the compass.

"Look, dot's lovely!" she cried suddenly, squirming around and flipping her glasses up onto her forehead. A reddish pinnacle loomed on our right, blotting out the dark sky for a moment, and then disappeared. "Just like a castle." And she flipped the glasses down again and returned to the map.

I do not doubt that the rock formation was *The Castle*, but there was no way of finding out. You could pass The Sentinal, Steamboat Rock, and The Cathedral, nowadays, and no one would bother to mention that you had just seen the scenic wonders of the Union Pacific line. The bartender had deserted his post just when he might usefully have identified The Witches or Thousand Mile Tree; when he did come back, clutching a bottle of vodka in each hand, he lurked in a corner and rolled his eyes eloquently every time I turned his way.

The canyon wall rose steeply on our right; over on the left, the open side, you could see a distant row of perfect, cone-shaped peaks. Their whiteness against the dark sky was like a photonegative of summer mountains. Deep ravines filled with snow formed luminous creases that would have been streaks of dense shadow on a sunny day; and the line of the ridge looked pure white against the blackness above it. On the other side, where the Mormons once hid among the rocks to fight off invaders from the States, a highway now runs parallel to the tracks. We passed a billboard, undoubtedly intended for the eyes of motorists and not train passengers, that said: "This Is Ford Country. What Are You Driving?"

Having driven a giant toboggan at least part of the way, I smiled scornfully at the thought of lesser transportation. But my companion did not like the service.

"Dammit," she said, "why do dey bring us here when it's so dark? Dot's a lovely place, but who can see it?"

She finished her study of the map and handed it back to me with a frown.

"I t'ink we're turning sout' now. Not so cold."

All I could see by this time was the reflection of our own faces on the glass and, now and then, the lights of a small station or a farmhouse, half-buried in drifted snow. But my Argus-eyed friend discerned innumerable palaces and peristyles of sandstone.

"Dot's lovely," she reported. "Look! Dot one's lovely, too. I'll have to come back here and see it in my car."

And she took a long draught of her honey-colored drink, having spoken her epitaph upon the scenic railroad line. □

THE DEVIL'S SLIDE, IN THE WASATCH MOUNTAINS.

of pure, bright water running along each street. These roadside streams also water the cottonwood and poplar trees than line the street on either side and keep the grass vividly green. There was no dust, no mud, no litter of any kind.

In the main street we noticed the Merchant's Cooperative Union Building or "Co-op," as it is popularly termed, with its inscription, "Holiness to the Lord," in black and gold above the door; a profusion of neat shops, especially flourishing millinery establishments; and several fine book and stationery shops.

We paid a visit to the principal photographer, an old acquaintance of our Chief and a very civil and gentleman-like proprietor. He freely admitted himself to be a Mormon, somewhat defiantly stating that he had nailed his colors to the mast. But he considered it very unlikely that any of our party, even the women, would be able to "interview" any of the upper class of Mormon wives.

"The ladies here don't like being made subjects of curiosity," said he. "Their homes are just as sacred to them as yours in the East are to you, and they are very sensitive about being questioned."

Then he cited the case of a titled English lady, recently passing through Utah, who had "as much cheek as a government mule" and, "wanting to know, you know," had called upon several of the Mormon ladies and put them to their catechism with the vigorous candor of a parish visitor. The consequence was that she got terribly snubbed, learned nothing, and went away next day to make up her notes of travel as best she could.

Having furnished this little narrative, our friend paused significantly and then indulgently added: "But I'll give you an introduction to the leading Mormon editor of the city."

Then he showed us some portraits of the various Mesdames Young, first the recreant Ann Eliza,[3] who "bolted," as he phrased it, upon the very day the President was about to present her with the title deeds of the house she lived in.

"And here's the house," he continued, producing a picture of a neat little villa. "That's the *hovel* she talks about in the East."

When President Young was informed that she was gone, or at least had removed with all her effects to the Walker House, the Gentile hotel, he just opened his desk, took out the title deeds and, tearing them across, said quietly: "So much saved!"

The next picture represented a lady of about thirty, well-dressed, a little stout, with a strong, sensible, pleasing face and something of a stylish air. This was Mrs. Amelia,[4] said to be Mr. Young's favorite wife. But this assumption our photographer scouted indignantly: That was only Eastern talk. There was a lot of nonsense talked in the East about the Mormons, and Ann Eliza had set a whole raft of stories afloat. Mrs. Amelia was a born nurse and had taken care of Mr. Young through some bad times; and so he always took her traveling with him and liked to have her near him at home.

To a delicate suggestion about Amelia's picture, the artist shook his head. No, he couldn't sell that, nor the picture of any private lady. He had been offered a hundred dollars for it, but it was not for sale. We appreciated the fine feeling of this little speech, and silently wondered how long our friend's position in Salt Lake City would be tenable if he offended Mrs. Amelia. We concluded that he was a wise as well as an amusing and instructive photographer; and so took our leave.

The editor of the Mormon paper proved a very intelligent and cultured man, and after a little talk he escorted us to see the "Woman's Union," where the work of the women of Utah is offered for sale. It is under the charge of a lady called Miss Snow[5] (although she is one of Brigham Young's wives), two of his daughters, and Mrs. Davis. The large room on the ground floor was decorated with the American flag and three large mottoes done in white on a blue ground:

"KNOWLEDGE IS POWER"
"IN UNION IS STRENGTH"
"SUCCESS TO INDUSTRY"

The goods consisted of every sort of home manufacture: clothes, shoes, bonnets, straw hats, artificial flowers, laces (including some beautiful wrought Honiton), and a piece of the first silk manufactured in Utah —a silver-gray fabric resembling Japanese silk.

Miss Snow greeted us pleasantly. She is a lady considerably past middle age, with a good and pleasing face, a quiet refined manner, although cold and reserved, and a very precise and deliberate mode of speech. She seemed perfectly willing to talk upon any subject. She had been abroad, and told me she had taken cocoons to Palestine to compare with those of that country and had found the Utah article fully equal to that of Oriental growth. She acknowledged herself the principal mover in the Woman's Union, the object of which is to encourage self-reliance and perfect independence of the outside world; and she added, with a smile of conscious strength and power, "We consider ourselves among the finest women in the world and aim to compete with our sisters elsewhere in every pursuit and every branch of education."

Women, she said, had as much interest as men in the prosperity of the territory, and their rights and privileges were equal. At the two colleges of Utah the course of study was the same for male and female students, and the progress of the one was fully equal to the other. Education had necessarily been neglected in the first hard years, when everyone had had to labor for bare existence; but now good schools were established everywhere, and the rising generation would be admirably trained.

In this connection she spoke of the hard journey across the plains thirty years ago. Leaving the place where Omaha now stands[6] on the twelfth of June, they had not arrived at Salt Lake until the second day of October.

We touched upon the "peculiar institution" of Utah, and I asked if the various wives of one husband got along among themselves. She replied: "Perfectly so, their religion inculcates it. Besides, their work is so large and their aims so high that they have no time and no capacity for petty jealousies."

We noticed a volume of "Voyages" by Miss Snow, and also a collection of poems; but she herself was more interesting than her books and seemed so strong and earnest, so full of ideas, aspirations, and plans for her chosen people that we left her with real regret.

From the Woman's Union the editor led us to the Deseret National Bank, a substantial brick building, and presented us to Elder H——, president of that institution and twice Representative from Utah to Washington. We found him a fine looking man with marvelously expressive eyes, as courtly and imposing in manner as appearance.

Mr. H—— spoke freely upon Utah matters, especially of its faith, professing himself a Mormon but not a polygamist. He said he had always respected his wife's feelings too much to take another. Very few polygamic marriages now took place in the city, he said, although they are still common enough through the rest of the Territory. He did not hear of more than half a dozen a year. Formerly, polygamy had been a different matter: more patriarchal than was now possible. Women had been content with the simple necessaries of life, and each had borne her share in the hardships and toil of the infant settlement. But now—

"But now," we interposed, "the railway has come and brought a whole train of French milliners and fashion plates."

"Yes," he replied, with a good-humored twinkle of the eye, "harbingers of a higher civilization, I suppose you think."

"Yes. Before them, the evil of polygamy will melt away as it never would have done before either civil or moral legislation. Don't you think so?"

"Perhaps, perhaps," replied the Elder, stirring a little uneasily in his chair. "That is, if it be an evil."

The women of Utah had an unusually elevated and respected position, he said. Their actions were free, their opinions sought and regarded. They had been offered the privilege of a vote on polygamy, which they had declined to accept; they had the right of legislation in school matters; and they could obtain almost any position they chose to try for. Certainly, the wives in polygamic families harmonized. Why should they not? Each, if she chose, had her own house, where she lived in perfect privacy with her children; or, if they preferred, all combined in one household.

A genial, hearty gentleman entered the room, and Mr. H—— at once presented him. He was, we learned afterward, one of the principal merchants of Salt Lake City and a man of large means; an Englishman, but quite free from English reserve. Mr. H——, evidently

SOME OF THE RESIDENCES OF THE LATE BRIGHAM YOUNG:
1) THE OLD RESIDENCE, 2) THE NEW RESIDENCE,
3) MRS. EMMELINE YOUNG'S HOUSE, 4) MRS. AMELIA
YOUNG'S HOUSE, 5) MRS. COBB YOUNG'S HOUSE, 6) SOCIAL
HALL, 7) METROPOLITAN SCHOOLHOUSE.

One Man's Family

Brigham Young had nineteen wives. Fifteen of these were his own for time and eternity; the other four were proxy wives, being widows of Joseph Smith. The children of their union with Brigham are credited to Joseph Smith and go to swell his kingdom. All plural wives are known by their maiden names, to distinguish one from the other. His wives in the order of marriage were: Mary Ann Angel, Lucy Decker, Mrs. Augusta Cobb, Harriet Cook, Clara Decker, Emeline Free, Lucy Biglow, Zina D. Huntington, Susan Snively, Margaret Pierce, Mrs. Twiss, Emily Partridge, Martha Bowker, Eliza Burgess, Eliza R. Snow, Harriet Barney, Amelia Folsom, Mary Van Cott, and Ann Eliza Webb, the nineteenth and last.*

He had forty-five living children. Most of them are grown and married. There are twenty-nine girls and sixteen boys. Seven of Brigham's daughters have plural marriages. Two of the seven call Hiram B. Clawson husband, two are allied to George Thatcher, and two to Mark Croxall. The seventh is the second mate of Thomas Williams.

Amelia Folsom was the only wife Brigham lived with at the time of his death. Upon this favorite wife was lavished all the care and attention the most devoted monogamist could possibly bestow upon his companion.

In the President's household they had what is called "ration day." Once a month each family received five pounds of sugar, one pound of candles, a bar of soap, and a box of matches. The rule with all the Prophet's wives — except the favorite — was that all food beyond the plainest fare, and all clothing except what nature demands for the protection of the person, the wife was expected to provide for herself and children. When about to seal another wife to himself either for time or eternity, the President (as he always insisted upon being addressed) promised a good house and $1000 per year for pin money, the result of which was quite an accumulation of private dwellings belonging to his family.

Leslie's Illustrated Newspaper, Sept. 15, 1877

[* Although Ann Eliza called herself "Wife Number Nineteen," Brigham Young actually had between twenty-six and twenty-nine wives.—*Ed.*]

enjoying the idea of seeing someone else put through the same inquisitorial questionings, said: "Madame wishes to know if the women of Salt Lake City are a jealous race."

"Jealous!" exclaimed the merchant, Mr. J——. "They have no time for such nonsense. They have their houses, their children, their sewing, their affairs to attend to, and if idleness is the mother of mischief, occupation is the parent of contentment. Look at my wife, for instance: to be sure, she is an only wife; but if she were not, what time would she have for jealous fancies, with a large household, a family of fourteen children, their governess, and four servants to look after?"

"Fourteen children!" we echoed, involuntarily.

"Yes," replied Mr. J——, with pious fervor, "we hold with the psalmist that children are an heritage of the Lord, and man can have no surer sign of God's approval and kindness than a large family."

We spoke of Miss Snow, her remarkable intelligence and attainments, and Mr. J—— explained that, although she was indeed one of Brigham Young's wives, she was merely "sealed to him for time," having been the widow of Joseph Smith, whose wife she would be in the next world. In fact, she had long since ceased to live among the President's wives. A woman once sealed, or married, to the man of her choice was his to all eternity. So long as he lived she could think of no other partner; but after his death she might, if she chose, seal herself to another for the remainder of her mortal existence; a mere marriage of time, not at all to the prejudice of those eternal relations. We were struck very forcibly by positive faith in another existence that is implied by such definite arrangements for its duties and pleasures.

Divorce is possible under the Mormon law, but it is seldom applied for and never granted except in case of ill-treatment, flagrant neglect, or the gravest offenses. It is not considered creditable to either party.

Mr. J—— closed by inviting us to call and see his wife in the afternoon, which we gladly promised to do. While waiting, we visited the theater, which is neatly but not very expensively decorated, the colors pink and gray. We did not see the rocking chair in which Mr. Young is fond of sitting in one of the aisles to witness the performance; but two of the four proscenium boxes, we were informed, belonged to him. Members of his family are generally to be seen there, as he is a zealous patron of the drama and encourages a large attendance.

From the theater we drive to Mr. J——'s house. The

fine sweep of the carriage drive cuts a lawn of emerald velvet, bordered with symmetrical beds of tulips, geraniums, and other brilliant flowers. Our host conducts us into a drawing room, noticeable in any city for its elegant and tasteful furniture, ornaments, and mirrors, and presents us to Mrs. J——, a fine looking, dignified English matron surrounded by several of her children —two young ladies, perfect in manner; a girl of twelve, very pretty and stylish in her polonaise of brown velvet; a little boy of about three; and a toddling baby, sweet and dainty in its Valenciennes lace and soft blue ribbons. The other nine children did not appear.

Mrs. J—— conversed much as any other cultivated lady might do until the gentlemen departed for a visit to the stables and conservatories. Then, with much circumspection, we introduced the subject of polygamy. Instead of being snubbed, we found our hostess pleasantly willing to converse upon that, as on all other subjects, giving us information in a courteous manner, saying neither too much nor too little, and convincing us that here, at least, we had a true woman view of this great and vexed question. And, once again, the assertion was made that there was little or no dissension between wives of the same household.

We remarked, somewhat impetuously, that we could scarcely imagine such a state of things. Mrs. J—— replied, with quiet significance:

"We control ourselves and make it a duty to subdue all jealousies and tempers that would injure the harmony of our home."

"But are there no women among you of such disposition and temperament that they cannot endure a rival in the affections of their husband?"

"If there are, and if they have accepted polygamy as part of their religion, that religion steadily trains them in the duties it involves and enables them to carry out whatever it teaches."

"But does not the favorite wife assume authority and privileges which the others are slow to admit?"

"Oh, there are no favorites," replied the lady, confidently. Then she added, a little dubiously: "Or at least there *should* be none. It is especially inculcated that if the husband has any preference he should be very careful not to show it, and if a wife suspects herself to be the object of more than her due share of regard, she should keep the suspicion strictly to herself."

"That is a very fine theory, Mrs. J——," we declared, laughing. "But you have never tried it personally and cannot be sure."

"Yes, but I *have* tried it and am very sure," replied our hostess, as courteously as ever. Turning with an affectionate smile to the eldest daughter, she added: "Jennie's mother and I lived in the same house for years and were always the best of friends!"

Our confusion at the horrible blunder we had been led into baffles all description. No doubt our hostess perceived it, but with perfect tact she went on speaking; and presently we recovered ourself enough to listen.

"The women of Utah," she said, "consider themselves quite on a par with the men in all respects. Not only can they live happily and peaceably with each other, but they are faithful and devoted wives and intelligent and affectionate mothers. It is the duty or the privilege of the first wife to present the newcomer to her husband, and if she is an elderly and motherly person, she generally helps and guides the junior, instructs her in household matters, advises her in the conduct of her new life, and sustains and encourages her in every way. And I speak of these matters from experience."

The writer, still a little nervous, turned to the young ladies and asked their views of Mormon life and Mormon marriages. They replied, with the gay insouciance of youth, that they enjoyed themselves very much for the present; and as to the future, perhaps they should never marry at all, although it was evident they had no horror of polygamic union. Their mother, however, remarked that she should prefer to see them each the only wife of a good husband. Otherwise, she had no doubt their religion would enable them to bear cheerfully and patiently whatever might be in store for them.

The gentlemen here returned, and the conversation took a different turn. But in recalling it minutely afterward, it seemed to me that the keynote of the whole system, so far as it related to women, was struck when Mrs. J—— said:

"It is ordained by their religion, and their religion enables them to bear it."

Cake and champagne were served; one of the young ladies cut us some beautiful flowers; and we took leave, feeling that we had at last gained some reliable information in the ways of Mormon homes and the feeling of intelligent Mormon women.

LAKE POINT, A SUMMER RESORT FOR THE CITIZENS OF SALT LAKE CITY.

MONUMENT ROCK, AT THE NORTH END OF THE GREAT SALT LAKE.

From Leslie's Newspaper: It had been our plan to spend the following day in Salt Lake City; but we learn upon rising in the morning that the great sight of sights — the "President" himself — is absent. Accompanied by the favorite wife, "Sister Amelia," he has traveled for his health to St. George,[7] his favored resort in the southern part of the Territory.

What is Salt Lake City without Brigham Young? It is hastily determined to postpone further exploration of the town until our homeward journey and in the meantime make a partial circuit of the lake — a tiny inland sea eighty miles long by fifty wide, dotted with rocky islands, each one a mine of mineral wealth; fed wholly by fresh water rivers and with no known outlet; yet loaded with saline deposits, and with a specific gravity of 1.170.

The shores surrounding Great Salt Lake are crusted with salt and alkali; the skin of the bather, emerging from his pickle, is coated with a white scaly armor, only to be dislodged by vigorous sponging with fresh water. Life there is none, in or around the lake, except a tiny insect like a gnat,[8] which floats in large masses like a

PROFILE ROCK, LOOKING EAST FROM BLACK ROCK HOUSE — THE WASATCH MOUNTAINS IN THE DISTANCE.

scum upon the surface and, when dead, forms a soft and unutterably nasty deposit at the bottom, to be stirred up by the bather's feet at the expense of his olfactory nerves. The waters of the lake for a long distance from the shore are excessively shallow, necessitating quite a walk before the would-be swimmer ceases to touch bottom. To sink is impracticable; "treading water" out of the question. Whatever position one assumes, and with whatever rigidity and tension of the muscles he may try to keep it, in less than a minute he will be quietly turned on his back or tilted over on his side. The tonic properties of the waters are said to be immense and a bath therein the most exhilarating and delectable of treats.

The little railroad skirts the base of the Oquirrh Mountains, a small range uniting with the Wasatches, and passes along the southern shore of the lake. Mountain, sky, and lake are veiled with a faint violet haze —a film of mist that is never quite lifted, caused by the incessant evaporation from the surface of the lake.

Certain points of interest are announced — "Monument Rock," rising sheer from the lazy sheet of water not far from shore; "Profile Rock," a steep promontory in whose jagged outline one can detect a dozen profiles as easily as one; and "Observation Point," from whose elevation on a clear day may be seen the snowy peaks of the Goose Creek Mountains, no less than one hundred and fifty miles north of us.

In the very shadow of Observation Point, and close to the edge of the beach, is a stone house, now empty, formerly occupied as a hotel and resort. From its windows one might look down into the glassy ripple of the waters or away over their shining level to the little, rocky knoll of Kimball's Island, twenty-two miles distant, or Church Island, fourteen. We might almost skip a stone to either, if the eye could be trusted; or, catching sight of Promontory Point, might account it a pleasant hour's sail and refuse to believe that it is eighty miles away.

Lake Point, twenty miles from Salt Lake City, is the principal pleasure resort of the Saints as well as of profane tourists. The railroad company has established a good hotel under Mormon management and has also furnished a wharf and a stern-wheel steamer, the *General Garfield*,[9] which is usually moored at the end of her long pier when not transporting picnic parties and such prosaic freight as ore from the numerous islands. A bathhouse stands in a prominent position — tempting to those who would personally test the tonic qualities of Salt Lake water, and tempting also to those observers who take a malignant joy in viewing human kind when fashion has no hand in the make-up and a simple flannel bag becomes the one thing needful.

Mrs. Leslie continues: On our second visit to Salt Lake we obtained an interview early one afternoon with the Prophet of Mormonism, preceding this by a visit to the principal edifices of the faith.

On Temple Street, behind a plastered wall twenty feet in height, we found the foundations of the new Temple,[10] which is to replace the Tabernacle as the scene of all the functional rites and ceremonies of the Mormon Church, such as ordination, baptism, "sealing" or marriage — both monogamic and polygamic — and

burial. This new building, ornate and imposing in style, is being built from white granite quarried in the northern part of the Territory. Teams of oxen were dragging in great blocks of stone, and a score of workmen were busily hammering them into shape. Five years and a good deal of money have already been expended upon this building, but its walls are only about ten feet above the ground, and the date of its completion is not named. One cause, if not *the* cause, of its delay may be found in the fact that it is built entirely by voluntary contribution. Even Brigham Young's earnest desire to see the work completed has not brought in the funds for very rapid results.

The Tabernacle,[11] as nearly all of us know from pictures, is a huge, bare, and very ugly building with an oval, tiled roof, brick pillars, and no attempt at out-

---

The Latter-Day Saints

The endowments, or secret rites, of Mormonism are a sort of allegory in blank verse, paraphrased from the Scriptures and Milton's "Paradise Lost." There are rooms fitted up with scenery adapted to the performance of a drama representing the creation of man, his fall, the coming of Christ, and the priesthood of Joseph Smith. In the performance President Young took the part of Elolm, or head God, while other prominent men represented Jesus, Satan, Michael, and the Apostles. Different degrees of the Aaronic and Melchizedek priesthood are conferred, at each stage of which the candidate is required to take oaths of secrecy, accompanied with penalties should he dare to violate them. They are also given a new name by which they will be known in the kingdom of God. The entire ceremony is of little interest to the outside world, except where the candidate takes a solemn oath to "bear eternal hostility to the Government of the United States and avenge the murder of the prophet Joseph Smith."

In this ceremony the women wear a long robe, which is placed on the right shoulder, gathered at the waist with strings, and flows to the floor. There is an apron of linen covered with green silk and embroidered with fig leaves —the nearest approach to the paradisiacal apron that is consistent with our climate. The men wear a cap of linen similar to those worn by stonemasons. The ladies' caps are of Swiss muslin, with a veil of the same. This is the costume in which the Mormons are prepared for the grave.
Leslie's Illustrated Newspaper, Sept. 15, 1877

---

ward decoration. Inside, it is quite as ugly but a little less monotonous, for in the center is a fountain with four *couchant* plaster lions about it; and from the dreary expanse of white plastered ceiling, concave yet scarcely a dome, hangs a great star with pendants of artificial flowers. Galleries, supported by three rows of pillars painted to imitate marble, extend along the sides, and the whole floor inclines like that of a theater. The seating capacity is twelve thousand; yet so fine are the acoustic properties that a speaker upon the rostrum is audible in any part of the house. In this respect, the Mormons claim the Tabernacle to be unsurpassed by any building in the world.

At the end of this great hall, 250 feet long, 150 wide, and 80 feet high, hangs a monstrous blue banner, blazoned with a golden beehive and the inscription:

"Deseret Sunday School Union."

At the other end is the great organ, of which the Mormons are justly proud. It is said to be second in size only to the Boston organ, which is taller but not quite so wide, and it possesses a sweetness of tone really wonderful. It is of absolute home manufacture, the wood grown in Utah and the plan and construction by an English convert named Ridges, who built it in the Tabernacle.

It contains twelve hundred pipes, and the case, although only of stained pine, is elegant in design.

Between the organ and the auditorium are seats for the Elders and leaders of the congregation: first and highest, a little desk with an ancient blue sofa behind it, used by Brigham Young and his two councillors; below this, a long straight bench and a small semicircular one to accommodate the twelve apostles; and below this, a similar arrangement where the Elders sit and speak. Other seats around the organ may be used by the choir and dignitaries of the Church.

Altogether, the Tabernacle impressed us as the sort of place where we would rather not spend the hours of a rainy Sunday in November. Having conscientiously looked it through, we gladly turned our backs upon it; viewed the Endowment House, where ceremonies of the Church are celebrated and where preaching went on until the Tabernacle was built; and then went to deliver a letter of introduction to Brigham Young himself, who had signified his readiness to receive us at his office at an hour now approaching.

We found the President's houses and other buildings enclosed by a high stone wall, filled in with adobe, with arched gateways and wooden gates before each building. Over the gateway to the factories and stables is a double arch, surmounted by a beehive in the clasp of a monstrous eagle.[12] The largest building, which is occupied by a dozen or so of the Mesdames Young, is also distinguished by a beehive over the door, and is called "Beehive House." The other principal residence is called Lion House. Mr. Young generally breakfasts at the one and takes dinner or tea at the other, except when he visits other of his wives living in a house by herself; for each wife, we were informed, has the title deeds of a house of her own, if she chose to accept the documents. Several of them, having rural tastes, live on farms a short distance from Salt Lake City and raise vegetables, etc., for the tables of the others.

The schoolhouse for the President's seventy children stands next the Beehive, and all these buildings, finished in smooth yellow plaster with white trimmings and green blinds, are crowded close behind the high stone wall that shields them from the street. We could think of nothing but the closely guarded seraglio of some Turkish prince. But change the scene from Stamboul to the United States of America, Territory of Utah; for the Sultan substitute Brigham Young; for Zoraide, Zuleika, and Dinorzade read Ann and Harriet and Susan; and it would be more difficult to write "A Thousand and One Nights" than the Book of Mormon.

We look in at the Tithing House, whither the people come, year by year, bringing literal tithes of all they possess, of whatever nature, and pay them into the common treasury. But the finest building within many hundred miles, perhaps, is the Amelia Palace,[13] a really magnificent house, nearly finished, designed for the wife whose name it bears.

The office at Lion House is a large, unattractive room with a private sanctum railed off at the end, plainly furnished as a business room and hung with portraits of the founders and leaders of Mormonism — among others, Joseph Smith, who may be called the Father of that religion.

(So blindly was it revealed to him that one of the first laws was a stern prohibition of polygamy or concubinage; and Smith's name is still on record, as President of the Church of Latter-Day Saints, in Nauvoo, Illinois, excommunicating a certain Hiram Brown for preaching polygamy and "other false and corrupt doctrine." Three years from that time, Smith and nearly all the Mormon leaders were living in authorized and undenied polygamy.)

We found President Young standing in the middle of his office to receive us, with an expression of weary fortitude upon his face and a perfunctoriness of manner suggesting that parties of Eastern visitors, curiosity seekers, and interviewers might have become a trifle tedious in Salt Lake City.

"How do you do! Glad to see you! Pass on, if you please!"

When nearly all had passed on and sat down, and the host had resumed his own seat, an awful pause fell upon the assembled company, broken presently by a sonorous assertion from the President that it was a pleasant day.

This was eagerly assented to by our Chief, who added that the weather had been fine for some days. The conversation flowed on in this agreeable strain for some moments, during which time we studied the lion we had come to see. We found him both formidable and attractive: a fine, tall, well-developed figure; a fresh, ruddy complexion almost befitting a young girl; keen, blue eyes, not telling too much of what goes on behind them; a full mouth; a singularly magnetic manner; a voice hard and cold in formal speech, but low and impressive when used confidentially; altogether, a man of mark, and one whose wonderful influence over the minds and purses of men and the hearts and principles of women can be much more fully credited after an hour's conversation than before.

Perceiving that the interview was but a "function," we approached the sacred sofa and murmured to the Chief, who was seated there, that we would change places with him as we had something to ask of the President.

The Chief rose with suspicious alacrity. For the first time a gleam of interest shone in Brigham Young's pale blue eyes. The first question of the bold intruder was:

"Do you suppose, Mr. President, that I came all the way to Salt Lake City to hear that it was a fine day?"

"I am sure you need not, my dear," this cavalier of seventy-six years responded, "for it must be fine weather wherever you are."

The rest of the party began to talk among themselves, and presently our conversation took a confidential and interesting turn. Glancing at Joseph Smith's picture, we ventured the opinion that it did not show any great amount of strength, intelligence, or culture. Mr. Young admitted the criticism. He said that Smith was not a man of great character naturally, but was inspired by God as a prophet and spoke at times not from himself but by inspiration; he was not a man of education but received enlightenment from the Holy Spirit.

"And this is my own case also," pursued Mr. Young, quite simply. "My father was a frontiersman, unlearned, and obliged to struggle for his children's food day by day, with no time to think of their education. All that I have acquired is by my own exertions and by the grace of God, who sometimes chooses the weak things of earth to manifest His glory."

This want of education, he went on, was one of the greatest trials to the older generation of Mormons. Almost without exception, they had been poor and unlettered people, gathered from all parts of the world, and obliged, especially after their arrival in Utah, to use all their time to make life-sustaining homes from the desert. Only thus, shut off from other men, could they hope to enjoy their religion unmolested.

"But all this is over now, thank God!" said the President, with a gesture of relief. "Our homes are made, our country is prosperous, and our educational privileges are equal or superior to any State in the Union. Every child six years of age in the Territory can read and write, and there is no limit to what they may learn as they grow older."

I said that I had spoken of these matters with Miss Snow — "formerly one of your wives," as I somewhat diffidently phrased it. But the patriarch, with a calm smile, amended the sentence. "My wife still, if you please, my dear. Once having entered into that relationship, we always remain in it, unless" — and his face clouded — "unless under very peculiar circumstances."

We presumed him to be alluding to Ann Eliza, and longed to hear his views upon that recreant spouse; but we refrained and only made a eulogy upon Miss Snow, which her husband heartily indorsed, saying that he had placed two of his daughters under her training and had the utmost confidence in her judgment.

We spoke of the magnificence of the Amelia Palace, and he characterized it as "absurdly fine." We suggested that nothing could be too much for so good a wife. He assented emphatically. "Besides," we went on, "the Beehive looks to me rather shabby for a man of your position."

But at this he shook his head, saying: "There it is, there it is. Extravagance and ambition come creeping in and destroy the simplicity of the first ideas. The Beehive was good enough for me and has been so for many a year, but the world is changing — changing! '

"But nothing will change the Mormon ideas of polygamy, I suppose?" Having approached the subject, I could no longer refrain from a direct attack. Mr. Young glanced at me keenly.

"No, nothing can, since it is given to them by the grace of God. It is not obligatory, of course, but it is a blessing and a privilege vouchsafed by Him to his chosen Saints."

I asked if the children of different mothers could live amicably in the same house.

"I'll tell you something about that," replied Brigham Young. "My sister came to make me a visit some years ago and stayed here until her death. She was not a Mormon and did not believe in polygamy, but she said she had never seen a family of four children as peaceable and orderly and happy as my family of twenty-four, as I had then. She talked of it all the time and never ceased praising this domestic harmony of which you speak. You see, they are trained to it by their mothers from earliest infancy. It is made a part of their religious teaching."

"Yes, but who trains the mothers?" I inquired audaciously. "What religion can make a woman happy in seeing the husband whom she loves devoted to another wife, and one with equal claims with herself? Any woman, I should think, would spend all her strength, use every effort of mind, body and soul, to attract and retain his love, admiration, and attention. Isn't it so, Mr. President?"

Brigham Young answered meditatively: "You look like just the woman to do that sort of thing, but fortunately, perhaps, there are not many of that mind among us. As a rule, our women are content in trying to make their husbands happy and their homes pleasant—"

"Just what I was suggesting. She should make it so pleasant that he would not seek another."

He laughed a little.

"That would be agreeable to the husband, no doubt, but it would be contrary to the teachings of the wife's religion. She would not be a good Mormon wife if she allowed herself to follow such a course, nor could it, in the end, make the husband happy to alienate him from those whom he was bound to love and care for equally. For my own part, I always endeavor to show perfect impartiality and allow no one division of my family to claim time or thought too exclusively."

"Then do Mormon husbands feel no preferences?"

Laughing outright, he replied: "Well, perhaps. Human nature is frail. But our religion teaches us to control and conceal those preferences as much as possible. And we do — we do."

In two or three generations, the President said, Utah would present the finest men and women to be found in this country, for they would spring from marriages of pure affinity and a society impossible except under polygamy. In fact, he said, the children of today were a finer race than were to be found elsewhere, and he was going to have all of his photographed as specimens of childish beauty.

"But are all the women of Utah sure to marry?" I asked. "Suppose nobody offers for them?"

"A woman feeling herself drawn in affinity to a man, and feeling inclined to seal herself to him, should make her ideas known to him without scruple. It is her duty, and there can be no indelicacy in obeying the voice of duty."

With this cheerful and hopeful vision of Mormonism before our eyes, we at last obeyed the urgent gestures of those who had not been so well entertained as ourself and rose to depart, Mr. Young taking leave much more impressively than he had greeted us.

An Interview with Brigham Young

An interview was obtained with the Prophet early one afternoon in his well-known office in the Lion House. The apartment was comfortably, though not richly, furnished. On the wall on one side were hung several unframed oil portraits of Mormon dignitaries, and on another side of the room were a number of commissions issued to Brigham Young by the United States Government. A few simple ornaments stood upon the mantelpiece, and an antique screen stood before the stove which imparted warmth to the room.

President Young received the party as he was accustomed to receive all visitors, whether Mormons or Gentiles, in an affable but somewhat restrained manner. He spoke in a low tone, scarcely audible to others than those to whom he was directly addressing himself at the circular table in the center of the room.

His appearance at first meeting reminded one of a well-fed, well-kept senator or bank president. He was six feet high and uncommonly compact and well muscled. He measured forty-four inches around the chest, and such was his breadth in midperson that strangers who saw him for the first time, in his short, gray business coat, imagined him a rather "stumpy" man, several inches shorter than he was. His head was of moderate size, with strong development of the basic and posterior regions of the cranium, and was by no means lacking in anterior breadth. His hair was chestnut, abundant in growth, and combed in a pedantic style into a foretop to the right side, with somewhat of the lop of a rooster's comb.

The interview lasted for about three-quarters of an hour.

The Lion House forms with the Beehive House the city residence of the President. The two are connected with the owner's business offices, the general or sitting office being to the west of the business office.

The Beehive is a large and peculiar but by no means imposing house. There is a private schoolhouse for the education of the Prophet's children, but he made no appropriation for the education of others. Nearly opposite the Beehive, a new structure of the modern style of customhouse architecture is nearly complete, which is intended for some part of the Prophet's numerous family; and a little distance from this is Ann Eliza's cottage, which, although more aristocratic in appearance than the generality of cottages here, did not satisfy the ambition of that personage.

Since this writing, news has come to us of President Young's sudden death at Salt Lake City on the afternoon of Wednesday, August 29, 1877. All that struck us as doubtful, wrong, or ludicrous in the strange system of life he upheld disappears in the solemn respect with which one remembers the dead whose lives have, even for an hour, intersected one's own. He was an honest believer in his own theories and lived up to his own convictions of duty. How many of those who sneer at him dare say the same? His parting words to us were: "If you put me in a book, promise at least that you will print me as you have found me, and not as others have described me." We have tried to do so.

VIEW ON MAIN STREET, SALT LAKE CITY, IMMEDIATELY AFTER THE ANNOUNCEMENT OF THE DEATH OF BRIGHAM YOUNG, AUGUST 29TH.

Immediately after Brigham Young's death, the Mormon papers came out with eulogistic reviews of his career. The Cooperative and other principal stores were closed and dressed with crape; flags were displayed at half-mast; and groups of Mormons and Gentiles gathered along Main Street and quietly discussed the probable effect of his death upon the vast institution. The funeral services were set for Sunday, September 2d at 12 M., in the Tabernacle, which has a capacity of about eight thousand. His remains are to be deposited in his family vault of stone in the Lion House grounds in the city and covered with earth.

Brigham Young was born at Whittingham, Vermont, June 1st, 1801. He joined the Mormons in 1832, at Kirtland, Ohio, and his energetic shrewdness soon secured for him an influential status. In 1835 he was one of the twelve apostles sent out to make converts. On the death of Joseph Smith in 1844 he was chosen President and Prophet. After the disasters at Nauvoo, he, with a majority of the sect, abandoned that location early in 1846. He then announced that the Salt Lake Valley had been revealed as the Promised Land, and founded Salt Lake City in July, 1847. In the spring of 1849, immigration having greatly increased the Mormon ranks, a State was organized by the rulers, which they termed Deseret, but which Congress refused to admit into the Union, constituting instead the Territory of Utah, of which, in 1850, Brigham Young was appointed United States Governor.

Up to 1854 this state of things existed, but the Mormons subsequently defied the laws and officers of the Federal authority. In 1857 President Buchanan appointed Alfred Cumming Governor of Utah, and sent an army of two thousand five hundred men to enforce his authority. In November, 1857, Governor Cumming proclaimed the Mormons as in a state of rebellion; but in 1858 a compromise was effected by which the Federal authority was to be respected, and Brigham Young left in power as President and Ruler of the Mormon Church. □

1967: A Revolution in Deseret

THREE OF US SAT DOWN to lunch this afternoon in a handsome stone clubhouse on a slope above Salt Lake: Tim (Roman Catholic), his wife, Mary Anne (Mormon), and I (sometime Presbyterian). With fresh crab and avocados on our plates, vodka in our glasses, and the city crouching at our feet, we felt benevolent, approving, and proprietary toward the whole State of Utah.

Just below us on the terrace was a pool in which a talented machine was swimming to and fro to keep the water free of ice. A green glass dormitory glittered in a crevice of the hills, outshining the older buildings of the University; and down in the valley, beyond the leafless elms, a young crop of office towers, industrial parks, and freeways bloomed exuberantly in the January mist.

This frenzy of building caught me by surprise. I remembered Salt Lake as a diligent, domestic, horizontal town, refreshing and clean to the eye, but somewhat lacking in gusto. Now, I saw indications of astonishing vitality, and I was eager to hear what my Salt Lake friends would say about it. To me, Tim and Mary Anne are the very essence of Salt Lake. Even their cross-pollenated marriage represents, in an acute form, the symbiotic mixture of Mormons and "Gentiles" that gives the place its unique, self-contained, rather inverted personality. If Salt Lake were to change from a cozy, parochial town into a sophisticated city, worthy to be the capital of a world religion, Tim and Mary Anne undoubtedly would be among the architects of the transformation.

I had noticed some changes in Ogden this morning, but they were hardly revolutionary. The train had come in at daybreak, over the saline margin of the lake. Snow lay on the salt ponds, white on white; crystals of brine clung to the faded wooden posts along the tracks; and Ogden appeared, as always, to be about ninety per cent railroad yard and ten per cent town. The station is fittingly awesome and echo-y: a drafty, oversized, Romanesque basilica, with golden oak benches, back to back, in ranks across the room, and buffaloes in bas-relief above the doors. It stands smack-dab at the foot of one of those great, wide, straight, flat avenues, four-square to the compass, that are the mark of early Mormon city planning; but this grand boulevard, unfortunately, is lined with prosaic three-story buildings of red and yellow brick, and it is powerfully dull. Down near the station, it unravels in a scatter of cantinas, thrift shops, chow mein parlors, and loft hotels with tattered shades and broken panes; and the neighborhood along the tracks has the depressed, end-of-the-road look that was typical of the mountain states in the 1930's, when nobody was getting anywhere but out. Although I walked six blocks before getting aboard the bus to Salt Lake City, I saw fewer than a dozen of my fellowmen, and two of those were asleep in a barber shop. It was reassuring to observe from the bus that Ogden does have districts that are more effervescent — bright with root beer stands, Mayfair stores, and lime green cottages with fir trees at the door.

(Ogden is lively, also, in the field of municipal technology. A few months ago the city began incinerating solid garbage in a high-temperature burner that leaves no residue. In my opinion, this innovation came none too soon, because Wyoming is bound to overflow one of these days, and the surplus auto parts may flood westward.)

Our bus meandered through the fertile flatlands of the Wasatch Front, crossing and recrossing the main highway and stopping in all the little towns that are bypassed by the intercity road. I was struck by the Yankee tidiness of the countryside: the brick farms, the stone barns, the big sycamores, the neoclassic meeting houses of the local Mormon "Stakes." Even the names — Clearfield and Layton, Farmington and Centerville — evoked New England. (No aboriginal Yakimas or exotic Albuquerques in this part of the West!)

Passengers waited in the snowy lanes, beating their gloved hands together and puffing out steam. The bus snorted impatiently at every stop, and then we hustled along without delay, goaded by the ubiquitous sign of the beehive on highway markers, service stations, dry cleaning shops, motels, banks — a constant reminder that this is a land of prudent industry, of gainful toil, of busy hands.

There is nothing new or startling about the beehive emblems, the meeting houses, or the white picket fences. They are the familiar hallmarks of the Latter-Day Saints, physical evidence that this is Mormon country. While other theocratic colonies (Rhode Island, Pennsylvania, Maryland) have faded into indistinctive secularity, Utah has retained its strong religious coloration. It is *visibly* Mormon in a way that no other state is Quaker, Baptist, Presbyterian, or Catholic. Utah is younger, of course, and relatively undiluted: seventy per cent of the population of the state is Mormon. But the Land of Deseret would not have kept its architectural and social particularities for 120 years had not the Latter-Day Saints deliberately held themselves aloof from many of the novelties that have enchanted other Americans. Almost from the beginning of their self-imposed exile, the Mormons faced economic, political, and social competition from Gentiles both outside the territory and in their very midst. There always were gold seekers, soldiers, and camp-followers. Anti-Mormons, Godbeites, Catholics, Protestants, and Jews bumping against the walls of the intimate, devout, exclusive, family-centered, mildly socialistic, Mormon utopia. Inevitably, the Mormons and Gentiles absorbed some of each others' ways, for better or worse, and began to resemble the secular, cosmopolitan people of the United States.

Coming in from the rustic countryside, I sensed that this process of reconciliation with America has speeded up. It was a nippy, pearl-gray morning, and crowds of rosy, lavender-scented housewives and substantial businessmen in scarves and overcoats were flocking the wide boulevards, getting and spending as if they were in Denver or Detroit, and showing hardly a trace of their unique religious heritage. On all sides, new commercial buildings were springing up. The office of a mining corporation towered above the Gothic spires of the LDS Temple, and a pit stood open at the edge of Temple Square, waiting to accommodate a Mormon headquarters building that will soar even higher.

Reminders of Mormon peculiarity abound, but they are historic, not contemporary. Tim and Mary Anne drove me to dozens of metal plaques, affixed by sodalities of good Mormon wives on mill wheels, stone walls, corner blocks, and old adobe houses, stuccoed pale yellow, beige, or salmon. We saw the house that Mary Anne's great-grandfather had built, and we made a pilgrimage to that infinitely touching relic of the American frontier, the "First Tree"—a poor, twisted, whitened wisp of desert driftwood, long ago dead and mummified in the fine, dry air, but sheltered in a tender little temple. When the Mormons came, this stick was the only tree standing in the Salt Lake Valley. The fact of its preservation speaks eloquently of the instincts of the people who saved it.

Later we stopped at Beehive House, a bower of polygamous cohabitation where Brigham Young maintained a wife, seven children, and a commissary for his other wives and offspring. It is a gracious structure, as frontier houses go, infused with longing for places that the Mormons left behind. The soft timbers of the Rockies have been painted to look like Eastern hardwood, and the plaster walls are overlaid with swirls of paint resembling the colors of Tennessee marble. Several of Young's successors as president of the Church lived in Beehive House, and the women sometimes baked forty pies a day. Beehives are carved on the newel posts and embroidered into the lace curtains.

"Handwork, handwork," Mary Anne murmured, lifting her hands in an ambiguous gesture of amazement, admiration, and disgust. She was reminded of her aunts and cousins, who endlessly turn out quilts, silk dolls, and samplers. In the gift shops on South Temple Street you can buy their products: handbags fashioned from rug samples, pillows stuffed with shredded stockings, pincushions stuffed with lint, along with beehives of metal, fabric, and ceramic, disguised as salt shakers, jam pots, and bracelet charms, and made in Japan.

Tim had more masculine souvenirs in mind. The male principle of Utah history is embodied in a monumental statue in a rift in the hills east of the city. It stands more or less on the spot where Brigham Young, lying feverish in the back of a wagon, looked down at the valley and said: "This is the right place. Drive on." A few hundred yards away is an older, simpler, far more poignant token of the same event—a small obelisk, decorated with a relief of a buffalo skull and the words: "This Is The Place. Brigham Young. July 21, 1847." The old monument was a shrine to primitive Mormon achievement. The new one, although it was designed by a grandson of Brigham Young, is syncretistic. Spanish soldiers, French trappers, and mountain scouts cluster in rigid tableaux. For all I remember, there is a Pioneer Woman, shading her eyes with her hand, and a man with a flintlock rifle cradled in his arms. In any case, it is a grandiose cliché on the theme of the Westward Expansion. Ruskin might have discerned between the two memorials the decline from spirituality to corruption; an historian perhaps would read in them the transition from insular self-importance to a wider patriotism. Tim apparently did not care for the newer statue. He spent the time in a curio shop across the road, buying some postcards with small bags of salt attached, which he brought back, making a terrible face, and offered to me as "absolutely the squarest souvenirs on earth."

(My boys considered them bold; but Paul, who is eleven, opened and sampled one of the sacks and said it tasted like stagnant water.)

By the time we left Emigration Canyon, I was helplessly fascinated with the Mormons. Tim insisted that we look at some of the Gentile landmarks: the Gothic mansions of the Irish mining millionaires, the Alta Club, the Roman Catholic cathedral, the banks, museums, hospitals, and libraries that have been built by the "outsiders" who are, Tim reminded me, two-thirds of the population of Salt Lake City. But the Gentile institutions of Salt Lake, like its industrial parks and commercial buildings, seemed to me rather ordinary.

"The excitement is in the interplay," Tim said, getting quite excited. "Salt Lake is rigidly defined. The world is Mormon and Gentile. The Mormons are preoccupied with social organization, good works, profit and loss. The Gentiles provide a creative stimulus; the Mormons provide a balance. We keep each other honest."

"Don't you get more and more alike?" I asked.

Tim glanced at his wife and shrugged his shoulders. "Salt Lake is changing fast. Maybe we are getting just like everybody else, in our own, odd way."

As we were walking into the country club for lunch, I asked Tim if he resented having the United States finally take over the Territory of Utah.

"Not at all," he said, with a grand gesture toward the valley. "As a matter of fact, we've been planning for a long time to take over the United States." □

VIEW NEAR CORINNE, UTAH — THE BEGINNING OF THE GREAT AMERICAN DESERT.

CHAPTER XII

Nevada–
High, Dry, and Aboriginal
1877: A Dash Across the Desert At Twenty Miles per Hour

A FEW HOURS AFTER we say goodbye to Salt Lake City, we are steaming back to Ogden to reunite ourselves with the Central Pacific road. There, as the last light of sunset is dying away, we are fairly embarked upon the Great Desert, that dreary waste so lately a *terra incognita* to tourists—the "unexplored lands" of school atlases. For a few miles the gray sage desert has frequent oases — Mormon farms, orchards, and an occasional tiny village or town over which the beautiful Wasatches still keep guard. Then comes a dreary level of wet marsh, white with alkali, from whose shallow pools the yellow sunset strikes fire; a distant glimmer of the Great Salt Lake and the ghostly range of the Promontory Mountains beyond; and then a roaring pile bridge, spanned in a moment as we run into Corinne.[1]

It is ten o'clock, but there is a clear, rising moon, brighter, we think, than any eastern moonlight. To those who choose to defy the cold winds and take an airy seat on the platform, there is a wonderful shadowy picture spread out under the stars. So we have our glimpse of Corinne, a small town that once stood preeminent among its fellows for all the vices, misdemeanors and manifold offences against law and order whereof a frontier town can be guilty. There is not much to see: the long, low, station buildings; the shabby shops; the staring, square, white saloons, from whose windows blaze the brightest lights in the whole

town; the dreary absence of a single cozy cottage, green tree or garden patch, or anything that savors even slightly of a *home*. There may be cheerful dwelling-houses farther back in some of those wide, straggling, dusty streets, and without doubt there are bright firesides and happy family circles; but we have never seen them in our flight westward, and can only take them on trust.

Fifty-two miles west of Ogden we come to Promontory, famous in the history of the West as the meeting point of the two railroads—the spot where the last ties and the last rails were laid by Chinese workmen, the last spike driven, and the marriage of the Union with the Central Pacific declared in the presence of a thousand witnesses.[2] An insignificant little dot of a place is Promontory; but we have been reading this afternoon the guidebook's account of that "great railroad wedding," and we take off our hats to it as we pass, and the long train roars its faint echo of the cheers that went up here nine years ago.

The moonlight, shining upon ghostly white alkali, gives the desert the aspect of a stagnant sea. Little woolly tufts of sagebrush dot it everywhere, and the alkali glimmers between. Waves of naked brown rock or arid land—we cannot tell which it may be—roll away in long, low swells against the horizon. Nothing stirs; there is not a leaf to quiver, not a bough to rustle, nor a solitary living thing in sight to cross the dead

SHIPPING CATTLE ON BOARD A TRAIN FROM A CORRAL AT HALLECK.

face of this forsaken land. You cannot imagine that a drop of dew has ever lain here, or that a green blade could ever grow; and yet, sixty miles behind us, there are orchards and young grain where the dry alkali dust used to drift to and fro.

We have ceased to measure distance from Omaha; a black and white lettered sign, hung out at the little center of civilization called Kelton, counts the miles from San Francisco: seven hundred and ninety. The place is a center for stage lines into Idaho and Oregon, and there are several large corrals for the cattle used in this extensive freighting business. Often we have had a glimpse of these enclosures in construction — the driving of stakes and the filling in with saplings to make a strong, six-feet-high fence circling a space of two or three hundred feet; and we have watched the struggling, savage, frightened herd driven with a vast expenditure of noise and profanity into the cattle cars that waited to hurry them east. Near Kelton there is said to be good summer grazing — enough to make up for the winter diet of sagebrush; to us, however, there are no visible signs that a grass blade ever did or could grow within the barren circle of this gray horizon.

A heavy upgrade brings us to the summit separating the Great Salt Lake from the desert valley beyond, and we catch our last glimpse of the lake, bounded by a shining white belt of salt-covered plain. Far away to the south stretch the "bad lands"—acres of baked, cracked soil where even the sagebrush withers up and disappears.

At Tecoma we pass the dividing line between Utah and Nevada — a heap of stones and a rough granite monument — and touch the mining district, where every little station has its "leads" and "pockets" and "claims," its smelting works in operation or in visionary prospect, and its stage lines to other busy centers where miners swarm like moles in gloomy burrows. Outwardly the country is still the same — alkali, sand, sagebrush, greasewood, and, far away, Pilot Range and Pilot Peak, the grand old landmarks of the first weary travelers over this waste.

Wells marks our entrance into the valley of the Humboldt. To this spot the old emigrant trains made haste by three converging roads[3] to water their starving brutes and quench their thirst at the springs of the Humboldt. There are some thirty natural wells, filled with slightly brackish lukewarm water and said to be bottomless. The theory of investigating visitors is that they are openings to a hidden lake over whose surface matted vegetation and drifted sand have gradually formed a dense floor, through which these orifices pierce like little trapdoors. Recent soundings to a depth of 1500 to 1700 feet have failed to touch bottom, and all the so-called wells, large and small, abound in fish, chiefly minnows and such small fry.

Leaving Wells, our moonlit ride crosses the dreary alkali plain and brings us by seven o'clock of a sharp, cold morning to the breakfast station of Elko.

Before arriving at this oasis, the wakeful eyes at the curtained section windows have discovered certain dark cones sprinkled among the sagebrush, around which small, moving figures may be seen, all tending rapidly toward our train. With this preparation we are not surprised by a shriek of "Indians!" from the young lady on the platform. As the cars slow up before the long station, the artists dive out, sketchbooks in hand. A crowd of Shoshones have come down from the dirty, smoke-blackened tepees on the bluff and are pressing around the steps of the cars — women and children all of them, and all as dirty as their lodges.

It is not for their picturesqueness, certainly, that we study them: there is none of the traditional feather and quill and beadwork, no plaited locks and braceleted and moccasined limbs — and no pretty faces. There is one old, dried-up, withered, hideous squaw who looks at least a hundred years old, an animated bundle of filthy calico, with a few matted gray locks blowing out from the ragged handkerchief around her head and a torn blanket wrapped about her shoulders. There are five or six stout, heavy women, anywhere from twenty to thirty, also covered with calico gowns from which all vestige of color or pattern has departed — hard-faced, repulsive-looking creatures, each with a thick, shaggy mane of jet-black hair hanging on her shoulders and her papoose basket on her back. Children of all sizes scamper after them — girls, gowned and blanketed and hooded like their mothers, and boys in calico leggings and blankets.

All of them, parents and children, unite in a guttural cry of "Muc-ca-muc-ca,"[4] and "Hungry!" and hold up their grimy hands as the passengers descend. Crackers, stale cake, cheese from ravaged luncheon baskets — anything that *can* be eaten — is grabbed in ungrateful haste and bundled up in the filthy blankets. Then the cry changes to "Money! Money!" and all the grimy hands go up again. On the grimy faces there is not a shadow of eagerness in the asking or of disappointment at a refusal — nothing but sullen, fierce stolidity. Only the old squaw stands mutely in the background, hustled aside by the younger, and we single her out for alms of cake and silver money, over which she closes her skeleton of a hand, with a positive smile puckering her face into wrinkles more multitudinous than ever.

INDIAN LODGES NEAR CARLIN, ON THE CENTRAL PACIFIC RAILROAD.

In the meantime a brisk traffic is going on over the unconscious forms of the papooses. Their parents refuse to lift the calico from their faces for any inducement short of "two bits," and, as every woman on the train is crying out for a sight of them, the coin circulates with amazing rapidity. The papooses are of all ages, from a few weeks to eighteen months — all fat and dreadfully thriving, dirty as young pigs, and absolutely silent. Their so-called baskets consist of an oval board covered with stretched skins, in some cases ornamented with beadwork, upon which the child is bound by flaps of skin laced across with rawhide; arms and legs alike are imprisoned, and nothing but a round black head and a stolid face are visible over the bundle. Nor is even this visible for more than a minute at a time, for, at least in the presence of the palefaces, the poor little wretches are made yet more miserable by a calico rag twisted round their heads and carefully secured, lest a glimpse should be caught of the prize beneath. Our artists, who are bent on getting sketches, dodge and hover about the ragged group. The squaws, catching sight of a sketchbook, however, scatter suddenly. Only two or three, unable even in their terror to forego the joys of begging, stand their ground, mingling

SETTLERS BUILDING A CORRAL NEAR WELLS, NEVADA.

DUGOUTS ON THE PLAINS NEAR WELLS.

113

THE TOWN OF ELKO, NEVADA, ON THE HUMBOLDT DESERT.

the torrent of Shoshone abuse with such broken English as "No good! no good!" and other less moderate ejaculations.

The town of Elko is a considerable one, as towns go on the Humboldt Desert. The bright, white-painted hotel and the two or three neat stores and station buildings have a thriving and busy look in the cheerful, early sunlight. The platform swarms with stalwart, bushy-bearded, long-booted natives, big hunting dogs, loping along, and clamorous representatives of the Shoshone nation. A few men — supposably "braves" — come straggling on the scene, deplorably ridiculous in civilized cloth pantaloons, calico shirts, and long, narrow blankets drawn up around their necks like an old woman's shawl. Their stiff-crowned, straight-brimmed black hats are tied by a string under their chins. One aged chief, with the thinnest legs possible to walking humanity, has a scarlet-striped blanket, and has stuck a tall, limp turkey feather in his hat. His long black hair is divided and plaited into two thin tails, which are loosely tied under his chin; and his countenance strongly and painfully resembles that of a withered monkey. He begs a little tobacco — or rather, demands it as his due; and as he is the only "brave" who solicits alms in person, the others delegating their squaws to the ignoble task, we reward him with a liberal supply.

According to the guidebooks, Elko has a future as a watering place, boasting of six hot and cold mineral springs, one of which is agreeably known as the "Chicken Soup Spring" and requires only pepper and salt and a willing imagination to make it a perpetual free soup kitchen. A bathhouse is already erected, and a large hotel is to follow which, it is confidently expected, will bring fashion and civilization by the carload into Elko.

We roll away over the hot, bare desert, shimmering in the sunlight; past the low, sandy bluffs, the sage-brush and white alkali, and the scattered Indian tepees, with their ragged, blackened skins fluttering in the lazy winds; through a narrow canyon whose walls are water-worn into fantastic turrets, spires, and needles; over some shallow, thirsty little creeks, gone astray on the great dry desert; and so at last into Carlin, a brisk little railroad town five hundred and eighty-five miles from San Francisco.

An inquisitorial man boards our train with paper and pencil to get the names of passengers bound for the Golden Gate and telegraph them straightway across the Sierra. Indians swarm here as at Elko, their faces flaming with scarlet paint. These children of the Great Father are allowed free transport on the platforms of the Central Pacific trains and are extremely fond of taking airy trips from one station to another; so it is by no means unusual to see a little group huddled on the steps, steaming over the desert which they once scoured on their war ponies. It would be worth something to catch a glimpse of the mental process going on as they stare upon the white man and his inventions!

It is hard to decide whether the impression left upon one by this desolate, death-smitten valley of the Humboldt is one of newborn incompleteness or of ancient ruin. Sometimes we could fancy it a new world, marred in its very making; again it seems older than Time itself, a mere wreck of dead matter — a wide, weary waste whose blossomtime lies so far back that the mind of man cannot find it. The very rocks seem decaying as they stand; the deep cracks in the dry white soil show how all the sap and life are drained out and only dust and ashes left behind. Even the sage is a very ghost of a plant, with its silvery-gray tint and its dry woolly leaves crumbling to fine dust in the hand; and the thin bunches of reedy grass that grow in hummocks among the alkali patches have no semblance of verdure about them.

Three things are stirring: the white, cumulus clouds overhead; the trail of brown smoke from our engine, floating back like the plume in a cavalier's hat; and, here and there, a tiny speck along the bald face of some brown hillside. As we near the stations, a few blackened tepees dot the bluffs; and high up in the shadeless blaze of sunshine we can see some brown specks, scarcely distinguishable at first from the soil, that rise and travel down toward the plain. A dot of bright scarlet resolves itself into a grim Indian, sitting at watch; but down he comes, too — they all come, as the train rushes in, and the old story is repeated until

Yawning Caverns and Hollow Niches

At Twelve-Mile Canyon, or, as it is also called, the Palisades of the Humboldt, we pass into a narrow gorge between steep, bare mountain walls broken into sharp, serrated ledges, and stretching away in great yawning caverns and hollow black niches. For twelve miles we wind and curve between these grim Palisades, the Humboldt River creeping below us at the foot of the bluff and above us the gray old rocks, colorless even in this hot blaze of sunshine.

Through this canyon — untraveled even by a horseman before the rails of the Central Pacific Road — we pass to the little town of Palisade, the tiniest of settlements, lodged between towering gray walls that must cast a shadow over it even at noonday. A very short distance below is another nucleus of human life: a cluster of blackened and tattered tepees, around which lounge a few idle figures quite as aimless as brutes, and far dirtier. These are "civilized Indians"— peaceable wards who live on their reservations or near them, with no greater object in life than to beg, steal, sleep, and eat; and, so far as the casual observer can see, not the slightest attempt is made to suggest any other aims to their minds.

Where are the Peace Commissioners? Where are the missionaries and the Indian schools, to teach the mysteries of cleanliness, decent living, and honest labor to the peaceable Shoshones and Paiutes of Nevada? Or is it really true, after all, that missionary work is wasted, that the savage will be a savage, fiercer, meaner, more desperate and more degraded than the beasts of the forest to the very end of the chapter?

THE PALISADES OF THE HUMBOLDT RIVER.

there is not a stray "bit" left in our pockets.

It is as well to explain here the mystery of the "bit" system, which begins after passing Ogden. A "bit" is ten cents in silver; but a twenty-five cent piece counts for two bits, fifty cents for four bits, and so on. A year or two ago, paper money was refused west of Ogden, except on discount, and everything but silver and gold was regarded with suspicion. The "bit" was the smallest coin in circulation — five-cent pieces and cents belonging almost exclusively to the "effete East"; but at present one may get along almost as well with a pocketful of greenbacks as with a ponderous bag of silver. One young lady explorer, after having laid in a heavy store of "bits" and fifty-cent pieces that tore new holes in her pocket every twenty-four hours, was deeply disgusted in a shop in Ogden to find that the accommodating tradesman smiled upon dollar bills and professed himself "glad to get them" — or anything else of the sort he could lay his hands on. Later, while shopping in San Francisco, we found that even in the Chinese quarter a greenback was dropped into the till without a murmur.

But here we are on the Humboldt Desert with the faintly rutted lines of the old emigrant road traveling with us.

Ranches, distant corrals, steaming hot sulphur springs fly past us and are left behind; and we cross the line between Paiute and Shoshone reservations.

The Indians around Battle Mountain are principally Paiutes and differ in nothing from the Shoshones except a slight variation in the fashion of papoose baskets. Instead of skins, these are of woven basket work and decorated with a little penthouse over the baby's head, mercifully shading the poor little victim's skull. But the babies themselves are identical with their neighbors, and neither in squaws nor bucks do we see any varying features. There are squads of them stalking up and down the platform, the wind rioting in their rags and blowing their shaggy hair around faces that flame with sanguinary scarlet. In the lee of the depot you may see huddled together half a dozen squaws, gambling with sticks on an outspread rag, while the older children in rabbit skin cloaks and calico leggings roll in the dirt, and the basketed papooses, set on end like mummies, lean against the wall and stare with calm, unwinking beads of eyes at the shifting panorama.

"What do you pile on all that red paint for, old fellow?" demands an irreverent youth of one of the highly decorated braves.

"Look nice!" grunts the child of nature, folding his blanket around him as he marches away.

Red blankets flourish, and almost all the children and many of the squaws rejoice in short cloaks of gray rabbit skin, the pelts twisted into furry ropes and woven with a loose warp of animal sinews or with cord made of hemp or willow bark.

The Paiutes' chief occupations are rabbit-catching and fishing. They are a tame and groveling race with no touch of romance or mystery attaching to their manners save in their superstition regarding the burial of the dead. No white man, it is affirmed, has ever known

THE "MAIDEN'S GRAVE" NEAR GRAVELLY FORD.

Lucinda's Cross

At Gravelly Ford, the Humboldt River runs shallow and lazy over its sandy bed. Near this well-known camping place of emigrants in the old times ten years ago is the "Maiden's Grave," where Lucinda Duncan — we know her name and no more — was buried on one of those weary marches. For years there was only a little mound with a low, decaying headboard; but the road builders, laying their rails across the desert, came upon it, fenced it tenderly, smoothed the mound, and planted above it a tall, white cross with the name of the girl whom perhaps no one else remembered on earth.

Dinner Stop

THE ARRIVAL AT BATTLE MOUNTAIN STATION, NEVADA

Battle Mountain, the thirty minutes' stop for dinner, conveys joy to every passenger in the train.

"The town," the guidebook naively remarks, ' is mostly on one street south of the railroad." On that one street are grouped the public buildings, the schoolhouse, the hotel, the freight depots, and the few stores, with their little knots of loungers always sunning themselves on the long, low "stoops." The headquarters of the Indian Agency is within a stone's throw, and the usual dirty, tactiturn braves may be seen inside and outside. Away to the south rises the long, blufflike eminence where, some time in the indefinite past, a band of Indians and a camping party of emigrants had a hard fight for life and booty. Upon the oral testimony of the Indians rest the facts of the case: "Heap white man killed."

of a Paiute funeral or seen one of their graves; the body in such instances is secretly conveyed away when it is scarcely cold, and its hiding place is kept inviolate.[5]

From Battle Mountain we sweep westward over the desert on a twenty-mile stretch of straight track, cutting shining parallel lines through the dusty alkali. In summer, when this fine white dust is blowing incessantly, the traveler finds his passage a trying one, for the face and lips are literally rasped by these simooms of alkali. Even during the spring months one feels this annoyance, although to a lesser degree; and a box of camphor ice and a little glycerine are indispensable adjuncts to an overland "outfit."

"Stone House,"[6] 504 miles from San Francisco, is an old overland stage station, once famous for good meals and now notable for nothing in particular except the legends of old border fights, a few graves, and the inevitable hot sulphur springs. These natural phenomena crop out again at Golconda, farther along, and the hottest is turned to good account by the thrifty settlers as an extempore kettle for scalding pork.

The next place of importance — if one can misapply that word to such a poor, insignificant, accidental freak — is Winnemucca, the county seat of Humboldt and the progressive namesake of the great chief of the Paiutes. This aged dignitary, whose photograph is furnished us in the glories of a general's uniform, lives on the Paiutes' and Bannocks' reservation in Oregon, where he is said to be almost worshipped by his dutiful children of the Paiute Nation. The portrait is anything but seductive. Winnemucca presents a nearer approach to

WINNEMUCCA, CHIEF OF THE PAIUTE INDIANS.

THE DAILY STAGE FROM WINNEMUCCA TO BOISE CITY.

INDIAN RAILROAD EMPLOYEES AT WINNEMUCCA.

the baboonish physiognomy than any Indian we have seen, and the native beauty of his countenance is not enhanced by a mysterious little metallic object run through his nose, which lifts the nostrils in a singularly unbecoming manner. Nor does the civilized garb sit well upon a savage-born. Like the clothes of the Native in *Dombey and Son*, Winnemucca's clothes "present the anomaly of being loose where they ought to be tight and tight where they should be loose," and his very boots have a random and inconsequent expression. What a pity that a "civilized" Indian should ever masquerade in cloth pantaloons and a felt hat, or that a soft-footed, sinuous Chinaman should ever drop his voluminous bag of a shirt to wriggle into the abomination of a European coat!

We watch the departure of the daily stage from Winnemucca to Boise City, Idaho, with its cheering load of humanity, armed to the teeth for their 275-mile journey; and we wish — a few of us — that we were bound with them. Then we seize the opportunity for a sketch, presented by a group of working Indians — working, not begging — absolutely performing the manual labor of loading up a freight car, with faces guiltless of paint and forms unshrouded by the distinctive blanket. True, they work in a rather languid manner, but still it is work, a refreshing spectacle. We are told that a small number of them are regularly employed here upon the railroad, co-laborers with the Chinese, receiving the same rate of wages — one dollar per day — with this difference: the Celestial "finds himself" in pork and rice, the staff of *his* life, while the Indian is allowed to draw his rations from Government.

The monotony of the glaring white flats, the tufted gray sage, and the long, low ranges of brown sandhills begins to pall upon some of the travelers. In two or three of the sections we observe recumbent forms with hats over their eyes, heads abased, and boots aloft — let us suppose lost in meditation. But to a few of us there is no monotony in these Plains. Their barrenness is grandeur and tragedy; their wide sweeping level is, to all other stretches of level country, as the stormy ocean to a stagnant pond.

All afternoon we glide over the hot, dusty land, passing only three little stations between Winnemucca and the supper station, Humboldt, which every traveler, certain he is uttering an original sentiment, calls an "oasis in the desert." We can predict with perfect certainty at given points in the journey what stock quotation each individual will repeat, unconscious that it was ever said before. A sensitive gentleman of the party has been driven to frenzy by the daily allusion to "cattle on a thousand hills," which the glimpse of a horned beast is sure to evoke from somebody.

But one may almost be pardoned for calling Humboldt an oasis, it is so green, so fresh, so unexpectedly pretty. There is a square yard sown with bluegrass and planted with willow trees, locusts, and poplars, among which a tame antelope is feeding; there is a flourishing orchard of apple trees and a fishpond filled with trout, and before the door plays a spasmodic little fountain, fenced in with an iron rail and bedded in a ring of bright green grass.

Inside the bar is, as usual, a grand depository for "Rocky Mountain Curiosities" — petrifactions, crystals, fossils, and mineral wonders; on a shelf above the bottles there is even an ancient-looking human skull with an ominous fissure running across its occipital region. Besieged with questions, the man at the bar has nothing more marvelous to tell us than that it was "dug up roun' yere somewhere." He guesses it was a nigger or an Injun, evidently considering it, in either case, beneath interest.

Emerging from the bar, we find everyone collected around a group of Indians, gorgeous in buckskin and beadwork. The men have eschewed the regulation black hat, tied on with a dirty string, and one of them actually has a bow and quiver of arrows slung at his back. They are good-looking, too, after the Indian type: fringed leggings and moccasins, blankets girt at the waist with a strip of rawhide, and hair, after the fashion of the genuine Plains Indians, parted through the middle and collected into two long braids over each ear. Some of the blankets are striped and some beaded; the squaws are all wrapped in blankets of dark blue,

with only a pair of moccasined feet visible; and the children — there are no babies — are clad in tight leggings and short blankets, with their hair braided in tails and stuck full of such ornaments as colored papers, brass buttons, and beads. An old chief with his squaw and his son, aged about ten, attracts us especially, for the woman presents the only specimen of a comely female Indian that we have seen. She sits curled up on the ground at the feet of the man, with her hands clasped round her knees, so wrapped in her blue blanket as to hide all the outlines of her figure; but her face, in its framework of shaggy, blue-black hair, is young and fresh, even sweet-looking, and she laughs with her white teeth together as she tells us her tribe, "Shoshone," and her name — some soft, liquid combination of syllables that we fail to hold in memory. She ends

by selling her brass earrings to one of us, first turning to the chief for permission. He is a surly old villain who sits humped up in his blanket, watching us with eyes full of cold venom, never moving a muscle or vouchsafing a sound. The inquisitive young lady of the party is tortured with curiosity respecting a certain brass knob planted in the parting of his hair, resembling a brass-headed nail driven into his skull; and she wanders round and round him, inspecting the phenomenon and endeavoring to account satisfactorily for its presence, until the train conductor summons us all aboard, and we are forced to leave the mystery forever unsolved.

All around Humboldt lie sulphur mines, with a little sprinkling of gold and silver, and the dreariest section of the desert stretches westward from its acre of green. The Humboldt River runs north of us, but it is sunken

HUMBOLDT STATION — AN "OASIS IN THE DESERT."

119

deep between its bluffs and cannot be seen; the Humboldt Mountains on the left lean shadowy against the sky, and the plain around us undulates like the ocean. We are going rapidly down toward the "Sink of the Humboldt," where the Humboldt and Carson Rivers sink into the marshy plain and disappear. The sun sets; the miles of gray sage look grayer and more ghastly still; and the shapes of cattle loom like specters in the dim light. Although the mere observer fails to see what the cattle can possibly find to eat, the natives tell you they thrive and grow fat on the bitter, ill-smelling sagebrush: the tall bushes, which reach a height of three or four feet; the white sage, with its dusty, woolly leaf never going beyond a foot.

In the rising moonlight we can see distinctly the shapes of the low hills, the rusty-brown, ragged formations of lava and loose stone that remain to speak of old volcanic convulsions; later, the moon, shining white upon the alkali, touches brighter upon a sheet of water which they tell us is the beginning of the Sink of the Humboldt.[7] In that moonlit patch of water, we have our last glimpse of the Humboldt River as it soaks out of sight in the great salt marsh. According to the residents of the country, its waters, with those of the Carson, are not only absorbed into the thirsty earth but also taken up into the air by a process of evaporation so rapid as sometimes to drain vast areas of submerged land in a few days, and it is possible that by both methods the drainage of the two rivers is performed. No other outlet to the "sink" is known to exist, at all events. □

THE "SINK OF THE HUMBOLDT," IN THE NEVADA BASIN.

Joys of the Warpath

Here and there, over the bleached plain of sand and alkali and against the low, brown hills, we have seen a red light smoldering and guessed it to be a Paiute lodge fire; and imagination has gone visiting inside the flapping screen of skins, to speculate upon the household economy of the dirty Ishmaelites who are sleeping there under the stars — dreaming, we may suppose, not of the joys of the warpath, nor of the great buffalo herds of old times, nor of raids upon stage stations and the burning of stray, pale-faced captives; but only of such tame, ignoble matters as rabbit hunts and weekly rations, the sole excitement of these degenerate days.

Rabbit hunting and fishing now constitute the business of life to the Paiute warrior, since the buffalo have traveled north and the antelope is fast following them; and in the capturing and killing of such small game he is exceedingly expert. His fishing tackle consists of a bit of light rope, weighted with a stone at one end and grasped by hand at the other. To this line are attached half a dozen or more hooks, made of rabbit bones, in the form of a narrow letter V; and to the angle of each V is fastened a short line made of sinews and baited with a snail or a freshwater sucker. The fish, swallowing the bait, swallows also the hook, which by the tension of the line expands its two prongs and fastens them firmly in the victim's throat. The fish struggles and whirls and darts about, attracting all its family and neighbors to swallow the same snare, until the angler has a bite for every hook and quietly draws in his main line, heavy with spoils.

Still more simple are the "rabbit drives," in which

five hundred to a thousand "head of game," if we may so use the expression, are caught in one hunt. A V-shaped fence is put up, made of slight saplings, across which is stretched a wide-meshed net of hemp or willow bark. In the angle of this enclosure an Indian or two take position while the rest of the band, including squaws and children, start off to beat up the game. Ten or twelve miles from the trap they start the "drive." The entire company scatters into a wide semicircle and with whoops and yells beats the sagebrush with sticks and clubs. The frightened rabbits start up by the hundreds and are chased by the shrieking, hooting hunters down toward the trap.

Gradually contracting their ranks, the hunters force the fleeing creatures into the enclosure. The men within the trap start up with yells rivaling those of the hunters outside, and the luckless rabbits, dashing themselves against the net to force a way out, fasten their heads in the meshes. When every one is a prisoner, the brave huntsmen make a tour of the net and with their sticks dispatch the game, which the squaws collect and pack home to the lodges. Then follows a great feast of rabbit meat, and after that the squaws have their hands full, making robes and cloaks out of the soft, downy, gray skins. The rabbits that are left among the sagebrush have a rest from persecution until the next fall. The Indians value a rabbit skin robe very highly and much prefer it to a blanket, though it takes a good deal of time and patience to make one. This work, however, is all done by the squaws and is taken as a matter of course by the bucks of the tribe.

1967: Some Vanishing Americans on the Ogden-Carlin Run

IN THE DARK NIGHT of eastern Nevada, I had an opportunity to satisfy a lifelong curiosity about certain operations of the railroad. While sitting with the brakeman at a table in the coffee shop, I steered the conversation around to passenger trains, and then, as if the question had just popped into my head, I asked: "What does a brakeman do? I mean . . . what does he do on the *train*?"

The brakeman — I'll call him Mr. Carlson — stared at me with his mouth wide open and his bushy white eyebrows halfway up his forehead.

"You watch the train," he said. "When it goes around a curve, you look at it. You look for hotboxes and make sure there aren't any fires. When the train stops, you get out and look at it. You look for weak couplings and passenger problems."

"Oh," I said. "Passenger problems?"

"All sorts of passenger problems," Mr. Carlson explained.

"Oh, I see," I said. I felt that somehow I had raised a vaguely indecent subject and was being as nosy as Dr. Kinsey, but I persisted.

"How do you like it?"

Mr. Carlson deliberated for a moment, staring down at his lantern and his fur-lined gloves, which he had arranged in a little corral around his coffee cup. With his head down and his eyes half-closed, he looked like a sleepy French gendarme — blue uniform, polished visor, gray mustache, sharp-pointed nose.

"It's a pretty good life," he said at last. "You do pretty well for an uneducated man with no particular brains. On this run you usually work an eight- to twelve-hour shift. It's about two hundred miles, and that's longer than most runs. Out one day and back the next."

Mr. Carlson's home is in Ogden, but he often spends the night in Carlin, Nevada, at the west end of the division. There are worse things in life, he said, than spending a night in Carlin, Nevada. The railroad gives you $1.50 for a meal and $1.50 for a room, and there are some clean hotels around the station.

Up to a year ago, Mr. Carlson was a conductor, which is a higher-paid and more prestigious position than brakeman; but the railroad canceled some trains and eliminated several conductors' jobs, and he took a demotion rather than a move.

"I suppose you'd call it a dying business," he said. "But what can you do when it's all you know?"

I assured him that I, too, was in a dying business. Offhand, about the only business I could think of that *wasn't* dying was launching rockets.

"You ever fly?" Mr. Carlson asked. I admitted that now and then I have rushed impetuously to Los Angeles on some slapdash airline. Mr. Carlson shook his head morosely.

"All the passengers came back to us last summer during the airline strike," he said. "You couldn't get on this train for weeks. Extra cars. Extra diner. Plenty of those executives said how they'd love to take the train all the time, only the company won't let them. Takes too much time."

I glanced around at the dimly lighted car, which served as a restaurant, bar, and sitting room, and tried to imagine it crowded with air-minded executives whose wings had been clipped. It seemed unlikely that they had been able to recapture the easy camaraderie that used to prevail on transcontinental trains in the recent but departed days of the Overland Limited. A train trip in those days had no resemblance to a modern air journey, which is merely a lapse of time-space. The old trip was an entity, like a pilgrimage to Canterbury. Often, the passengers would form a harmonious little society, eating and sleeping in matey intimacy and plotting adventures at every five-minute stop; and companions of the observation platform would trade addresses and exchange Christmas cards until the last delicious memories of the voyage had faded from their minds. Some of that communal atmosphere remains in the Dome Lounge of the Union Pacific, but it has disappeared completely from the Ogden-Carlin run.

"I suppose they noticed how things have . . . changed," I said, trying to choose words that would not be offensive. But Mr. Carlson snorted and glared around at the empty car.

"Who could miss it?" he said. "Some of them laughed — sarcastic and insulting. Most of them were just sad. One man said to me, 'You can't compete with the airlines for speed, but what's wrong with competing in other things like comfort and service and so on?' I told him I don't run the damned railroad." Mr. Carlson showed his teeth in a mirthless smile and then began somberly rearranging the tools of his profession around the coffee cup. "Airlines carried 110,000,000 passengers last year. Even with the strike. All these cattle-growers around here have got private planes. Only the cows travel on the railroad nowadays."

"Well, I suppose everybody hops a plane now and then for convenience," I said.

"I've never tried it," said Mr. Carlson firmly. "Sure, you get there faster. But what do you do when you're there? Also, I'm scared of them."

It was obvious that airplanes were a sour topic; so I raised some less controversial questions about the hot springs at Elko and the Indian tribes of Winnemucca. Mr. Carlson answered perfunctorily. All at once he leaned toward the window, cocked his head in recognition of a landmark that was quite invisible to me, and began to pull on his gloves.

"I don't call what's happening *progress*," he said, getting up. "And I'm not just thinking about my own

122

job. Hell, if I lose my job I'll retire. I'm thinking about the country. Everybody's in such a big hurry, and where are we heading? The way things are going, in morals and all, we'll be eating each other with mayonnaise in another ten years."

Leaving me with that prospect, he took his lantern and left. A few moments later, the train stopped among an unimpressive scatter of motels and gambling casinos —downtown Elko, I assumed. Like all Nevada towns, it glittered extravagantly: scarlet neon is the state flower. Twitching electric arrows directed the visitor to the slot machines and blackjack tables of The Stockmen's and the Hotel Commerce; but I did not follow. I sat with my empty coffee cup and thought about the cattle-growers hopping over to Las Vegas and Denver in their small planes, and about the strange paradoxes of railroad travel: the poor can afford the time to travel on trains, but not the rich; when we were a poor country, we could afford many luxuries that we cannot afford today.

After we left Elko, Mr. Carlson came back to the coffee shop, smiling and swinging his lantern. Someone on the platform had regaled him with a rollicking tidbit of local news. The state highway department, it seems, had been planning a section of interstate freeway on the outskirts of Elko. After months of debate, a route on the north side of town, smack through the golf course, had been adopted, and a new 18-hole course had been laid out and planted in another place. The highway engineers were about to start work when— wham! A tribe of Indians had thwarted the whole project by asserting their own claims to the right-of-way.

"A treaty or something," Mr. Carlson said gleefully. "Imagine—a tribe of Indians!" He showed his teeth in a genuine smile, and he bought each of us a fresh cup of coffee to celebrate. It was a mean emotion, I suppose, but I shared his enjoyment of the comeuppance to highway engineers. When Mr. Carlson left the train at Carlin, he was still gloating.

Next day in Carson City, I called the Nevada Department of Highways to ask about the Indians who had blocked Interstate Highway 80. The engineer I talked to said I must be kidding. The department had just finished negotiating a financial settlement for the Indian lands, and the project was moving ahead on schedule. As a matter of fact, the Indians seemed extremely pleased with the price they had got.

This struck me as a miserable outcome to the last rebellion of a defeated breed, and I am sure it would have plunged Mr. Carlson into bitter gloom. After all, he, too, is a vanishing American. □

CHAPTER XIII

The Gracious Life of the Palace Car Traveler

1877: Oyster Soup by Lamplight

One of the ladies of our party gave vent to her enthusiasm for railroad-hotel life in a sketch entitled, "Thirty-three Hundred Miles in a Pullman Hotel Car."

IT SOUNDS APPALLING. Still more appalling were the accounts of friends who had gone before us, following the setting sun at twenty miles an hour.

"You will be worn out with fatigue. You will be cramped and stiff with the confinement. You will turn blacker than the Ethiop with tan and cinders and be rasped like a nutmeg grater with alkali dust. You can never sleep a wink for the jarring and noise of the train, and never will be able to dress and undress and bathe yourselves like Christians. Above all, your nearest and dearest, under the influence of the fatigue and the monotony and the discomfort, will be ready to turn and rend you before you get down into the Sacramento Valley—and *you* will desire nothing better than to make a burnt offering of them and every one else insane enough to shut himself up seven days and nights in a railway car!"

"Scenery?" I venture to suggest.

"Oh! the scenery is grand at the end of the route—Echo and Weber Canyons, of course, and the Wasatches. But the Plains! So dry and brown and monotonous—you'll hate the sight of them before you're twelve hours out from Omaha!"

This was the sketch held up to us. What is the reality? Look through *my* glasses—not *couleur de rose*, I assure you—and take twenty-four hours on the Pullman hotel car as a fair sample of the rest.

Peep in at us by lamplight, when Howells is majestically working his way between the berths, making them up in strict rotation, regardless of the prayers of sleepy wretches whose numbers come last in his list.

Howells is a severe autocrat who patronizes the women and condescends to be playful with the men. His daily life is passed in struggles to suppress our light baggage and keep track of lost penknives, sketchbooks, gloves, and purses. Berth after berth is spread with fresh, clean sheets and heavy rugs, piled with little square pillows, and duly shut in with voluminous curtains; while under each are stowed the occupants' belongings—the satchel, the half-cut magazine that is never read, the portfolio and sketchbooks, a pair of slippers, or a whiskbroom.

We are divided by a curtain across the aisle: four women, each rejoicing in "a whole section all to herself," at one end; and at the other, the turbulent masculine element, "doubled up," so to speak, in upper and lower berths and making night gleeful in their own peculiar fashion.

And do you sleep? The springy roll of the cars, the slight monotonous rocking of your easy, roomy bed, and the steady roar and rattle of the train lull you into dreamland as a child is rocked by his nurse's lullaby. There is a little struggle with sleep at first, for the mysterious moonlit country is so full of fascination. A dark shape slides swift and shadowy across the picture, vanishing with great flying leaps. It may be a prairie wolf, a coyote, or a mountain lion. Another faintly outlined shadow points a motionless cone up to the stars. It is a Shoshone tepee, the moonlight falling on its smoke-stained, ragged skins and the ashes of its smoldering fire. Your eyes shut lazily and forget to open again. But they shut in a picture of those melancholy, awful wastes that will be a part of you henceforward.

Then the waking—perhaps with a flash of new-risen sunshine across your pillows, or only the first scarlet streak of dawn above the tawny divides. You draw the blankets and rugs closer round your shoulders, for it is chilly, and, pushing the pillows higher, you lie staring out for the next hour or two upon the shifting wonder of the great Plains. There is no sign of life among the other sleepers; nothing stirring but Howells, who will presently pull open the curtains of the berth with a bland "Wake up—open your eyes, lady!"

And then the womanly soul gives itself up to one great problem—how to dive into the washroom with the greatest expedition, eluding other candidates and locking them out in triumph.

If you step out on the back platform, you can investigate the process of breakfast and have a chat with the cook. Our car is the last of the train, and its tiny kitchen opens on the platform, the steps of which are guarded by strong iron gates. In the tiny cupboard adjoining, where the caterer reigns supreme, is an incredible store of potted meats and vegetables, preserves and fruit, and close-packed dainties of all sorts. The portly chef almost fills up his small quarters and risks knocking down an army of saucepans at every

124

turn of his elbow; but he moves deftly and beams upon us over his little stove while he turns the beefsteaks and stirs the mushroom sauce.

At nine o'clock Howells fastens the little tables in place, lays the white cloths and napkins, and we slip into our places. Breakfast comes by dainty courses: fish, fresh-caught at the last station on our way; beefsteak and *champignons;* hot rolls and cornbread; broiled chicken on toast; and potatoes stewed in cream or fried Saratoga fashion, with the best of coffee and tea, or a glass of milk, half cream. You eat with an appetite unknown east of Missouri, and meanwhile your eyes are drinking in their fill of the great, solid sea of the plains, new-bathed in morning sunshine.

Breakfast is scarcely over before you rush to the platform to see some wonderful line of buttes, or look for antelopes, or watch a slow emigrant train winding past; or else, in a fit of sudden industry, you spread your little table with sketchbook and pencils and work out, as much as the almost imperceptible jar of the car will let you, the last group of Indians sketched at Elko or Evanston.

The party scatters into groups, twos and threes, as parties inevitably will. Somebody scribbles notes in a tiny book; another hurries off a file of postal cards to drop at the next station. Lady Bountiful opens her work box to darn a rent in a flounce or a coat sleeve; and Madame brings out her French *brochure* to read, when any one will let her.

At the farther end of the car, in the gentlemen's quarters, the tiny smoking room has always a tenant or two; and so we drift our several ways and dream or work away the miles until the sun is high overhead and Howells announces luncheon.

Our little table is set this time with sandwiches and a salad, or some biscuits and a dish of fruit, never very long ignored, though every one declares that he is "not the least bit hungry." An hour afterward, perhaps, the train stops for dinner and twenty minutes at the wayside station; we rush for our hats and the blessed opportunity of a "constitutional" on the platform while the rest of the hungry passengers besiege the dining-room.

The afternoon is never a minute too long. If it should be, there is the couch in the middle section, with its bright rugs and fresh pillows. We see freaks of archi-

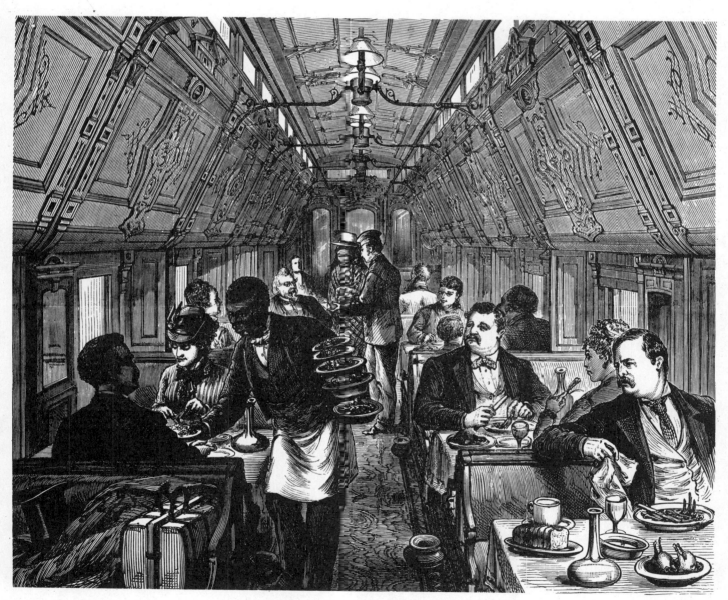

DINING AT TWENTY MILES AN HOUR.

125

tecture among the ochery-red buttes; we slide through miles of prairie dog villages, alive with frisky little tenants; we throw silver "bits" and handfuls of crackers and cakes to painted squaws, reaching up greedy hands at every station; we whistle herds of cattle off the track, and the sportsmen impotently pop their pistols at fleet-limbed antelopes skimming by like shadows; and never for one second do we grow tired of it all.

Now the afternoon light is getting low, and Howells and the little tables come on the scene again. We sip our oyster soup, discuss turkey and antelope steaks and quail, and trifle with ice cream and *café noir*. When the wild cloudy masses in the west are flushed and hot with the sunset's last fires, we take our places on the platform again and keep them until the stars are out and the moon is high above the snow peaks of the Rockies.

Inside, the lamps are lit and swinging overhead. Between the windows, the looking glasses are slid up on their panels, and a candle behind each burns in a bright reflector. You will join the group at cards yonder, and I shall order a table laid for me at the farthest end, away from the clatter and laughter and fun, and shall scribble a half-dozen letters to tell the friends at home how I have gained five pounds already, how I am burnt brown as an Indian by the western sun and wind, and how the rarest and richest of all my journeyings is this three thousand miles by rail. □

1967: The Creme of the Automatic Buffet

AT OGDEN THE PASSENGER CARS for San Francisco are severed from the Union Pacific dining car, with its dome of tinted glass, its pink tablecloths, and its vases of fresh flowers. Union Pacific turns southward, taking with it the portion of the train designated *City of Los Angeles*, and Southern Pacific takes command of the *City of San Francisco*, the overland route.

In place of the departed dome car, we are provided with a Coffee Shop Lounge, which resembles a lunch counter in the financial district on Saturday afternoon. Supplementing this, one car forward, is a fairly recent refinement in railroad catering called the Automatic Buffet, to which every traveler is expressly invited by a printed notice left on the seat of his roomette, along with two coat hangers, three clean towels, and a supply of paper cups.

"Over the past few years," the invitation says, "budget-minded SP travelers have found that snacks and light meals in the Automatic Buffet Car help ease the costs of travel—and children find it fun."

This exactly confirmed what we had been told by a budget-minded traveler of our acquaintance who once ate lunch in the Automatic Buffet on the Southern Pacific *Lark*, between San Francisco and Los Angeles. Her children, she said, had found it fun.

The Automatic Buffet of the *City of San Francisco* turned out to be a railroad car of standard size, rather murkily lighted and painted a neutral beige throughout. At either end were eight tables, topped with gray Formica, and at the center was a long row of vending machines on both sides of the aisle. The only decorative touches on the pristine expanse of enameled metal were two large representations of Automatic Buffet full-course dinners, done in warm colors: the roast turkey dinner with stuffing, buttered peas, and sweet potatoes ($1.25), and the barbecued chicken dinner in a four-compartment aluminum tray (also $1.25 but not served on this car). These brilliant photolithographs, which invited comparison with the finest work of Andy Warhol, were obviously masterpieces *sui generis*, strikingly appropriate to the Early Factory Lunchroom decor, and their visual impact was accentuated by the solitary prominence of their position.

I immediately sensed a mute efficiency about the vending machines that contrasted favorably with the independent disposition of the waiters in the Coffee Shop Lounge. The only sound was an occasional low grumbling when one of the machines would respond to some internal, thermostatic urging and turn its compressor on or off. With the vast, dark desert slipping past the windows, the dim light gleaming on the Coca-Cola signs, and the gentle purring of wheels underfoot, the buffet evoked some of the cosmic awe one feels in a great hydroelectric powerhouse late at night, when the dynamos are throbbing tirelessly and a solitary engineer sits near the control panel, reading a comic book and eating a Milky Way.

Silently, I wandered up and down on the rubber matting between the rows of machines, pricing the ice cream bars (vanilla, fudge, or creamsicle, 15¢), the cold drinks with crushed ice (orange-pineapple, carbonated or noncarbonated, Coca-Cola, or Lemon Hi, 15¢), and the sandwiches (ham, 75¢, cheese, 60¢, bread, butter, and jelly, 30¢). Next to the dispensary of "hot casserole dishes" (or canned goods, as they often are called), I found a cunningly designed Self-Service Counter stocked with paper plates, paper napkins, paper straws, plastic knives, forks, and spoons, paper envelopes of salt, pepper, and sugar, and plastic ampules of syrup, catsup, and mustard.

I decided, perhaps rashly, to begin dinner with a

plastic bowl of Campbell's Tomato Soup (35¢). This choice necessitated a search for change. I had only two quarters; but I woke up an accommodating porter two cars back who was willing to give me two dimes for one of my quarters. Returning to the Automatic Buffet, I inserted a quarter and a dime in the soup machine and was promptly delivered an 8½-ounce can, hot to the touch. At this point I discovered that there was no can opener in the Self Service Counter, although you could see a bracket on the wall to accommodate a crank-type opener. A brakeman who came by gave an opinion that the can opener had been stolen.

"Everything gets stolen in time," he said enigmatically.

For a minute or two I stood there, tossing the hot can back and forth between my hands. Finally I remembered that I had a beer can opener in my suitcase. I wrapped an edge of my jacket like an insulating pad around the can, carried it back four cars to my roomette, and set it on the lid of the toilet while I got my suitcase from under the seat and searched for the beer opener under several layers of dirty shirts and underwear. The opener eventually proved to be in a bag of pretzels on the hat rack above the mirror, but the soup stayed appetizingly warm throughout my ten-minute search. I poured it into a little wax paper porringer, printed to simulate a wooden tub (which I went back and got from the Self Service Counter), and I ate it with a pink plastic spoon. The soup needed a little salt, which I had forgotten; but I felt I could make up for the lack of seasoning on the next course.

By the time I got back to the Automatic Buffet again, an attendant in a white jacket had come on duty, and he fussed paternally over the next steps of my meal — offering me change, showing me where to find the little vials of syrup and mustard and packets of salt, pointing out the napkin holders and the drinking fountain. There also were some other customers — three men and a blonde girl in ski clothes and deerskin boots — who were playing cards at one of the tables and drinking Lemon Hi (15¢) from plastic cups. They openly stared at me as if they had never seen a budget-minded traveler eating in the Automatic Buffet.

I had intended to move on to a macaroni and cheese course (95¢) or one of the hot casserole dishes — say,

Silver Skillet Beans with Sliced Franks (50¢) or Nalley's Enchiladas with Meat in Sauce (50¢). The lack of a can opener ruled this out. (The attendant also thought it had been stolen.) I chose instead a salad course of fruit jello (30¢). Somehow, I punched the wrong button and got macaroni salad, which was in the tier immediately below the jello; but I really didn't object to the substitution. Both salads were the same price, and they looked as if they tasted quite a bit alike, anyway.

My doting attendant insisted that I permit him to insert the coins ($1.25) and carry to the Self Service Counter the *pièce de résistance* — sliced beef dinner, boiled potatoes, buttered corn. It was served in a divided aluminum platter of a convenient rectangular shape that emerged, fully cooked and well heated, from a glass compartment marked "Lift the Door When Package Is in View."

While the attendant and my fellow passengers looked on approvingly, I tore off the foil topping, seasoned the beef with a packet of salt and a plastic pannikin of catsup, and carried the whole steaming trencher to a table directly under the photographic view of the roast turkey dinner, steaming seductively in its gravy. The attendant offered to bring me coffee, but I was not again to be denied my direct encounter with the vending machine. The coffee machine offered four choices: black, sugar only, creme only, or creme and sugar. (I do not know precisely what "creme" is, but I think it is not produced, or only partly produced, by cows.)

After wavering between Stempel's Cake Doughnuts (25¢) and Raisin Pound Cake (25¢), I decided for a piece of berry pie (35¢) that was displayed in a transparent, wedge-shaped box just a few shelves below the fruit jello. I was careful not to get macaroni salad again, although I *had* enjoyed it. With the pie, of course, I had a paper cup of coffee (15¢), creme only.

For just $2.40, plus tip (35¢), I had had a truly memorable, budget-minded, light meal. Whatever it may have lacked in graceful cuisinage could have been remedied, I am sure, by the addition of a small bottle of dry, red burgundy. I undoubtedly could have bought this in the Coffee Shop Lounge, one car back, if only I had thought of it in time. ☐

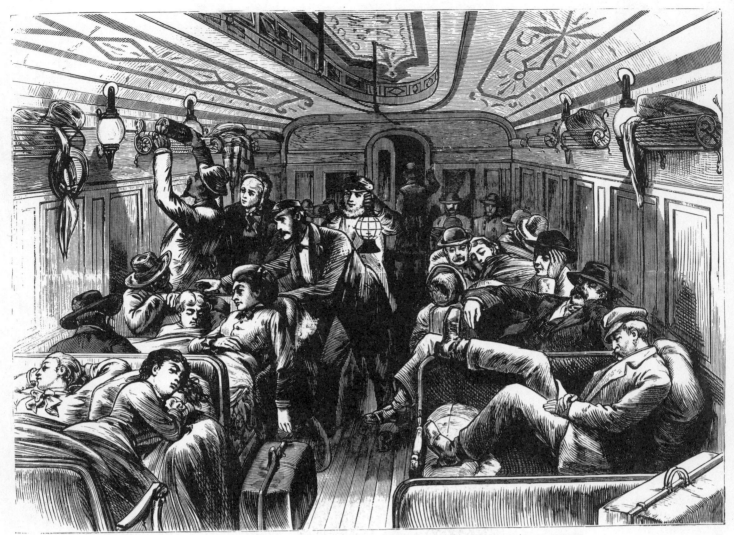

THE DISCOMFORTS OF TRAVEL: WEARY PASSENGERS SETTLING FOR THE NIGHT.

CHAPTER XIV

Fellow Travelers

1877: Newspaper Editors, Railroad Tramps, and a Parlor Organ in the Van

FROM OUR PULLMAN HOTEL CAR, the last in the train, to the way car that follows the engine, there is a vast scale of comfort, with as many steps as there are conveyances. It is worth one's while to tour the train and observe the manners of traveling humanity. The old assertion that man is at bottom a savage animal finds confirmation in a sleeping car; and as for woman, her claws will out, even under 5¾ kid gloves.

At 9 P.M. in the drawing room sleeper, we find a cheerful musical party howling "Hold the Fort!" around the parlor organ; three strong, healthy children are running races up and down the aisle and scourging each other with their parents' shawl straps; a

consumptive invalid is bent double in a paroxysm of coughing; four parties, invisible but palpable to the touch, are wrestling in the agonies of the toilet behind closely buttoned curtains and trampling on the toes of passers-by as they struggle with opposing draperies; a mother is engaged in personal combat (also behind the curtains) with her child in the upper berth; and two young lovers, dead to all the world, are exchanging public endearments in a remote corner.

Who could bear these things with perfect equanimity? Who could accept with smiles the company of six adults at the combing and washing stages of his toilet? Who could rise under the close personal scrutiny of twenty-nine fellow-beings, jostle them in their seats all day, eat in their presence, take naps under their very eyes, lie down among them and sleep — or try to sleep — within acute and agonized hearing of their faintest snores, without being ready to commit twenty-nine distinct homicides?

But if the "drawing room sleeper" be a place of trial to fastidious nerves, what about the ordinary passenger car, wherein the working men and working women — the miners, gold-seekers, trappers, hunters, and queer backwoods folk, who have left log homesteads in Wisconsin, Michigan, and Illinois to trail the sunset — congregate, all packed like sardines in a box?

It is pathetic to see their nightly contrivances at comfort: the vain attempts to improvise out of their two or three feet of space a comfortable sleeping place for some sick girl or feeble old person, and the weary, endless labor of the mothers to pacify or amuse their fretted children. Here and there, some fortunate party of two or three will have full sway over a whole section — two seats — and there will be space for one of them to stretch his limbs and rest luxuriously; but for the most part, every seat has its occupant, by night as well as day, a congregation of aching spines. The overland journey is no fairy tale to those who read it from a way car!

We climb into the baggage car sometimes to admire the orderly piles of trunks, valises, and boxes and peep at the corner fitted up as an armory, with its grated door and assemblage of weapons held in readiness for a possible attack. Or we take a furtive glance at some pretty girl who has been seized with an unconquerable desire to explore her trunk, and who, under close surveillance of the baggage master, is turning over the trays to rummage out a handkerchief, a clean collar, or perhaps a hat in place of one that a gust of wind sent whirling over the Plains.

THE BAGGAGE-MASTER'S ARMORY.

One might suppose that in shaking the dust of the "States" from his feet the overland traveler would leave behind him, among the other bones of civilization, the slouching figure of the tramp. But even on

A Source of Constant Amusement

CHINESE RAILROAD LABORERS GETTING A TOW.

We find constant amusement in watching the Chinese roadmenders along the route to Reno. Whole groups of them dot the roadside, bare-legged, ragged, dressed in a sort of hybrid mixture of Chinese and Caucasian styles, with pigtails twisted up out of the way and great straw platter hats tied under their chins. They are by no means the smooth, immaculate, well-shaven pictures of neatness that greet our eyes in the dining saloons. On the contrary, they are evidently of the lowest caste, with stupid, half-brutal faces, dirty and unkempt — though still, in these respects, falling short of the Irish or German laborer. They work diligently as beavers along the route, traveling from point to point with their tools on a little handcar, which they sometimes hitch to our train. We find an ever-fresh delight in looking down upon them from the rear platform, laughing and pelting them with "pidgin English," to which they scorn a response. They sit cackling among themselves in their own queer, chopped-up language, replete, probably, with opprobrious epithets for the "white devils."

A NIGHT CAMP OF TRAMPS NEAR BRYAN, NEVADA.

the broad plains west of the Missouri, in the shadow of the Wasatches, on the Humboldt Desert, one comes with a shock of surprise upon the old familiar features and sees a dusty figure or two trailing along the side of the track, pipe in mouth and bundle on shoulder.

TRAMPS THROWING A CONDUCTOR FROM A TRAIN.

As twilight is drawing over the desert, we rush past a group of them, camping out beside their fire — a jovial-looking company, with their pipes and bottles and cards to pass the time away.

They are in no way more agreeable to contemplate than their brethren of the East — neither morally nor physically an improvement upon those personages who solicit broken victuals at the kitchen door and set fire to the haymow when sent away empty-handed. The conductors along the route know them well and are thoroughly up to their tricks. It is one of our amusements, in crossing the tramp-ridden regions, to watch at every station the stealthy maneuvers of these officers, one of whom drops silently from the rear platform and, bending low, with hands on his knees, waddles the length of the train, peering under each car. For the tramp, when footsore, is wont to lurk around some station until the daily train comes in, then dive unseen under the cars, coil himself along the iron work between the wheels and, half-lying, half-hanging, be whirled away at twenty miles an hour instead of two.

It charitably occurs to us that any man who is willing to tie himself into a knot and suspend his aching frame in the midst of a simoom of dust, alkali, and cinders half-a-dozen inches from the railroad track ought at least to be let alone and allowed to torture himself in his own way. But the conductor is of a different opinion. He can tell you startling legends of personal encounters with these gentry of the road, who are forever watching their opportunity at dinner

130

TRAMPS RIDING ON THE RAILS.

CLEARING THE REAR PLATFORM OF AN OVERLAND TRAIN.

or supper stations to slip up on the rear platform and into the cars, where they may work their wills upon the absent passengers' valises.

Occasionally, a sharp tussle takes place on the platform, and the strong-armed conductor, with a reinforcement of brakemen, pitches the intruders right and left without much regard for their personal feelings. But upon one occasion within the memory of our conductor the tables were turned, and one of his contemporaries, while engaged in a tug-of-war on top of a freight car, was hurled into the road and seriously hurt. □

Two Ways of Going West

An emigrant train is by no means a rare sight, even in these days of steam and Pullman hotel coaches. We have passed several of them along our route, yet it is always a source of interest to watch the slow-moving caravan crossing the great, illimitable waste.

There is the great wagon packed with bedding, household stuff, ancient trunks, ironmongery, and crockery, with a calico gown and a sunbonnet or two perched in front, and a guard of stalwart male emigrants on foot and in the saddle, each carrying his gun and pack—a sturdy, resolute, and possibly dangerous customer. There they go, toiling beside us for one second and then left far behind, the children waving to us with ragged straw hats and little flapping aprons, and the women turning to look half-wistfully after our flying train.

A NEBRASKA EDITORIAL PARTY PUBLISHING A PAPER ON BOARD THE TRAIN.

The Wayward Press

We have exchanged civilities within the past few days with a party of Nebraska editors out on a holiday like ourselves—a cheerful company who, strangely enough, have chosen to bear with them a printing press and types and consume the fleeting hours of their overland trip in editing a paper. This small sheet is circulated through the train each day. If not actually scintillating with wit, it is about as cheerful as one could hope for under the circumstances. We have been courteously invited to inspect its "setting-up," so in we go, and our artist takes a hasty sketch of the scene. The crowded way car, with its dim lights, its weary-looking company of travelers packed for the night in their hard, uncomfortable seats; the inevitable crying child or two; the black, dingy presses and the shirt-sleeved men hard at work, all shaken up by the jolting and swaying of the car in rude contrast to our smoothly gliding Pullman —these make up a curious "side-scene" in our panorama, one which even a "special artist" must fail to render in its full oddity.

Replenishing the Palace Car

At almost every station our conductor, whose duties include those of commissariat, goes forth on a foraging expedition and lays in stores of whatever delicacies the place affords—trout from some mountain stream, antelope steak, game of all sorts, or such vulgar necessaries as eggs and milk. Then there is the frequent process of supplying our kitchen tank with fresh water by a long hose through a pipe in the roof. All the ice coolers and washing room tanks are filled throughout the train, and the supply of water is plentiful, although in quality none of the best.

TAKING IN WATER FOR THE KITCHEN.

132

1967: India-rubber Men and Tattooed Ladies

MY WIFE ONCE COMMENTED, regarding a friend of ours who had sprouted a piebald goatee: "The trouble with beards is, they always make you wonder why."

I felt a similar curiosity about my fellow passengers on the overland route, and it caused me a twinge of bad conscience. Nobody questions the hidden motives of automobile or airplane riders — why should railroad travelers be subject to conjecture? I suppose our minds have been warped by the hypnotic persistence of airline advertising.

Having accepted air travel as "normal," we expect to find trains occupied by a conspicuously abnormal residue of humanity. When I boarded the *City*, I already had the word of the Stanford Research Institute that trains do not appeal to businessmen or young people. (In any case, it was not a season for student travel or family vacations.) Accordingly, I anticipated meeting an assortment of acrophobes, invalids, sideshow freaks, and little old ladies in diamond chokers.

The first passengers I encountered seemed to live up to this expectation. They were farm folk, apparently, and dressed in resolute defiance of current fashion. The two women, who were built on an ample scale, wore tiny, pink pillbox hats and tailored wool suits with nipped-in waists, broad shoulders, and skirts that hung to a point midway between the knee and ankle; their husbands had on double-breasted brown suits and high-crowned beige hats with turned up brims. A scent of plug tobacco clung about them like an aura of innocence.

I took them for old believers in the cult of ground transportation, indissolubly wedded to the train habit and prejudice. But later I saw them in one of the chair coaches, sharing out canned meat and soda crackers from a picnic basket, and I realized they were riding the train simply because it was the cheapest way to travel. The coaches were half-filled with others like them: pasty old men in flannel shirts, who sat bolt upright and coughed all through the night; sailors wrapped in peacoats; and mothers with tired children, rearing up and whining and spilling cups of water.

In the sleeping cars there was a cheerful clique of Midwestern couples who were in no hurry. My mousy looking friend from Madison, Wisconsin, had formed them into a peripatetic retirement club, with members from St. Paul, Duluth, and Manchester, Ohio, and a schedule of frequent meetings at the bar of the Dome Lounge. In late morning, late afternoon, and immediately after dinner, they held plenary sessions at which inadequately conservative politicians were ritually disemboweled; at other hours there were rump caucuses to discuss foreign travel, dude ranches, mutual funds, and other matters of common interest. Although I did not ask them, I surmised that all the members of the club had taken the train merely because they liked it. I imagine they soon will be compelled to travel instead by rocket, pneumatic tube, or some other hyperaccelerated form of propulsion, like it or not.

Obviously, there are many Americans to whom the relative slowness of train travel seems disgustingly indolent. I was puzzled when a woman of evident hustle settled into the seat across the aisle from me on the slow mail train. She put on a pair of black stretch pants and a turtleneck sweater, hung her dress in a garment bag, did several limbering-up exercises, and then opened two large suitcases. One contained a supply of raw carrots, green peppers, celery, cauliflower, jars of puréed fruits and of wheat germ, and a copy of *Let's Get Well*, by Adelle Davis. The other held several dozen plastic jars and bottles of lotions, unguents, capsules, and powders. For ten hours she napped, did exercises, ate vegetables, took pills, and applied compounds to her neck, forehead, and elbows.

"Must choose the train for health reasons," I said to myself. But it turned out she was taking the slow mail only by necessity. She was going from Ogden to Columbus, Nebraska, and the train was faster than connecting flights. Besides, she had no one in Columbus to meet her at the airport.

Shortly after she left the train, her seat was taken over by a windburned, blonde man from Elko, Nevada, who was on his way to Lansing, Michigan, for a probate hearing on his parents' estate. He was going to be two days late for the hearing.

"How come you didn't fly?" I asked. "Bad weather?"

"You know what?" he said. "I was so upset when I got this wire about the hearing, I didn't pay no attention to what day it was. I just got on the train by mistake." □

CHAPTER XV

To Carson and Virginia

1877: Fresh Milk and Boston Brown Bread

RATTLING OVER THE ASHEN-GRAY PLAIN in the dark hours of the night, we are nearing Reno where, for a while, we shall turn our backs on the Central Pacific and branch off into the mountains of Nevada. We pass a few stations in the moonlight, speed over many a mile of desolation, and, turning over in our soft-pillowed berths, wake up with a start as the train stops at the junction of the Virginia and Truckee Railroad,[1] the shortline that connects the main transcontinental track to the riches of the Comstock silver mines.

At seven o'clock of a Sunday morning we reach Carson City, the capital of the state and a sort of "half-way house" between Reno and Virginia City.

Carson considers itself a fine, thriving, full-grown town—quite an old established one, having had twenty years' time to improve and beautify itself and to run up its population to three thousand, five hundred souls.

It is not fair to look upon—few of these Western centers of young civilization are. It is only a straggling place, set on a flat plain with the glorious, snowy Sierra stretching away north and south. There are the usual broad streets with stone-paved channels of clear, running water on either side in lieu of our muddy gutters of the East; sparse rows of cottonwood trees with smooth, pale yellow bark; square, two-storied houses in a most severely simple style of domestic architecture; planked sidewalks; stores; saloons; long, low railroad buildings and platform; and a little square enclosure of fresh, thick, green grass, in the midst of which a fountain is playing. Indians lounge along the line of the cars, of course—calico rags, red paint, blankets, and papooses are *their* distinctive features; a few American citizens, garmented with that careless, self-sustained, half-barbaric freedom that influences the

VIEW OF THE PRINCIPAL STREET IN CARSON CITY, NEVADA.

THE UNITED STATES MINT, CARSON CITY.

THE NEVADA STATE CAPITOL.

very cut of hair and beard and the putting on of clothes in a Far Westerner; men and boys of all sizes; but, as always, no women.

We leave our car and wander off on a stroll through the streets. They don't invite the pedestrian to a very extended ramble; in ten minutes one could make a brisk circuit of them all. There is the main street, running north and south, with its two goodly stone buildings, the Mint[2] and the Capitol,[3] and its straggling show of shops (most of them with open windows and doors and a view inside of the proprietors making ready to open business for the day); and the cross streets, with their few neat and many shabby dwellings, all of the peculiarly bare and utilitarian type prevailing in this part of the world. Many of the cross streets terminate in dreary waste lots, strewn with ashes, old timber, and barrel hoops, and given over apparently to the Indian population. The solemn figure of a man in a red blanket disappears into a low hovel in the lee of a great lumber yard, followed by two or three squaws, barefooted and with generously molded figures compressed with difficulty into their ragged calico gowns.

Passing a little shop in whose windows hangs an inviting sign, "Fresh Milk and Boston Brown Bread," we step in for a taste. A civil man, whose linen is of a somber color and whose morning toilet evidently has not included the ceremony of ablution, receives and serves us — not with the Boston brown bread, for we are too early, but with a species of very solid jumble and glasses of milk, suspicious in color and decidedly weak to the taste. Criticism is disarmed, however, by the voluntary statement of the man at the counter that "milk's quite skeerse in Carson. Every drop has to come down from Virginia, and the supply ain't regular."

So we drink our portion from tall beer glasses and pay our ten cents apiece without a murmur.

"Don't you close your places on Sunday?" one of us asks. "I see nearly all the stores opening."

"Oh, they shut up at noon, most of 'em."

"And what time are the churches open for service?"

The man looks dubiously at us, meditates, and looks out of the window at the Mint opposite for information.

"Well, I do'no exactly. I think some of 'em one time and some another. I couldn't tell you for certain."

Evidently the subject of church services is entirely alien to his experience. He is able to tell us, however, that there are in Carson four sacred edifices — Roman Catholic, Episcopalian, Methodist, and Presbyterian — and even as we leave his shop, the bells of one of them ring sweetly.

Besides the churches, the Capitol, and the Mint, Carson has a large and very excellent schoolhouse; three good hotels on the main street; two daily newspapers; and a "Society" that is said to be unusually good. The last statement we must take on faith, our social observations being confined to Indians and those of the male population who tuck their pantaloons in their boots, cultivate manly beards, and eschew "biled shirts."

Leaving Carson, our Pullman car pursues the windings of the Virginia and Truckee Road, en route for the city of big bonanzas. From Carson to Virginia City the distance by a bee-line is only twenty-one miles; by the erratic line of the railroad, however, it measures fifty-one and three-quarters, sweeping round curves of fourteen and nineteen degrees and climbing a steady up-grade. Two and sometimes four engines are required to drag the long train. Like a ship in a storm, our great unwieldy car goes swinging around jutting promontories and sharp, capelike spurs. One or two of the more imaginative members of the party avow themselves seasick. Nowhere on the journey have we passed through a wilder and more desolate land than this; nowhere have we found ourselves so completely *in* the mountains, or felt so shut in and overshadowed by their grandeur.

Down in the deep hollows there is a faint tinge of springing grass, but up on the dreary slopes, toward the sharp cones of the summits, it is all one uniform tint of russet brown — the whole vast landscape dashed in with one brushful of somber color, unrelieved by any sparkle of light but lying back in dead monotone against the warm brilliance of blue sky. The Carson River winds through its narrow canyon far below us. Here and there, we look down upon a quartz mill and a long flume, or great floating masses of timber and cordwood drifting down the river; and in one place we catch a glimpse of the operation of "tailing," the running of streams of discharged ore over blankets to catch the tiniest atoms of gold and silver that remain after the process of amalgamation.

At Merrimac the road turns aside from the river and twists up the side of Mount Davidson, among whose highest peaks Virginia City is perched. Every hillside has scars of pick and shovel, tunnels or pockets, gray heaps of refuse quartz, or simply a score or more of stakes, planted deep in the soil to mark somebody's "claim." After a short season of prospecting and the discovery—or, in some cases, the deposit—of a few promising nuggets, the gold-seeker stakes out his claim and opens the sale of shares, either on the spot or away in the marts of civilization. Hundreds of these claims are marked out on either side of us, and every stake suggests to impecunious travelers the cave of Aladdin, where money difficulties exist only in the form of *l'embarras de richesses*.

We look down on Silver City, lodged in a green canyon, and American Flat, round which the road sweeps in a great semicircular curve to Gold Hill—a huddled cluster of houses, pricked with the smokestacks of countless mining works and tunneled with abandoned shafts. The city lies in Gold Canyon, where the first discovery of precious ore in any considerable quantity was made in 1856. As early as 1833, Kit Carson is said to have camped in the ravine while making his way across the Plains with a band of Crow Indians; and from 1843 to '45 it was a camping ground of Colonel Frémont's, where he and his party are reported to have panned for gold and found—if any—only a paltry handful. Now the great quartz mills are jarring and reverberating all day and all night, and the bare, brown sides of the canyon are riddled by hundreds of human moles, working away as if all heaven and earth hung upon the yellow dust.

Only two miles from Gold Hill lies the Silver City itself, with its close-packed population impartially distributed above and below the surface. Every man who has handled a silver dollar has heard of the famous Comstock Lode and is familiar with the names of such bonanza kings as Jones, Sharon, Flood, and O'Brien,[4] whose magnificent wealth has rendered the West famous; but it is doubtful if many persons are as familiar with the aspect of this unique city that is the home of our silver wealth.

A succession of terraces winds along the mountainside, with tier above tier of houses clinging to a bare, brown slope; not a green tree, not a garden spot, not a patch of grass is visible. Below us the brown hills fall away into a confused sea of scattered peaks, sinking gradually to the faraway level of the Nevada plains. Just at our feet is an unpeopled solitude; above our heads, the intense, concentrated life of that strange, struggling city. Behind it towers Davidson, the highest of the brown cones, and every house shines out, a distinct white speck against the dull background.

In this first glance the whole aspect of the city is one of intense shabbiness and instability; the low frame houses strike one as only elaborate tents, hastily thrown together to meet a temporary need. The soul of the place concentrates, not around the homes, but about these long, low sheds, these smokestacks and flumes, this network of crossing and recrossing railroad switches, these great, gray mounds of crushed quartz —signs of a tremendous labor that never rests, never stops for breathing space, never for one moment relaxes its grip upon the men who are its tools. The mines and shafts are the city; the houses are the accessories.

On the main street are shops whose window fronts would not disgrace Broadway or Kearny Street, and here and there a tall building of brick or gray stone towers above its two-storied wooden brethren. But brick and stone seem to be viewed with disfavor by the dwellers in Virginia City, possibly from an accurate knowledge of the wind's capacity up among these

SILVER MINERS PROSPECTING ON THE SLOPES OF MOUNT DAVIDSON, WITH A VIEW OF ABANDONED "PROSPECT HOLES."

136

VIEW OF THE MAIN STREET IN VIRGINIA CITY.

Nevada mountains. The distintegration of parts in a slight frame structure and their disposal abroad is attended with comparatively little danger to life and limb.[5]

The principal structure is the hotel, a new and handsome brick building opened only a few weeks before our arrival. Its newness is apparent as we cross the threshold, so fresh and spotless is its white paint, so immaculate are its appointments, from the flaming red velvet and snowy lace curtains of the parlor to the least accessory of the large dining room. Farther along the terraced hillside is Prospect Hall, a less imposing edifice, whose name suggests its principal attraction, and on the same street is the Assay Office, a dingy little place to look at, which promises to reward us well for a more minute inspection tomorrow. Predominating over all are the familiar saloons—the "Union," the "Yosemite," the "Montana," all the local names with their flavor of the Pacific Coast which we have met already in a dozen different towns.

Mrs. Leslie writes: To call a place dreary, desolate, homeless, uncomfortable, and wicked is a good deal, but to call it God-forsaken is a good deal more. We never found a place better deserving the title than Virginia City.

To commence with, the conditions of its being are highly disagreeable, for it is hooked, as it were, to the precipitous side of a barren and rocky mountain. One is always apprehensive that the adhesive power may become exhausted and the whole place go sliding down to the depths of the valley below.

The streets are mere narrow terraces built along the face of this precipice, like the vineyards along the Rhine or the steps of the Pyramids, whose arid and dusty desolation they imitate, without the grandeur and mystery.

Leaving the station, we climbed a steep and long flight of wooden steps to the street above, where stood the hotel (a very good one, by the way), flanked by some substantial stone and brick buildings. This block is the exception in architecture. The rule is frame houses, as loosely and carelessly put together as a child's card house. The style may be inferred from the fact that about two years ago the whole town burned down one night and was rebuilt as good as ever in six days.

Nowhere does one find a level. The streets are all parallel, with the exception of one that leads up the mountain from the depot. Standing in any of them, one looks across the tops of houses and over the chimneys of quartz mills and mining works lower down until vision loses itself among the crowding brown peaks, never coming to any resting point of level or greenery before the horizon closes the dreary scene.

The fierce, cold wind sweeps through the narrow streets with force enough to take one off his feet. Very

137

little rain falls, but plenty of snow, coming early and remaining late. Indeed, it is possible in any month of the year, sometimes lying three feet deep in May, in which jocund month we paid our visit.

Virginia City boasts of forty-nine gambling saloons and one church, open this day for a funeral, an event of frequent occurrence in this lawless city. The population is largely masculine, with very few women, except of the worst class, and as few children.

Chinese are rare, not being in favor with the miners, who have a horror of cheap labor and show their dislike of Orientals in vigorous fashion when the opportunity occurs.

A carriage took us zigzagging from one steep, narrow street to another until at length we dismounted at the great building over the shaft of the California or Bonanza Mine.[6]

The Superintendent, Mr. Taylor, one of the most courteous and attentive of men, invited us first to his own charming bachelor apartments in the mill building, then took us all over the works and showed us the entire process: the cages, running night and day, hauling up masses of quartz rock that the miners have shoveled out of its natural bed; the crushing of the quartz and its agglomeration with water in great vats into a dingy, lead-colored pudding; the amalgam, mixed with quicksilver, pouring out into iron vessels; the crucibles; and, finally, the residuum of metal run into bars and stamped.

We saw machinery enough to drive one crazy and were almost suffocated with its hot, oily smell, besides being deafened by the stamping and banging and crashing of the quartz-crushing machines, which keep that whole section of the building in a state of jar and quiver like an impending earthquake. We saw the pumps which are always at work taking water out of the mine; and we looked down the shaft used by the miners — two square black holes, close together, with a cloud of white steam floating up from them, product of the heat and damp below.

At last, postponing further investigations until the morrow, we left the mills and drove about the city; returned to the hotel for dinner; and, after a while, strolled out to see what changes might have been wrought by night and moonlight.

The changes were noticeable but not beautifying. Two policemen who followed close at our heels were by no means a guard of ceremony but a most necessary protection. Every other house was a drinking or gambling saloon, and we passed a great many brilliantly lighted windows where sat audacious-looking women who freely chatted with passers-by or entertained guests within.

Cheyenne did not seem to us to deserve its mournful sobriquet; Virginia City did, but it has not received it.

Next morning we returned to the Bonanza or California Mine. The Chief and some others of the party had resolved to explore its depths.

This mine is principally owned by Messrs. James C. Flood, William S. O'Brien, and Mr. James G. Fair.[7] The two former kept a small drinking saloon in San Francisco and were on intimate terms with some of their miner customers, one of whom, in his cups, informed them of a wonderful "lode" just discovered.

PREPARING FOR A DESCENT INTO THE MINES.

DESCENDING THE SHAFT OF THE CONSOLIDATED VIRGINIA MINE.

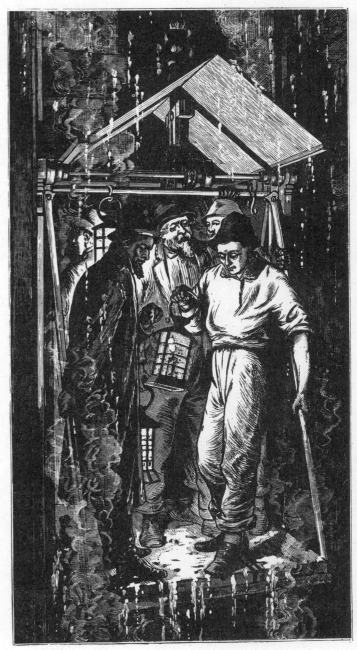

They sold all they possessed, invested every cent, managed to get control of the whole mine, worked it wisely and fortunately, and today are said to be worth fifteen millions each.

Mr. Fair, equally rich, resides on the spot and passes three hours daily down in the mine, personally superintending its operations. The receipts for this mine during fifteen months were $24,850,524.85 — and for over a year it has divided a million monthly, with no signs of exhaustion.

It was Mr. Fair who took us to the large room where the miners change their clothes. Miners' shirts and trousers hung all around, while on a long frame down the middle of the place stood their big heavy shoes or brogans.

We encountered a party of miners just dressed to go down. They looked very wild and strange in their great solid hats, like roofs, stiff enough to protect the head from falling bits of rock, their uncouth clothes and great brogans, each man carrying a lantern in his hand.

Nine men crowd onto the elevator. At a given signal they go dashing down into the hot, white steam, disappearing in a moment, absolutely swallowed up in the earth.

A set came up while we stood looking, and such ghosts one never saw: pale, exhausted, dripping with water and perspiration, some with their shirts torn off and naked to the waist, all of them haggard and dazed with the long darkness and toil. The heat in the shaft is fearful, and although the galleries are cooler, it is still so warm that the men are obliged to work half naked, sometimes wholly so, and word is always sent down when ladies are about to visit the mine.

The men are mostly Cornish — no Irish and no Chinese allowed. The owners would like to employ Chinese but the Miners' Union is too strong, dictating eight hours a day as the period for labor, wages of four dollars per diem, and no competition.

Presently the Chief, with the "forlorn hope," who had volunteered to accompany him underground, retired to the dressing room. They returned so queerly metamorphosed that it was hard to recognize them. Various quizzical comparisons accompanied them as they somewhat gingerly stepped upon the elevator.

But a sudden thrill of vague horror superseded laughter as the car swiftly and suddenly took our friends from our midst, leaving only the black shaft with its ghostly clouds of steam to show where they had been. I, for one, turned away shuddering and afeard. □

1967: The Mystic Allure of the Bell, Plum, and Cherry

THE TRAIN GETS INTO RENO, Nevada, at 4:25 in the morning, and I suppose if you have to arrive somewhere at 4:25 in the morning there is no place more invigorating to do it in than Reno, Nevada. The Sierra forms an inky stain against the darkness to the west; but Reno is ablaze with signs of commerce and conviviality. A spotlight illuminates the emblem on the roof of Harold's Club, which already is illuminated by a swath of neon tubing. Enormous cocktail glasses, root beer mugs, and bubbles of luminous plastic whirl around in the murky sky, and a large billboard announces: "Hart Skis Turn You On."

At this hour, I prefer to be turned on by a cup of coffee; so I stowed my suitcase in a locker at the station and walked uptown to look for a restaurant. Rounding a corner, I was astonished to find that Reno's most famous landmark — an arch over Virginia Street embellished with the words, "Biggest Little City in the World" — has been replaced by a more pretentious structure with the same inscription. The new monument has thousands of electric light bulbs twinkling in the vaults and a gigantic sphere revolving on the cornice, and it looks remarkably like the facade of a prosperous gambling casino. As a matter of fact, six of the largest casinos in town caused it to be constructed in 1964 "in common bond for the betterment and advancement of a greater Reno." I don't know whether the sign actually has bettered and advanced Reno, but it is a doozy, as signs go, and exactly appropriate to a town devoted to the raptures of hasty marriage, casual divorce, and short term speculation.

Reno has other industries, of course: stud farms, dude ranches, stone yards, creameries. There are sleek little office buildings on the river bank, chemistry labs at the university out on the north side of town, and rows of neat, brick houses with Norway spruces on the lawns and water skis in the garages.

But it is not for these homely attractions that travelers tumble out of their cozy roomettes on the *City of San Francisco* at 4:25 A.M. and rush eagerly toward Virginia Street. It is for the roulette wheel at Poor Pete's, the crap table at the Primadonna, the blackjack game at Harrah's, the $25,000 Keno at Bill Fong's New China Club. It is, above all, for the slot machines. At a quarter-to-five in the morning, you can hear them from a block away — the whirring and clanking of myriad wheels, embossed with cherries, plums, bells, oranges, and lemons.

Actually, four-forty-five is a rather quiet hour, even for the largest of casinos. Only three of the crap tables at Harold's are in action; most of the roulette wheels are silent; and several of the blackjack dealers are sitting idle, with no one across the green felt table muttering, "Hit me easy." The bar is stagnant. Less than a dozen bon vivants are toasting the dawn with draught beer and bourbon neat.

Yet the slot machines grind ceaselessly, like the old stamp mills of the Comstock Lode. Thirty or forty men and women with rigid faces are tugging away at the handles. Just inside the door, a woman whose hair and skin are the color of a glacier is manipulating half a dozen machines. She moves to and fro like a frosty, blue bee pollenating a row of metallic flowers. Her tote-bag of polished white calfskin hangs open, and she dips into it occasionally to replenish the supply of coins in her fist. Now and then one of the machines gasps, crepitates, and hawks a splatter of nickels into a basin; but the woman pays no attention. Nothing breaks the cadence of her work: coin in, handle down . . . coin in, handle down. . . . When she comes to the machine that has regurgitated, she darts out her hand without glancing downward, scoops the coins into her white leather reticule, and moves on.

The sight of this tedious, unrelenting labor gave me a terrific appetite. I took the moving stairway up to the second floor, where a three-piece orchestra was playing "Hello Dolly" for breakfast *dansant*, and on up to the third floor coffee shop. A number of early birds in riding pants and satin blouses were chatting at the counter. At first, I assumed they were a day shift of slot-machine feeders, warming up for work, but on closer view most of them showed name badges over the heart that identified them by name and place of origin as employees of the club. I sat with Margi, Spokane, Wash., and Jimmie, Paterson, N.J., and we were served coffee by Matt, New York, N.Y.

The badges, I think, are supposed to stimulate fraternal chitchat between dealers and players, as in: "Hey, Margi — I'm from Spokane, too! Hit me light, Margi old girl . . . . Ooops! Well, win a few, lose a few. How long since you been back in Spokane?"

At the moment, however, the only conversational opener I could think of was: "Margi! What on earth are you doing in Harold's Club at 5:00 A.M.?" Since this would have sounded impertinent, I kept my mouth shut. After breakfast, I saw Margi on duty at a blackjack table on the first floor, and she looked so comfortably habituated to the casino that I was glad I hadn't said anything. The glacial slot machine addict also was in action. She looked right at home, too.

I caught the 6:00 A.M. bus to Carson City at a Greyhound depot a block from Harolds. We started almost empty and gathered passengers at laundromats and furniture stores on Mill Street and Wells Avenue. Everybody said good morning to the driver, threw a briefcase up onto the baggage rack, and settled down with a pleasant, coffee-scented sigh. It was a wholly different aspect of Nevada life than I had seen before

—commuters on their way to work—and the landscape was as pristine as Virginia Street is tawdry. Palomino stallions and little chestnut mares stood in the frozen pastures; hot springs fumed up in the silent air; and pink sunlight burnished the snowfields of Mount Rose.

But my mind was filled with the clatter of slot machines. I kept thinking about a friend of mine whose wife is a hopeless addict. Whenever they come to Reno, my friend gives his wife a gambling allowance of fifteen or twenty dollars, and she changes it all for nickels and dimes. For half an hour or so she wanders among the machines, cocking her head like a percussionist tuning his timpani. It is her unshakable belief that a few machines in every casino are adjusted to pay favorable odds in order to keep women occupied while their husbands are chancing high-stake games. These philogynous devices, she says, develop an audible rumble when they are about to enter a fertile cycle. When she finds a machine coming into heat, she settles down and plays for as many hours as it takes to lose all her money. Then she says: "Well, I've had my fun," and immediately begins nagging her husband to take her back to the motel.

If this woman's affliction were rare, it would not have preyed on my mind. As far as I am concerned, slot machine playing is no worse than a lot of other pastimes. But the craving is epidemic in California, where slot machines are illegal; and this means that sick Californians must come to Nevada to play. They flock eastward every weekend to insert dimes and pull handles until they are relieved of the unbearable pressure of their accumulated coins. Palaces for their accommodation rise on the Nevada shore of Lake Tahoe. Neon signs and phosphorescent banners guide them through the pine trees; diesel oil and carbon gases float in their wake; and sterilized sewage from their casinos, their nightclubs, and their skyscraper hotels seeps into the sapphire water and stains it with green algae. Looking up toward Mount Rose, you can imagine a great tide of effluent oozing downward to pollute every lake and stream of the Sierra. And this is too much to endure, now and forever, as the price of some five-dollar jackpots.

Carson City, surprisingly, looks undefiled. The bus stops at a red brick post office, and a crisp little woman in a faded-blue jump suit trots out with a hand cart to take in the mail. The sun is shining; the streets are clean. The attractions of Carson City apparently are not the kind that appeal to effluent-making gamblers: the Old Mint, which is a museum now; the State Capitol, with its granite walls and silver cupola; the station house of the abandoned Virginia & Truckee Railroad, painted pea-green and used as a Masonic Hall.

Most visitors give a quick inspection to the monuments and then take in a wedding or two at the Ormsby County courthouse. In Carson City, as elsewhere in Nevada, loving couples get married 24 hours a day. Wedding licenses cost $5 during business hours and $10 after 5:00 P.M. and on weekends and holidays. Some friends of mine got married in Carson City a few years ago (during business hours), and they reported the arrangements were refreshingly informal. The man and woman just ahead of them in line were dressed in levis and sandals, and the bride had her hair done up in pink plastic curlers.

When I looked in at the Justice of the Peace, however, the waiting room was empty. A secretary came out and asked if I wanted to get married. I fled to the nearest restaurant, which naturally turned out to be a casino. It was full of slot machine players with the same sugar-glazed expressions and tireless right arms as their brethren in Reno.

I walked among the dime machines, listening for telltale rumbles of parturition and wondering what it is about these nondescript machines that makes them more precious than a sapphire lake to the people of our republic. They are only metal boxes, filled with whirling wheels, and their operation requires no physical or mental skill whatsoever—not even the ability to read the alphabet. A well-trained dog with a sturdy paw could play a slot machine; but most dogs show little interest. Only higher animals are fascinated by the bell, plum, and cherry.

Finally I gave up my somber meditations and went into the coffee shop for lunch. A good-looking man and woman at the next table were absorbed in eating pancakes. They fed steadily, swiftly, and silently, without saying a word to one another, until the man finally raised his eyes, wiped his lips with a paper napkin and said, "You ready?" The woman nodded. They stood up, paid their bill, and at once began pumping coins into the slot machines.

The girl at the cash register smiled over at them fondly as I was leaving.

"Look at them!" she whispered. "Just married." □

WATCHING SILVER MINERS "PICKING" ORE IN THE CONSOLIDATED VIRGINIA MINE.

CHAPTER XVI

Comstock Silver

1877: English Noblemen and Busted Millionaires Pick Paydirt 1500 Feet Down

IT REQUIRED A STRONG DEGREE OF COURAGE to face the fancied perils of a descent 1600 feet below the surface, though the miners think nothing of it.

Entering a large building, we were deafened by the clatter of a ponderous, 500 horse-power steam engine that lifts and lowers the "cages" carrying the small, deep, wheeled trucks used as receptacles for ore. As we entered the building, a truck was landed and run off to the crushing department, a part result of the labors of a thousand men in the caverns beneath us. Men work as low as 2500 feet in some mines, though the lowest level in the Con. Virginia is 1750 feet.

In the visitors' dressing rooms we divested ourselves of every article of clothing and assumed the garb of a miner, which consisted of blue-jean overalls, a woolen shirt of the same color, a pair of gray worsted socks many sizes too large for an average foot, an ancient pair of boots, and a hat of nondescript shape. Repairing to the shaft, we found the cage in readiness for our descent.

The sides of the well-like shaft are shored up with timber, and as there is very little space between the walls and the platform we were cautioned against protruding our arms. With one hand we grasped the iron support which connected the platform with the suspending chain, and with the other we held on tightly to the person next to us. Including the guide, there were five of us.

"Stand steady," said the guide. A gong sounded. The heavy machinery was set in motion, and we began to go down with a startling and decidedly unpleasant rapidity. The darkness became profound, a rushing noise was heard, and big drops of cold water fell upon us, increasing in volume as we progressed. At times the machinery caused the cage to jerk and bump against the side timbers, which did not add to the peace of mind of the victims. Though the entire time consumed in this descent was only forty seconds, it appeared to be a great deal longer. About two-thirds of the way down, we caught a sort of magic lantern

THE LANDING IN THE SHAFT, 1500 FEET BELOW THE SURFACE OF THE EARTH.

glimpse of men at work in an upper level; their naked backs gleamed in the light of the candles as they wielded their picks. The next instant we were plunging again into the abyss, our frail platform shaking and trembling, while the lowering chain creaked overhead.

At length we come to a standstill. We have reached the 1550-foot level or drift. Half a dozen men are here whose business is to place the trucks of ore on the cage for their upward journey, the richly laden trucks being propelled along tramways from the different workings. Each of us was here supplied with a lantern containing a lighted candle.

The miners eyed us with silent curiosity, without desisting from their work. Because of the oppressive heat they operated naked to the waist, and even then the perspiration ran from them in streams. Buckets of pure, clear water with large blocks of ice in it were placed at intervals, and cups were handy. Scarcely were we equipped with our lanterns than the miners near us ceased operations and crowded to the cage. It was time to change the shift; they had performed their allotted labor, and were to be relieved by others, for night and day, Sundays and holidays, the hive of human ants is busy. A day in the Comstock is not a mere trifle of twelve hours, as with the idlers above ground, but of twenty-four, in which there are three shifts of eight hours each; and right glad are these serfs of the silver king to be permitted to breathe fresh air once more. A good many of the solid Virginians, however, repair to the tobacco-laden atmosphere of a saloon, where spiritous liquors are retailed and the seductive game of poker can be indulged in; but hard work and solitude make the miner long for a little gaiety, be it of ever so cheap a kind.

The forms of the men we saw elicited general admiration. All were strong, muscular, and well developed. The nature of their work and the continued cleansing process of the heat render them lissom and athletic. The men employed in the mine represented nearly every nationality—the native American worked side by side with the Italian; the British lion was jostled by the Russian bear; and the Frenchman evinced no particular antipathy to the German. There is the scion of a noble English house, while French and Spanish counts are not unique. A judge is on the payroll, with several army and navy officers who have graduated at West Point and Annapolis; lawyers, doctors, and politicians of every grade; and men who have been shoddy millionaires in days when Con. Vir. was up in the hundreds instead of being at twenty-two, as it is today. Working in the bowels of the earth or sheepherding in the Sierra is too often the only reward of the enterprising young man who has gone West.

As we push on through the galleries, we notice an increase of the heat which, in spite of the ventilation, is oppressive. By and by this feeling wears off, and we experience an elasticity of mind and body that is decidedly agreeable. In some places the heat is almost incredible in its intensity. Pools of water will be struck in which an egg will boil in one minute. It is related that a miner once stepped into such a pool and was so badly scalded that he died.

The drifts run in every direction. They resemble spacious tunnels. Here and there the rocky ore presents a beautiful sight as it reflects the numerous lights which are constantly kept burning. The number of candles consumed annually is simply enormous. Eight hundred are burning at once in this mine, and it is

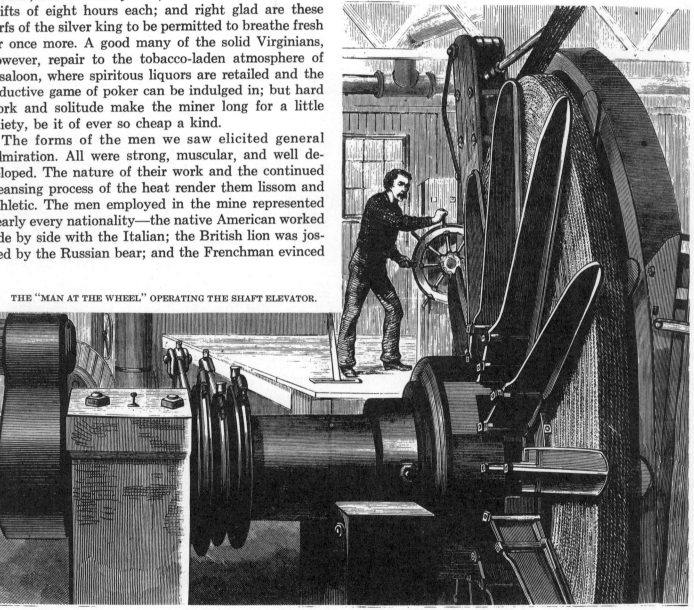

THE "MAN AT THE WHEEL" OPERATING THE SHAFT ELEVATOR.

reckoned that one candle will not last more than four hours on an average. This will give a grand total of 4800 every twenty-four hours.

Frequently, crystallizations are encountered, composed of silver mingled with chlorides and bromides that throw out brilliant scintillations worthy of a fairy palace. This effect is said to have been particularly noticeable in the old Crown Point Mine when it was a bonanza some five years ago.

Our progress at times is interrupted by an abrupt termination, requiring a descent to still lower regions by rude ladders. Here and there are dummy engines, hissing and panting. At many points we come upon the toiling miners. A man raises his pick in a close working; at each blow the brittle ore comes crashing down. Twenty minutes of the labor is about as much as the picker can endure; he will then give way to another and go to a cool spot, where he can recuperate with a drink of ice water.

In the drifts all is bustle and confusion. The men are forcing their way through the solid earth — boring, drilling, pounding, tunneling. The hammer, drill, and pick go clink and clank with a noise like that of Vulcan's workshop. At times a blast takes place, making a detonation like the bursting of a bomb — deafening yet grand, terror-striking but impressive.

Each of our party essayed a little amateur mining by borrowing a pick from a perspiring workman and chipping off pieces of ore to be carried off and shown to those at home. In the ore we detected the presence of lead. After some working, a draught of the cool water in the miners' buckets was very acceptable.

Our formidable array of sketchbooks and notebooks did not seem to strike the gnomes of the mines as anything out of the common, for they had been written about before. They favored us with a stare and scarcely interrupted their work on our approach. Several times we were compelled to crouch up against the wall, as the sudden rumbling noise of the ore trucks warned us of their coming. No horses or mules are used here, the men pushing the trucks before them on the smooth rails.

Though a man of resources, our artist found it difficult to sketch in the imperfect light. He had drawn landscapes in a lightning express, but to make pictures with nothing but a glowworm glimmer to indicate phantom forms was more than even his cunning hand could accomplish. A rough-and-ready, horny-handed miner solved the difficulty by holding up his lantern at an angle that cast a ruddy glare upon pencil and paper. Several others were immediately volunteered, and by the light of three or four our artist succeeded in making his hurried designs, which he reduced to shape and

MINERS CHANGING SHIFTS AT 1600 FEET.

SKETCHING IN THE MINE.

DESCENDING TO A LOWER LEVEL.

order on his arrival on *terra firma*. The miner in question little thought that his Rembrandt-like head would serve as a study; but if he sees this picture, he will not fail to recognize the portrait, which we can fancy attracting considerable attention when it reaches Virginia City.

Another noticeable figure was Aquarius, the water-carrier. This very agreeable sign of the zodiac followed us as our rear guard, tall and erect as one of the pines on the neighboring mountains, with a skin as clear and white as that of a woman and a staid, self-possessed air that would have befitted a member of the legislative body.

A year bèfore he had been working in Boston as a clerk in a lawyer's office, his home being Augusta, Maine. Hard times caused his employer to cut his salary. Piqued at the reduction, he threw up his situation, collected all the money he could from his relatives, and went West to seek his fortune. But, like the character in Dickens' novel, he did not find it. Going first to Chicago, he found every avenue of employment filled. From there he went to Omaha, where no better luck attended him. At Cheyenne he discovered that a good education, a knowledge of Latin, a good hand, and a thorough acquaintance with mathematics and the exact sciences was of no service to him whatever. So he bought an outfit and took the stage for Deadwood City. Here were too many of his own class, and no work offered itself, though he would gladly have handled pick and shovel for a bare subsistence. The natural law of progression in the West took him from the Black Hills, which have ruined the expectations and blasted the hopes of so many men, to Nevada, and after a short and fruitless stay in Reno, he went on to Virginia City.

Now our pilgrim had reached his Mecca, and he felt sure of making his fortune. But again he was mistaken, for all the mines were full-handed, and numerous applicants were turned away daily. After waiting and starving for nearly three months, he got put on a shift in the Consolidated Virginia, where we found him. As he ended his graphic recital, we fancied we detected a sigh of regret for that obstinate pride which had induced him to leave home and friends in the good old city of Boston for the imperfect civilization of the West, where the struggle for daily existence is, if possible, fiercer than it is in the East.

Having pretty well exhausted the novelties of the 1550-foot level, we descended deeper into the earth. Our journey now reminded us of Jules Verne's ingenious story, "To the Center of the Earth." We saw before us a series of ladders almost perpendicular. The sensation was like that of going down into the hold of a ship. The perspiration was streaming from us, and our hands were begrimed with the impalpable dust which encompassed us.

By "levels" is meant a series of drifts that are cut horizontally in all directions of the compass, each level being, as the name implies, parallel with the surface of the ground in which it is commenced. As a drift is abandoned, so is a whole level deserted when the vein is found to be extinguished; and then a lower one is established. The different levels are accessible by ladders, and in course of time a large silver mine becomes a vast series of excavations, forming a veritable underground

146

MINERS PAUSE TO REFRESH
THEMSELVES WITH ICE-WATER
1600 FEET UNDERGROUND.
THE GREAT HEAT OF THE MINE
AT THIS LEVEL REQUIRES MANY
SUCH INTERRUPTIONS OF THE WORK.

Things That Go Bump in the Dark

*Every now and then a noise like distant thunder
fell upon our ears. At first we looked up in
fright, thinking that we were going to be favored with an explosion, at least. The management, perhaps, had arranged this amusement
for our sakes. How relieved, and yet how disappointed, we were when the truth dawned upon
us! It was simply a car laden with ore that was
coming our way, propelled from behind by a
very harmless miner. Not wishing to be run
over, we stepped out of the track and crouched
up against the wall, while the car ran at the
speed of four miles an hour from Slope Station
to the depot in Shaft Street.*

ALLOWING A CAR TO PASS IN THE SHAFT.

147

A "STOPE" AT THE END OF A LEAD OF ORE.

Dissertation on Excavation

As in all trades and occupations, the miners of Nevada have a phraseology of their own. For instance, we were stopped suddenly at the end of a drift and informed that we had come to a "stope," whatever that might mean. We found that a stope is an excavation of considerable dimensions and marks the end of a drift. It sometimes happens that the miners find the vein of silver growing weak, and this attenuation indicates an exhaustion of the "lead" or a total running-out of profitable ore. It is not likely that the quartz all around will be barren, and the course is to search on every side for a continuation of the silver-bearing ore. The miners strike out here and there, until at length their perseverance is either rewarded by the discovery of a continuation of the old vein or of an entirely new one Should their efforts on all sides be unsuccessful, the drift is abandoned and timber is sent down to board up the excavation so as to prevent the much-dreaded catastrophe called a caving in; for being buried alive is a fate that the miner fears above all others. In these mines it is the principal danger, for the gases which generate the chokedamp of a coal mine do not here find a home. The atmosphere, though heated, is comparatively pure and harmless.

It has occurred to us that stope may be derived from "stop." We make the philologist a present of this hypothesis, and he is at liberty to take it for what it is worth.[1]

We may remark here that the size of these drifts is ordinarily something less than that of a common car tunnel. They are shored up by a continuous lining of huge timbers on either side, and the top is braced in the same substantial manner, so that there is no risk of any falling rock. Having arrived at our stope and inspected its gloomy surroundings, we returned to the scene of active operations. Being the last of the party, we confess to a slight nervousness lest we should fall out of the line and so lose connection with the man in front of us. Unpleasant indeed would be the position of one lost in the depths of this honeycombed rock. Who knows but that the unwary explorer might take a wrong turn and wander in solitary amazement until, weak and weary, he sank to his eternal rest, a victim to starvation and despair? The numerous, deserted, cell-like openings suggest being lost, with death as the ultimate result. It was with delight that we came once more in contact with the busy miners and banished all lugubrious fancies from our mind.

148

A DRAFT REGULATOR.

Reveling in the Cool

The currents of air through the galleries are carefully regulated by heavy canvas curtains placed at intervals. One of these draft regulators, when pulled aside, allows a steady stream of air to rush along like a boisterous current in a storm area. This is very agreeable to the tired and gasping miner, who experiences a feeling at times akin to suffocation. All he has to do to gain relief is to come into one of the levels and inflate his lungs, reveling in the cool and grateful atmosphere.

"How Long Will It Last?"

A supply of partially pulverized ore shoots, like a lot of small coal for stove use, down a shaft. It is falling into a bucket by the side of which stands a man who is prepared to carry it away when it is full. The supply of ore seems to be inexhaustible, and this raises the important question: "How long will it last?"

No other discovery has ever created half so much excitement as this famous ore body. Soon the telegraph wire had spread the important news around the world, and the most exciting anticipations were formed as to its present and future. Some experts then estimated the value of the ore body at not less than $1,700,000,000. It has since been worked continuously, and nothing more may now with certainty be said of its possible yield. It has been worked for five years — we are speaking of the Consolidated Virginia and California Mines — and has in that time yielded nearly $80,000,000, of which over $40,000,000 has been paid in dividends. The Consolidated Virginia alone has paid double what the Belcher has done. Prior to the opening up of this wonderful bonanza, the Belcher was the greatest dividend-paying mine on the coast.[2]

A Low Passage

In the course of our peregrinations we encountered a low passage. We do not hesitate to say that this is the meanest contrivance that the mind of man could descend to. When a person glorying in five feet ten-and-a-half finds himself suddenly compelled to double up and creep and crawl and stumble along a narrow, dwarfed passage fifty or a hundred yards long, he is apt to use expressions which would be deemed unparliamentary at Washington.

We made the transit inspecting the ground as if searching for a lost quarter, stumbling over detached pieces of rock, and contracting pains suggestive of rheumatism in the lumbar region. To a fat man, this mode of progression was extremely repulsive, as emulating the antics of a toad was not at all in our line of business.

Having emerged into a comparatively open space, we summoned the rear guard, took a libation, and enjoyed a brief rest. While our artist began to limn the sharply defined outlines of the low passage, we were pressed into the service of lighting the knight of the pencil. It was not exactly holding a candle to a certain person who shall be nameless, but it was weird and picturesque nevertheless.

LOADING A BUCKET FROM A CHUTE.

149

city with streets, avenues, lanes, alleys, elevators, and even railroad cars. In the building of one of these mines more care, money, labor, and engineering skill are exercised than in the erection of those congeries of buildings which in the West are dignified by the name of cities.

In this lower level the same ceaseless activity was visible. The human moles were tunneling and removing the debris, penetrating ever deeper and deeper, extending their ramifications, and creating an almost endless series of caverns. We could not refrain from casting an uneasy glance overhead from time to time, but the ponderous wooden supports allayed all fears. Scarcely a particle of dirt was able to fall down, so closely allied were the transverse beams and solid uprights.

Sightseeing is proverbially hard work, and few undergo more severe and continuous toil than the conscientious tourist. This is as true underground as above; but we enjoyed small stoppages occasionally, which were usually ordered by the artist whose practiced eye perceived some object of interest that he deemed worthy of a place in his sketchbook. Until he had metaphorically brought down his prey with his penciled shaft, we could no more proceed than a battalion without the command of its officer.

During the time thus consumed, we got into the way of gathering round the sketchbook, which became as gossipy as the park surrounding Congress Spring of an afternoon at Saratoga. We talked and chatted as if we were quite at home in mines and rather liked being down in one than otherwise.

One raconteur, bolder and hardier than the rest, boasted of his experiences in Mexico, where he had been captured by brigands and condemned to work at an incredible depth until he escaped during the confusion attending an explosion; but as the gentleman was connected with the San Francisco press, his story did not receive that amount of credence which would otherwise have been accorded to it.

The guide was not talkative, but as he was a well-informed man we drew him out. He had been a long time in Nevada, his father was one of the celebrated '49ers, and he himself was born on the Pacific slope. His relations had been pioneers. They had worked in the gold placers of California as well as in the gold and silver lodes of Nevada.

"Look at this little state," he said. "It is only 112,000 square miles. Its population is but 54,000, and yet this year its production of silver has been $50,000,000. If you want gold, you will find it all along the Pacific coast, from Frozen River to the borders of Sonora and from the eastern foothills of the Rocky Mountain range to the blue waters of the ocean. You can find gold right here, too, under your feet, all around you."

In his dislike for the Chinese, our guide was vigorous and pronounced. He declared that they would work for nothing and live upon nothing; by this he meant that they reduced their expenses to a minimum.

"Why, sir," he said, "they would come to a claim that we had worked out and abandoned. They'd wash our dust over again and get something out of it. I've seen them cut up a dead dog and make a stew out of it, and a sewer rat is a delicacy to them. A heathen Chinee is not fit to live on our continent! If you were to ask me about their manners and customs, I should say that manners they have none, and their customs are simply beastly. Talk about hoodlums! What makes our young men hoodlums? I answer, Chinese cheap labor! The Chinese cut down the wages, and by monopolizing the work, take the bread out of the mouths of the whites of the West. Thank goodness we don't have them here. I believe if I saw a Chinaman in the mine, I should go for him with a pick, and you wouldn't find a jury in Virginia City to bring it in murder either."

An agreeable draft of air came along the passage, and our attention was attracted by a miner who was sitting down, enjoying the cooling current.

"Taking it easy, friend?" we observed.

"Why shouldn't I?" was the reply. "A man ain't a machine, is he? Can't oil his joints and run him by steam night and day, can you?"

"I wouldn't mind changing places with you," we continued.

"You won't say that, colonel," he answered, "when you sit down to dinner at the International, where I guess you're hanging out your sign — fine hotel, ain't it? Ha, ha! time's changed, that's certain. I came out here in '59, and then there was three houses in Virginia City. The first frame house ever built here was run up by Jimmy Hickman that winter, and cruel cold it was too. He located it on A Street, between Union and Taylor. We had a touch of a gentle zephyr the following May, and that took the roof off. Lord, how Jimmy did cuss!

"Then, Johnny Connell built the first International Hotel on the corner of B and Union. They made it of lumber, whipsawed down in Six Mile Canyon, and, hang me, if Johnny didn't go and saw the planks himself. It was one story high and had a barroom, dining room, and about a dozen lodging rooms, 's well 's I can recollect. We didn't have no mahog'ny furniture, nor no walnut, yet the first day Connell opened he took in $700.

"In '62 Johnny and Paul, his pardner, concluded to draw stakes, and they packed up the hotel in two wagons and moved to Austin, where I'm blamed ef it ain't standin' to this day.

"There's some difference atween now and then. I was prospectin' in these parts when we had to stop in the sagebrush on the mountain side and look spry for fear the Indians 'ud come and steal our blankets. Yes, and I've lived in a 'hole in the wall.' The weather was so durned rough we were obligated to dig holes in the hillside and creep into them for warmth's sake. I've seen a hole in the wall, south of Tom Buckner's house, whar the engine house now stands, in which were two billiard tables and room for twelve men. I tell you a chap's got to house somewhar when there's five foot of snow on the hills.

"I could tell you a heap of things, for I've known everyone West worth knowing, from Comstock to Old Zip Coon. I ought to write a book, but I ain't got the hang of the pen, somehow. I can talk, but durn my hide, I can't write. Queer, ain't it? You've saw Gold Hill? That's where the 'ristocrats live — the lucky speculators, the bosses, and chaps that have made their pile. I knowed the first locators of Gold Hill. There was Johnny Bishop, Aleck Henderson — he was the original

Smart Aleck—'Old Virginny', Vigneau, Comstock, Camp, Sandy Bowers, Joe Plateau, and a chap named Rogers who'd been born a Mormon but didn't cotton to the Saints, and so drew stakes and run for the hills. Bishop and Camp located the present Yellow Jacket, which was a queer name they got from the Australian diggings. This was April, '59. I've heard that the name 'Yellow Jacket' first came from the prospectors comin' acrost a nest of wasps; but yer can't tell how half of them get to be christened. It's the fancy of the locators that does it. I once named a claim the 'Ann Eliza'—that was after my gal. She's dead an' gone, now. So's the claim.

"The miners came in fast 'bout this time, and we had to put up a shanty for them. Jessup, of the Ophir, turned in and helped. After it was finished, Jessup and Tides sat down to play a game of cards for drinks. They quarreled over the cussed bits of painted paper, and Tides cut Jessup with a bowie.[3] This was May, '59. I ought to know, because I was thar' and saw the cuttin' done and was one of the witnesses at the trial. Tides was taken to Carson—it was called Eagle Valley then. But nothin' war done to him. The boys did not want him hurted, and he went free. Jessup's was the first death on Gold Hill. Have there been many since? Well, I reckon. After the death of Jessup, and while the boys were over in Eagle Valley with Tides, O'Riley and McLaughlin jumped his claim, and that's how they got the

credit of being the first discoverers of the Comstock."

It appears that the Comstock claim has received several names; at least, the name Ophir was given it. Yet the lode is generally known as the Comstock, this person being the only one who was fortunate enough to achieve immortality as the discoverer. As a matter of fact, if the lode should have been called after the *first* discoverers, it ought to be known as the "Grosh" lode, as the brothers of that name located claims for themselves and others long before the days of Virginia and Gold Hill.

From 1859 to 1871 no very thorough exploration was made of this group of claims, the deepest shaft put down—that on the Central—having attained no greater depth than 620 feet. Then the owners of the several claims incorporated a company under the name Consolidated Virginia. This shaft reached 400 feet.

In 1873 the shaft had reached 600 feet, while the drift being brought in from Gould and Curry had been well advanced. In time the daily ore extraction exceeded 200 tons, and the shipments of bullion had risen to a quarter of a million dollars a month. In 1873 the California Company was organized, the Virginia management conveying to them the California claims. In January, '74, the shares were quoted at $85; in October they went up to $110, and by the close of the year Consolidated stock was sold in San Francisco for $580 per share.

EXHAUSTED MINERS COOLING OFF.

The Comstock Lode

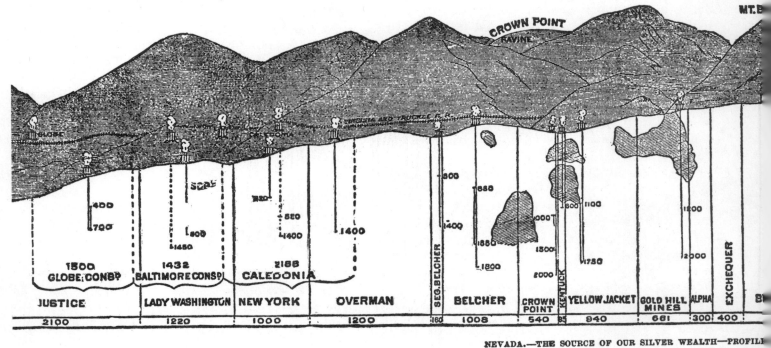

$3,000,000,000 in Paper

The history of the Comstock Lode is, to a large degree, identical with that of Nevada. Those who, in the early days of the California gold fever, went overland by this route found parties working surface claims in the canyons about Mount Davidson. A settlement of Mormons was there as early as 1847. A little later a party of Mexicans digging for gold are known to have brought considerable silver from croppings of what is now recognized as the Comstock Lode.

In 1853 two brothers named Hosea and Ethan Allen Grosh,[4] who had a practical knowledge of minerals, reported the discovery of a ledge of silver. The first location was called "Pioneer," and it was made where Virginia City now stands. These men were deterred from working their valuable find for want of means, and both died within five years.

H. T. P. Comstock at that time was keeping a general trading store at Carson, which was much resorted to by miners. The Grosh brothers had placed in his keeping their personal effects and the records of their discovery, and upon their death he took possession of the location and began at once exercising exclusive ownership. During 1859 a great furor was raised over Comstock's claim, and the entire country for miles around was soon dotted with locations, each locator setting up a little wooden slab to mark the claim, giving the side of the mountain the appearance of a large and thickly populated cemetery. The chief search, even then, was for gold, and immense quantities of silver ore were thrown aside as practically worthless.

By 1876, mining in and around the Comstock Lode had assumed such vast proportions that over four hundred companies had been formed, representing a nominal capital of over three billion dollars, and over one hundred different mines were being operated.

400 Gallons a Minute

The pump room is essential to the safety of the miner. If water is allowed to accumulate, working within its depths will become impossible. Therefore the water is pumped to the surface, where it arrives quite hot and steaming. It then flows through a brooklike bed, cooling as it goes along to the stamping mills and the amalgam rooms, where it is turned to good account.[5] The pump in the Consolidated Virginia raises four hundred gallons per minute. In addition, the company has to buy water brought from the Sierra Nevada.

152

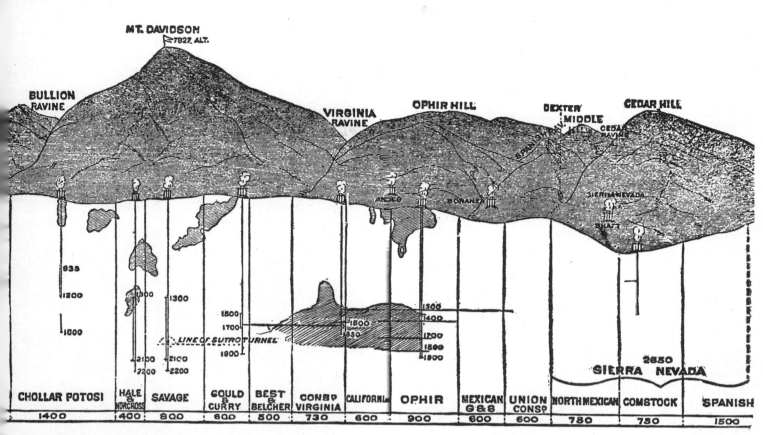

CHOLLAR POTOSI	HALE & NORCROSS	SAVAGE	GOULD & CURRY	BEST & BELCHER	CONSP VIRGINIA	CALIFORNIA	OPHIR	MEXICAN G&S	UNION CONSP	NORTH MEXICAN	COMSTOCK	SPANISH
1400	400	800	600	500	730	600	900	600	600	780	750	1500

TIONAL VIEW OF THE COMSTOCK LODE AT VIRGINIA CITY.

200,000,000 Feet a Year

At least two hundred thousand feet of lumber are annually brought to Virginia City by the Virginia and Truckee Railroad. Every drift must be shored up When the timber is brought into the mining quarters it is taken to the shop where it can be trimmed and shaped. The gnarled trunks of large trees are sliced into boards or cut into beams, which, having lorded it above ground in their principal forests, must now hide their diminished heads underground, to be discovered perhaps, by future generations who, wondering over the evidences of a past civilization, will in vain try to guess how they got there.

When the beams are prepared, they are sent to men who are constantly engaged in lowering the timber by special elevator. When the beam reaches the point at which it is to be used, the miner draws it out of the elevator and throws it upon the ground, whence it is hauled to the destination it is to occupy.

LOWERING TIMBER BY SPECIAL ELEVATOR.

WORKMEN IN THE TIMBER SHOP PREPARING MATERIAL TO SHORE UP THE MINE ONCE THE ORE IS EXTRACTED.

Onward and Downward

Several men were at work erecting a bulkhead. It was very substantial and appeared calculated to last for centuries. It seemed the irony of fate for trees to be stowed away in ground so sterile as never to have been known to produce one. Very carefully, the miners placed the several pieces of wood, fitting them together as diligently as if they had been engaged in building a ship. Each upright resembled some fabled Atlas, supporting a mimic world.

MINERS STOWING THEIR CANS BEFORE WORK.

A BULKHEAD, SHOWING HOW THE MINE IS FILLED IN WITH SOLID TIMBER.

STARTING A NEW DRIFT.

In an Argentiferous Vein

In a quiet corner a man was boring into the solid rock with what some would have called a crowbar. He was starting a new drift. The dull, sullen thud of his blows was accompanied only by his deep respirations. (The almost oppressive silence of some parts of the mine was a strange contrast with the activity of the machinery above.) Our miner's blows fell in slow and labored succession. A candle stood on a transverse beam near him, and by its imperfect light he worked with the precision of an automaton. Stopping to speak to us, he wiped the perspiration from his brow with the back of his hand and, resting on his battering apparatus, said he thought the new drift would be a profitable one, as it was rich in "auriferous and argentiferous veins." Having delivered himself of the two words, he appeared to be much relieved. He had been working three years underground and did not feel much worse for it. His appetite, he said, was more capricious; he could not eat everything; he wanted something nice, like the tidbits that French cooks put upon the table. This want we could understand, for the confined air was not calculated to inspire anyone with a healthy appetite.

154

Our explorations below the surface having been extended as far as it was deemed advisable, the party decided to return to the outer air. The ascent was not nearly so formidable as the descent. We reached the top in safety and hastened to the dressing room, where the luxury of a warm bath and the restoration of our own clothes speedily made us feel that we had come back to the refinements of civilization. In a corner of the room was a glass case containing specimens of silver quartz, some of which were given to those desirous of preserving a souvenir of the Consolidated Virginia. With languid air and somewhat heavy steps, we sought the cozy parlors of the International Hotel, the question of dinner being more important than that of silver, for a time.

The next morning we were early on the scene of our previous day's exploits. The courteous superintendent, who was indefatigable in his attentions, had provided a splendid carriage and four magnificent horses for the convenience of the ladies. The first department that called for special attention was the crushing or stamp mill. As soon as the ore is hoisted to the top it is taken to the stamp mill, where a diabolical din reigns supreme. The crushing is done by huge, cylindrical iron weights, arranged perpendicularly and propelled up and down by steam. Some of these weights are as heavy as nine hundred pounds — an enormous pressure, when we think of a hand or a foot caught accidentally under it. At least fifty were at work when we entered, stamping at the rate of a hundred times a minute and all striking at different intervals, as if there was no preconcerted action but each of its own sweet will worked its wicked design upon the ore.

It is estimated that each of these stampers will crush to powder five tons of rock per day. There is no escape for a piece of quartz when once it gets within the herculean pale of the crusher; and when it emerges on the other side it is like fine dust. Then, mixed with water,

INSPECTING THE LIQUID ORE, OR "PULP."

it goes through a sifter and falls into a box. This liquid ore, resembling a dirty white mud, the miners call "pulp."

The silver, of course, is retained in this composition, but a great deal yet remains to be done. It has to be subjected to further ingenious processes which all tend to show the absolute and indispensable importance of machinery in modern mining operations. Labor is positively powerless without capital, and the extraction of the precious metals from the bowels of the jealous earth cannot be accomplished unless the gloved hand of the millionaire joins the horny fist of the laborer.

In the pan mill there are rows of large vats in which dashers are agitated, somewhat on the principle of a revolving churn. In these vats the pulp is placed and undergoes a thorough amalgamation with quicksilver, sulphate of copper, and salt. The amalgam is then allowed to flow into still another vat where the silver and quicksilver — now thoroughly combined — settle to the bottom, the copper and salt having been consumed in the process. These pans are denominated "settlers." The residuum in the settler is an amalgam of quicksilver and gold.

On entering the pan mill and beholding the many wheels and handles in motion, we fancy we are in some weird ballroom peopled with strange creatures belonging to the iron age. Each pair of pans seems to be happily waltzing to some wild, forgotten music.

It requires 200 pounds of quicksilver, priced at approximately 50¢ per pound, to work one ton of ore, or 60,000 pounds per day for the reduction of 800 tons, an expenditure of $30,000. If this were the end of the quicksilver, it would be an expensive operation indeed, but the quicksilver is saved and can be used over again.

CRUSHING THE ORE IN THE STAMPING-MILL.

Crush, Add Water, and Stir . . .

Silver ores, no matter in what combination the metal occurs, are completely chloridized if they are mixed with salt and then fall against a current of hot air rising in a shaft. The ore is mixed with the necessary amount of salt in a dry kiln and very finely crushed, being afterward run through a screen. The screened pulp is taken by an elevator to the top of the furnace and discharged into a hopper, whence it is fed into a furnace.

The next step is the process of amalgamation. When mercury is brought into contact with metallic silver, the two readily unite to form an amalgam. If mercury and chloride of silver are brought together, a portion of the mercury takes away the chloride, leaving the silver free to combine with another portion of the mercury to form an amalgam.

The operation is performed in a large pan. Wooden mullers, shod with iron, revolve in this pan, bringing the ore into contact with the mercury. Water is added

SETTLING THE SILVER BY AMALGAMATION WITH QUICKSILVER IN THE PAN HOUSE.

to the pulp, which is next run into the separator. The liquid amalgam is drawn off, carefully washed in clean water, dried in flannel, and strained through thick canvas bags. The dried amalgam is finally placed in cylindrical cast iron retorts and the mercury distilled off it at red heat. When cold, the retorted silver is broken up, melted in graphite crucibles, and cast into bars.

In the early stages of Western mining the process of amalgamation was conducted after the primitive manner of the Mexicans, but this has long been superseded. The "slimes" from the stamps in Nevada, which were formerly wasted, are now saved, and the "tailings" are also collected on a series of inclined planes covered with blankets.

The process of raking the bullion from the retorts is extremely simple, but when the crude heap falls from the furnace it is difficult to think that it will ever be made into bright, solid, shining dollars.

To start a mill of this size an outlay of $50,000 for quicksilver alone would be required. The Consolidated Virginia keeps 75,000 pounds of quicksilver on hand all the time. A few years ago quicksilver was up in price to 90¢ per pound, nearly double the present outlay.

The amalgam, after coming from the settler, is first strained to relieve it of the superfluous quicksilver. The balance is placed in a retort as a final operation. The retorts are simply large iron cylinders subjected to an immense amount of heat. The quicksilver passes off by evaporation through channels made for that purpose, so that nothing but the crude gold and silver remains, and this is called "crude bullion." The quicksilver vapor is recovered by condensing pipes.

The crude bullion is finally taken to the assay office, where it is melted in crucibles and run into bars, in which state it goes to the mint at Carson, San Francisco, or Philadelphia. Before the bars are complete, each one has to have the comparative weight of gold and silver marked on it. This is obtained by a very close system of weighing. The operation is performed on a small piece of crude bullion, chipped from the mass before it goes into the smelting furnace. We asked whether mistakes are often made and were told that forty millions of bullion has left the assay office of the Consolidated Virginia Mine without a single cent of reclamation being made. The process is so fine that

MARKING THE VALUE OF THE COMPLETED SILVER BARS.

MANIPULATING SILVER AMALGAM AND DISTILLING QUICKSILVER IN THE RETORT HOUSE.

MELTING AND MOLDING THE BULLION IN THE ASSAY OFFICE.

PREPARING TO SMOKE THE MOLDS IN THE ASSAY OFFICE.

weight to the fortieth part of a milligrain can be detected.

Few people, when receiving or expending a silver dollar, think of the amount of skill, labor, and ingenuity that has been employed upon it before it is put in circulation; but our readers have now been able to gain some idea of the manipulation of silver coin from the mine to the mint. We are not to blame if they are not well educated as to the production of the silver dollar, which, if we are not mistaken, is destined to play an important part in the future history of this country. The rising generation will soon forget that we ever had a paper currency, and the gold and silver idol will be raised in their midst to the utter confusion of the rag baby, which since the war we have fondled in our financial arms.

Having exhausted the objects of interest in Virginia City, we prepared to take our departure. The Golden Gate and the wonders of California beckoned us onward, the attractions of San Francisco inflaming our imaginations while the orange groves of Los Angeles tempted us in our dreams.

It was, however, with regret that we took leave of the enterprising city. The inhabitants were unobtrusive, yet unvaryingly kind and attentive. None of the alleged roughness of Western manners was perceptible, and the civilization of the East was in no way burlesqued in this out-of-the-way but rapidly growing and important landmark of human progress in the faraway West.

Most of the party were presented with lumps of pure silver; and, as a mark of special distinction, we believe, the Chief was given a solid silver brick, such being a Nevada mode of conferring honor on distinguished visitors. ☐

1967: Getting By on False Coin

THERE WERE NO OTHER PASSENGERS on the two o'clock bus from Carson to Virginia City, so the driver stopped and let me off in front of the motel, a row of red and white cottages with vinegar cruets and cut-glass pickle castors on a shelf in the office window. When I paid for my room, the landlady gave me change in paper dollars.

"This is the new Nevada silver," she said, shrugging her shoulders. "Awful, huh?"

In Nevada they used to give change in big silver dollars that rang like cash registers and made your pockets sag auspiciously. If you pulled one out in San Francisco, people said: "You been up to Reno? How did you do?"

It was Nevada's whim in those days to traffic exclusively in coins. The purpose was not to stimulate mining. Most Nevada silver mines had been closed for years, and the Government stopped minting silver dollars in 1935. The purpose was to bewitch tourists. Every silver dollar was a reminder of the cushy days when an Irish saloonkeeper could turn into a millionaire pumping blue mud out of the steaming penetralia of Mount Davidson, when Mark Twain wrote gags for the *Territorial Enterprise*, and the political divisions of Nevada were "Silver Democrat" and "Silver Party." Jingling a couple of jolly little cartwheels in your trousers pocket gave you a warm, expansive, open-handed feeling toward the whole state. And, wherever you went, your silver dollars advertised the bounties of Nevada gambling.

In Reno and Carson City, however, I had noticed that the casinos now use *artificial* dollars—lackluster, gray, dollar-sized, plastic tokens. They fall on the green felt tables with a feeble, epicene click, quite unlike the inspiring, masculine clang of *real* money. Without that tough, metallic sound, a crap game seems as unsubstantial as Monopoly. And who wants to take a plastic token to lunch?

"Where did they go?" I asked my landlady.

"The silver dollars?" She lowered her voice and glanced around. "All of a sudden, they just disappeared. All's I know is, I don't think we'll ever see them again." She changed the subject to the operation of the electric heater.

The motel was out on the west side of town in a neighborhood dominated by large yellow signs with red and black letters, indicating an obsessive local fascination with silver. Directly across from the motel, a billboard invited tourists to peek into "Fabulous Mansion of Comstock Millionaire," and farther along the road other signs implored visitors to fill a cup at the Silver Queen, tour a bona fide underground mine, and revel in mining nostalgia at the House of Memories ("A Must for Your Children").

It seemed grossly unfair that a town absorbed in a single commodity should be deprived of a few measly metal disks to hand out with the after-dinner mints. It would not have surprised me to find Virginia City moping in despair; but the mood of the town was jubilant. Even on this midwinter afternoon, when most of the bars and soda fountains were padlocked and the streets nearly empty, the old silver capital was preening itself for the next onslaught of admirers. A woman in pink stretch pants was polishing the front window of the Real Old Fashioned Ice Cream Parlor and Home of the Famous Basket Burger; half a dozen Jumbo Rollo-Broiled Hot Dogs were writhing on a greasy steel rack in the window of the Red Garter Saloon; and down by the parking lot, next door to the Bucket of Blood, a sign painter was stenciling six-inch scarlet letters on a chrome-yellow background: "DON'T MISS TH------"

The air was clear; the weather was mild; the view was splendid. Through a gap in the hills you could see west, across the Carson Valley, to the white Sierra. In the other direction, you looked at the tops of sunken mines and huge, eroded pyramids of tailings, yellowish-white and sterile, and, beyond the plain, another range of snowy peaks. What better grounds for soaring spirits? Admittedly, Virginia has a trifling shortage of retail institutions. (I could not find, for example, a drug store, hardware store, bank, jeweler, butcher, cobbler, dry cleaner, clothier, realtor, automotive supply, furniture store, stationer, appliance shop, lumber yard, or laundry.) But who needs petty commerce in a village so well supplied with bars and curios?

In Virginia City, you can get drunk and go to museums from morning to night. Every other door on the main street swings open to disclose a long mahogany buffet, with mirrors and whiskey bottles behind it and ranks of slot machines in front of it; and each of these enterprising taverns has its private reliquary stuffed with dolls' heads, rusty pistols, photographs, and clippings. Upstairs at the Sharon House, which used to be a branch bank in the days when Jim Fair was parboiling Cornish miners at the Con Virginia, portraits of the Silver Kings gaze down as you savor your New York cut with baked potato, sour cream, and chives, and your green salad with French, Thousand, or Roquefort. Downstairs at the Delta Saloon, you can read placards about Mark Twain and Dan DeQuille as you feed your last two bits into a *fin de siecle* pianola.

There are half a dozen places where you can gorge in historic surroundings on homemade fudge or chicken-in-the-basket; and an equal number of establishments where you can order your name imprinted in a 144-point Gothic headline on the front page of a mocked-up historic newspaper. ("Tom Watkins Jailed in Virginia City . . . ;" "Roger Olmsted Wins Kissing

Contest. . . .") In all of them, the management reminds you with a yellow, red, and black billboard that you are not in some ordinary penny arcade but truly in the historic city of the Big Bonanza, a shrine of relics "replete with memories."

Sometimes the relics get a little esoteric. In one historic shrine, I found a picture of "Organized Labor's Booster Dinner to Jack Dempsey, January 22, 1932," which I suspect would be replete with memories only for those who were in it; and in a grog shop across the street there was a photograph of William Faulkner, pipe in mouth, taken at the Greek waterfront resort of Turkolimano in company of Mrs. Duncan Emerich, wife of the American cultural attaché in Athens, in 1959.

I suppose there are not enough verifiable mementos of the silver bonanza to meet the demands of interior decoration. (It is rumored that raiding parties from Virginia City have to comb New England every few years to replenish dwindling supplies of pickle castors.) Even the weekly *Territorial Enterprise*, which is a Dead Sea cave of Comstock incunabula, occasionally runs short of material and has to fabricate items about mountain lions spotted on "D" Street.

The *Enterprise* is a souvenir paper started in the early 1950's by the late Lucius Beebe as a medium for his quaint literary style and political prejudices. It took the name, the office, and even some of the typefaces of the celebrated Virginia City paper of bonanza days — the paper that took such brutal revenge on Mrs. Frank Leslie for her snooty comments.

By a remarkable transmogrification, Beebe's *Enterprise* embodied the revived spirit of the original paper — or, at any rate, so many people *thought* it did that everything Beebe wrote got mixed up with history, legend, and illusion and became a sort of Instant Past. Although Beebe sold his *Enterprise* almost a decade ago, and it has passed through the hands of half a dozen publishers, it is still the leading spiritual institution in Virginia City.

It was the revival of the *Enterprise* that reminded most of the five hundred residents of Virginia City that they were sitting on a gold mine, so to speak; and the paper has continued to perform a valuable service to local tourism by exhuming and publicizing defunct Virginians whose careers could become the inspiration for new museums and saloons.

The most successful project of this type was the resuscitation of Julia C. Bullette. Miss Bullette, a harlot of obscure origin, was murdered at her place of business in January, 1867, and given an elaborate public funeral by her grieving admirers. From this poignant but inconclusive incident, her modern apostles have raised Miss Bullette to the archetypal Tart of the Golden West. Her picture hangs in nearly every saloon; her biography is for sale in all the souvenir shops; and the centennial of her death was solemnized by a torchlight cortege of E Campus Vitus, a not-very-serious historical and drinking club based in California. It was one of the best things to happen to business in Virginia City for several months.

Walking down "C" Street a few days after the parade, I was pondering the disappearance of silver and the emergence of Julia C. Bullette in the economy of Virginia City. It reminded me of similar modifications that numismatists have discovered in primitive religious shrines. Half a block away, I noticed a saloon called the Silver Queen, and I assumed it must be making a synthesis between the old and new forms of worship — silver and sex.

But the Silver Queen turned out to be an ordinary Virginia City bar (antlers, Chick Sales postcards, pickle castors) with a Free Wedding Chapel at the rear for the convenience of customers: three church pews, an altar, and a mural of St. Francis feeding some pigeons. Not a sign of Julia C. Bullette. The "Silver Queen" was a twenty-foot high painting of a blonde in a blue evening dress embossed with 3,261 silver dollars.

I told the bartender I was relieved to find out where the silver dollars had gone.

"Them? That's a drop in the bucket," he said, mopping up. "We used to use a million cartwheels a week in this state."

"Where did they all go?"

"Oh, they're in piggy banks and mattresses. Some dame sounded off in Washington a couple of years ago there was going to be a shortage, and everybody started hoarding them."

"Too bad," I said. "No more dollar slot machines."

"Why not?" he said. "We still got 'em."

Sure enough, I saw a dollar slot machine, later on, in a place festooned with Julia C. Bullette keepsakes. You just feed a crisp, new Federal Reserve note into a handy slit, Washington's face up, and pull the crank. □

CHAPTER XVII
Over the Sierra
1877: Fresh Strawberries for Passengers and Silver Bullion for the Mint

LATE ONE WET, CHILLY AFTERNOON we leave Virginia City and by nine o'clock or thereabout are once more at Reno, waiting to be picked up by the westbound train on the Central Pacific Road. Between us and San Francisco loom no more delays, side trips, or erratic switchings-off from the regular route — nothing but the slow tug climbing the Sierra, then the swift, rushing descent to the Sacramento Valley.

In the darkness we pass a host of little stations, cross and recross the noisy, foaming Truckee River, and always steadily press upgrade. It is cold enough to frighten away most of the enthusiastic patrons of the rear platform and to make berths and blankets more seductive than sharp winds and an airy exposure. Nevertheless, one or two of us are kept on the alert by the prospect of Summit Station and Donner Lake at midnight, and with a few extra wraps and a cigar apiece, we manage to brave it out.

The clouds break up for our especial good, and the moon comes struggling out to show us the great snow peaks, glittering in long ranks against the blue-black sky, climbing and crowding above us until they seem to meet the stars. All along their sides is a fringe of black pine forest. Here and there is a clearing, shining out ghastly white with its untrodden covering of snow: black and white alternating in a broad patchwork and crossed now and again by some brawling baby river rushing down from the high snow summits. We are cognizant of Truckee, a brisk little town, only by its long line of station buildings and the twinkling lights clustered round about them. The guidebook tells us that it has fifteen hundred souls — a good many of them of Celestial origin — and that it has been four times burnt out in three years and as many times revived like a true phoenix from the ashes of its ruin.

The snowsheds are very much in our way at this stage of the journey. In fact, we wish that they had never been built, or at least were portable commodities, to be taken down in the spring and packed away for next winter's use. Wherever the action of the snowplow — a trifle weighing thirty tons — is too much impeded by the lay of the ground, then come the long gloomy tunnels, winding along for miles, with only here and there an opening that serves to show us in one little glimpse what sort of world this is. Between Strong's Canyon Station and Emigrant Gap, a distance of twenty-five miles, there is scarcely a break in the monotonous succession of sheds, and it so happens that some of the finest points of scenery are congregated along this section of the route. The road, turning aside from the Truckee River, passes near the site of Starvation Camp, where in the winter of '46, the Donner party[1] perished by cold and starvation.

Just before the train arrives at Summit Station, Donner Lake can be seen, usually through "observation holes" cut in the side of the snowshed; but we are lucky enough to have a better view. The road curves round a steep mountain side directly overhanging the lake, and about a mile of shed has recently been blown down or otherwise obligingly leveled. We have a splendid view of the oval sheet of quiet water, bedded deep in gloomy, black pine forests. Leaning far over the platform, we look down into the reflected moonlight on its bosom and up at the glittering snow crests of the Sierra closing around it — only for a moment, it seems — and then we go roaring into the black arch of the snowshed again. But one of the most vivid pictures of all our journey is this of Donner Lake, with its weird, tragic story clinging round it, lying white and shining between the dark forests and the snow peaks under the quiet stars.

At Summit Station the upgrade comes to an end at an altitude of 7017 feet. The largest and best hotel on the line of the road is said to be at this point, but we have no opportunity of testing its merits. In ten minutes we are rushing downgrade, in and out of the snowsheds again; past Cascade and Tamarack and Cisco, little signal and telegraph stations half-buried in the pine woods; along the side of the divide which separates the waters of the Yuba and American Rivers; through canyons and around sharp bluffs; until at Emigrant Gap the divide is pierced by a tunnel through which we dash, emerging in Wilson's Ravine.

Daylight is creeping up. Vast walls of forest sweep above us; unsounded depths of shadowy ravines fall away on either side; and it is all in somber masses of quail color: drifted snow and olive-black pine foliage, the dark gray-green of a winding stream, and overhead the tender opal changes of the sky. The very trees are giants, crowded together in solemn companies whose ranks dwindle gradually as they ascend, until the last of them are drawn like a fringe of grass against the mountaintops. Passing around Trail Spur, we catch the first glimpse of the American River, far down in its deep, narrow canyon, a cleft of two thousand feet worn by the slowly moving glaciers of another age.

At Dutch Flat the first flavor of California is apparent. Hydraulic mining is in actual progress, and here are all the evidences of its past operations — gravel heaps, naked boulders, ragged cones and pyramids of rock washed white and bare and shining by streams of water poured at a range of two or three hundred feet through a six-inch nozzle.

Why Dutch *Flat* it would be difficult to say, unless because there is not a square foot of level soil to be seen anywhere in the vicinity, only a tumbled sea of mountains stretching east, west, north, and south into the distance, and close at hand steep, ragged precipices, gulches, and a wilderness of rock and ravine. But it is already summer here: the greenest and softest of grass and the glossiest fresh leafage — such vivid shades of green on a groundwork of bright, ochery-red soil, with a dash of blue here and there in the shape of blossoming wild flowers! — making Dutch Flat beautiful in our eyes as we go dashing by.

Gold Run is passed, in whose neighborhood is Red Dog — familiar to the readers of Bret Harte; likewise You Bet and Little York and Ophir, all given up, like Dutch Flat, to the desolating influences of hydraulic mining. And then we come to Secret Town, so called by some early prospectors who wished to involve their discoveries in mystery; and Secret Town Ravine, crossed by a spider-like trestle bridge. Coming round a side hill, we look from this airy span and see the mountains sink away below us — sink down, down into a shadowy abyss, darkened with forests and threaded by a lazy stream of water almost as gloomy.

Now comes Cape Horn, the jutting promontory that frowns at the head of the Great American River Canyon. The train swings round on a dizzily narrow grade, with a wall of rock towering above and the almost vertical side of the abyss sweeping down to the narrow bed of the river. The canyon is two miles long and 2500 feet deep. Between its walls there seems just space enough for the narrow stream to slide and no more — not a trail wide enough for a jackrabbit on either side. The forest grows unbroken from the very edge of the river up to the sharp, clear-cut line of the mountain summits — two steep, dusky walls, shutting in a little, winding ribbon of emerald green and narrowing in the southwest to a gap through which you may see the peaks like a long line of frozen surf.

Twenty minutes are given us to revel in this one, long look — our first and last at the Great American River Canyon. While the train waits and the photographer runs hither and thither with his tripod, we wander along the edge of the track and scramble a few feet down the side of the precipice after wonderful wild flowers. We lie in the fresh, dewy green grass and stare down into the gloomy shadows of the canyon; and the twenty minutes, crowded so full of beauty, seem to be but a second in passing.

We recall that memorable February day in 1848 when John Marshall, assisting in the erection of a mill for John A. Sutter, picked up a small lump of yellow substance. It seems that we can see the aged Sutter, whose face is still familiar to Washington society, closeted with his employee, applying test after test to the pebbles, watching every change in color, and only giving expression to his pent-up feelings when the last resort, *aqua fortis*, has convinced him that the yellow lumps are virgin gold. Then the two men, flushed with pride and nervous with anticipation, clasp hands together and pledge each other to keep secret the great

discovery, at least until Sutter has completed the building of his mill.

But the event, most fortunate to the world, most unlucky to the hardy pioneer, is divulged before the appointed time; and now we hear the wail of Sutter, as hundreds have heard it since (for it will be remembered he is still seeking of the Federal Government the possession of his own property) —

"The scum of the world came. They cared nothing for law, property, or anything. They took from me what they wanted, and I was powerless. After a year or so, civil authority was established; but in the meantime, my stock had all been taken and my land occupied by squatters."

The brakeman shouts to us. The photographer, shouldering his camera, runs past and scrambles up on the car again. Time is up, and in another hour we rush down into the Sacramento Valley.

From Cape Horn to Colfax there is little break in the grandeur of the scenery. The last patch of snow has disappeared, and at Colfax, in the foothills, we find full-blown summer, a real June morning with the sun an hour high above the forests.

Colfax was a bright, pretty little place, and an army of little boys was waiting to pounce upon us as soon as we alighted, each boy holding up strawberries, ripe cherries, or a big bouquet of blue lupines and flaming California poppies. Nobody could keep a "bit" in his or her pocket in the face of such lures. We walked up and down the platform and ate strawberries and peeped into the baggage car at a precious freight come down with us from Virginia City — bars of solid silver for the Mint at San Francisco.[2]

We strayed across the track and up a hillside to a tiny village of Chinese huts, huddled away by themselves, as well they might be. They were the dreariest little dark holes imaginable — mere frame shanties set in a row, with a single room each, into which, in most cases, were crowded eight or ten breakfasting Chinamen.

One of these dens was a butcher's shop as well as a dwelling; and most horrible to see was the array of meat, cooked and otherwise — great chunks, hacked indiscriminately from the animal, and whole halves of roasted swine hung up by the heels, to be served piecemeal to customers. Three or four men were busy in this foul and evil-smelling retreat — some cutting up the meat, and one stringing unsavory-looking fragments of an unknown nature upon long straws.

Next door we peeped into a close, dark, little room at a party of a dozen Chinese crowded round a table, eating with chopsticks from bowls of rice, and drinking tea from dark blue cups. Nobody seemed offended at our curiosity, and no one scowled in response to our stares — only a bland stare from the many pairs of slanting black eyes.

Leaving Colfax, we speed down through the foothills to the broad, green plain. The coloring of the whole landscape has grown strangely brilliant; the sky is like a great hollowed sapphire; the tossing sea of foliage runs through every shade of vivid green; and the soil along the roadside and in the cleared spaces is a warm, rich red.

Through all this flush of color, however, we look

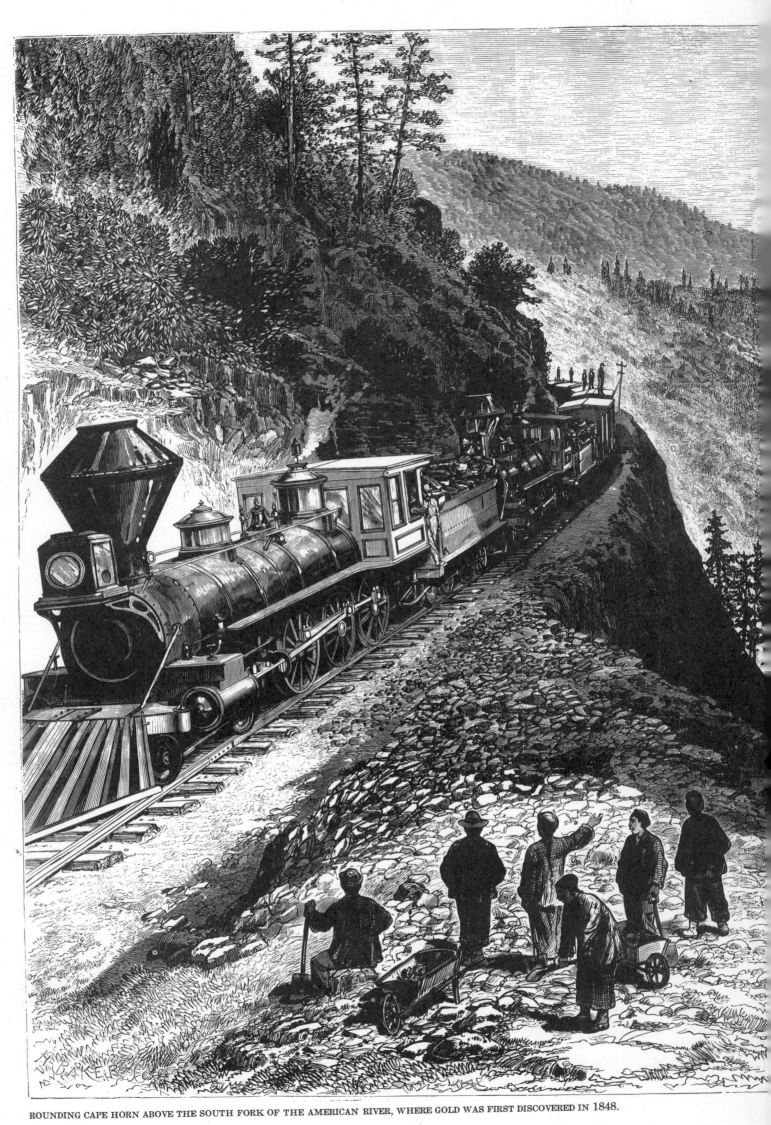

ROUNDING CAPE HORN ABOVE THE SOUTH FORK OF THE AMERICAN RIVER, WHERE GOLD WAS FIRST DISCOVERED IN 1848.

away over a soberer level of plain below us, and a great, wide, gray-green flat whose boundary line is a misty purple range of mountains lying against the far western horizon. This is the Valley of the Sacramento, and those are the Contra Costa Hills, on whose far slope beats the white surf of the Pacific. We are almost at our journey's end, and each little town reminds us more vividly of it—they are so widely different from the "cities" of the plains.

The whole landscape is rapidly losing the savage character of its beauty. There are pretty little glimpses of white houses sheltered in trees, great masses of flowering shrubbery, and shady roads, traversed perhaps by a horseman who sits as if grown fast to his flying mustang; long, low, white stations near the track; cozy little two-storied hotels; a church steeple here and there; and gardens where great, luxuriant, red roses revel in the sunshine. At Newcastle we even catch a glimpse of an orange tree growing strong and vigorous in the open air.

The first settlers in the valley found these plains overgrown with wild oats, nodding above their horses' heads as they pushed through; and now, instead of grass, almost all the California meadows bring forth "volunteer" crops of oats or barley, sown through and through with wild flowers.

The Sacramento River comes in sight, crossing the green plain lazily; and in ten minutes we are running into Sacramento City. The train stops under a long arcade, gay with little refreshment booths and lunch counters and crowded with people, without whose limits stands in waiting a long line of hacks and buses, with the broad, sunny main street for a background. Straightway we rush from our car to one of the said hacks. In less than five minutes we are rattling over an uneven pavement, through a blaze of semitropical sunshine and a cloud of dust, up K Street.

Shall we ever forget that half-hour in Sacramento? Under that blue midsummer sky, in that clear atmosphere and soft, bracing, flower-scented air, it seems to us the very most delectable spot that man might ever call home. It looks so quaint and foreign, with its low, wide buildings and wooden arcades, its great, broad, sunny streets, planked sidewalks, and white and yellow adobe houses, each half-buried in its lovely, crowded garden.

The stiff, dark evergreens are all clipped into fantastic shapes, and huge rose-trees run wild with masses of flowers—scarlet and snowy-white and golden. Every porch and veranda is a bower of yellow-starred jasmine or pale purple passion flowers. The aloes grow thirty feet high and throw up great spikes of dull white blossoms; the tall prickly cactus shoots out its fleshy lobes side by side with the poplar and the elm; and the palm trees grow next-door neighbors with the walnut of our Eastern woods.

Oh, there never were such homes and such gardens as we see in Sacramento! Every street down which we whirl is shadier and prettier and more picturesque than the last; every cottage, just a little more enticing to eyes that have looked at the bare Plains and the savage mountain passes for so many days.

But there is another side to Sacramento: business streets, ugly brick stores, and long rows of business blocks not a whit more interesting in themselves than those of other cities. We pass the Court House, the College, and all sorts of "Halls"—Pioneers and Odd Fellows and Masonic and the like; churches and schoolhouses; and the handsome half-granite, half-brick Capitol, standing in its terraced park. After a fleeting glimpse of a very dirty Chinese quarter and some attractive Chinese bazaars with windows crowded full of curios, we pass some comfortable-looking brick hotels with wide verandas and porticoes sheltering the side-

A STREET SCENE IN SACRAMENTO.

SNOW-SHEDS AT SUMMIT STATION — THE END OF THE UP-GRADE ON THE C.P.R.R.

walk; and then we are back at the depot again. We have just time to run from the carriage to the cars and swing ourselves aboard before the long train starts in its dignified and noiseless fashion, and we glide out of Sacramento City.

The day's journey across the Sacramento Valley is dusty, dreary, and monotonous. For the first time since our train puffed out of Omaha, we find no attraction on the platforms and very little outside the windows. We have come upon California in a dry season and, as a consequence, we are wrapt in heavy clouds of penetrating, brown dust. Dust tones down all the fresh green that was so lovely around the foothills east of Sacramento; dust obscures the distance and begrimes the foreground; and through dust we speed along, over a dull, drab-tinted plain whose only features are glaring white ranches, whirling windmills, way-stations, and little, scattered villages dotted at short distances along the route.

We pass ten or a dozen of these small places before reaching Stockton — one of the largest, hottest, and most important of California towns, which only commends itself to our notice for the superior unattractiveness of its position on the flattest level of all the great, flat, dusty plain. In the matter of heat, however, it is fairly rivaled, if not outdistanced, by our bewitching first love, Sacramento; in fact, all the towns of this great Central Basin of California are subject to very furnace blasts of heat.

"Stockton," Mrs. Leslie writes, "has fewer handsome houses than most California towns of its size; almost every house, however, possesses a croquet ground with an awning over it and a board about six inches high around it to keep the balls within bounds.

167

"We also noticed a great profusion of clipped cedar and arborvitae trees; and in the suburbs we came across one of the prettiest public gardens we have seen anywhere, laid out with nicely graveled walks, tall hedges, and great masses of brilliantly colored flowers. Trellises covered with passion flower and other vines were artfully placed to conceal the boundary walls, and there were watering tubs fed by whirring windmills close by the little greenhouse where the plants are started.

"Stockton is the location of the State Lunatic Asylum, which is one of the finest of this melancholy nature in the country."

From Stockton many tourists branch off from the Central Pacific and commit themselves to a short railway connecting with the line of the stagecoaches to the Calaveras Grove of Big Trees. Passing by this magnetic point, however, we push on to Lathrop, where ten minutes is given us to exercise on the platform and visit a caged grizzly bear. Then we are off again, with eighty-two miles more between us and San Francisco.

The heavy upgrade through Livermore Pass in the Monte Diablo range seems rather like child's play to us after climbing the Sierra; but they put on an extra engine, nevertheless, and our train goes winding up and around the rolling foothills, between high gravelly embankments, through deep cuts and a single, short tunnel at the summit, to descend with a rush into the Livermore Valley. An inland sea once rolled over these acres of grain and wild flowers. Beautiful rainbow-colored abalone shells are still found scattered around the old ranches near the town, and in 1836, the scattered skeleton of a whale was discovered, lying high and dry above ground, among the wild oats and poppies.

We pass through the canyon of Alexander Creek, past little, white towns and miles of salt marshes and green fields, masquerading now in a Quaker-like disguise of dust; past orchards and groves of live oak and blue gum eucalyptus; past Melrose and Alameda and Brooklyn; and then we are at Oakland.[3]

If San Francisco is a city of business, Oakland is a city of homes, where half the merchants and bankers and brokers of Montgomery and California Streets across the bay have beautiful villas and pleasure grounds. The cold winds that draw through the Golden Gate and the heavy sea-fogs that wrap the harbor for the greater part of every day seldom reach Oakland; the air is milder and warmer and the climate less variable than in the city, although the points are but seven miles apart. Of the beauty of Oakland we obtain not so much as a suggestion; in fact, we are not so much interested in the glimpse of the town as in a group of Chinamen, newly landed, who are just being moved eastward to work at road-mending on the Central Pacific. There they stand, huddled together, with all their personal effects done up in queer bundles of straw matting and piled on the ground around them. Some are dressed in the common dark blouses and pantaloons; others wear paler blue, quilted knee breeches and white stockings; but all are immaculate as to the hose and the thick, white soles of their clumsy shoes. They give a curious, foreign look to the landscape.

And now all the parcels, the odds and ends and impedimenta of travel, are collected together from every corner of our car. The train passes through an unsavory suburb, past flat, marshy lands and low, straggling houses, and reaches a great dockyard, where the railroad companies have their repair shops, roundhouse, etc. All the framework is built here for bridges, stations, hotels, and other necessary buildings on the lines of the Central, California, and Southern Pacific Railroads.[4] From this point, a trestle some two miles in length runs out into the bay. Over it pass daily an enormous num-

LATHROP STATION, AT THE JUNCTION OF THE CENTRAL PACIFIC AND SOUTHERN PACIFIC RAILROADS.

THE WHARF AT OAKLAND, WESTERN TERMINUS OF THE CENTRAL PACIFIC.

ber of freight and passenger trains; and at its three slips and four piers, eight seagoing ships can be loaded at the same time with grain or lumber.

Here we take our leave of the traveling hotel whose hospitalities we have enjoyed so thoroughly. Without much time for tender farewells or any but substantial benedictions upon our friend Howells and the fat cook we hurry, baggage-laden, from the cars to a ferryboat that lies waiting for us at its slip.

Hurrying to the upper deck, we prepare ourselves to be electrified by a grand *coup d'oeil* of San Francisco Bay, with the distant city reposing on its sand hills and the afternoon sun slanting down toward the shining gap of the Golden Gate. But we see nothing. There is a luminous haze, a golden fog wrapped about everything through which the black and white seagulls dart and flash their wings. Nothing else is visible to our intensely disappointed eyes.

As the boat starts, however, and the strong, cold wind sweeps in our faces, there is a slight lifting, or rather a thinning, of the fog, and the shadowy shapes of islands and mountain ranges shimmer through. Then we see, across the rough, white-capped, gray-green waters of the bay, a long line of low hills, like domes of windswept sand — silvery-gray, tawny yellow, and crested with the dark roofs, the crowded towers and spires of a great city.

To the right lies the round, hilly island of Yerba Buena or, as it is now called — heaven knows why! — Goat Island,[5] with its military reservation. Beyond it is a luminous opening in the hills that circle the bay, a mere tiny pass, guarded by a dim, blue promontory on either hand; and that is the Golden Gate. And exactly facing this narrow entrance lies the little island of Alcatraz,[6] with its steep, red banks, its red-roofed forts, and green-sodded earthworks, and the flag on its tall staff flying in the soft, hazy sunshine and the riotous trade winds of the Pacific Ocean. □

CROSSING THE BAY FROM OAKLAND TO SAN FRANCISCO BY FERRY-BOAT.

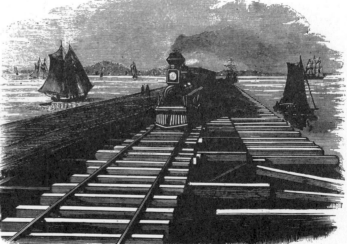

RAILROAD PIER AT OAKLAND, LOOKING TOWARDS GOAT ISLAND.

1967: A Non-Passenger Train for the Convenience of Non-Passengers

A TRAVELER FROM RENO TO SAN FRANCISCO may choose between two daily trains: the *City of San Francisco*, which romps through at 4:30 A.M. and reaches the Bay Area a little past noon; or the Night Mail, No. 21, which chugs west at 6:40 in the evening and gets to San Francisco around three the following morning.

Having sampled the Reno station at 4:30 A.M. a few days earlier, I decided against the *City*. Besides, the Night Mail has a reputation for austerity that is unique even among the monastic passenger trains of the Southern Pacific, and I was curious to see what new nadir of comfort this imaginative railroad might have in store. As I came into the station, fresh from dinner with a throng of bon vivants who were playing keno and eating pancakes, I could hear a woman announcing over a loudspeaker that the Night Mail had no diner, no sleeping accommodations, no lounge, and was running a trifle late.

In spite of this pretty unappealing format, the Night Mail had attracted a dozen or more passengers to the station. They were pacing up and down the platform, laughing and talking, their cheeks flushed pink in the glow of the neon crucifix that surmounts the nearby Sunset Motel and Wedding Chapel. There were two couples in their late fifties who were telling another couple that they had come up from Oakland for a midweek keno orgy, a brace of Air Force enlisted men, three adolescent boys in white Levi's and sheepskin jackets, and some soberly dressed men with sample cases. From the cheerful tone of their voices, I gathered that no one had as yet abandoned all hope.

It is natural to be exuberant when one anticipates a railroad trip from Reno to San Francisco. The train follows the most celebrated emigrant trail to the Golden Gate, and it is a route with inherent geographic drama, like the approach to Manhattan from Staten Island or the descent to Florence from the heights of Fiesole.

First, you climb over the hump of the Sierra and slowly descend the western slope, through fir and pine forests, into the red foothill country of the Gold Rush. You cross the great valley, with its peach orchards, rice fields, and cities oozing pastel ranch houses. You slip through a gap in the coastal hills to the upper shallows of the bay, wander for an eternity through a damp, hummocky region of dead ships, slag piles, petroleum tanks, sedge grass, and smokestacks, then burst at last upon the glittering, windswept water and the city gleaming on the western headlands of the continent.

The Reno-San Francisco route is an overture to California, sounding all its various motifs in a crescendo that is sometimes disappointing but always unforgettable. Even at a peculiar hour, it is an important trip.

A little after seven o'clock, the Night Mail came in from the east, and we passengers climbed gleefully aboard. The voice on the loudspeaker pursued us gloomily, giving a final warning about the shortage of amenities on board. As a matter of fact, the accommodations *were* rather unimpressive: a single coach, ancient and dusty, with patched upholstery, a lack of paper in the men's room, and an odor of cigar smoke throughout. But the women from Oakland who had been on the keno binge bustled about with happy cries, raising footrests, passing around steamer robes and looking for a place to unpack a picnic basket they had brought along.

I stowed my suitcase in a rack near the vestibule, got out some magazines and settled into a chair toward the back of the car. It occurred to me that we probably would not be able to see much of the famous Sierra crossing in the dark. On the trip east, too, we had crossed the mountains at night, and the train had seemed strange and lonely, slipping along like a wraith in the snowy forest. Only one other man had been sitting in the lounge car. He was reading an article about American Youth in *Time* Magazine and yawning prodigiously; by the time we passed through Cisco he was asleep.

The Night Mail promised to be sprightlier. One of the Oakland women was asking her husband: "Sandwich now or later?" There was a comfortable rustle of newspapers and some comradely chatter across the aisle.

Five minutes out of Reno, the brakeman, a ruddy, gray-haired man with a bulldog jaw, strode down the aisle, saying: "I'm turning off the lights now."

No one made a sound as he went to the switchboard at the end of the car and one-by-one turned out the lights: the ceiling lights, the reading lights above each chair, the hall lights to the vestibule, the small blue nightlights near the floor. When the metal door of the switchboard clanged shut, the passengers let out a plaintive wail.

"You can save your breath," the brakeman said. "I'm in charge of this car, and this is the way I run it. If you don't like it, you don't have to ride it."

"I want to read!" one of the Oakland women cried petulantly. "It's not fair. I don't *want* to go to sleep!"

"If you wanta read, go sit in the men's room," the brakeman said. "The lights in this train go off."

"What am I supposed to do?" the Oakland woman complained. "Take my picnic to the men's room?"

"If you think that's a nice, dignified, refined, ladylike thing to do, you go right ahead," the brakeman said. "I can't stop you if you think that's proper conduct for a lady."

There was a gasp of annoyance from the darkness. A man's voice said consolingly: "We can eat our sandwiches in the dark. The only problem is pouring the milk."

I asked the brakeman why he had turned the lights off at ten minutes after seven.

"Look," he said, "who's running this car? You or me?"

As a warm-tempered Quaker friend of mine used to say, I could think of nothing reconciliatory to reply; so I groped my way back to the men's room and sat there for several hours, breathing second-hand cigarette smoke and mentally composing a letter to the chairman of the board of Southern Pacific ("Dear Don: Dammit, Don . . ."). From time to time, someone would stagger in, blinking, and plop down for a few minutes before getting up with a groan and plunging back into the shade.

Part way through the evening, we got a report that one of the Oakland ladies had stumbled and fallen down while making a dash for the women's lavatory with a quart of milk, a chopped olive sandwich, and two deviled eggs. I could believe this, because when I went back to my seat once to get a pencil from my jacket, I ran smack into another passenger in the middle of the aisle. We both said "Ough!" or a word to that effect, and quickly disengaged ourselves, and I never found out whether I had bumped a man or a woman.

Around midnight, as the train was approaching Sacramento, I again questioned the brakeman, and he informed me that as far as Southern Pacific was concerned, this was not really a passenger train at all. You could not find it advertised anywhere nor listed in the train schedule. (Actually, you could, but don't bother.) The only reason they sold tickets on it, he said, was for the convenience of a few passengers.

Once I understood this public-spirited sacrifice by the SP, I was grateful that the brakeman had left on any lights at all, even in the toilet; and my cup ran over when a new brakeman came aboard at 12:30 A.M. and turned on all the overhead lights for an hour for our further convenience.

The new brakeman really was solicitous. After looking at the ankle of the woman who had fallen down, he wired ahead for aid and comfort, and we were met in Oakland by an ambulance, a stretcher bearer, a doctor, and a lawyer employed by the railroad. Everyone said it was the most festive arrival of the Night Mail in some time.

By day, passengers ride from the station in Oakland across the Bay Bridge to San Francisco in a forty-passenger Greyhound bus. But so few were going to San Francisco at 3:00 A.M. that the railroad put both of us into a taxi. It seemed anticlimatic to be making the last miles of a transcontinental journey in a Yellow Cab. But the passenger train goes no farther west than Oakland, and it never will. I had ridden the overland train to its end, its bitter end. □

THE WESTERN TERMINUS OF THE CENTRAL PACIFIC RAILROAD.

CHAPTER XVIII

Extravagant San Francisco

1877: Haphazard Social Standards and a Hotel Bursting Out with Bird Cages

A SOFT, HAZY, GRAY SKY OVERHEAD; a strong, fresh wind blowing clouds of dust; a Babel of shouting hackmen, car drivers, newsboys, and vendors; a jostling crowd of carriages, drays, and hotel coaches; and a scurrying stream of foot passengers courting destruction under the horses' heels — these receive us at the western terminus of the Central Pacific Road.

Before us is the city on her many sand hills, with Market Street for the immediate foreground of the picture — an unalluring picture enough, painted with dusty drab. Were it otherwise, we, in our garb of railroad dust and ashes, would be sad blots on the local coloring. It is not without a thrill of joy that we welcome the prospect of clean linen, a bath, and a luxurious hotel apartment.

In less than five minutes we are hastening toward these felicities, jolting over the cobblestone pavement that still prevails in San Francisco and taking an eager glimpse from the windows.

Between the Ferry and the Palace Hotel lie chiefly the business streets, with here and there a short block of private residences, curiously dropped down among the rows of warehouses and stores — pretty little frame houses, stuck full of bow windows, with grassy dooryards and clipped cedars. There is a good deal of eccentricity in the way of road-making, an occasional stretch of Russ pavement alternating with old-time cobblestones, agreeably varied on the lesser streets with primitive planking, while the sidewalks are variously composed of wood, asphalt, and the blue stone familiar to the feet of New Yorkers. These we notice, and the crowd that treads them — the indifferently dressed men (dandyism and the ultra-refinements of the tailor's art are left behind us, it would seem, on the Atlantic Slope); the few, rather showily dressed women; and the frequent blue blouse and pigtail, drifting along with the general tide. There is a suggestion of a more intense energy than comes to us from a Broadway crowd. Idlers are fewer, and the individual man appears to be in just a little greater hurry. And something better than anything to be seen in New York is the gray background of hills — the long, low, sweeping sand hills that seem to close every vista and the picturesque streets that climb them.

In ten minutes the hotel looms in sight — a white marble palace in truth, monopolizing the whole block with its majestic front: eight tiers of windows, and every window bowed, looking, as the British tourist is said to have remarked, "as if the whole blarsted thing had broken out into bird cages!"

Whirling around the corner of Market Street, we are at the main entrance, fronting on a quiet, sunless, little side street called New Montgomery. Under a great, wide archway guarded by tall gates of wrought iron, we drive into the grand court, the center of the hollow square upon which the hotel is built, and find ourselves in an enchanted region, all light and brightness.

In the center of the court is a circular carriage-sweep wherein half a dozen lumbering hotel coaches could turn at once; this is half-surrounded by a wide sidewalk paved in blocks of white and black marble, dotted with light settees, and bordered by many-branched candelabra alternating with tall, tropical plants. On the right is the entrance, through a cool, marble vestibule, to the reception rooms, while to the left lie the offices and the more exclusively masculine haunts. On all four sides rise the galleries, bright and airy, with their white balustrades and rows of glittering gaslights; and above all, roofing us in, is the clear glass dome that lets through such a generous flood of sunshine and blue sky.

If there be a drawback to the Palace, it lies in the very grandeur of all its appointments, in the colossal scale on which everything is drawn, almost precluding the possibility of a real "home" feeling under its great roof. The suites of rooms are large and lofty, cheerful with their bright, bowed windows and Eastlake furniture in sunny-colored native woods; but once outside of these, one loses himself in the immense corridors, down whose long vistas passing figures are dwarfed and interminable distances appear to open with every intersecting hall to the right and left. An army might tramp down the great staircases; and as for the grand dining room, one has a fair chance to walk off any twinge of after-dinner dyspepsia between the table and the exit. The parlors, with their tall Chinese vases and quaint delineations of California scenery on the walls, could harbor in their nooks and corners any number of flirtatious *tête-à-têtes* at once; but the galleries are the chosen spots where most of this small warfare is carried on.

It is eight o'clock before most of us have emerged from our rooms, and then instead of daylight, there is a flood of gaslight; for every chandelier from the marble pavement to the dome is brilliantly lighted, and every gallery is full of loungers and gayer than any flower garden with the most gorgeous of dinner toilettes; while down in the court the band is playing, and our welcome to San Francisco comes floating up in the very sweetest tone poems of Rossini and Offenbach.

Mrs. Leslie writes: The climate of San Francisco seems a point as difficult to settle as the standard of feminine beauty or the intrinsic value of Wagner's music. Everyone agrees that it is exhilarating, that the air is highly charged with ozone, that the brain worker can accomplish more here than anywhere else,

MAIN ENTRANCE TO THE PALACE HOTEL.

and wear himself out faster. But this ozone is borne upon high, cold winds, alternating with fogs and dampness fatal to any rheumatic or neuralgic tendencies and unfavorable to pulmonary complaints.

One person says: "The climate of San Francisco is all that keeps me alive." The next one shudders: "The climate is killing me; I must get out of town to warm my blood, or it will congeal altogether."

The climate, like the society, the morals, and the social habits of San Francisco, is a little mixed.

Accents of almost every language meet one's ear in all the thoroughfares, and to accommodate these various tastes, amusements, shops, theaters, and restaurants are established at every corner. The Frenchman, scanning the menu of the Maison Dorée, may fancy himself at the Trois Frères in Paris; while the German finds his sauerkraut, the Italian his macaroni, the Spaniard his picadillo, and the Welshman his leek, each at his own house of refreshment.

To live in lodgings and eat in a restaurant is San Franciscan as much as it is Parisian. Even families possessing houses and domestic conveniences are often to be found at one of these establishments, dining or lunching, "just for variety" — and also, perhaps, to see and to be seen.

A fashionable restaurant for gentlemen is "The Poodle Dog." "Campi's" is as Italian as Naples; and the "Maison Dorée" is Delmonican in every respect. The code of social law in San Francisco permits young ladies to visit these establishments freely, even at the risk of occasionally encountering a male acquaintance.

On the whole, we would not advise the widowed mother of a family of lads and lassies to carry them to San Francisco for social training. Although there is a large class of charming, unexceptional, and rigidly moral society, there are several other classes shading into it by almost imperceptible degrees. The bygone days, when every man was a law unto himself, have left their impress in the form of a certain recklessness and willfulness pervading every circle.

The style of street dress is more gay and showy than is consistent with the severest taste. An afternoon promenade upon Kearny or Montgomery streets reminds one of a fashionable "Opening." It has been said that in other cities the *demi-monde* imitates the fashions of the *beau-monde*, but that in San Francisco the case is reversed. It may be a libel; but we certainly saw very elegant toilettes and very fine jewels on pedestrians to whom we had no letters of introduction.

Noticing a goodly proportion of churches among the buildings of San Francisco, we inquired if anybody ever visited them and were indignantly informed that religion was flourishing. Everybody knows, of course, that the city was founded as a mission by the Franciscan Fathers. The Presidio and fort erected to protect the monks was called San Francisco, and the adjoining town took the name of Yerba Buena, from a medicinal plant growing abundantly in the vicinity.[2] It was not until 1847 that the name of San Francisco was formally given to the little town, just upon the eve of its marvelous upward bound. The Roman faith has kept its ascendancy in the city of San Francisco de Asis and claims today about one-half of the population. St. Mary's Cathedral, St. Francis', St. Patrick's, and St. Ignatius' are large, wealthy congregations, and there are ten more Roman churches in the city. The Presbyterians are most numerous among the Protestant denominations, and Calvary Church is one of the handsomest in the city. Grace and Trinity are the most prominent of the Episcopal churches; and the Congregationalists, Methodists, Baptists, and other denominations are in a hopeful condition.

Returning from our first tour of the city, we dined in the grand hall of the Palace Hotel, where stand four rows of tables with space for three persons to walk abreast between them, the whole lighted by twelve great crystal chandeliers.

Hotel residence is a popular mode of life in San Francisco, and surely a lifetime might contentedly be spent in some of the apartments of the Palace Hotel. Among the guests with whom we made acquaintance were the Admiral and officers of the Russian Fleet, then in harbor. We especially noticed one handsome young baron, for whom our sympathies were strongly enlisted when the Russo-Turkish war began. He sailed away with his ship, leaving his heart with a fair American to whom he could not give even an address, since the squadron sailed under sealed orders.

We passed a delightful morning at Woodward's Gardens.[3] The place was originally Mr. Woodward's private grounds, and the building now serving as a museum was his private house. Having transformed the grounds into a terrestrial paradise and the house into a rare collection of every sort of curiosity, he daily throws the whole open to the public. For twenty-five cents one may spend the day rambling among shady groves, lawns, lakes, streams, waterfalls, conservatories, and ferneries; using swings, trapezes, and merry-go-rounds; or listening to fine music and witnessing theatrical dis-

LADIES' PARLOR IN THE HOTEL.

BILLIARD-ROOM IN THE HOTEL.

174

In the Shadow of the Bananas

No picture can give an idea of the sunshiny lightness and brightness which is one of the strongest attractions of the Grand Court. All day the court is full of carriages coming and going, great hotel coaches, and groups of idlers in the armchairs and settees under the shadow of the bananas and palms. With its arched glass roof, it affords a charming resort and promenade which no other American hotel has as yet offered. It is similar to the court of the Grand Hotel in Paris, but even the most loyal lover of France is obliged to confess that the copy has in every respect surpassed the original.

Six tiers of balconies circle the four sides. Brightest and pleasantest is the upper gallery, whose balustrade is bordered with great tropical plants and bright flowers. Almost all families resident at the hotel have their suites on this upper floor, where the children can run riot.

The court is gayest, perhaps, of a Monday evening, when the guests hold their informal reunions in the great parlors, all the galleries are lighted up, and the band plays its best. Between the dances everyone drifts out for a promenade on the gallery, where the air is cooler, music sounds sweeter, and there are cozy little corners with broad velvet sofas that invite just two and no more.

VIEW OF MARKET STREET, SAN FRANCISCO, LOOKING TOWARDS THE PALACE HOTEL.

Montgomery Street

Market Street is fast becoming the leading business artery of the city. Every horsecar line in San Francisco except one either traverses or crosses it, and all connect with the ferry at its foot. From the windows of the Palace Hotel we look down upon the width of Market Street, with Lotta's pretty iron fountain trickling in the center and the long lines of twinkling lights along Montgomery Street stretching up over the heights of one of the many hills.

The trade and financial operations of San Francisco are pretty evenly divided between Sansome and California Streets, Kearny and Montgomery. The two latter, however, are also the centers of fashion, where the San Francisco belles gravitate for their serious business of shopping. California Street is almost exclusively devoted to large importing and jobbing houses, while in Sansome Street most of the banking houses and bankers concentrate around the Bank of California and Stock Exchange. It is a wide, handsome street, with solid brownstone buildings. More interesting to an observer is the incessant stream of hurrying, crowding buyers and sellers, speculators, and competitors in the tremendous race that is forever running in San Francisco's busy thoroughfares. At noonday the crowd is thickest and the hurry seems greatest, and each face, as you catch a glimpse of it in passing, seems strained and concentrated on one point only, with self-interest for the solitary, universal aim.

Leslie's Illustrated Newspaper, July 20, 1878

SANSOME STREET, SAN FRANCISCO, SHOWING THE CENTER OF THE JOBBING TRADE AND THE BANK OF CALIFORNIA.

AN ELEVATED VIEW OF MONTGOMERY STREET.

plays in a great arena, which is also used for dancing, parlor skating, and acrobatic performances. Connected with this is an excellent refreshment room.

An underground passage leads from the gardens proper to the Zoological Gardens, so called, a fine collection of wild animals: the ferocious ones languid and disgusted, as wild beasts in iron cages always are; the beautiful ones more beautiful because they are at liberty within their fenced paddocks. In a cool grotto was an admirable saltwater aquarium, supplied constantly from the Pacific Ocean and fitted up with stalactites, barnacled rocks, masses of coral, and sand at the bottom. A similar freshwater aquarium adjoins this, and also a machine for hatching fish spawn. The tanks for seals and kindred monsters were large, well kept, and very popular, especially at feeding time, when the barking and roaring are really terrific.

Next morning, we started out to the Cliff House in the fog that is nearly inevitable at this season but is guaranteed to clear by nine o'clock. This especial morning the guarantee failed, but unlike gloves and boots, the day could not be returned or exchanged. So we made the best of it and took out our annoyance in grumbling. The drive through the suburbs is not especially attractive until one enters Golden Gate Park, which, like many other things in this wonderful city, is destined to become one of the finest in the world.

Just at present, things are in a rather rudimentary state. In four years the park gardeners have done much work upon the thousand acres of shifting sand hills and wild ravines, thinly clothed with evergreen. But much is left to be accomplished. The first object was to form soil, or rather to hold the sands in one spot until soil could be laid upon them. This has been done by the extensive planting of lupines, whose spreading roots interlace the surface while the coarse leaves form a shelter for finer growth. Trees are profusely planted, and the hard, red roads are perfect of their kind. The commissioners are active, the citizens liberal, and the climate propitious; so the baby of today, on her bridal tour to San Francisco, may find this melancholy waste of sand dunes transformed into a park that will delight the continent.

After three miles' drive, we emerge from the great, gray drifts on the western side and see the long level line of the Pacific, its breakers rolling heavily in upon the flat beach and their low roar filling the air. The Cliff House perches on a rocky eminence, sweeping up abruptly from the beach. Its piazza literally overhangs the surf. A few hundred yards off the shore rise the picturesque Seal Rocks; and the long swell of the Pacific, meeting this obstacle, breaks from its majestic placidity into an angry roar of surf, sweeping among the rocks and churning itself into a foamy fury.

The ocean was dull green that day; the sky, gray; the wind was wildly scattering the feathers of the sea fowl who fled before it. Far to the left stretched the sandy beach, with the soft fog drifting down upon it, while to the right the jagged cliffs cut sharply against the sky. From their summit we could have looked across the Golden Gate; but we sat instead upon the piazza to watch the sea lions playing, fighting, filling the air with cries and roars that mingle with the tumult of the surf. Every age and size is represented, from the soft baby a few weeks old to the barnacled, clumsy patriarch, turning the scale at three thousand pounds and rolling hither and thither in majestic disregard of the small fry, who scuttle out of his path to avoid annihilation. The biggest, ugliest, and most belligerent of the seals is called General Butler,[4] and he evidently is not considered an agreeable or safe neighbor, for everyone else gave place to him with a haste more of fear than of reverence.

After breakfast — elaborate, prolonged, admirably cooked and served — several of us descended the cliffs by a winding wooden staircase of one hundred and forty steps to a little sheltered bay and sandy beach, with a huge rock towering up just on the edge of the surf. We stood and gazed far out upon the lovely, opal-green expanse of water. Its great, heaving swells seemed lifted above our heads, gathering forces to roll over and submerge us.

On the drive home we passed Lone Mountain,[5] upon whose summit stands a gigantic cross. The hills around its base are covered with gleaming stones, and the Roman Catholics, Protestants, and Chinese have their cemeteries here. The sun came out, and by the time we reached home about two o'clock, it was overpoweringly hot, and we were glad to shelter in the comfortable hotel.

One day we visited the Board of Brokers by invitation of the president, and assisted at the throwing away, as he plaintively styled it, of some mining stocks. The scene was one of wildest excitement — a jostling, yelling, frenzied, purple-faced struggle. At each call of a new stock, the bidders crowded to the center, gesticulating, pushing, ready to tear each other to pieces.

Not one word could we understand; but the excitement was contagious. I would have given worlds to be six feet high, a baritone, and in the midst of it all!

From the Brokers' Board we proceeded to the County Jail. Passing through Chinatown, we entered an objectionable region called the "Barbary Coast,"[6] inhabited by the vilest class of poor whites, as much worse than the "Heathen Chinee" as a vile woman is worse than a bad man. This region is said to resemble San Francisco in the early days, when gold attracted every desperado on the continent and scarcely one respectable woman was to be found within the city limits. It is surprising that out of such vile soil the fair flower of the present city could ever have grown.

In broad daylight, protected as we were, we saw nothing objectionable except dust an inch thick upon the sidewalks, and numbers of hollow-eyed, sallow-cheeked, vicious-looking men and women lounging in doorways and windows or exchanging scurrility from house to house. At the northerly border of this unhallowed region, in a street called Broadway, we found the County Jail, an unpretentious brick building, rather shabby and dirty. A placard upon the huge iron door stated that positively no visitors could be admitted. Ringing the bell, we philosophically waited and presently perceived four human eyes inspecting us through a small grated aperture in the door. Our escort made known our names. The iron door swung suddenly open, admitted us, and swiftly clanged to.

A stone corridor, whitewashed severely, runs through the building, with a row of black iron doors opening at intervals. In every door appeared a little window, scarcely large enough to frame a human face; and in every window, two human eyes coldly and incuriously inspected the visitors. No model prisoners these, such as were exhibited to us in England, but men whose depravity required no other warrant than those horrible eyes. Far from appearing ashamed, they compelled us to lower *our* eyes and hasten our footsteps to escape those bold and loathsome looks. Few of these men were imprisoned for less than four years, and one was to die on the morrow. He was a Chinese, the second ever executed in San Francisco. He had committed a hideous murder, thoroughly proven, and he well deserved his doom. But in the leering eyes at his window one could read no remorse for the crime, no dread of the impending punishment.

Upstairs we looked into the yard of the prison. Among the men were a good many Chinese, squalidly dressed in shirt and trousers, barefooted, and shorn of their pigtails — the greatest punishment short of death that the law can inflict upon one of their nationality. They are said to cry and shriek like little children while undergoing this penalty; and they never recover the self-respect or confidence they previously had.

A straw mattress, a tin pan, plate, and spoon constitute all the furniture of the cells, and no effort is made for the physical, mental, or spiritual improvement of these unfortunate beings. □

THE GREAT PANIC IN MINING STOCKS, 1878. READING QUOTATIONS ON THE BULLETIN OF THE STOCK EXCHANGE, SAN FRANCISCO. (FROM A SKETCH BY WALTER YEAGER.)

1967: Will the Real San Francisco Please Stand Up?

CROSSING THE BAY BRIDGE TO SAN FRANCISCO at three in the morning, I focused my somewhat bleary eyes on the lights of Market Street and tried to imagine that I was entering an unfamiliar port of call for the very first time.

This trick is easier than you might imagine, for San Francisco is a city that continually shows new faces, even at three in the morning. One can never be certain whether she will greet the weary, way-worn wanderer with a beguiling grin, a scowl, or a lubricious leer. We natives who pass our lives in her shoulder-to-shoulder houses, under the damp umbrella of her summer fogs and the incandescent azure of her balmy Februaries, are constantly astonished by her changing moods. She is whimsical, eccentric, as obviously schizophrenic as a dotty old actress who keeps slipping in and out of costume — partly because she enjoys showing off but mainly because she has gotten her real identity hopelessly confounded with her dramatic roles.

Seen from a distance, she looks like a mellow dowager: aloof, pearl gray, and angular — a city of banks and brokerages, devoted to long lunches, English secretaries, and conservation of capital. On closer view, she turns out to be an earthy broad with a raucous laugh and permissive morals.

At her worst, San Francisco is self-centered, indecisive, self-indulgent. Her newspapers are brassy; her architecture is prosaic; her restaurants are overpriced; her libraries and museums are second-rate; her government has seldom been exemplary and often been execrable. She is afflicted with social diseases. Her people have a notorious thirst for alcohol and a sinister predilection to suicide. Her Skid Row is the tag-end of the continent, the last stop for losers; and its ruinous figures persistently totter north to haunt the glittering streets with silent testimony to the failure of the last bonanza, the closing of the last frontier.

Yet, San Francisco's soul is warm, her heart is kind, and her beauty is imperishable. Few cities in the world — perhaps only Rio, Naples, Istanbul, Vancouver, and Hong Kong — can rival the splendor of her setting. She is always redolent of salt spray, violets, and spices (*not* burning peanuts, as my friend in Chicago imagined). Tenors leave their hearts beside her blue and windy sea. She is the best-loved, most ingratiating city in North America.

Some of the elements of San Francisco's personality are so contradictory that they can never be reconciled. The myths and the reality, the masks and faces, can never jibe. This fact became clear to me when a friend of mine visited the city for the first time. He is an intelligent, inquiring man, and I was sure he would want to sample the bitter side of San Francisco along with the sugar and spice served up by the Convention and Visitors' Bureau.

In preparation for George's visit, I made a list of things he ought to see. I planned to deliver a preliminary briefing on Bay Area geography at the crest of Twin Peaks, surrounded by views of a couple of dozen political subdivisions, all as mutually intolerant as the ancient city-states of the Aegean and the Adriatic. Later, we would make a sort of field trip around the Bay, spending two or three days and touching lightly on each of the major problem areas. As a starter, I intended to stop at Brisbane, just south of the city, for a full investigation of San Francisco's problems in garbage disposal. Then, we would head south for a look at bay filling and urban sprawl in the Santa Clara Valley. Along the way, George and I would discuss the tax base and assessment rates, racial integration in the public schools, street crime, narcotics addiction, parking problems, traffic congestion, urban renewal, rapid transit, public libraries, metropolitan financial support for cultural activities, higher education, water pollution, smog, jet transportation facilities, sonic boom, automobile freeways, low-cost public housing, school drop-outs, unemployment among minority groups, and other topics of regional importance.

When I picked George up at the airport, I asked if he was well rested and ready for the full tour.

"I want to see San Francisco from top to bottom," George said, rubbing his hands together. "*Everything!* Chinatown, the cable cars, Golden Gate Park, the bridges, the redwoods, Alcatraz. . . ."

"Alcatraz?" I said.

". . . Seal Rocks, Fleishhacker Zoo, Russian Hill, Fisherman's Wharf, Mission Dolores. . . ."

"Nobody goes to Mission Dolores," I said with authority.

"What do you mean?" George said. "The city *started* at Mission Dolores." And he showed me a guidebook he had been reading on the plane.

To placate him, we stopped at the Mission and looked at the chapel and the graveyard. George was delighted to find the graves of a couple of hoods who were hanged by the Vigilance Committee in 1856. He then suggested we drive on to Fisherman's Wharf, where he could look at Alcatraz through the binoculars and we could have a bite of lunch at Joe Di Maggio's Restaurant.

I thought I had better give George the benefit of a native's advice.

"You know, you're not going to see Di Maggio there," I said. "I mean, he doesn't stand around, frying scallops and saying hello to the customers."

George said of course he knew that, but he had always been crazy about Joe Di Maggio, and he would not feel he had been in San Francisco if he hadn't eaten at Di Maggio's place.

It was a Friday, and we had to park eight blocks away from Di Maggio's and walk down to the Wharf in a nippy wind. On the way, I suggested we order some fresh cracked crab, a romaine salad with oil and vinegar, a big loaf of sourdough French bread, and a bottle of Wente Brothers' Grey Riesling. George's face fell.

"Gee," he said, "that sounds a little . . . well, don't you think we ought to test the abilities of the chef a little more?"

I told him that was a *very* San Francisco lunch, well balanced and reasonably light, providing you didn't go hog-wild on the French bread. George shook his head doubtfully. He ordered fried Louisiana prawns, a baked potato with sour cream and chives, and a salad with choice of French, Roquefort, or Thousand Island. Afterward, we looked at Alcatraz.

"Wait until you see the view from Twin Peaks," I said as George was putting a dime into the public binoculars for the third time. "That really gives you an overall picture of the Bay Area."

"Later, maybe," George said, without much enthusiasm. After studying a map in the back of his guidebook, however, he concluded that Twin Peaks would be too far away. In any case, he would rather climb Telegraph Hill and take the elevator to the top of Coit Tower.

"What makes you think they've got an elevator?" I said, trying to sound friendlier than I felt. George showed me the relevant passage in the book. It made Coit Tower sound like the Empire State Building on top of Mount Fuji overlooking the Grand Canyon. The elevator got an asterisk.

"Ah, yes," I said. "I must have been thinking of the Old Coit Tower."

"*Old* Coit Tower?" George said.

"Before the Fire," I said.

Running his finger along the lines, George reread the part about Coit Tower.

"They don't say anything about an old tower," he said.

"Poor job of research," I said. "You can't rely on these books."

While walking to the car, I had a sudden and distinct intuition that there never had been an Old Coit Tower, merely some crude sort of signal rig that was used to announce the arrival of sailing ships during the Gold Rush, but I decided not to mention it to George; visitors always think we San Franciscans are obsessed with the past. When we got to the top of Telegraph Hill, I instead directed his attention to the Golden Gateway redevelopment project — another example of the kind of thing that is ignored by the average guidebook.

"Who lives on Alcatraz now?" George asked, training his binoculars in the opposite direction. "Can you go and visit it?"

"Oh, a few caretakers," I said. "The trouble with urban renewal, aside from aesthetic considerations . . ."

"Do the harbor cruise boats stop there?" George interrupted, dredging another dime out of his pocket to reactivate the binoculars. "What do you suppose that pink stuff is on the side of the island? Some kind o plant? How come they don't open it to tourists? It would be a great tourist attraction."

"And then there are the damned highway engineers," I said, poking at George until he reluctantly peeked at the Embarcadero Freeway. "Now they're even talking about running a new bridge from here to Marin County,

over the widest part of the Bay."

"Great!" George exclaimed. "What a view that will give you!"

"No, no!" I said. "It will be a disaster. Wreck the looks of the whole north Bay. And think of all those commuters, dumped right into the heart of the city with no place to park!"

But George was callously unconcerned about San Francisco's transportation problems. He headed for the Coit elevator to scrutinize Alcatraz from another angle. While he was upstairs lending support to the binocular business, I stayed in the lobby and looked at the murals that Diego Rivera's California disciples painted under the patronage of the Federal Government in the 1930's. The murals, which I had not seen in many years, were neither as radical nor as interesting as I had remembered. I kept glancing at my watch and wondering whether we would have time to tour the urban renewal areas of Oakland before the evening traffic congealed on the approaches to the bridge.

It developed that George had a positive loathing for urban renewal projects; and he laughed so hilariously at the idea of visiting Oakland that I had to remind him pretty coldly that Jack London, Joaquin Miller, and I had been proud to call Oakland home.

"All right, but what about the cable cars?" George said. "What about the Japanese Tea Garden? Aren't we going to see the Japanese Tea Garden? What about Chinatown?"

I sighed, smiled indulgently, and reached for the guidebook in George's hand. For the rest of the afternoon, we followed the Forty-Nine-Mile Scenic Drive. We stopped at the Marina Green, the Palace of Fine Arts, the Presidio Officers' Club, and the Cliff House. George spent fifty cents on binoculars aimed at Seal Rocks. At sundown, chased eastward by tendrils of incoming fog, we rushed downtown again (by way of Golden Gate Park) and took an elevator to the Top of the Mark. We sat on the Alcatraz side.

My capitulation was complete. We ate dinner at a restaurant on Van Ness Avenue where they pushed roast beef around in a cart, and George had his second baked potato of the day, with sour cream and chives. Afterward, we did *not* go to the Fillmore Auditorium, which is locally celebrated for its loud noises, swirling lights, and rampant hair. George preferred the classic entertainment of North Beach, which he had read about in *Playboy*.

"The Silicon Surprise?" I said. "Never heard of her."

We did find, however, a Topless Girls' Volleyball Team. Their athletic ability was not striking.

I was afraid George was getting a terrible impression of San Francisco. Sure enough, when I asked him how he liked the city, he narrowed his eyes and said: "You want me to speak frankly?"

I squared my chin and tried to smile.

"It's a lovely city," George said. "But I get the feeling you're all living in the past. Nostalgia. Self-love. Myth-making. Not getting your teeth into the issues of today, if you know what I mean. It's a kind of wonderful, never-never land, cut off from reality. You see what I mean?"

I told him I had a rough idea. □

CHAPTER XIX

A Night in Chinatown

1877: Dark Alleys, Opium Dens, and Dancing Acrobats with Horns

BRIGHT WITH GASLIGHT from a thousand windows, noisy with rolling carriages on the cobblestone pavement, and swarming with idlers almost as numerous as at high noon, Kearny Street at 9 P.M. is a gayer sight than ever New York can show. Turn the corner of Washington Street — past the Plaza, and the gray, old house from whose window the first victim of the Vigilantes swung in 1851, and a pall of darkness appears to drop upon us. The noise of wheels dies away; the quick-footed, jostling crowd vanishes; and in its place, a dark phantom or two slides past us in the darkness, creeping close to the gloomy walls of the unlighted houses. One more turn into Dupont Street, and here, just a block away from the gaslit gaiety of Vanity Fair, lies the dark labyrinth of Chinatown.

It is a long, narrow street — so narrow that only two people can walk abreast on the rickety, uneven wooden sidewalks. It is very dark, for scarcely a street lamp can be seen dotting its entire length; and from the small shop windows (and every ground floor window in Chinatown comes under that denomination) glimmers only the feeblest light, thrown from queer, tumbler-shaped lamps in which a long, coiled wick — the stalk of some imported Chinese weed — floats in dark, ill-smelling oil.

The crowd is as silent, as stealthy, and as melancholy as a company of ghosts. Up and down they go, their cork-soled slippers making no sound on the plank walk: dusky specters in baggy, dark blue and plum-colored clothes, with low-crowned black hats pushed back from their listless moon-shaped faces and long, slim pigtails switching like whiplashes down their backs; old men with wizened, saffron-colored faces and big, round spectacles that give them the look of aged, half-human owls; young men, placid and smooth as infants; and boys that look scarcely younger than the men.

Here and there a tiny, childish figure in wider, baggier, shorter garments than the rest toddles by on little wooden pattens; and if it should turn in the direction of the light, you see the face of a woman, white and

pink with paint, and framed in stiff, wing-shaped puffs of hair shot through with bright, gold pins. But these figures are rare; the crowd is essentially masculine, and the stray woman is quickly lost to sight, swallowed up in the blacker darkness of some blind alley.

The Royal China Theater on Jackson Street has a long, narrow entry, bare and unpainted, but brightly lighted, leading back into the house. At the threshold sits a vendor of fruit and confections, whose little wooden stand is spread with saucers of black-looking sweetmeat, broken sections of coconut, plates of salted almonds, bunches of cherries, stalks of sugarcane, and smooth, white slices of betel nut, wrapped up cornucopia-wise in a green leaf and held at the end with a daub of red paint.

The vendor never turns his eyes to look at us as we pass in. American visitors are no novelty at the Royal China Theater, for this is one of the standard "shows" of Chinatown. Of the two theaters, it is decidedly the favorite; and if it cannot be strictly called the most fashionable, it is certainly the largest and best. Its hours of performance are from 8 P.M. until 4 A.M. The prices of admission to its native patrons vary from two to one bit, according to the lateness of the hour, but Caucasian visitors are charged fifty cents.

Inside is the barest skeleton of a theater — unpainted, undecorated, comfortless, and gloomy. There is a single gallery for women, who are not allowed on the floor of the house; rows of hard wooden benches, dark and slippery with age and dirt; and, as a stage, a mere raised platform connecting by two little flights of steps with the pit. There are neither "wings" nor "flies," curtain nor orchestra — nothing but the bare, boarded platform with two little doors at the back, shaded by scant curtains, and the musicians sitting in a row against the wall.

The auditorium is closely packed with dingy blue blouses and black felt hats; the air is dim with smoke and heavy with that peculiar odor inseparable from Chinatown. Upstairs, the women are crowded together

—more dingy, dark blue sacks and, instead of the felt hats, shiny black pates glistening with gold pins. Through the narrow aisles moves a vendor of sugar-cane and oranges, with his bamboo tray poised on his head; but he utters no sound, only strolls apathetically up and down, glancing about in search of customers with his dreamy, slant eyes under the shadow of the tray.

These are the spectators. As for the actors, they are like nothing in the world but a Chinese nightmare. The first thing you perceive is the noise, and for the first few minutes every other sense is nullified by the agony that smites your sense of hearing. The sound proceeds from the men who sit at the back of the stage, with bland, infantile faces addressed to the audience, banging upon brass gongs, pounding cymbals, belaboring little three-legged drums, scraping madly and monotonously upon Chinese fiddles, and extracting the concentrated din of pandemonium from mysterious instruments without name. There are no words in any European language to describe this unearthly racket; but it evidently tickles the ears of its Oriental listeners, for it never ceases, never abates one fraction of its violence. Men may come and men may go, but from eight until four it rages relentlessly.

The performance is partly in pantomime; but occasionally there is an accession of agony when all the actors burst forth into high-pitched, falsetto shrieks and storm at each other with seesawing inflections of

BRUSHING UP FOR THE THEATRE.

A PERFORMANCE AT THE ROYAL CHINA THEATRE.

183

AN ALL-NIGHT SUPPER IN THE DRESSING ROOM OF THE ROYAL CHINA THEATRE.

the voice. In and out of the two little curtained doors rush streams of grotesque figures, hideous in half-human masks, bearded, horned, blotched with black and scarlet paint and gilding, costumed in flowered and embroidered robes, jeweled breastplates, and flashing scimitars, with peacock's feathers nodding over their heads and clusters of gay flags flapping at their shoulders like wings — tricked out of all likeness to men by every ingeniously grotesque device of form and color that the fantastic Chinese mind can conceive.

There is a battle raging on the stage, and the God of War himself, more terrible than all the rest with paint and tinsel and flags, a great black beard half way to his knees, and two pheasant's feathers four feet long arching out from his helmet, comes prancing and stamping out, screaming at the highest, grating pitch of his voice; and he performs a pirouette on one leg exactly in the center of the stage. After him rush a body of warriors, naked to the waist, with queer, horned head-pieces, and spears in their hands, who follow in single file, whirl in like manner upon one leg apiece, and then, having dismounted in this easy manner from imaginary steeds, fall to fighting.

Suddenly, in the strangest way, the fighting merges into lofty tumbling. The half-naked warriors chase each other round and round the stage, throwing double and triple somersaults high in the air, forward and

backward, alighting on their feet, on their hands, and flat on their backs with their feet stretched out straight and their arms close on their sides. Reinforcements rush out — more men, stripped to the waist, bare-armed and barefooted, with a single, hornlike unicorn sprouting from their foreheads and their noses painted a staring white. One huge, fat man, without a perceptible bone or muscle in his body, stands on his head, walks on his hands, on his elbows — anyhow but on his feet — ties himself into horrible knots, leaps backward over piled-up chairs and tables, throws himself into the air rolled up like a ball, does everything but turn himself inside out, and retires, bland and expressionless, amid a storm of applause from our small party of Caucasians, which causes all the almond-eyes to look askance at us and a faint smile of contempt to cross a few of the placid faces.

Behind the scenes, the actors and acrobats make merry over a supper in their dressing room — a spread of roast pig, rice, tea, and Chinese sweetmeats, ranged on a great, clumsy table of black teak, with smoking joss sticks and red and yellow candles burning around and great globe lanterns swinging overhead. Downstairs, in a dark, bricked kitchen, others of the dramatic corps take turns at cooking mysterious native messes amid dense, greasy vapors and smells even more uncanny than those which salute our noses above.

184

AN ITINERANT FORTUNE-TELLER AND HIS MYSTERIOUS APPARATUS.

Face for Sale

Outside, we jostle the rickety table where a fortune-teller has established himself and his mystic apparatus. A dried-up old man, with huge, round spectacles and the ghost of a pigtail struggling out under his black silk skullcap, sits juggling small coins, tossing them into the air, and, as they fall, reading off the characters they cover on a great sheet of paper spread out before him. He is unfolding the future to a meager countryman of the lowest caste.

At the back is a woman in gala dress, a bright patch of color that seems to catch all the sunshine in the narrow, dark street. Her hair, stiffened with gum, stands out in two oval wings on either side of her pale olive face; two long gold pins flash through it, and in her ears swing double hoops of gold and light green jade. Her blouse is apple green silk with a border of black satin, and her wide, baggy trousers are a brilliant pink. On her plump arms are jade bracelets, and circlets of jade clasp her bare ankles above the tiny, black cloth slippers with their inch-thick soles. Behind this luminous figure are great banners of colored paper; an old, weather-beaten, wooden house front with patches of red paper plastered over it as if to cover the scars of time; and the somber figures of men in dark blouses.

185

"Have Smoke?"

From the theater to the opium den is but a short step in Chinatown. We follow our guide blindly through a network of black passages and grope our way after the glimmering star of his little candle-end. Turning a corner, we come suddenly upon a dimly lighted window, breast-high from the ground. He pushes open a low, battered door and straightaway we are standing in the Chinaman's paradise.

Such a close, stifling den it is! Eight or ten feet square, barely high enough for a tall man to stand in, with every inch of its whitewashed ceiling and roughly boarded walls blackened with smoke and greasy with dirt. Strips of red paper — Chinese prayers — are pasted about, but that is the only decoration. Around three sides of the wall runs a narrow shelf, scantily covered with ragged matting, upon which the smokers lie with heads and feet together like sardines in a box. Some have their blouses rolled up for pillows; some use blocks of wood or bundles of rags. Under the shelf are rough bunks, each holding one or sometimes two men, coiled up in the smallest possible space. In the middle of the den a single lamp throws a disk of sickly light upon the table. All the corners are in black shadow, made dimmer by the blue smoke which hangs heavily in the air.

The only smoker who seems in full possession of his senses is a big, powerful Chinaman spotlessly dressed in a clean white shirt, with his pigtail coiled up like a smooth black snake and his head resting comfortably on the neat roll of his dark blouse. Beside him is the opium smoker's apparatus: the square tray, glass lamp, and tiny horn box filled with opium paste. In his mouth is the long bamboo stem, with its curious stone bowl screwed half-way up, which he holds in his long, listless, thin fingers; the other hand, looking like carved, yellow ivory in the lamplight, is busy working the lump of opium into the bowl at the end of a long wire. He glances up at us with twinkling eyes but never moves the pipe from his lips nor stops the mechanical motion of his right hand.

"Why do you smoke that horrible stuff?" asks one visitor. He simply looks at her and gives a short laugh.

"Have smoke?" he says politely, taking a fresh lump of opium from the little box and holding it to the candle-flame for an instant.

But the lady declines and forever afterward regrets that she did so.

Our friend laughs again — a contemptuous, compassionate laugh — and applies himself to his pipe. In half an hour he will have sunk into the trance; and, with his pipe fallen from his lips and his body lying like an insensate log, will be reveling in bowers of bliss, embraced by almond-eyed houris and lulled by a Chinese orchestra.

All of Chinatown is encompassed within the eight or nine blocks of Dupont Street and the network of alleys branching out from that main stem. At high noon, as at midnight, these narrow streets are crowded with men, while in the alleys women flit to and fro or lean over the crazy wooden balconies that cling, all awry, to the decaying housefronts. From nearly all these balconies hang scraps of colored scarfs or gilt paper. Strips of red paper, scrawled with Chinese characters, are pasted about every door; and over the lintels are

THE CHINAMAN'S PARADISE ON KEARNEY STREET, A FAVORITE HAUNT OF OPIUM-SMOKERS.

fastened bundles of joss sticks, sending up thin, blue smoke and the odor of sandalwood to scare away the devil and his emissaries.

The little shop windows are crammed full of the strangest articles, huddled together with no attempt at display: opium pipes, bracelets of green jade, shoes, teapots, queer little embroidered bags like tobacco pouches, gold and silver earrings, and paintings like long strips of wallpaper, sold by the yard. The provision stores have a distinct smell, never to be effaced from the recollection—a smell of brine, rancid lard, and pork that has been kept, say, a month too long; fish, dried, salted, and fresh; ducks split down the middle and flattened out like a sheet of paper, looking as though preserved in oil for a half-century or so; leeks and other green vegetables; halves and quarters of roasted pork; dried herbs; and platters of square cheeses, or what look to be cheeses, of the brightest mustard color. □

The Happy Computer

Here is a tiny, dark den with two little windows whose sole ornaments are some gold and silver wares and a chubby-faced, laughing-eyed little Chinese, whose long, slim fingers are flying over a square tray, where he seems to be playing some inexplicable Chinese game. He looks up and laughs so enticingly that we all turn without more ado into the shop. There are five or six men behind the two narrow counters, one of whom, an ancient, shriveled, but excessively beaming Chinaman, we take to be the proprietor, Mr. Tie Lang Tong. Our little friend in the window, who receives us with a shower of nods and smiles and "How are you's?" is apparently the bookkeeper, at this moment engaged in casting up the accounts of the day.

With inexhaustible good humor he proceeds to show us the process. Across his little square tray are stretched a number of wires, each strung with large round beads representing units, tens, and so on. Running over these like a keyboard, slipping them this way and that, he balances his accounts without pen or ink. All this he explains in the prettiest broken English imaginable, with a perpetual laugh in his bright little black eyes. His name is Lee Yip. He is 17 and has a wife in China, where he intends to rejoin her as soon as he has made enough money. He shows us his thin, smooth, brown hand with its long pointed nails, proof of his being "high caste." Then he writes his autograph for each of the feminine members of the party — or rather, paints it with a brush on a strip of red paper; and then we make him show us his assortment of silver bracelets, tongue-scrapers, tweezers, probes for the ears, ring-shaped thimbles, and broad hoop earrings, or "eelings," as he calls them. He talks to us all the while with the air of a painstaking and gracious host; and before we leave San Francisco we go several times back to the shop of Mr. Tie Lang Tong and his laughing-eyed bookkeeper, Lee Yip.*

1967: Some Discordant Notes On the Flower Drum

LIKE MOST SAN FRANCISCANS, I get to Chinatown every week or so, sometimes more often. It is the best place in the city to stock up on dried sea horses, ivory back scratchers, mahjong sets, and other household necessities, and there are innumerable small, Cantonese restaurants on Washington and Jackson streets where you can gorge on snow peas, chicken with almonds, fried rice, and black mushrooms for a couple of dollars. I can (and usually do) supply friends from out-of-town with the names of a dozen Chinese cafes, bars, nightclubs, and souvenir shops virtually unknown to non-Orientals except me; and I can say "Happy New Year" in Cantonese. In short, I have dangerously little knowledge of Chinatown. Bearing this in mind, I took a day off to recuperate from the Night Mail and

then went over to Chinatown to look at it with the clear eyes of a tourist.

The Chinese, as any stranger can see, are the most influential and popular people in San Francisco. All along Grant Avenue, Caucasians wander night and day in silent homage. A Democratic club from Russian Hill was having a cocktail party at the Kuo Wah Restaurant, and ruddy, blond statesmen kept rushing out to greet small, dark, sleek-haired men and draw them inside, firmly gripped by the elbow. Conventioneers with badges on their breasts were trampling one another in their eagerness to buy kimonos, teapots, teakwood screens and puzzle boxes; and what looked like an entire college student body was trying to crowd through the door of a night club called Dragon-a-Go-Go.

This Sinomania is a form of compensation. For more than half a century, the Chinese were grossly mistreated and misunderstood in California. There was legislation to prevent their staking claims in the gold fields. They were forbidden to organize unions, forbidden to bring suit or give testimony in court, forbidden to become citizens. But they were not forbidden to work. The Central Pacific Railroad imported thousands of coolies to lay the transcontinental track; then, when the work was over and the Chinese drifted to San Francisco in search of jobs, they were blamed for causing unemployment, for turning poor Irish lads into hoodlums, for living on little and laboring much, for being abstemious, thrifty and, worst of all, stubbornly different. The police, with their usual solicitude for constitutional rights, would snip off the queue of any Chinese who happened to be arrested; and the Board of Supervisors passed an unusually repulsive ordinance that made it almost impossible for a Chinese to own property or do business in San Francisco.

All this vicious nonsense happily has been forgotten and forgiven now, at least by the white folk. The photographs of Arnold Genthe, the watercolors of Dong Kingman, the prose of Charles Caldwell Dobie and Jade Snow Wong have revealed to the Occident the elusive charms of the Chinese; and San Francisco has taken gleeful possession of its own Far Eastern Disneyland, complete with pretty little inhabitants who serve tea and fortune cookies, peddle joss sticks, and provide evocative background material for newspaper columns and Chamber of Commerce brochures.

Every night, the tour bus rumbles along Grant Avenue, and no guide fails to mention the dear, dead days of the Old Chinatown, with its opium dens, tong wars, lotus feet, all-night theatricals, and child prostitutes, shivering in gilded cages. Chinatown is San Francisco's most adorable historic treasure, and the Chinese—well, it is hard to overpraise their diligence, their studiousness, their pride of family, their passive courage. In fact, the virtues of the Chinese are rather frequently served up to the Negro race as an instructive example, and many good-hearted San Franciscans are surprised that Negroes regard the lesson as irrelevant, not to say ambiguous.

The trouble is that Chinatown, this adorable enclave of racial segregation, is a slum. It has the most alarming incidence of tuberculosis, the worst congestion, the poorest labor conditions, and the highest suicide rate in San Francisco. Immigrant couples from Hong Kong sometimes work 135 hours a week to make $125. The Chinese are welcomed everywhere in the city as students, social acquaintances, political allies, and PTA ladies, but they are not equally welcomed as neighbors, club members, and employees. Although they are six per cent of the city's population, they never have enjoyed much political representation. Last year, San Francisco had only one Chinese fireman (out of 1,635), two Chinese police patrolmen (out of 1,722), and no Chinese sheriff's deputies (out of 155).

While I was walking along Grant Avenue, I encountered a Chinese lawyer I know. He was on his way to the Democratic cocktail party, smiling mysteriously in anticipation of fried Won ton, sweet-sour spareribs and a martini on the rocks. I told him I was trying to see Chinatown through a visitor's eyes and was getting visions as through a glass darkly.

"A bourbon and soda," he said helpfully, steering us toward the Kuo Wah.

But I raved on about my somber doubts. Why should there be a Chinatown, a sort of extraterritorial enclave, within which poverty and exploitation were permitted to exist on the comfortable assumption that "the Chinese take care of their own"? Couldn't the culture of the Chinese be preserved without packing everybody into a smelly ghetto?

"Write anything you like against Chinatown," the lawyer said airily, "just as long as you say we are energetic, well-disciplined, dignified, modest, witty, etcetera, etcetera. And be sure to mention the beautiful girls."

And he marched on, briskly, crisply, in his Brooks Brothers suit and his Nettleton shoes.

"Don't forget," he called back. "We also are inscrutable." □

CHAPTER XX

Barons and Bounders

1877: Stanford, Sharon, and "Lucky" Baldwin—and Accessible Ladies with Names on Their Doors

WE RECEIVED A PLEASANT CALL from Mr. A. J. Bryant,[1] the Mayor of San Francisco, a most genial gentleman with the frankest and most honest of blue eyes and a mouth and teeth just formed for gracious and contagious mirth.

He had brought his horses, and presently he took us out to see the new City Hall,[2] which will not be finished for about three years. It is of brick, and they claim that it will be the strongest, most perfect structure of the kind ever erected and will outlast any public building in the country.

We went on the workmen's elevator to the roof and saw tantalizing glimpses of a magnificent view partially hidden by the summer fog, which, as usual, rested soft and gray and fleecy upon the bay. The wind blew a gale, but it was so fresh and warm that one forgave its rude toying.

Later in the day we took a Market Street car for the Mission Dolores—the nest egg, so to speak, of San Francisco. It was built in 1776 by the Franciscans, but the original adobe building has been restored almost to annihilation. One passes through a little wooden gateway into the graveyard, a wild and tangled place overgrown with ivy and myrtle. Each grave is sheltered in its own little picket fence with a high board at the end like the headboard of a bedstead. We left the sunshine and entered the church, where a century's gloom and damp seemed centralized. One aisle divided the rows of uncushioned benches, and the floor was bare and worn by the feet of those who now filled the neglected graveyard. The main altar was rather bare and tawdry, and at each side of the chancel was a shrine containing statues of saints, not badly executed. The altars are decaying, the gilding tarnished, and the paint dingy; but there were many little bouquets at every shrine, and the smell of roses was as heavy and sweet as incense.

By way of severe contrast, we went that evening to Baldwin's Theatre. It is really the prettiest to be seen in any part of the world—a perfect little gem, fitted up like a *bonbonnière* in crimson satin and gold.

Mr. E. J. Baldwin[3] later invited us to go over to the hotel connected with the theater and likewise bearing his name. It is not quite complete, but has been open for visitors for a couple of months and is a most admirable house. We viewed improvements such as a revolving post office, with boxes arranged in a cylinder; a chronometer which regulates the sixty clocks of the hotel; an apparatus for gauging the heat of each apartment, another for reporting the movements of the bellboys; and an elevator for sending up parcels to each floor. The parlors were unfurnished, but we could admire their graceful proportions and elaborate frescoing. The private apartments were charming, finished in black walnut and furnished in crimson velvet and gray satin, with fine, large bathrooms rich in hooks and shelves. The upper floor, or sixth story, furnished in light California wood, is devoted to bachelor apartments where smoking is *not* forbidden!

The theater connects with the hotel, and two minutes before each act the prompter touches a bell that rings in the bar. Thirsty souls may appease the pangs of drought with no danger of losing any part of the play. Altogether, Mr. Baldwin's hotel,[4] like his theater, is quite the model building of its class in this, our model country.

The steep hill-streets of San Francisco are adorned with handsome residences. Many are perfect palaces, built of wood and ornate to excess. The late William Ralston's city house is a huge caravanserai, absolutely without beauty, the grounds a mere waste of weeds and rubbish. Most of these places, indeed, fall short in grounds; everything looks crude and unfinished to Eastern eyes.

Two fine houses are in process of building by Mr. Mark Hopkins[5] and Mr. Charles Crocker. On the estate of the latter stood a small cottage which he wished to purchase and take down, but the owner refused to sell under some fabulous price. Mr. Crocker, declining to be imposed upon, has instead built a high frame wall around three sides of the cottage, completely shutting it out from his view and from viewing. The proprietor threatens to erect a Chinese laundry on the roof of his house in revenge.[6]

We dined at the home of ex-Governor Leland Stanford, the most magnificent house on this Continent. It covers an entire block at the corner of Powell and California Streets, and its appointments are simply pala-

VIEW OF BALDWIN'S HOTEL AND THEATRE.

Lucky's Place

The Baldwin Hotel is located at Market, Powell, and Ellis Streets. A leading feature is its roof, which affords a most picturesque and complete panorama of San Francisco. It is enclosed by a pretty iron railing such as is used for public parks. In every direction are walks festooned with flowers twining themselves gracefully around antique urns. In the cool of the afternoon, ladies may resort to a charming nook, "The Ladies' Reading Room," with their needle or fancy work, crocheting, books, papers, games, etc., and amid the perfume of the flowers will often lose themselves in slumber. There are stationed on the roof fourteen large tanks, containing upward of eighty-two thousand gallons of water. The precautions against fire seem almost complete.

Mr. Baldwin, the owner and founder, is a man of a pleasing, courteous, and affable nature, but with a self-reliant, tenacious will that makes circumstances bow to him, not him to them. His success is well known. We have often known him as "Lucky Baldwin." It seems that some more honorable appellation than this is due him. He has laid his course upon principles, and he defends them, regardless of what consequences stare him in the face. That is the secret of his success.

BAR-ROOM OF THE BALDWIN HOTEL.

191

Leland's Place

From the windows of the magnificent Leland Stanford mansion in San Francisco, there is a varied view of land and water extending from the coast range to the Pacific, and from Angel Island southward, until the landscape fades away in the hazy distance. The building, which is in the Italian style of architecture, has a width, east and west, of 155 feet, and a depth of 130 feet. Without counting a number of apartments of small size, there are sixty elegant rooms in the dwelling. An elaborate portico, 50 by 14 feet, is reached from Powell Street by a flight of thirty broad, marble steps and is illumined by gaslamps surmounting massive posts.

Passing through the vestibule, the guest enters the grand hall. Corinthian columns of red Aberdeen granite flank the entrance. Blue is the prevailing color; Florentine, the style; and a heavy gilt cornice, the marginal relief and setting. Tasteful allegorical representations of Peace and Plenty are shown in beautiful colors, and the Latin legend, Pax Vobis, stands out in bold characters.

At the farther end of the hall rises a solid mahogany staircase with balusters in imitation of antique vases and the most elaborate newel post ever made in the United States.

The rotunda is octagonal and opens through a circular well 25 feet in diameter to the roof. In each corner is a lofty mirror, flanked by double columns of red granite 12 feet high and a foot in diameter— 16 in all. Huge sliding doors of mahogany, ebony, and mirrors open on one side into the library and on the other into the music room and art gallery, two of the largest rooms in the house.

The dining room is in the southwest corner. It has two immense bow windows and a pleasant outlook over the southern part of the city and the bay. It is about 50 by 30 feet. The woodwork is French and American walnut, with rosewood and ash-root sinkage; the buffet, in the same combination of woods, is the largest ever made in this country. The butler's pantry adjoining is finished with light-colored woods and has all the modern improvements, including an electric annunciator, burglar alarm and plate warmer. The furniture of the dining room, which is made to match the ceiling, is covered with a richly brocaded stuff not often seen in house furnishing.

North of the dining room are the art gallery and music room in the style of Louis Seize. The wallpaper is of garnet-colored floss velvet of a deep, rich hue. The ceilings are finished in soft, harmonious colors to avoid unpleasant interference with the pictures on the walls. The apartment devoted to art is decorated with heads of Rubens, Raphael, Van Dyck and Michelangelo, painted in medallion. The other portion of the room has music trophies and medallion heads of Beethoven and Mozart.

The sleeping, billiard, family, and reception rooms and library are furnished with corresponding liberality, nearly all having distinctive names.

Governor Stanford appears to be utterly devoid of the selfish element, and his friends in all parts of the world acknowledge him to be unequaled in the princely character of his entertainments.

tial. One drawing room is furnished in Pompeian style from designs which were the joint work of its tasteful mistress and her friend Miss Harriet Hosmer, the sculptress of whom America is so proud. The dining room is as superb as it is spacious, and nothing that taste could suggest or wealth provide is here wanting. The sleeping and dressing rooms are luxurious, dainty, magnificent, and the picture gallery is a worthy home for its choice paintings and statuary.

The dinner was superb, the thirty guests well selected and harmonized, the hostess a tall, stately woman with regal manners, fitly borne out by her costume of crimson velvet, softened with rare old lace and embellished by a magnificent *parure* of diamonds and glowing opals. Her unmarried sister,[7] who aided her, is a charming lady, genial and courtly of manner; but the pet of the house is a splendid boy, some ten years of age, the only child of parents who waited nineteen years for his arrival. The little fellow was presented after dinner and charmed us by his graceful manners. He has great artistic talents, all carefully fostered under the charge of his adoring mother. On a subsequent occasion, Mrs. Stanford took us to see the boy's apartments. They consist of study, music, and play rooms, bathroom, dressing room, and bedroom, all fit for a prince — or better, for the splendid American boy whose manhood should be the perfection of our race, so nurtured and protected.[8]

We gladly accepted an invitation from Senator [William] Sharon to pass some days at his country house, Belmont, a name intimately associated with that of its late master, William A. Ralston, whose life and death form one of the extraordinary episodes of San Francisco history. Through Ralston, hundreds of persons fell from affluence to penury; yet those very persons spoke of his death with tears in their eyes, as of a public loss and misfortune.

Ralston, the Napoleon of speculators, rose from small beginnings to the position of banker and broker before he was thirty years old. During the Civil War he managed the business of his firm so successfully that his correspondents in New York urged him to move to the East and consolidate his business with theirs.

"No," said Ralston, "we have made our money in California, and if it is the nucleus of a business that shall bring credit and advantage to the city where it is established, that city shall be San Francisco, and the men who profit by it shall be San Franciscans."

That sentence was the keynote of his subsequent career. The millions he lavished upon business undertakings, palatial residences, or hospitality were all expended at home; the money passing into his hands from hundreds of wealthy and confiding fellow citizens passed through to thousands of other fellow citizens who lived by Ralston and adored him.

As president of the Bank of California, Ralston found ample opportunities for fostering the prosperity of his adopted state, and used them grandly and fearlessly. It was in these days that he built Belmont, a palace costing $1,500,000, standing in the midst of two hundred acres of pleasure grounds.

It was no uncommon thing in the days of Belmont's glory for its master to engage a special train of cars,

fill it with guests, a band of music, flowers, and all that could add to the sumptuousness of a banquet, and make a sort of royal progress to his palace to spend a night and day of feasting and merriment. Abstemious and frugal in his own habits, he never wearied of heaping attentions upon his guests; and the story of his sending $10,000 to a man who in his early days had lent him $500 is but one of a score of similar anecdotes lovingly told today.

It was at the very height of his splendor that the crash came. The Bank of California suspended payment. While the city, state, and financial country stood aghast, the management summoned Ralston, in whom they had reposed the blindest confidence, for an explanation. He had none to offer, but he offered his princely fortune to throw into the gulf. The sacrifice was accepted, and Ralston was removed from his managerial position. He acquiesced in this decision, spoke bravely and collectedly of the future and then — driving alone to North Beach — went into the water to bathe and was brought to the shore a little later a corpse.

Some men gave an ugly name to this death; others, more charitable, called it an accident. Who shall decide?

Senator Sharon was his friend and partner. Together they built the Palace Hotel, costing $6,000,000. In addition to his share of that property ($4,000,000), Ralston was, at the time of his death, building a million-dollar private residence on Pine Street, carrying a million or more in the Grand Hotel, supporting several manufacturing companies, and keeping the credit of the Bank of California to a $10,000,000 standard when it was really nothing but an insolvent shell. He died owing $16,000,000, and it is impossible to say what the real height of his fluctuating fortune ever was.

The public excitement at his death was intense. Bankrupt men stood crying in the street — not that they were ruined, but that Ralston was dead; the garb or badge of mourning was everywhere displayed; flags in the harbor drooped at half mast; bells tolled; business was suspended; great meetings of Ralston's friends collected to pay him every honor that the dead can receive. The funeral procession was four miles long, and when its head reached the grave, the rear had not yet stirred from Calvary Church, where the obsequies took place.

Belmont[9] lies twenty-five miles south of San Francisco and is reached by an hour's ride over flat, uninteresting country, cut up into fields and market gardens, irrigated by ditches, and cultivated by bare-legged Chinamen. Every house has its water tank, with a whirling mill to fill it; and the scene is quite Dutch, in spite of the Chinese in the foreground and the mountains in the distance.

There is a pretty little station at Belmont, built by Ralston for his own accommodation; but we left the train at San Mateo, where Senator Sharon's four-in-hand and other carriages were waiting for our party.

The scent and feeling of the soft air, lazily drifting across our faces, was delicious. We drove through the grounds of several private houses, as is the friendly custom here, and noticed that they are not as precisely laid out as in the East. The live oak is the principal tree, and many of the trunks are massed with ivy climbing riotously up the stem and waving green tendrils from the upper branches. The wonderful eucalyptus also abounds, and cypress, palm, and olive; while roses blossom upon trees fifteen or twenty feet high.

At sunset we drove into the precincts of Belmont, passing a large pleasure ground known as Belmont Park, the favorite picnic spot of the Italians of San Francisco. The carriages passed slowly between rows of tulip trees, catalpas, magnolias; and, as we neared the house, a lower growth of feathery pepper trees, laden with dull red berries; hedges of geranium and roses; trellises of passion flowers and stephanotis. The great house, made of wood and painted white, is not perhaps so imposing as one is led to expect from so magnificent an approach; but like Oriental mansions, it reserves its wonders for those so happy as to enter.

Driving under a *porte cochère* covered with climbing yellow roses, we entered what seemed like the disordered vision of an architect. Beyond saying that there is a pervading effect of lightness, brightness, airiness, cool repose, luxury, and comfort, it is all but impossible to give any idea of this delightful house.

In the first place, there are no doors throughout the first story. A wide corridor, once a piazza, runs around three sides, its floor of native woods polished like a mirror. Cane and bamboo chairs, Chinese settees, inlaid tables, and tall vases of flowers furnish this gallery. French windows open to the parlor, dining, billiard, and drawing rooms, while at the left lies a superb music and dancing room, lighted by day through a glass dome and at night by elaborate chandeliers of silver and crystal. The furniture is Chinese — light, elegant,

and curious. The great dining and billiard rooms have waxed floors, but the parlor, in which a bright, cheery fire was burning, is a cozy little carpeted room with some fine bronzes, a wonderful Chinese center table, and some Indian armchairs of carved wood, big enough for three people. In the center of the house is a square hall upon which all these rooms open. Here stands a tall, old-fashioned clock such as was familiar to some of us in our childish visits to our grandparents, with the sun and moon beaming jollily from its dial, and on a pedestal, a brazen Chinese bowl used as a gong to summon the faithful to dinner.

The numerous bedrooms are spacious and luxurious, with dressing and bathrooms. Every marble bowl is fitted with a plated pipe that supplies a small shower bath for washing the head — a great comfort, especially to gentlemen, in this dry and dusty country.

Before dinner we took a little stroll in the grounds, looking at the stables niched into the side of a hall and spending some time in the fernery, which is really exquisite, with a lovely fountain trickling into a mossy stone basin, grottoes, rock work, and every graceful species of fern. The barbaric tones of the gong summoned us before we had half done with this, and we sat down fourteen at the table which, in Ralston's time, often accommodated a hundred guests.

Mr. Sharon, the friend and partner of the unfortunate Ralston, is a man of wonderful, instinctive appreciation of character, a gift affecting his general manner. Frank and outspoken among those whom he finds congenial, he is chilling to those who impress him unfavorably. He is a man of comprehensive ability, and

BELMONT, THE COUNTRY-SEAT OF THE LATE WILLIAM A. RALSTON.

he has need of it in attending not only to his duties as United States Senator from Nevada, but to the care of his own colossal fortune and domestic duties. But with all of these, he has Byron, Moore, and some of our more modern poets at his fingers' ends and is a vivacious and entertaining conversationalist. His immediate family is made up of two daughters: the younger a pleasant schoolgirl; the elder a fragile, graceful young woman, married to one of the most promising young lawyers of San Francisco, whose sister's marvelous musical talents added greatly to the charm of our stay.[10]

The most distinctive feature of the dining room was a great sideboard of carved, black wood, inset with a large mirror upon which are engraved the numerals of the hours. Two slender, gilded hands steal silently round, and the stately, noiseless motion of the hands across the mirror has a most weird and fascinating effect.

After dinner, we went to the music room to spend the evening in conversation, music (in which our host's son-in-law and his sister are proficient), and dancing. We were also introduced to a novel musical instrument, which, upon being wound up, performs as a full band of instruments.

After breakfast on Sunday morning we again went for a drive. Taking the old San Jose post road through the little town of Redwood, we wound among picturesque foothills and beautiful private grounds.

During the first part of this drive, the air was mild, fragrant, and warm as our New York July; but as we returned through Redwood, the sea wind came in so chill and damp that we were glad to put on the sealskin sacques that had seemed absurdly inappropriate in the morning. Indeed, it is never safe in the neighborhood of San Francisco to leave home for an hour without some substantial wrap, and nothing is more common than for a lady to dress in white muslin or lace, find herself perfectly comfortable for two or three hours, and then hasten to wrap herself in furs or shawls.

As the day of our departure drew near, every member of the party began to make those frantic, futile snatches at the delight they were about to lose.

For our own part, we haunted the Chinese quarter. We visited Lee Yip as usual, and found the shop crowded with customers; and from this favorite haunt we wandered through several little dark alleys, seeing the dirt we had only smelt during our evening expedition. The sidewalks are wide enough for only one person to pass at a time, and the doors of the houses open directly upon them. Each door is provided with a sliding panel at the height of a man's head, and one cannot fail to get a pretty clear idea of the internal economy; in many, however, the view was obstructed by a female face, highly decorated, perfumed, and painted, looking out as we were looking in. Over many of these panel windows, a bunch of joss sticks were slowly burning, although I fear quite as much evil dwelt within as could approach from without.

Just back of Chinatown is the French quarter. We coyly promenaded through several streets of one- and two-storied houses, consisting, as the open window assured us, of little more than a front parlor and a bedroom behind, some of them elegantly furnished. The half-doors are furnished with a little cushioned ledge where the occupant may lean with folded arms to enjoy the outer scenery; while a little silver plate below is engraved with her Christian name only. A glass door within is decorated with lace curtains, and the whole is prettier than the Chinese houses. There are, however, no joss sticks above the doors, no amulets or charms, alas! to avert the evil that stalks through these quarters of the town.

At the very last, we made a sorrowful promenade through some of our favorite haunts: the steep hills that slope up from Kearny Street; the flower stands enclosed in glass and mounted on wheels, filled with bouquets; the brown foothills circling the town; and the heights, crowned with the homes of rival capitalists, which a vivid imagination can readily convert to castles.

As *l'envoi*, I can say no more and no less than this to all the dear public who year by year wander up and down the earth seeking and not always finding delight, and expending money, which by no means always brings its *quid pro quo* of enjoyment. To them, I say, Go West, my friends, Go West! Within the Golden Gate lies all that you desire. Go West! □

1967: From SFO to LAX
By Escalator, Conveyor Belt, and Butterscotch Velocipede

A FEW DAYS after reaching San Francisco on the great transcontinental railroad, I had to make a business trip to Los Angeles. Naturally, I went by plane.

I suppose this scandalous confession is quite out of place in a book devoted lovingly and mournfully to railroad travel. But the truth is, it never occurred to me *not* to fly. Air travel between the two great, rivalrous city-states of the California coast is so incessant, familiar, and effortless that other forms of transportation have almost been forgotten. It is easier — and probably less hazardous — to take a "Commuter Jet" from SFO (San Francisco International Airport) to LAX (Los Angeles International) than it is to ride a municipal bus from the Cliff House to the Ferry Building.

To reach the San Francisco terminal, you drive for three-quarters of an hour through tiers of stuccoed houses, hillsides gouged and layered into yellow ziggurats, and garbage dumps enclosed but not concealed by hedges of blackish-green wattle. You leave your car in an enormous automotive storehouse that professes to be, for the instant, the largest parking garage on earth — an honor that it probably will have relinquished to some other stable by the time these words are in print. From here you continue on foot, with your tape recorder, your toilet kit, your suitcase, your dispatch case, your paperback mystery novel, and your *Wall Street Journal* dangling about you like trophies of economic warfare. The course is marked by a trail of yellow light bulbs on the ceiling. These lead by a labyrinthine route through avenues of Chevrolets and Karmann Ghias to a moving sidewalk, an ascending escalator, an obliging door that opens automatically, and a conveyor belt that whisks away your suitcase.

The only delay occurs when half a dozen pea-green steamer trunks arrive just ahead of you at the conveyor belt. Each trunk is decorated with swirling pink and orange calligraphy that apparently spells "The Butterscotch Velocipede." Four young men in lavender sackcloth trousers and glistening purple sausage curls accompany the baggage. All are en route to LAX.

At the ticket counter, a girl with pearly white lips gives a ghastly smile and says: "You'll have to hurry along, sir." You sprint toward the concourse, circle back to the counter to reclaim your toilet kit, shoulder through a crowd of air force sergeants rioting at the door to the pancake palace, cast a last, despairing glance at the coin-operated machines that sell life insurance, and plunge down a carpeted chute leading into the plane.

Among air travelers it is considered unsporting to look at the outside of an aircraft until you have committed yourself to the flight. After you have strapped yourself to your chair, felt under the seat for hidden bombs, located your Sick Bag, and quickly scanned three out-of-date copies of *Look*, you may lean over and peer out a smeary porthole the size of a dinner plate, through which you can see one of the wings trembling feebly while the plane stands on the runway, making growling noises and shuddering from nose to rudder.

At this point, in the manner of a Victorian novelist, I shall draw a curtain. Behind the curtain I am reading *Look* for the fifth time and breathing deeply and calmly through my nostrils. (I often have told my wife that she would enjoy flying more if she could learn to breathe deeply and calmly through her nostrils, but she assures me that she *already* enjoys flying, except for the takeoff, the landing, and the part when you're up in the air.)

When the curtain discreetly parts, we have lunged forward and upward with a whooshing roar, skimming over the frothy, brick-red salt ponds, the glittering bay, the wandering sloughs. The pilot comes onto the loudspeaker to introduce (on our left) Mount Hamilton and (directly below us) the blotchy banlieues of San Jose. The air fills with cigarette smoke, and there is a handicap race to the lavatory.

I have been told that SFO-LAX is the most heavily traveled air route in the world. This is credible, especially on Friday evening. One of the airlines recently bragged in a newspaper advertisement that it never makes its passengers feel like penned sheep; but it was not this airline. We sit elbow to elbow, handing our *Look* magazines and *Wall Street Journals* to and fro, holding our tape recorders on our laps, while the stewardesses relentlessly deliver coffee from a metal cart that they push along the aisle at frantic speed.

If you are close enough to one of the portholes to see out, you are struck by the dryness, the vastness, the emptiness of the California landscape. On the ground, you get a definite impression that entirely too many people, urged on by the likes of Horace Greeley, Mrs. Frank Leslie, and the All-Year Club of Southern California, have forsaken the East and come west to find their hearts' desires. California shows everywhere the ravages of hasty exploitation, careless technology, and wasteful stewardship. Up in the air, however, you enjoy the comforting illusion that it is still a virgin land. Endless rows of tawny mountains, dotted here and there with little storage lakes and clumps of oaks, roll westward to the sea. It is possible to imagine that you are seeing the desert coastland that enchanted Richard Henry Dana during his two years before the mast: the brown and fogbound margin of New Spain, with its hides and tallow, its orange poppies and white surf.

Inevitably, you are reminded of its beauty and its decadence. How much has vanished or been irremediably spoiled! What will remain in fifty or a hundred years?

Two-thirds of the way to LAX, you pass the bony spires of the Tehachapi Range. Here the nostalgic from San Francisco is expected to wrinkle his nose in anticipation of a repellent encounter with Los Angeles. This sibling rivalry is partly sham, of course, and partly habit. But at its heart there is a fundamental difference of personality. San Francisco is tough, broad-minded, sentimental, mystical, impulsive, self-centered, Latin; Los Angeles is pious, ambitious, grandiose, aggressive, militant, Teutonic. For sixty years — from 1846, when the United States took California, until 1906, when the eminence of San Francisco was shaken with its buildings — the northern city dominated California. San Francisco was the undisputed western terminus of North America; Los Angeles was a cattle town, some orange groves, a spa.

Then, Los Angeles began to grow. For years it was no more than an immense, uncultivated town, eccentric, untidy, and prosaic. In its adolescent awkwardness, it was reviled and persecuted by its older rivals. Its hyperbolic press agents, its movie actresses, its religious cults, its mausoleums, its oil wells, its politics were objects of hilarity from sea to shining sea.

But Los Angeles has changed. The northerner looks down with uneasiness at the long, straight boulevards, the long, low roofs, the parking lots, the shopping centers, the swimming pools — my God! the countless, bean-shaped, palm-girt, sun-drenched, tile-lined, copper-sulphurated, turquoise-and-crystal swimming pools! — and he thinks about the energy and power of Southern California. He feels a terrible, reluctant awe for the Dorothy B. Chandler Music Center, the Art Museum at Hancock Park, the Santa Monica Freeway, Century City, Disneyland. He has a more than slight suspicion that the West has moved from SFO to LAX and that the enormous Southern California basin, writhing in its perpetual beamish haze, is the *real* terminus of the overland route.

For almost an hour we circle above the hidden towers of LAX, waiting for clearance to land in a ground fog that covers the field. I draw a curtain on our landing. The Butterscotch Velocipede precedes us to the waiting room and down the escalator and along the moving sidewalk. LAX is one of the few international airports I have seen that posts signs warning against riding escalators while barefoot; but The Velocipede and I are fully shod.

We wait for our baggage in a breezy loggia at the nether end of a conveyor belt. In a car rental booth across the way, a girl with pearly white lips gives us a ghastly smile. Chevrolets and Karmann Ghias slip past the curb.

I am not yet ready to concede that Los Angeles is, indeed, the new terminus of the West; but I think SFO-LAX might do as a transitional co-terminus. Somewhere in between, the dear wandering public will find the West. If they insist. □

FOOTNOTES

CHAPTER I *(pp. 12–18)*

1. THE WAGNER DRAWING ROOM CAR, designed by New York wagonmaker Webster Wagner (1817-82), went into service on Commodore Vanderbilt's New York Central Railroad in 1867. A few years later, Wagner contracted to use George Pullman's invention, the folding upper berth and hinged seats, on the New York Central. A breach-of-patent dispute developed when Wagner also used the Pullman design on Vanderbilt's Lake Shore and Michigan Southern line. The lawsuit was unsettled when Wagner died — in a train collision on the New York Central.

2. THE ERIE CANAL, a 350-mile barge route between the Hudson River at Albany and Lake Erie at Buffalo, was a major factor in opening the old Northwest to immigration and commercial development after the War of 1812. Completed in 1825 at a cost of $7 million, the canal has been enlarged many times and is now incorporated as the New York State Barge Canal.

CHAPTER II *(pp. 20–25)*

1. CHICAGO had a population of 4100 when its first city charter was drawn in 1837. During the next four decades, it grew more rapidly in population and commercial importance than any other community in the world. By 1857, it had 93,000 inhabitants; by 1870, 300,000. Its name in popular speech was Slabtown, "The Mud Hole of the Prairie," because the houses of the burgeoning city were crude, box-like structures, hastily thrown together of boards or split logs. In 1877, the city covered slightly over 35 square miles. Its area today is more than 226 square miles, its population in excess of 3,500,000.

2. THE CHICAGO FIRE of 1871 began on Sunday evening, October 8, in Patrick O'Leary's cowbarn. It burned for two days, destroying more than $200 million in property; 90,000 persons lost their homes, and 300 died. By 1875, few traces of the disaster remained except the bad reputation of Mrs. O'Leary's cow; which historians have exonerated of blame for starting the conflagration.

3. GRAND PACIFIC HOTEL, located on Jackson, La Salle, Quincy, and Clark streets, had just been completed when it was destroyed by the fire of 1871. Rebuilt at a cost of $1,500,000, the "new" Grand Pacific was six stories tall, had the most up-to-date fireproofing system in Chicago, and proclaimed itself "the most perfect hotel structure in the world and the largest edifice representing private enterprise in the United States." In 1874, a year after the reopening, John B. Drake (best known as the proprietor of the Drake Hotel) bought out the two original operators of the Grand Pacific and soon made the hotel famous for elaborate decor and lavish game dinners. The Michigan Southern Railroad, a Vanderbilt property, also owned a large interest in the hotel.

In 1877, transient rates ranged from $3.50 to $7 for each of the 435 rooms. Breakfast was $1, dinner $1.25, and supper $1. There was an extra charge for burning gas after midnight, and children were under no circumstances to be permitted in the drawing rooms unless accompanied by their parents.

4. TREMONT HOUSE, a four-story brick structure, was the largest building in Chicago in the early 1850's, and like the rest of the business district, it suffered from soil subsidence. Guests entering the lobby had to walk down a flight of wooden steps from street level. In 1855, engineers concluded that the only practicable solution to the mud problem was to raise the entire commercial district of the city 12 feet above the level of the lake by covering it with fresh soil. The proprietors of the Tremont saw no alternative but to tear the building down and start over again. As a last resort, they asked George M. Pullman, a 27-year-old contractor from New York, to inspect the doomed building. Pullman pledged himself to lift the Tremont without disturbing a teaspoon in a coffee cup or breaking a single pane of glass. He employed 1200 workmen and used 5000 jackscrews, placed at regular intervals in the basement. On signal every workman gave the lever of the jackscrew half a turn. The building rose to street level without damage. Pullman, remaining in Chicago, later developed the sleeping car that made his name famous.

5. UNION STOCKYARDS opened Christmas Day, 1865. By 1891, they had a capacity of 40,000 cattle, 200,000 hogs, 25,000 sheep, and 5,000 horses. Swept by fire in 1934, the Stockyards were largely rebuilt and the old Amphitheater was replaced by a new convention hall. The old stone gate and water tower are mementos of the early yards. In recent years, the Stockyards Amphitheater has been used for the annual International Livestock Exposition and for many national political conventions.

6. THE WATER TOWER, a crenellated, limestone castle at the northwest corner of Michigan and Chicago avenues, is the city's most famous historic landmark — the only major structure to survive the 1871 fire. The tower is no longer in use, but a pumping station across the street serves the neighborhood.

7. PERRY H. SMITH (1828-85) was the chief legislative advocate of the Chicago & North Western Railway in its formative years, and his two-hundred-thousand-dollar mansion at Pine and Huron streets was one of Chicago's architectural landmarks. Born in Augusta, New York, Smith learned politics as a lawyer, county judge, assemblyman, and state senator before moving west to Chicago in 1856. He represented a newly formed railway company seeking land grants from the United States government; and when this company became the Chicago & North Western, Smith was installed as vice-president. As confidant of William B. Ogden, the president of C&NW, Smith was virtually the policy director of the railroad, a position he fulfilled with implacable hostility toward the town of Milwaukee and loving solicitude for the interests of Chicago.

8. GEORGE MORTIMER PULLMAN (1831-97), built his first two sleeping cars in 1858 from old day coaches of the Chicago and Alton Line. Makeshift sleepers had been in use for twenty years when Pullman entered the field, but these were ordinary day coaches with bunks built into one side. The beds had mattresses but no sheets, blankets, pillows, or curtains. Passengers slept fully clothed — and badly. For several years after Pullman's more comfortable sleepers went into service, they were poorly patronized. In 1870, fewer than one hundred Pullman cars were in use in the United States. Some Americans considered them effete and snobbish, and many women regarded them as indecent. In 1863, Pullman introduced his first cars on the principle of the hinged upper berth and folding seats. His "Palace on Wheels" cars cost an average of $18,000. By 1881, Pullman shops were producing 114 cars a year, and ten years later the Pullman Palace Car Company had seven thousand employees and operated one thousand sleepers and parlor cars.

9. THE CHICAGO BOARD OF TRADE, organized in 1848, opened its first offices at 101 South Water Street. After several changes of location, it moved in 1865 into the Chamber of Commerce Building at La Salle and Washington streets, where it operated until the 1871 fire. The "new" Chamber of Commerce Building described by the Leslies was built at the same site in 1872. The Board's present building, a 45-story tower at the foot of La Salle Street, was completed in 1930. The Board of Trade now handles 80 per cent of the world's trading in grain futures. Its 1964 dollar volume — $51 billion — was less than that of the New York Stock Exchange ($60 billion) but greater than the volume of most other financial institutions in the United States.

CHAPTER III *(pp. 28–34)*

1. PARMELEE TRANSPORTATION COMPANY was founded in 1853 by Frank Parmelee, a young stagecoach driver and steamship clerk. In partnership with Liberty Bigelow and David Gage, Parmelee contracted to transport passengers and baggage among the separate depots maintained by five railroads entering Chicago. This exclusive contract existed without major challenge for more than a hundred years. Parmelee rigs, painted a distinctive shade of dark green, met all trains. By 1881, ten years after the fire had virtually wiped out his business, Parmelee was operating 75 omnibuses and 75 wagons, owned 250 horses, and employed 130 men. In 1903, Parmelee sold out to a financial syndicate headed by Marshall Field. The following year he died at 88. The Parmelee Transportation Company is now a diversified system with substantial interests in the Yellow Cab Company, and other taxi and bus companies in several cities. Checker Motors Corporation of Kalamazoo, Michigan, owns the controlling interest.

2. THE CHICAGO & NORTH WESTERN RAILWAY CO., third largest in the United States in operating mileage (nearly 10,800 miles), was formed out of the Galena & Chicago Union Railroad (1848) and the Chicago, St. Paul & Fond du Lac Railroad Co. (1855), which consolidated in 1864. For years it was an immensely profitable enterprise. Then, in the 1930's, hounded by depression, drought, and competing forms of transport, the C&NW went into receivership. Reorganized in 1944, the railroad began an extensive program of mechanization and modernization, and discontinued many unprofitable intercity lines.

3. DOM PEDRO II (1825-91), became Emperor of Brazil in 1831, succeeding his father, Pedro I, who had declared the country's independence from Portugal nine years earlier. Noted for his scholarly tastes, Pedro II ruled peacefully until revolution drove him out in 1889.

4. WHEATON COLLEGE was founded in 1853 as Illinois Institute, an orthodox Methodist school "for Christ and His Kingdom." When the college was reorganized under Congregational auspices seven years later, Warren Wheaton, the unusually generous founder of the town who had given the college its original campus, deeded to the college every other lot in town. Renamed for its benefactor, Wheaton today is nondenominational and ranks among the leading liberal arts colleges of Illinois.

5. COLONEL JOHN DIXON, the first white settler in Lee County, opened a trading post, tavern, and ferry on the Rock River in April, 1830. Factories later were attracted by the abundant waterpower, and the town of Dixon became a cement-manufacturing center.

6. THE BLACK HAWK WAR arose from the impact of numerous white settlers on the territory of the Sauk and the Fox Indians along the Rock River in 1828. It resulted in the virtual extermination of both tribes, the opening of northern Illinois to extensive colonization, and the capture of Black Hawk, the courageous and intelligent Sauk chief, whose *Autobiography* is a classic of American aboriginal literature. The tragic war, which ended in 1832, marked the passing of the Indians from Illinois. Black Hawk died in 1838 in Davis County, Iowa.

7. THE MISSOURI RIVER BRIDGE between Council Bluffs, Iowa, and Omaha, Nebraska, was started in 1868 and opened to railroad traffic in 1873. The year before the Leslie excursion, two of its nine 250-foot spans had been carried away by floods and cyclones, and Council Bluffs, which had been on the riverbank, found itself three miles inland from the new riverbed. In August, 1877, the bridge was again partially destroyed. Quickly rebuilt, it was replaced with a new structure in 1887 and again in 1916.

CHAPTER IV   *(pp. 37–41)*

1. OMAHA'S POST OFFICE AND COURTS BUILDING, completed in 1873, was built of freestone transported from Ohio. It was four stories high, fronted on 15th and Dodge streets, and with its furnishings cost $450,000.

2. GEORGE FRANCIS TRAIN, one of the West's quirkiest capitalists, was an enthusiastic land speculator who listed himself in the Omaha City Directory of 1871 as "owner of 5000 lots, a hotel and ten other buildings in Omaha; 1000 lots in Council Bluffs, and 7000 lots and a hotel in Columbus." In 1867, while breakfasting with some friends in the municipally-operated Herndon House, Train noticed that a sudden windstorm had sprung up, and he ordered a Negro waiter to stand against a window to protect the patrons in case the glass broke. When the hotel steward protested this insult "to the Negro race," Train swore angrily that he would build a better hotel of his own within sixty days. His Cozzens House, on the southeast corner of 9th and Harney streets, opened within two months. Train appended the letters N.P.A. to his name, and these were understood to stand for No Party Affiliation or Next President of America. In either case, he ran for President in 1872 as an independent candidate. Jailed at "The Tombs" in New York shortly afterward for distributing obscene literature (namely, certain passages from the Bible), he lost his Omaha real estate —but he already had made and kept several fortunes.

3. MR. GREELEY'S MOTTO, "Go West, young man," has entered the American language and outlives the other writings of Horace Greeley (1811-72), abolitionist editor of the New York *Tribune*. In fact, the phrase originated with John Babson Lane Soule, who used it in an article in the Terre Haute, Indiana, *Express* in 1851. When the saying gained currency through a Greeley editorial, the *Tribune* reprinted Soule's article to show the source of the expression, still attributed to Greeley.

CHAPTER V   *(pp. 44–53)*

1. ARBOR DAY, which originated in Nebraska in 1872, is observed in most states of the Union and in Canada, Australia, and New Zealand as a public occasion for setting out trees. The founder of this institution was J. Sterling Morton, who established squatter's rights on a strip of rich farmland near Nebraska City, overlooking the Missouri River, in 1855. Morton made large experimental plantings of shade trees, evergreens, orchards, and vines, and in 1872, as president of the Nebraska State Board of Agriculture, induced the governor to proclaim a statewide day of tree-planting. In 1885, Arbor Day was declared a legal holiday and the date set at April 22, Morton's birthday. Morton was Secretary of Agriculture in the cabinet of President Grover Cleveland. His fifty-two-room mansion, Arbor Lodge, is a Nebraska state park.

2. FREMONT, NEBRASKA, was founded in 1856 by Pinney, Barnard & Co., a development organization, and named for Col. John C. Frémont, who was then a candidate for President. The first settlers suffered through constant threat of Pawnee attacks, bad crops, and lack of financial credit, and for a time the developers had to sell lots for seventy-five cents each to repay their debts. Immigration and agriculture brought prosperity to the town. It is the county seat of Dodge County and the site of Midland College, a coeducational Lutheran institution.

3. BISON were exterminated so recklessly during the period of white settlement in the Great Plains that the disposal of their corpses was a major problem. It has been estimated that more than thirty million bison perished between 1860 and 1880.

4. SCHUYLER, NEBRASKA, seat of Colfax County, was named — as was the county — for Schuyler Colfax, Vice-President of the United States in 1869, the year the town was laid out. Texas cattle, herded north for the Chicago market, first reached the Union Pacific line at Schuyler.

5. COLUMBUS, NEBRASKA, has continued to outstrip its rival Schuyler (pop. 2,500) and is now a town of about 7,000. Settled ten years before the arrival of the Union Pacific tracks, Columbus became an important supply point. It now has several dozen industrial plants.

6. KEARNEY, NEBRASKA, like nearby Fort Kearney, was named for General Stephen Watts Kearny but eventually adopted the misspelled name that its residents persisted in using. The town was originally called Kearney Junction. At one time, Kearney hoped to become the capital of the United States. Its population in the 1880's and-90's was greater than it is today.

CHAPTER VI   *(pp. 56–61)*

1. ELM CREEK and Overton are still "live" towns, but Stevenson, Josselyn [Joslyn?], and Plum Creek have disappeared from most maps. Plum Creek, a trading post and pony express station on the Oregon Trail, was the scene of a massacre in August, 1864, when Indians overtook a party of Iowans and killed all but one person — Mrs. Frank Morton — whom they held prisoner for five months. After the arrival of the railroad, the Plum Creek settlers moved to the north side of the river and renamed the town Lexington, for the battle in Massachusetts. Elm Creek, settled by a few families in 1873, had a disastrous series of blizzards in the 1880's, lost many of its inhabitants and most of its cattle. In 1906, it was almost wiped out by a fire.

2. MAJOR FRANK NORTH and his brother Captain Luther North enlisted a group of Pawnee Indians in the mid-1860's to oppose various hostile tribes that were attacking settlers on the Nebraska prairie. The "Pawnee Battalion" helped protect construction workers on the Union Pacific line, and the Norths gained national renown as Indian scouts. In 1877, the brothers joined William F. ("Buffalo Bill") Cody in establishing a ranch in the sandhills of Hooker County in western Nebraska, where they worked to suppress cattle-rustling and acted as hosts to many prominent visitors.

3. THE FETTERMAN MASSACRE was a disastrous setback to the U.S. Army's efforts to pacify the Indian country of northern Wyoming. The victims were Brevet Lieutenant Colonel W. J. Fetterman, seventy-nine soldiers, and two civilians, all of whom were dispatched from Fort Phil Kearny (near Sheridan, Wyoming) on December 21, 1866, to aid a wood-gathering party that was reported under attack by Indians. Fetterman, an inexperienced cavalryman who held the Indians in contempt, disobeyed orders and followed a group of fleeing horsemen into an ambush. Lookouts at Fort Phil Kearny lost sight of Fetterman's patrol, then heard rapid rifle fire from beyond a ridge. A second column hurried out and found the bodies of the entire patrol.

4. JULES RENI, also known as Jules Beni, Jules René, Jules Bené, and René Jules, was a surly French Canadian who established a small trading post near the South Platte River in northern Colorado about 1859. "Julesburg" (or "Julesberg") became a rendezvous of adventurers and desperadoes as well as a station for the overland stage. Reni, the station manager, reputedly was also the leader of a band of white and Indian marauders who preyed on the stage line. Restless with this type of management, the stage company replaced Reni with a swaggering

gunslinger named Joseph A. Slade (Jack Slade), who enjoyed such soubriquets as "The Little Terror of the Plains" and "The Bad Man from Bitter Creek." Reni spitefully peppered Slade one day with a volley of buckshot that would have killed a frailer man; but Slade was soon up and about, arranging for Reni's capture, torture, and death. In 1864, the Vigilantes of Virginia City, Montana, hanged Slade for incorrigible violence. His last words: "My God, must I die? Oh, my dear wife . . ."

The original Julesburg, with fewer than a dozen buildings, was destroyed by an Indian raid in 1865. It was followed by a second Julesburg (1865-67); a third (1867-81), that was a typical hell-on-wheels railhead center of bars and gambling halls; and a fourth (1881 to present), that was laid out on a curve of the South Platte to serve as a division point for Denver from the Union Pacific's overland line.

5. RANCH was spelled "ranche" in *Leslie's Illustrated Newspaper*. This Gallicization of a Spanish word (*rancho*) persisted for many years, although ranch, however spelled, has been part of the American language since the early nineteenth century.

6. SIDNEY, NEBRASKA, was named for Sidney Dillon, president of the Union Pacific Railroad during construction of the overland route. It began in the late 1860's as a crew camp around Fort Sidney, then developed into a major staging point for emigrants to the Black Hills during the gold rush of 1876-77. During the Black Hills fever, there were twenty-three saloons on a single block, and some 1500 travelers passed through the town every day. The wagon road to the Dakotas ran due west from Sidney along the Union Pacific tracks for about a mile, then turned north through a draw among the low hills and ran 265 miles to Deadwood. In commemoration of the Nebraska Centennial in 1967, the Deadwood run was reenacted by a group of equestrians and stagers.

7. FORT SIDNEY was established as a temporary encampment to protect railroad workers in 1867. For three years, it was a subpost of Fort Sedgwick, Colorado, and was called "Sidney Barracks." On November 28, 1870, the post became an independent fort. The trail from Fort Sidney to Fort Robinson in the Black Hills was of strategic importance during the Sioux rebellion 1874-77; and in 1878, during the uprising of Cheyenne Indians under Dull Knife, a troop train stood in readiness at Sidney to intercept the Indians at any point on the Union Pacific line. Fort Sidney was closed in 1894. In 1967, the Cheyenne County Historical Society restored and refurnished the post commander's home as a public museum.

8. PAWNEE SCOUTS protected white settlers and railroad workers from the traditional rivals of the Pawnee Indians — the Sioux, Cheyenne, Crow, Arapaho, Comanche, Osage, and Kiowa. The Pawnee, a generally peaceful nation of farmers and buffalo hunters, were at the time of the Lewis and Clark Expedition (1804-06) the largest indigenous tribe in Nebraska. In 1875, they ceded their large Nebraska reserves and moved to Oklahoma, but the move caused many deaths. By 1879, only 1,440 Pawnee remained, and in 1906, there were a mere 649 descendants of a nation that had numbered more than 10,000 a century before.

9. BOOTHILL CEMETERY was located on the east slope of the bluff north of Sidney. It was abandoned many years ago.

10. OUTFITTING SHOPS during the Black Hills gold rush included Oberfelder's Store and the C. L. Moore General Store. Both were on Front Street, facing the Union Pacific depot.

CHAPTER VII *(pp. 64–69)*

1. THE CHEYENNE-DEADWOOD ROUTE was served by a stage line from 1876 to 1887. In 1886, the Colorado & Southern Railroad (originally called the Cheyenne & Northern) built tracks from Denver to Cheyenne and thence north to Wendover, paralleling the old stage route. This line later connected with the Chicago & North Western at Orin Junction.

2. LANSQUENET, a card game of German origin, dates from the sixteenth century or earlier. The name is a French corruption of the German *land* (country) and *knecht* (foot soldier or subaltern.) In play, lansquenet resembles faro.

CHAPTER VIII *(pp. 72–74)*

1. "DEVIL AMONGST THE TAILORS" is the name of an English play, a Scottish reel, and a firework that spews out sparks and stars and whirling imps. The game at play in Colorado Springs probably was "Devil and Tailors," also called "Fox and Geese," a board game in which pegs or pieces representing tailors are moved forward in an attempt to corner the devil, a piece that can move in any direction and can remove tailors by jumping them.

2. HELEN HUNT (JACKSON), 1830-85, was a popular American novelist, best known for her *Ramona* a romance of the mission Indians of Southern California. Born in Amherst, Massachusetts, she moved to Colorado Springs in 1873 and married William S. Jackson the following year. Although she died in California, she is buried in Colorado Springs, where a waterfall is named in her honor.

3. GRACE GREENWOOD was the pen name of Sara Jane Clarke Lippincott (1823-1904), an American author of light poetry, sketches on travel and history, biographies, and informal essays. Born in New York, she took her pseudonym in contributing articles to the magazine *New Mirror* in 1844. She was intensely patriotic and visited many camps and hospitals during the Civil War.

4. BRIGADIER GENERAL WILLIAM JACKSON PALMER, a veteran of the Union Army, moved to Colorado in 1869 as construction manager for the Kansas Pacific Railroad. The following year he and his associates incorporated the Denver & Rio Grande Western Railroad and began developing coal and iron mines and founding towns along its route. Palmer was so impressed with the townsite of Colorado Springs (then called "Fountain Colony") that he induced his company to invest in 10,000 acres for $10,000. Palmer's home, *Glen Eyrie*, a few miles north of the town, set a new standard for Rocky Mountain bide-a-wees. Constructed of native stone, it had crenelated towers, turrets, and barbicans, and a tunnel in the hillside to carry away the smoke of the fireplaces. There is a bronze equestrian statue of General Palmer in downtown Colorado Springs.

———

CHAPTER IX *(pp.75–87)*

1. DALE CREEK BRIDGE, 650 feet long and 135 feet high, was at the time of its construction in 1868-69 the highest railway bridge in the world. The original structure of wood was soon replaced with an iron trestle, and the chasm it spanned has now been bypassed by a new grade with a long tunnel that is about two miles south and 237 feet below the original roadbed. The Sherman Hill route, now followed by U. S. Highway 30, was discovered in 1865 by Major General Grenville M. Dodge, later chief engineer of the Union Pacific, and a survey party that was trying to evade an Indian attack.

2. TIE SIDING originated as a railroad camp supplying ties to the Union Pacific from a heavy patch of timber on the southeast edge of the Laramie Plains. After the railroad was completed, Tie Siding became a supply point for ranches in the Red Buttes and Pole Mountain areas.

3. FORT SANDERS, three miles south of the present town of Laramie, was one of several army posts established in Wyoming Territory in the middle and late 1860's to pacify the Indians, guard mail and emigrants, and protect railroad workers. Originally named Fort John Buford, the cluster of log, frame, and stone buildings was completed in 1866, just in time to extend protection to tie-cutters and grading crews working their way west from Cheyenne. The fort was shortly renamed for Brigadier General William P. Sanders, a Union officer who had died of wounds in 1863. According to her own account, Calamity Jane was stationed at Sanders in 1871-72 as a scout. Later, she guided a party of soldiers to the Powder River country, where, in a foray with Sioux and Cheyenne, she saved the life of her commander.

4. RUSSELL, CARLIN, AND WALBACH were units in the network of frontier barracks built by the army in the late 1860's to protect the transcontinental railroad from Indian attacks. Fort David A. Russell, named for a Union general lost in the Civil War, was started shortly after the Union Pacific established a construction base called Cheyenne, and it was located just three miles northwest of the townsite. At first, it consisted merely of a log barracks, an officers' quarters, and a hospital. When other forts in the region were closed in the 1880's, these buildings were replaced with permanent brick structures, and the reservation was enlarged. In 1930, the fort was renamed Fort Francis E. Warren to honor the first governor of Wyoming. It is now one of the largest military bases in the United States. . . . Nearby Camp Carlin, established by Captain E. B. Carling [sic] in August, 1867, was a quartermaster depot for a dozen military posts in the Rocky Mountain region. Located two miles from a Union Pacific spur line, Carlin transshipped supplies to other forts by wagon train. It was incorporated into Fort Russell in the 1870's. . . . Camp Walbach, on Lodgepole Creek between Fort Laramie and the Laramie Plains, guarded a travelers' cutoff.

5. FAIRBANKS SCALES are a type of platform weighing machine patented in 1831 by Thaddeus Fairbanks of St. Johnsbury, Vermont. Through a system of multiplying levers, a heavy object on the platform can be counterpoised by a light beam with a small sliding weight and slotted weights on an extension arm. Fairbanks scales generally are used to weigh freight rather than New York ladies.

6. ROCK CREEK, now a ghost town, was a newly established freighting station in 1877. By 1883, it had become one of the liveliest small towns in Wyoming. Up to 175 teams carried freight in and out of Rock Creek, and the average shipment of cattle during the fall roundup was a hundred cars a day. A stage line connected Rock Creek with Junction City, Montana, four hundred miles away. When the Union Pacific carved out a new mainline route between Laramie and Medicine Bow, Rock Creek was bypassed. The station was abandoned in 1900, and a new shipping center established at Rock River.

7. AT WILCOX STATION, six miles west of Rock Creek, two armed men flagged down the Union Pacific express on June 2, 1899. They ordered the engineer to detach the engine, express, and baggage cars from the rest of the train. Leaving the passenger cars behind, they rode the lead cars across a bridge, stopped, dynamited the bridge to prevent interference, looted the express car of $60,000 in unsigned bank notes, and escaped into Montana. Wilcox was long ago bypassed on the new Union Pacific route.

8. MEDICINE BOW STATION, a supply center for oil drillers and livestock ranchers, was headquarters for the fictional hero of Owen Wister's novel, *The Virginian*.

9. FORT FETTERMAN, built in 1867 on the Bozeman Trail near the present city of Casper, Wyoming, was in such peaceful country that for seven years it was not equipped with cannon. Still, Fetterman was an important supply base during the later Sioux Wars, and after the Sioux Treaty of 1868, it was the last outpost to be maintained on the Indian border. Abandoned by the army in 1882, it was taken over by cattlemen, who turned the barns and warehouses into business establishments, the barracks and officers' quarters into homes. When Casper and Douglas were founded in the late 1880's, Fetterman declined, and was eventually deserted. The fort was named for Brevet Lieutenant Colonel W. J. Fetterman (see note on Fetterman Massacre).

10. CARBON, deserted for more than half a century, was located west of the thriving town of Hanna. In the 1880's, the six mines at Carbon employed up to six hundred men, but mining ended in 1902, shortly after construction of the Hanna cutoff put Carbon off the mainline of the Union Pacific.

11. FORT STEELE, the western anchor in the army's line of barracks across Wyoming, was built on the site of one of Lieutenant John Charles Frémont's 1843 camps. It was active from June 20, 1868, to August 7, 1886. A few log and frame buildings remain.

12. THE ASPEN GRADE, with its sharp curves and steep climbs, has been eliminated by a 5,900-foot concrete tunnel. Another tunnel, 6,706 feet long, carries the Union Pacific mainline under the Altamount summit.

13. BEAR RIVER VALLEY, like the Great Salt Lake Basin, was periodically plagued by grasshoppers. In the early 1870's, a reporter for the *New Jersey Journal* wrote: "An eastward-bound train which has just come in to Wahsatch is provided with evergreen brooms, covering the cowcatcher and brushing the track, to sweep off the grasshoppers. The engineer of our train informs me that at times they are so numerous on the track as to be crushed to death by thousands; hence they make the driving wheels and track so greasy that trains are often two or three hours behind their time."

CHAPTER X *(pp. 90–93)*

1. WAHSATCH, a village at 6,879 feet elevation, was the half-hour dinner stop of the transcontinental railroad during its early years. Travelers ate hastily at a hostelry called "Trout House," which was later moved to Evanston. "Truth to tell," said *Nelson's Pictorial Guide-Book to the Union Pacific Railroad*, "it bears a very malodorous reputation. A recent traveler was told that 'out of twenty-four graves here, only one held the remains of a person who had died a natural death, and that was a woman of notoriously bad reputation who had poisoned herself.'"

2. "GENERAL ALBERT SIDNEY JOHNSTON'S MEN" were the United States Army of the West, dispatched to Utah by President Buchanan in July, 1857, to terminate the governorship of Brigham Young and suppress the alleged Mormon rebellion. The army was at first commanded by General W. S. Harney, but the command was given over in the autumn to Brevet Brigadier General Johnston, who was later the brilliant commander of the Confederate Army. Although the Mormons made plans to fortify Utah and later contemplated fleeing to another refuge, Johnston eventually occupied the territory without bloodshed.

3. THE NAUVOO LEGION was an independent Mormon militia authorized by the Illinois Legislature to the impoverished Latter-Day Saints who founded the city of Nauvoo in 1837. The commander, Daniel H. Wells, was a member of the first three-man presidency of the LDS Church. In the fall of 1857, anticipating an attack by Federal troops, the Legion fortified Echo Canyon. It was Daniel Wells who delivered a classically terse funeral oration for Brigham Young in September, 1877: "I have no desire or wish to multiply words, feeling that it is rather a time to mourn. Goodbye, Brother Brigham, until the morning of the resurrection day...."

4. THE WEBER RIVER (pronounced *WEE-ber*) is presumably named for Captain John G. Weber, a Rocky Mountain trapper of the 1820's. At various times, the river and canyon have been spelled *Weaber* or *Weaver*, leading to speculation that the name may actually have come from that of Pauline Weaver, an Arizona frontiersman.

5. ECHO CITY was a rip-snorting encampment of tent saloons, gambling houses, and brothels during construction of the railroad in 1868. Men often disappeared during the night, and seven unidentified bodies were once uncovered in a pit under a saloon.

6. "GENTILE" is the term used by Latter-Day Saints to designate all nonmembers of the Mormon Church. The term "Jack Mormon" refers to a Gentile who is a Mormon sympathizer — or, in general parlance, to a professed Mormon who does not observe the church's rules of conduct.

7. Z.C.M.I. — Zion's Cooperative Mercantile Institution — was organized by the Latter-Day Saints as the transcontinental railroad neared completion, threatening to end the protective isolation of Utah Territory. Mormons were expected to trade with the church-owned store, which bore the legend "Holiness to the Lord" above its door. Gentile merchants, who always had been regarded with suspicion, were almost driven out by the competition of ZCMI. The main ZCMI store in Salt Lake City remains one of the major retail establishments of the mountain states.

CHAPTER XI *(pp. 96–108)*

1. THE GOLD SPIKE was one of many special ties and spikes prepared for the ritual meeting of the Central Pacific and Union Pacific railroads at Promontory, Utah, on May 10, 1869. There was a silver spike from Nevada, a silver, iron, and gold spike from Arizona, gold and silver spikes from Idaho and Montana, and two spikes of solid gold from California. California's Governor Leland Stanford — one of the "Big Four" capitalists of the Central Pacific—had the honor of pounding in the last gold spike, which was wired to complete an electric circuit with Stanford's silver hammer so that the blow could be transmitted telegraphically across the country. Stanford missed the spike entirely on the first swing, but a resourceful telegrapher simulated the blow, and cannons, fireworks, whistles, and cheers resounded from coast to coast. One of the two gold spikes was made into rings and distributed; the other is displayed in the museum of Stanford University at Palo Alto, California. A replica is in the Union Pacific Museum in Omaha.

2. UTAH CENTRAL RAILROAD was completed from Ogden to Salt Lake City in 1870 and extended south as the Utah Southern the following year. By 1880, the tracks had reached Milford. Brigham Young, disappointed that the transcontinental railroad line did not pass through Salt Lake City, took the task of completing the feeder line as a personal challenge, and it was he who drove in its "last spike" at a ceremony in Salt Lake. The line was later incorporated into the Union Pacific.

3. ANN ELIZA YOUNG, Brigham Young's renegade wife, returned to the East and published in 1876 a memoir called *Wife No. 19*, purporting to afford an intimate glimpse of Mormon polygamy to American readers insatiably curious about the subject. Whether Ann Eliza was, in fact, No. 19 or some other number is a matter of conjecture, because Young was not a source of much illumination about his wives. Born in the Mormon city of Nauvoo about 1844, Ann Eliza Webb had been married to James L. Dey and divorced before her "sealing" to Brigham Young in 1868. She sued Mr. Young for divorce in 1874. Estimating his worth at $8,000,000, she asked $1,000 a month pending a hearing, $6,000 in lawyer's fees, $14,000 in divorce payment, and $200,000 as a final settlement. The case was compromised by a payment of $3,600.

4. MRS. AMELIA YOUNG was the twenty-fourth wife of the president of the LDS Church, according to a semi-official directory of the Young household, published in Salt Lake City about 1900 by James H. Crockwell. Born in Buffalo, New York, Harriet Amelia Folsom migrated to Salt Lake City with her parents in 1860, when she was 22 — "tall, stately and queenly in appearance, of fair complexion, bright and intelligent." She married Mr. Young in 1863. The president's other wives were: Miriam Works, Mary Ann Angell, Lucy Decker, Harriet Elizabeth Cook Campbell, Augusta Adams, Clara Decker, Louisa Be-

man, Clara Chase Ross, Emily Dow Partridge, Susan Snively, Emmeline Free, Olive Grey Frost, Margaret Pierce, Naamah Kendell Jenkins Carter, Ellen Rockwood, Maria Lawrence, Martha Bowker, Lucy Bigelow, Margaret Alley, Zina Diantha Huntington, Eliza Roxey Snow, Eliza Burgess, Harriet Barney, Mary Van Cott, and Ann Eliza Webb. Mr. Young fathered fifty-six children and at his death left seventeen wives, sixteen sons, and twenty-eight daughters.

5. ELIZA R. SNOW, the "Sweet Singer of Israel," was widowed in her early forties by the murder of Joseph Smith in 1844. Shortly afterward, she was "sealed" to Brigham Young, although the marriage, at least at first, was apparently for her protection only. She was a prolific poetess and hymnist of the Mormon trek to Utah, and is regarded as an "immortal" of the LDS Church. Her brother, Lorenzo Snow, was the fifth president of the church.

6. COUNCIL BLUFFS was for twenty-five years the staging point for Mormon immigration to the West. In May, 1846, the vanguard of the migrating Saints formed a temporary settlement called Miller's Hollow, later Kanesville, at the heart of modern Council Bluffs; and by the following winter, the Mormons were encamped several thousand strong in this area, waiting for spring. The advance company departed in January, 1847, from Winter Quarters, a temporary camp on the west bank of the Missouri. It is now Florence, a suburb of Omaha.

7. ST. GEORGE, in a hot, windy badlands area, was founded by the Mormons in 1867 as the center of a major colonization of southern Utah's "Dixie." The early colonists suffered bitter discouragement trying to grow cotton, fruit, mulberry trees, and other warm-winter crops, but St. George is now a well-established town and stopping place for tourists to Zion and Bryce Canyon national parks. Brigham Young's winter home, a two-story adobe, is at the corner of First West and Second North streets.

8. BRINE FLIES and half-inch-long brine shrimp are the only inhabitants of Great Salt Lake. The flies, which pass their larval stages in the salt-laden waters, are similar to small house flies; the shrimp resemble primitive trilobite crustaceans of the Cambrian period.

9. THE GENERAL GARFIELD, a stern-wheeled steamboat, was built in 1871 to navigate Great Salt Lake between the mining districts and the smelters. The non-Mormon founders of Corinne (q.v.) saw the ship, which they first called *The City of Corinne*, as an economic boon to the town. But the steamer lost money. Renamed the *Garfield*, it became an excursion boat, and eventually was dry-docked at Garfield Beach on the south side of the lake, where it served as a tourist pavilion.

10. THE LATTER-DAY SAINTS TEMPLE at Salt Lake City is not the oldest temple of the Mormon faith (several earlier temples were burned or abandoned) but the largest and most imposing. Commissioned during the presidency of Brigham Young, the six-spired edifice, vaguely Gothic in design, took forty years (1853-1893) to complete and cost approximately three and a half million dollars. It is closed to non-Mormons.

11. LDS TABERNACLE, 250 feet long and 150 feet wide, is an egg-shaped dome that rests on heavy stone buttresses, forming an auditorium that seats five thousand. Its wooden beams are held together with rawhide thongs and wooden pins. The Tabernacle was constructed by William Folsom and Henry Grow.

12. THE EAGLE GATE, erected in 1859 at the entrance to Brigham Young's private estate, still stands as a landmark on South Temple and North State streets. It was made higher in 1891 to accommodate the passage of streetcars.

13. AMELIA YOUNG'S HOUSE, a pretentious edifice on the corner of South Temple and State streets, was intended as a "Mormon White House." Unfinished at the time of Mr. Young's death, Gardo House was left as a lifetime inheritance to his second wife, "Mother" Mary Ann Angell, and his twenty-fourth, Sister Amelia. Since both wives had indicated a desire not to live in the mansion, it passed to his other heirs. The site is now occupied by a Federal Reserve bank.

CHAPTER XII *(pp. 111–120)*

1. CORINNE, the first "Gentile" town in Utah Territory began in 1868 with high hopes of becoming the major city of the Salt Lake Basin. When the transcontinental railroad was completed the following year, thousands of freight handlers and miners swarmed in, looking for excitement, and turned the primitive settlement into a rakehell metropolis for prostitutes and professional gamblers. Frustrated by Ogden in competing for the railroad junction, Corinne went after Federal land grants, steamship trade on the lake, and other economic stimulants; but its isolation and its bad name defeated it. It is now a small agricultural town.

2. PROMONTORY became the meeting place of the Union and Central Pacific railroads by luck rather than design. Having selected various junctions that were unsatisfactory to one railroad or the other, the Congress in 1866 decided to allow the lines to build until they met. UP graded as far as Humboldt Wells, Nevada, while Central Pacific graded east to Echo City, Utah. At stake was not merely a future mainline but immense subsidies: 12,800 acres of public land for each mile of mainline track, plus $16,000 per mile on the plains, $32,000 per mile in difficult terrain, and $48,000 per mile in the mountains. Union Pacific received a total cash subsidy of $28,450,000 for the route from Omaha to Ogden; Central Pacific got $24,386,000 for its work from Sacramento to Ogden. Because Chinese and Irish workers were fighting hand-to-hand along the right of way, Congress finally picked Promontory as a compromise junction, although the actual division point was soon moved to Ogden. Waterless Promontory never thrived, and with the construction of Southern Pacific's Lucin Cutoff across Great Salt Lake in 1903, it lost all importance to the railroad.

3. EMIGRANT TRAILS that converged in the Humboldt Valley some miles southwest of Wells were the California-Oregon Trail, which turned south from the main Oregon Trail at Raft River, in what is now southern Idaho; the little-used Bidwell Trail, branching down from the Oregon route at Alexander, Idaho; and the harrowing Hasting's Cutoff from Fort Bridger, Wyoming, via Salt Lake City and the Great Salt Desert.

4. MUC-CA MUC-CA was probably *ne-muck-ah*, Shoshonean for "give me."

5. PAIUTE BURIAL CUSTOMS are known to anthropologists, despite the mystery that prevailed in the Leslies' time. Northern Paiutes buried their dead in shallow graves or in niches among the rocks. Mourners frequently cut their hair, and the name of the deceased persons was taboo for several years. The Washoe Indians of western and southern Nevada cremated their dead.

6. STONE HOUSE is now a ruin about two miles off U.S. 40 between Battle Mountain and Winnemucca.

7. HUMBOLDT SINK, a depression near the Humboldt Range, is the disappearing place of the Humboldt River, which rises in eastern Nevada and flows south and west about 300 miles, past Elko, Winnemucca, and Lovelock. The Sink was named by John Charles Frémont for Alexander Humboldt, the celebrated German geographer and explorer.

CHAPTER XV *(pp. 134–139)*

1. THE VIRGINIA & TRUCKEE RAILROAD has been called by its admirers (including the late Lucius Beebe) the most successful short line in history. It was established in 1869 by three officers of the Bank of California — William Ralston, William Sharon, and Darius Ogden Mills—after about ten years of mining activity on the Comstock Lode; its construction was completed shortly before the discovery of the unparalleled "big bonanza." As the need for heavy mining equipment, timbers, and supplies increased, the V & T turned a fabulous profit, bringing $100,000 a month in dividends to its three owners. Innumerable fortunes moved along its rails in its distinctive yellow and green cars. By 1933, when Ogden Mills inherited two-thirds of the railroad from his grandfather and purchased the remainder from the Sharon estate, the V & T had declined with the Comstock. Mills operated the railroad out of sentiment until his death in 1937, when it went into receivership until its final abandonment in 1950. Engines and cars have been sold, rails removed, and buildings put to other uses. The central station, on the southeast corner of Carson and Washington streets in Carson City, has been painted pale green, and functions as a Masonic Hall and real estate office. The stone roundhouse is an automobile repair garage. The famous Crown Point trestle at Gold Hill, regarded in 1869 as an engineering marvel, was torn down in 1936 to allow mining on the site, but it is depicted on the State Seal of Nevada—with a V & T engine puffing across.

2. THE UNITED STATES MINT in Carson City was built in 1866, and began making coins in January, 1870. During its years of operation, it pressed fifty-seven issues of gold coins and fifty-three issues of silver with its characteristic "CC" mark. Out of operation from 1885 to 1889, is was permanently closed in 1893. For the next forty years, the building was used as a United States Assay Office. In 1933, the State of Nevada purchased the Mint as surplus Government property. Through the efforts of Judge Clark J. Guild and other Carson City residents, the Nevada State Museum was established in the building and opened to the public in October, 1941.

3. NEVADA STATE CAPITOL, completed in 1871, is a sandstone building with a

silver dome. An octagonal annex was added in 1907, and north and south wings in 1915. Abe Curry, the founder of Carson City, supplied the sandstone from his nearby quarry. To lure the capitol to his townsite, Curry allegedly spread generous donations among the legislators, who were more disposed to locate the state offices in the more prosperous and better-located town of Virginia City.

4. BONANZA KINGS is a title usually reserved for the four Comstock millionaires who were associated in the "bonanza firm"—John W. Mackay, James G. Fair, James C. Flood, and William S. O'Brien. William Sharon, who was the Bank of California's sharp-dealing representative in Virginia City, and John P. Jones, a mine owner who became U.S. Senator from Nevada in 1873, were not associated with the "kings"; in fact, Sharon was their bitter adversary.

5. VIRGINIA CITY BUILDINGS impressed most visitors as unusually substantial, at least by the standards of western mining towns. Wood construction was used because of its cheapness and speed.

6. CALIFORNIA MINE was a portion of the bonanza controlled by the Mackay-Fair-Flood-O'Brien company. This fabulously endowed section of 1310 feet lay between the Ophir and the Gould & Curry. At one time, it had been owned by five separate companies — the California, the Kinney, the White & Murphy, the Sides, and the Central and Central No. 2. Later, 710 feet were brought together under the control of the Consolidated Virginia, and 600 feet under the California. The four major owners gained control of these two companies for about one hundred thousand dollars in late 1871 and early 1872. Within two years, they had uncovered an ore body estimated to be worth three hundred million dollars — the richest deposit of gold and silver ore ever discovered.

7. JAMES G. FAIR, a relatively impecunious mine manager from the California gold country, and John W. Mackay, major owner of the small but profitable Kentuck mine at Gold Hill, joined Flood and O'Brien, saloon owners turned brokers, in a daring and secretive project to corner the stock of Hale & Norcross Mine and wrest control from William Sharon in 1868–69. After capturing the company, the foursome installed Flood as president, Fair as superintendent, and Mackay and O'Brien as trustees. Several years later, they struck the "big bonanza" in the California and Con-Virginia.

Chapter XVI (pp. 143–159)

1. STOPE, according to Webster's New International Dictionary (Springfield, 1941), is akin to "step," not to "stop." Frequently, the excavation within a stope is shaped like a crude flight of stairs.

2. THE COMSTOCK LODE in its palmy days between 1859 and 1882 produced some $397,000,000 in gold and silver. Bullion production reached a maximum of more than $36,000,000 in 1877, largely as a result of the "big bonanza" and other ore discoveries at greater depth. Stock sales on the San Francisco Exchange that year totaled $119,699,731. The Nevada State Museum lists the following important mines with their year of bonanza and their payout: Crown Point, 1866, $34,201,525; Belcher, 1870, $36,-177,118; Imperial, 1859, $5,448,050; Yellow Jacket, 1870, $17,676,736; Kentuck,

productive 1866-73, $5,763,295; Chollar Potosi, 1870, $17,789,599; Hale & Norcross, 1866 and 1870, $10,299,736; Savage, 1862, $17,524,645; Gould & Curry, 1860, $15,686,749; Consolidated Virginia, 1873, $62,763,531; California, 1873, $64,-596,684; Ophir, 1859, $15,439,471.

3. JESSUP AND TIDES, the victim and the assailant in the first murder in Gold Hill on April 29, 1859, are identified in Thompson & West's 1881 History of Nevada as "one Jessup, alias 'Pike' " and William Sides, who stabbed and killed him over a game of cards.

4. ETHAN AND HOSEA GROSH, sons of a Philadelphia clergyman, found and assayed silver-bearing quartz while scratching for gold in one of the dry canyons of the Washoe Range in 1857. But Hosea, the younger brother, died shortly afterward of an infection; and Ethan, after panning enough gold to pay for his brother's medical expenses and funeral, left for San Francisco to raise funds to mine the silver ore. On the way over the Sierra, he was trapped for four days by a snow storm. Exhausted and frozen, he reached a settlement on the west side of Donner Pass, but he died in delirium a few days later — without disclosing the location of his silver claim.

5. THE SUTRO TUNNEL, opened in 1878, was the brainchild and obsession of Adolph Sutro, an immigrant from Germany who arrived on the Comstock Lode in 1860. Sutro obtained a franchise from the Nevada Legislature in 1864 to build a lateral under Mount Davidson to drain the hot water from the silver mines, provide ventilation, reduce temperatures within the mines, save timber, and decrease the cost of hauling ore. Sutro's implacable opponents in mining and banking repeatedly thwarted his plan, but in October, 1869, he began construction work with foreign capital and funds raised among the miners. The tunnel was five and one-half miles long and cost four million, five hundred thousand dollars, but was completed too late to serve the mines in their years of greatest activity. Sutro, however, became a multimillionaire in San Francisco real estate and was mayor of that city from 1894 to 1896.

Chapter XVII (pp. 162–169)

1. THE DONNER PARTY, a group of immigrants bound for California from Iowa and Illinois in 1846–47, took an unfamiliar cutoff west of Fort Bridger, and were delayed in crossing the Utah salt flats. Overtaken by early winter snows while still on the east side of the Sierra, they camped by a forlorn lake, where they suffered horribly from starvation, and were finally driven to cannibalism. Only about half the party reached California.

2. BULLION CARS have disappeared from the mainline over the Sierra, but at least one car remains in Virginia City (1967). The Territorial Enterprise has editorialized in favor of restoring the car and maintaining it as a public museum.

3. OAKLAND AND ITS SUBURBS were founded by Yankee squatters who settled in the early 1850's on the forty-eight-thousand-acre Rancho San Antonio, owned by Don Luis Peralta and his four sons. The villages of Clinton, San Antonio, and Lynn eventually were consolidated into the town of Brooklyn (now East Oakland) on the southeast side of the Lake Merritt tidal basin. Melrose, Elmhurst, and other villages

were annexed by Oakland during its prodigious growth after the San Francisco earthquake and fire of 1906.

4. THE CENTRAL PACIFIC MILL in West Oakland had a moment of creative splendor in 1879–80 when the railroad's land development subsidiary, Pacific Improvement Company, built the elaborate Hotel Del Monte near Monterey, California. All the framing timbers, interior panels, and "Swiss Gothic" gingerbread for the "Queen of American Watering Places" were cut and shaped in the Oakland shops and shipped to the building site by rail. The famous old hotel twice burned and was twice rebuilt. It is today (1967) a U.S. Navy postgraduate school.

5. GOAT ISLAND, a pyramid crowned with eucalyptus trees, has gone under many names. Early navigators called it Wood Island, Isla del Carmen, or even Alcatraz. The name Yerba Buena (Sp. "good herb"), was bestowed by Frederick W. Beechey, an English navigator, in 1826, but other visitors to the Bay called it "Goat Island" because of the animals pastured on its then-treeless slopes. The colloquial name endured, although many official documents designated the island Yerba Buena. In 1895, the United States Geographic Board officially adopted "Goat Island." But two decades later, Nellie van der Grift Sanchez, a California historian, began campaigning to have the more euphonious Spanish name restored. In 1931, the island officially became Yerba Buena. It is seldom called Goat Island today, but the Navy has popularized an even less dignified nickname: "Wye-Bee-Eye" — or Y.B.I.

6. ALCATRAZ, an infamous, twelve-acre island in San Francisco Bay, was named by Lt. Juan Manuel de Ayala, a Spanish explorer, in 1775. He apparently intended the name to apply to the island now called Yerba Buena, where he had observed a number of pelicans (alcatraces). From the time of the Civil War until 1933, Alcatraz served as a harbor fort and military detention barracks. Then it became a Federal penitentiary for incorrigible civilian criminals. It was abandoned as a prison March 22, 1963.

Chapter XVIII (pp. 172–179)

1. PICADILLO is a dish that seems to have originated and disappeared within the mind of Mrs. Frank Leslie. The peccadillos of Spaniards are well known but are not served in restaurants, whereas the piccalillis found in restaurants are East Indian, not Spanish.

2. THE NAME SAN FRANCISCO, honoring St. Francis of Assisi, was applied by Spanish and Mexican settlers to the Bay, the Mission, and the Presidio, but not to the secular village, or pueblo, founded with one tent in 1835 by Captain William A. Richardson, an English-born mariner then resident in California. Richardson's settlement was called Yerba Buena. The village kept this name until January 30, 1846, when Lt. Washington A. Bartlett, who had been appointed alcalde by the conquering American naval commander, proclaimed that the place would thereafter be known as San Francisco. His reason: several enthusiastic Californians, including Mariano Vallejo, were planning to appropriate the saint's name for a townsite on Carquinez Straits. The rival town was named instead for General Vallejo's wife, Benicia.

3. WOODWARD'S GARDENS, which covered two city blocks between Mission and Valencia, Thirteenth and Fifteenth streets, was originally the suburban pleasance of Robert Woodward, the proprietor of the What Cheer House (a hotel). Woodward, who had made a comfortable fortune in the gold rush, embellished his estate with bridges and ponds, pavilions and gazebos for the amusement of his guests, and in the late 1860's he began admitting the public to the gardens. Woodward's Gardens remained the most popular place in the city for family outings, even after the establishment of Golden Gate Park in the early 70's; but the Mid-Winter Exposition of 1894 finally tranferred the affections of San Francisco to the public park.

4. GENERAL BUTLER was the namesake of Major-General Benjamin Franklin Butler (1818–93), known to southerners as "Beast" Butler because of the severity of his military regime in New Orleans in 1862–63. San Francisco's "General Butler" was succeeded in the 1890's by an equally bossy herd leader named Benjamin Harrison Cleveland. The denizens of Seal Rocks are not actually seals but Steller sea lions.

5. LONE MOUNTAIN, a 468-foot hill on Turk Boulevard between Masonic and Parker avenues, was once encircled by four cemeteries: Laurel Hill, to the north; Calvary, to the east; Masonic, to the south; and Odd Fellows, to the west. On the hilltop, which was bought by the Roman Catholic Archbishop of San Francisco in 1860, there was until the early 1930's a large cross of white wood. When all cemeteries were ordered removed to San Mateo County (1912 to 1940), Lone Mountain lost it reputation as a necropolis and became a pleasant residential area. The name is now associated primarily with the San Francisco College for Women, a Roman Catholic institution, built on the hilltop in 1933.

6. THE BARBARY COAST was San Francisco's iniquitous neighborhood of saloons, dance halls, and brothels that centered along Pacific Avenue from the waterfront to Grant Avenue (Dupont Street). Probably named for the perilous shores of North Africa, where pirates preyed on shipping, the Barbary Coast was notorious for its "shanghai" saloons, where drunken or drugged seamen were impressed into the crews of outbound ships. The Pacific Avenue dance halls boarded up during Prohibition, reopened as the "International Settlement" in the 1930's and 40's, but Pacific Avenue is now occupied by respectable advertising agencies, decorators' shops, small restaurants, and import display rooms.

CHAPTER XX *(pp. 190–195)*

1. ANDREW J. BRYANT, Mayor of San Francisco for two terms, 1877–1879, is remembered for the rioting that swept the city during his administration. Aroused by Dennis Kearney and other "sandlot orators," thousands of white workmen stormed through the city in July, 1877, beating and tormenting Chinese laborers, burning Chinese shops, and threatening hanging and arson to the millionaire residents of Nob Hill. Bryant drowned in San Francisco Bay on May 11, 1888, at the age of 53.

2. SAN FRANCISCO'S "NEW" CITY HALL (1872-1906) at McAllister and Larkin streets, was undertaken with grandiose designs and a one million, five hundred thousand dollar price tag. The voters of the city, who had suffered repeated malfeasance from elected officials, refused to authorize a bond issue to construct the building, and the work therefore proceeded under annual appropriations. Often the contractor would work only three or four months before the year's budget had been expended. By the mid-1890's, work was still underway. The City Hall had become a standard joke for gaslight vaudeville comedians. When it was finally completed in 1898, the building had cost more than six million dollars. Less than sixty seconds after the first shock of the 1906 earthquake, the towering dome—335 feet tall, with 6,000 tons of brick, 1,000 tons of steel, and 1,000 tons of terra-cotta—crumbled and fell, leaving only the steel framework to haunt the city with another stark monument to municipal corruption.

3. E. J. "LUCKY" BALDWIN was a shrewd San Francisco businessman with an apparently insatiable appetite for money, land, and thoroughbred horses. He made his first fortune in the Ophir Mine in Virginia City; then, going "down below" to San Francisco, he amassed a second fortune in Comstock shares on the stock exchange. In 1875, he bought from Harris Newmark the thirteen thousand-acre Rancho Santa Anita, adjoining the present town of Santa Anita in Southern California. Moving to Santa Anita in the late 70's, he beautified the ranch with magnificent groves of eucalyptus trees, lakes, pavilions and race courses. The sobriquet "Lucky," which he often disclaimed, was attached to him after he had acquired a fortune by fluke. Instructing his broker to sell some Comstock shares, Baldwin left the country for several months with the key to the safe where the shares were stored. While he was abroad, the price of equities rose four million dollars.

4. THE BALDWIN HOTEL, at Powell, Market, and O'Farrell streets, burned in 1898. For many years it had dominated upper Market Street and rivaled the Palace Hotel for prestige. The Flood Building (1905) was built on the site — another monument to Comstock money — and survived the earthquake and fire.

5. MARK HOPKINS' HOUSE, at the southeast corner of California and Mason streets on Nob Hill, was an extravagant Victorian castle, the work of seven architects urged on by "Uncle Mark's" ambitious wife, Mary. When Hopkins, the most conservative of the "Big Four" railroad entrepreneurs, bought the corner lot in 1874, he hoped to build only a modest house. He died in 1878, a year before the Gothic pile was completed. In 1893, the house passed to the San Francisco Art Association, which used the building to house the Hopkins Art Institute until it fell victim to the 1906 fire. The twenty-story Hotel Mark Hopkins, world famous for its rooftop cocktail lounge, opened on the site in December, 1926.

6. CHARLES CROCKER'S "SPITE FENCE" towered forty feet high around the small residence of a Chinese undertaker named Yung, who refused to sell his twenty-five foot lot to the imperious builder of the Central Pacific. Eventually, Yung sold to Crocker, but not before the irony of the confrontation had impressed the people of San Francisco. Crocker's heirs gave all his property to the Episcopal Diocese of California after his death in 1888, and the land is now the site of Grace Cathedral.

7. MRS. STANFORD'S UNMARRIED SISTER was Anna Maria Lathrop of Albany, New York.

8. LELAND STANFORD, JR. was born May 14, 1868, and christened Leland DeWitt Stanford. At age 11, he became Leland Stanford, Jr. by court order, because he had told his parents he wished to resemble his father in every way. As the first and only child of prodigiously wealthy parents who had been married for eighteen years, Leland Jr. was as well favored as any child of his day. On family trips to Europe, he would gather priceless antiquities and bring them home for his private museum. When he was only fifteen, his parents arranged for him to visit Dr. Heinrich Schliemann so that the two might discuss their mutual interest in archeology. Shortly after this interview, the boy contracted typhoid fever. He died in Florence, Italy, on March 13, 1884, two months short of sixteen. As a living memorial, the grief-stricken parents established Leland Stanford, Jr. University on their immense stock farm near Palo Alto, California — so that, as Mrs. Stanford said, "the children of California shall be my children." The original endowment was three farms totaling eighty thousand acres. Later cash endowments of twenty million dollars made the bequest the largest in history. (It has since been exceeded.) Stanford died in 1893. Mrs. Stanford, after acting as the sole trustee of the university for a decade, died in 1905.

9. BELMONT, in the Canada del Diablo of San Mateo County, was originally a small villa owned by Count Lussetti Cipriani, an Italian patriot from whom Ralston bought the property in the early 1860's. Ralston and his wife developed the modest country house into a mansion famous for its charming architecture and lavish entertainment. After Ralston's death, his widow was allowed by Sharon to live in a small outbuilding on the property she had once commanded. In 1923, the estate was acquired by the Sisters of Notre Dame as a new location for their convent and college, established in San Jose in 1851.

10. SENATOR WILLIAM SHARON had five children by his wife, Maria Malloy, who died in 1875. The talented daughter and son-in-law who joined the Leslies at dinner in Belmont were undoubtedly Clara Adelaide and Francis G. Newlands, who had been married three years earlier. Clara died in 1880, leaving three small children. Mr. Newlands, a successful corporation lawyer, later married Edith McAllister, daughter of Hall McAllister, one of California's noted barristers.

205

INDEX

Page references in italics indicate illustrations. Notes are indicated in parentheses by Roman chapter number and Arabic note number.

Adams, Neb., 61
Alameda, Calif., 168
Alcatraz, 169, 204 (XVII, 6)
Alda, Neb., 53
Alexander Creek Canyon, 168
Alkali, Neb., 56
Alma, Wyo., 87, *87*
Amelia Palace, 104, 203 (XI, 13)
American Flat, Nev., 136
American River Canyon, 162–163
Antelope, Neb., 61
Arbor Day, 44, 57, *57*, 59, 200 (V, 1)
Aspen, Wyo., 85, 202 (IX, 12)

Bad Lands of Wyoming, Church Buttes, *84*
Baldwin, E. J. (Lucky), 190, 205 (XX, 3)
Baldwin Hotel and Theatre, 190–191, *191*, 205 (XX, 4)
Barbary Coast, San Francisco, 205–206 (XVIII, 6)
Batavia, Ill., 33
Battle Mountain, Nev., 116–117, *117*
Bear River City, Wyo., 86
Bear River Valley, 85, 202 (IX, 13)
Beebe, Lucius, 161
Beehive House, 104, 110
Bella Union gambling hell, 65
Belmont, Calif., 193
Belmont Mansion, 193–195, *194*, 205 (XX, 9)
Bené (Beni). See René
Bennett, Neb., 61
Berwison, Neb., 61
"Bit" system, 116
Bitter Creek Valley, 80–81
Black Hawk, 200 (III, 6)
Black Hawk War, 33, 200 (III, 6)
Black Hills, Wyo., 75, 77
  emigrants, 37–40, 60
  gold rush outfitting shops, 60, *60*, 201 (VI, 10)
"Bonanza kings," 136, 138–139, 204 (XV, 4)
Bonanza Mine, 138–139
Boothill Cemetery, 201 (VI, 9)
Bromley's Cathedral, 90
Brooklyn, Calif., 168
Bryan, Wyo., emigrant camping ground, 83, *83*
Bryant, Andrew J., 190, 205 (XX, 1)
Buffalo, extermination of, 47, 200 (V, 3)
Buffalo grass, 52–53
Bullette, Julia C., 161
Bullion cars, 204 (XVII, 2)
Burlington and Minnesota Railroad and machine shop, 33
Bushnell, Neb., 61

Calamity Jane at Fort Sanders, 201 (IX, 3)
California, 162–197. *See also* specific cities
California Mine, 138–139, 204 (XV, 6)

California Pacific Railroad, mill at Oakland, 168–169, 204 (XVII, 4)
Camp Carlin, 201 (IX, 4)
Camp Walbach, 201 (IX, 4)
Cape Horn, Calif., site of gold discovery, 163, *164–165*
Carbon, Wyo., *79*, 80, 202 (IX, 10)
Carson, Christopher (Kit), 136
Carson City, Nev., 134–135, *134–135*
  in 1967, 140–141
  State Capitol, 135, 203–204 (XV, 3)
  U.S. Mint, 135, *135*, 203 (XV, 2)
Cascade, Calif., 162
Castle Rock, 90
Cedar Rapids, Iowa, 33
Central Pacific Railroad, building of Hotel Del Monte, 204 (XVII, 4)
  Chinese labor on, 189
  mill at Oakland, 168–169, 204 (XVII, 4)
  western terminus, *172*
Chapman's, Neb., 52
Cheyenne, Wyo., 64–72, *68–69*, 75
  Cheyenne-Deadwood stage route, 201 (VII, 1)
  gambling, 64–65, *65*
  gold miners for Black Hills, 64, *66–67*
  in 1967, 70–72
  Old Zip Coon, 68, *68*
  stage coaches, 64–66
  theatres in, 67–69
Cheyenne Indians, Battle of Plum Creek, 56, 200 (VI, 1)
Chicago, 20–27
  Board of Trade, *24–25*, 24–27, 199 (II, 9)
  Conrad Hilton, 26
  Fire, 20, 199 (II, 2)
  Grand Pacific Hotel, 21, *21*, 199 (II, 3)
  growth, 199 (II, 1)
  in 1967, 26–27
  Police Department, 27
  scenes, *21–23*
  Tremont House, 22, 199 (II, 4)
  Union Stockyards, 22, 199 (II, 5)
  water supply, 22–23
  water tower, 199 (II, 6)
Chicago and North Western Railway Co., 28, *28*, 199–200 (III, 2)
Chicago River, 23
Chinatown, San Francisco, 182–189, 195
  fortune teller, 185, *185*
  in 1967, 188–189
  opium den, 186, *186–187*
  Royal China Theatre, 182–184, *183–185*
  shop bookkeeper with abacus, 188, *188*
  slum conditions in, 189
Chinese, at Colfax, Calif., 163
  discrimination against, 150, 189
  laborers, 86–87, 129, *129*, 168
  laundry at Hilliard, 85, *85*

Cisco, Calif., 162
City of San Francisco, 9, 35–36
  in 1967, 126–127
Clark's, Neb., *50–51*, 52
Clinton, Iowa, bridge over Mississippi, 33, *33*
Colfax, Calif., 163
Colorado Springs, 72
Colton, Neb., 58
Columbus, Neb., 49, *49*, 200 (V, 5)
Comstock, H. T. P., 152
Comstock Lode, 136, 151–152, 204 (XVI, 2)
Comstock millionaires, 204 (XV, 4)
Consolidated Virginia Mine, 151
Continental Divide, tree at, *92*
Corinne, Utah, 111, *111*, 203 (XII, 1)
Council Bluffs, Iowa, 34, *34, 37*, 203 (XI, 6)
  bridge over Missouri, 34, 200 (III, 7)
Creston, Wyo., 80
Crocker, Charles, "spite fence," 190, 205 (XX, 6)

Dale Creek Bridge, 76, *76*, 201 (IX, 1)
Deadwood, S. Dak., 66–67
Denver, Colo., 72, 74
Denver and Rio Grande Railroad, 72
"Devil's Gap," *93*
"Devil's Slide," 92, *95*
Dexter, Neb., 56
Dixon, Ill., 33
Dixon, John, 200 (III, 5)
Donner Lake, 162
Donner party disaster, 162, 204 (XVII, 1)
Dutch Flat, Calif., 162–163

Eagle Gate, 104, 203 (XI, 12)
Echo Canyon, 90–91, *91–92*
  in 1967, 94–95
Echo City, Utah, 91, *91*, 202 (X, 5)
Elkhorn River, 44–45
Elko, Nev., 112, 114, *114*
  in 1967, 123
Elm Creek, Neb., 56, 200 (VI, 1)
Emigrant Gap, Calif., 162
Emigrants, for Black Hills, 37–40, 60
  camping ground at Bryan, 83
  outfitting shops, 60, *60*
  "Ship of the Plain," 57
  trails into Humboldt Valley, 203 (XII, 3)
  trains, 112, 131
  wagon, 57
Erie Canal, 14, 199 (I, 1)
Evanston, Wyo., 86–89, *86–87*

Fair, James G., 136, 138–139, 204 (XV, 4, 7)
Fashions, ladies' Paris, 31
Fetterman Massacre, 56, 200 (VI, 3)
Flood, James C., 136, 138–139, 204 (XV, 4, 7)
Fort Carlin, 77
Fort David A. Russell, 201 (IX, 4)
Fort Fetterman, 56, 79, 202 (IX, 9)
Fort Francis E. Warren, 201 (IX, 4)
Fort John Buford, 201 (IX, 3)
Fort Russell, 77
Fort Sanders, 77, 201 (IX, 3)
Fort Sidney, 58, 201 (VI, 7)

Fort Steele, *79*, 80, 202 (IX, 11)
Fort Walbach, 77
Frémont, John C., 136
Fremont, Neb., *44*, 45, *45*, 200 (V, 2)

Gannett, Neb., 56
  bridge over North Platte, 56
Garden of the Gods, 74
Gardo House, 203 (XI, 13)
General Butler, at Seal Rocks, 178, 205 (XVIII, 4)
General Garfield, The, 103, 203 (XI, 9)
Geneva, Ill., 33
Gentile, in Utah, 202 (X, 6)
Glen Eyrie, Colo., 74
"Go West, young man," 200 (IV, 3)
Goat Island, 169, 204 (XVII, 5)
Gold Canyon, 136
Gold Hill, Nev., 136
  murder at, 151, 204 (XVI, 3)
Gold Run, Calif., 163
Gold spike ceremony at Promontory, 96, 111, 202 (XI, 1)
Golden Gate Park, 178
Grand Island, Neb., 52
Grand Pacific Hotel, Chicago, 21, *21*, 199 (II, 3)
Gravelly Ford, 116, *116*
Great American Desert, *111*
Great Plains, 44–71
Great Salt Lake, *102*, 102–103, 203 (XI, 8)
Great Salt Lake Valley Basin, 96
Greeley, Horace, 200 (IV, 3)
Green River, Wyo., 83
Green River Valley, 81–88, *81–82*
Greenwood, Grace, 72, 201 (VIII, 3)
Grosh, Ethan and Hosea, 151–152, 204 (XVI, 4)

Hale and Norcross Mine, 204 (XV, 7)
Halleck, Utah, *112*
"Hell on Wheels," 64–69
Hilliard Station, Wyo., 85, *85*
Homesteading, advantages, 40–41
Hopkins, Mark, mansion of, 190, 205 (XX, 5)
Hotel Del Monte, Monterey, 204 (XVII, 4)
Howell, Wyo., 78–79
Humboldt, Nev., 118–119, *119*
Humboldt River Palisades, 115, *115*
Humboldt Sink, 120, *121*, 203 (XII, 7)
Humboldt Valley, 112, 114–120, 203 (XII, 3)

Indian lodges near Carlin, *113*
Indians, 46, 52, *118*, 118–119
  Cheyennes at Battle of Plum Creek, 56
  Otoes, in Wyoming, 79–80
  Paiutes, 116–117, 121, 203 (XII, 5)
  Pawnees, *50–51*, 56, 58
  Shoshones, 113–114
  Sioux surrender, 31
  Washoe burial customs, 203 (XII, 5)

"Jack Mormon," 202 (X, 6)
Jackson, Helen Hunt, 72, 201 (VIII, 2)

Jessup and Tides, in Gold Hill murder, 151, 204 (XVI, 3)
Johnston, Albert Sidney, 90, 202 (X, 2)
Jones, John P., 136, 204 (XV, 4)
Josselyn, Neb., 56, 200 (VI, 1)
Julesburg, Colo., 56, 200 (VI, 4)

Kearney, Neb., 53, 200 (V, 6)
Kearney Junction, Neb., 53, *53*, 200 (V, 6)
Kelton, Utah, 112

Lake Point, Utah, *101*, 103
Lake Tahoe, pollution of, 141
Laramie, Wyo., 77–78, 88 *77–78*
Laramie Plains, 75–77, 88–89
Lathrop, Calif., 168, *168*
Latter-Day Saints, 96–110. *See also* Mormons
Leslie, Frank, *5–8*
Leslie, Miriam Squier, 7–8
Leslie, Sarah Welham, 6
Leslie excursion, background, 5–9.
Leslie excursion train, 13–14, *29–32*
  arrival in Chicago, 20
  arrival at Columbus, *49*
  arrival at Council Bluffs, *34*
  at Clark's, *50–51*
  daily routine in the Palace Car, 124–126
  departure, 12–13
  dining on, *125*
  fellow travelers in other cars, 128–132, *132*
  members of excursion, 7, 12
  paper wheels, 28
  the "President" hotel car, 28–32
  provisioning, 28–29, 132
  scenes on board, *128–132*
Leslie publications, 6
Lion House, Salt Lake City, 104
Lippincott, Sara Jane Clarke, 72, 201 (VIII, 3)
Livermore Pass, 168
Livermore Valley, 168
Lockport, N. Y., *13*, 14
Lockwood, Neb., 52
Lodge Pole, Neb., 57–58
Lone Mountain, 178, 205 (XVIII, 5)
Lone Tree, Neb., 52
Los Angeles in 1967 growth of, 197
  and San Francisco, differences in personality, 197

Mackay, John W., 204 (XV, 4, 7)
"Maiden's Grave," 116
Manitou, Colo., 72, 74
Marshall, John, 163
Medicine Bow Mountains, 76, 78–79
Medicine Bow Station, Wyo., 79, 202 (IX, 8)
Melrose, Calif., 168
Mennonites, 49, *50–51*
Mills, Darius Ogden, and Virginia and Truckee Railroad, 203 (XV, 1)
Mines, silver, draft regulator, 149
  drifts, 148
  interior of, *138–154*, 139, 143–155.
  levels, 146
  low passage, 149
  ore cars, 147
  pumping water from, 152

shoring up, 154
starting a new drift, 154
stope, 148, 204 (XVI, 1)
timber shop, 153
Mining silver, amalgama-
tion process, 155–158
assaying, 158
crushing or stamp mill,
155
loading a bucket, 149
pan mill, 155–158
processing ore, 138, 155–
158, *155–158*
prospectors, *136*
typical miners, 144–146
Mission Dolores, 190
"Missouri Bottoms," 33–34
Monument Rock, *102*
Morgan City, Utah, 93–94
Mormon Tabernacle,
103–104, 203 (XI, 11)
Mormon Temple, 103, 203
(XI, 10)
Mormons, 96–110
Gentiles, 202 (X, 6)
immigration from
Council Bluffs, 203
(XI, 6)
"Jack Mormon," 202
(X, 6)
Joseph Smith, 104–105
Nauvoo Legion, 202
(X, 3)
physical characteristics
and appearance, 97
polygamy, women's views
on, 98–101
present-day, 109–110
"sealing," 100
secret rites, 103
sermons, 97
Morton, J. Sterling, 200
(V, 1)
Mount Davidson, Nev., 136
"Mucca mucca," 113, 203
(XII, 4)

Nebraska, 37–61
Arbor Day, 44, 57, *57,*
59, 200 (V, 1)
homesteading, advantages
of, 40–41
in 1967, 42–43, 54–55,
62–63
oil in, 63
Nevada, 112–123, 134–162
Carson City, 134–135,
134–135
currency, 116, 160
in 1967, 122–123,
140–141, 160–161
Paiute Indians, 116–117
Reno, in 1967, 140–141
silver mines. See Mines,
silver; Mining silver
State Capitol, 135, 203
(XV, 3)
Virginia City, 136–139,
143–161, 204
(XV, 5)
New York Central Railroad,
Lake Shore route,
17, *21*
Niagara Falls, N. Y., 14–17,
14–16
Nichols, Neb., 56
North, Frank, 56, 200 (VI, 2)
North, Luther, 200 (VI, 2)
North Bend, Neb., 46
North Platte, Neb., 56
North Platte Valley, 80

Oakland, Calif., 168–169,
169, 204 (XVII, 3)
O'Brien, William S., 136,
138–139, 204 (XV, 4, 7)
O'Fallon's, Neb., 56
Ogden, Utah, 96–97, 109
Old Zip Coon, 68, *68*
Omaha, Neb., 37–43
bridge over Missouri, *40*
Cozzens House, 37, 200
(IV, 2)
depot, *38–39, 41*
"Emigrant House,"
38–39, 40

emigrant waiting room,
38–39
emigrants for Black Hills,
37–40
in 1967, 42–43
Post Office and Courts
Building, 37, 200
(IV, 1)
Ophir Mine, 151
Otoe Indians, 79–80
Overland Stage Company,
56
Overton, Neb., 56, 200
(VI, 1)

Paiute Indians, 116–117
burial customs, 116–117,
203 (XII, 5)
fishing technique, 121
rabbit hunting technique,
121
Palace Hotel, San Fran-
cisco, 172–175,
173–175, 177
Palisade, Nev., 115, *119*
Palmer, William Jackson,
74, 201 (VIII, 4)
Parmelee Transportation
Company, 199 (III, 1)
Pawnee Indians, 201 (VI, 8)
"Pawnee Battalion," 200
(VI, 2)
Pawnee Reservation, 52
scouts, *50–51,* 56, 58
Philadelphia and Reading
Railroad, and Union
Engineers, 31
Piedmont, Wyo., 83–85,
84–85, 87
Pike's Peak House, 73
Pine Bluff, Neb., 61
Plains, 44–71
Platte River Valley, 44–56,
45–47
Plum Creek, Neb., 56
Plum Creek Battle, 56, 200
(VI, 1)
Point of Rocks, Wyo., 81
Potter, Neb., 61
Prairie dogs, 49, *50–51*
Profile Rock, *102*
Promontory, Utah, 96, 111,
202 (XI, 1), 203 (XII, 2)
Pullman, George Mortimer,
28, *29,* 199 (I, 1; II, 8)
Pullman cars, description
of, 35
paper wheels, 28
patent disputes, 199 (I, 1)
the "President," 28–32
provisioning, 28–29, 132
sleeping cars, 199 (II, 8)
Pullman Company, present-
day activities, 35
Pulpit Rock, 90

Railroads. *See specific*
railroads.
Ralston, William A., 190,
193
Belmont Mansion, *194,*
205 (XX, 9)
and Virginia & Truckee
Railroad, 203 (XV, 1)
Rawlins, Wyo., 80, *80,* 88
Redwood, Calif., 195
René (Reni), Jules, 200
(VI, 4)
Reno, Nev., in 1967,
140–141
Rochester, N. Y., 13
Rock Creek, Wyo., 79,
202 (IX, 6)
Rock Creek House, *78*
Rock River Valley, 33
"Rocky Mountain Curi-
osities," 83, 118
Royal China Theatre, San
Francisco, 182–184,
183–185

Sacramento City, 166, *166*
Sacramento Valley,
166–167

St. George, Utah,
2–3 (XI, 7)
Salt Lake City, 97–101,
103–104. *See also*
Mormons; Young,
Brigham
Amelia Palace, 104,
203 (XI, 13)
Beehive House, 104, 110
Lion House, 104
Main Street at news of
Brigham Young's
death, *108*
in 1967, 109–110
President's houses, 104
"Women's Union,"
98–99
San Francisco, 172–195
airport, 196
Baldwin Hotel and
Theatre, 190–191,
191, 205 (XX, 4)
Barbary Coast, 178, 205
(XVIII, 6)
Board of Brokers, 178
business section, 176, *177*
Chinatown, 182–189,
183–188. See also
Chinatown, San
Francisco
churches, 174
City Hall, 190, 205
(XX, 2)
Cliff House, 178
climate, 173–174
County Jail, 178–179
French quarter, 195
Golden Gate Park, 178
International Settlement,
205 (XVIII, 6)
Lone Mountain, 178, 205
(XVIII, 5)
to Los Angeles by air,
196–197
and Los Angeles,
differences in
personality, 197
Mark Hopkins house,
205 (XX, 5)
Mission Dolores, 190
a modern tourist in, 180–
181
Montgomery Street, 176,
177
naming of, 174, 204
(XVIII, 2)
in 1967, 180–181, 188–
189
Palace Hotel, 172–175,
173–175, 177
personality of city, 1967,
180
restaurants, 174
Sansome Street view, *177*
seals at Seal Rocks, 178,
205 (XVIII, 4)
social classes, 174
women's clothing, 174
Woodward's Gardens,
174–178, 205
(XVIII, 3)
Zoological Gardens, 178
San Francisco Bay, 169
Scalping survivor of, 81–83
Schuyler, Neb., 48, *48,* 200
(V, 3)
Seal Rocks, 178, 205
(XVIII, 4)
Secret Town, Calif., 163
Sentinal Rock, 90
Sharon, William, 136, 138–
139, 193–195, 204
(XV, 4)
family of, 205 (XX, 10)
and Virginia & Truckee
Railroad, 203
(XV, 1)
Sherman, Wyo., 75, *76*
Sherman Hill route, 201
(IX, 1)
"Ship of the Plains," 57
Shoshone Indians, 113–114
Sidney, Neb., 58–61, *59,* 201
(VI, 5)

emigrant outfitting shops,
60, *60*
in 1967, 62–63
street of "dug-outs,"
58–59
Sierra crossing, 162–163
Silver City, Nev., 136
Silver Creek, Indians at, 52
Silver dollars,
disappearance of, 161
Silver mining, 143–159. *See*
also Mines, silver;
Mining silver
Sioux Army Depot, 63
Sioux surrender, 31
Skull Rocks, 75
Slabtown, 199 (II, 1). *See*
also Chicago
Slade, Joseph A. (Jack), 56,
75, 200 (VI, 4)
Smith, Joseph, 104–105
Smith, Perry H., 199 (II, 7)
Snow, Eliza R., 98–99, 100,
105, 203 (XI, 5)
Snow fences, *84, 89*
Snowsheds, 162
Soule, John Babson Lane,
200 (IV, 3)
Southern Pacific Railroad,
Automatic Buffet Car,
in 1967, 126–127
mill and shops at
Oakland, 168–169,
204 (XVII, 4)
Night Mail, Reno to San
Francisco, 170–171
Squier, Miriam, 6–8
Stage coach departure, 118,
118
Stanford, Leland, at gold
spike ceremony, 202
(XI, 1)
mansion of, 190–193, *192*
Stanford, Leland Jr., 193,
205 (XX, 8)
Steamboat Rocks, 90
Stevenson, Neb., 56, 200
(VI, 1)
Stockton, Calif., 167–168
Stone House, Nev., 117, 203
(XII, 6)
Stope, 148, 204 (XVI, 1)
Strong's Canyon, Calif., 162
Summit Lake, 72
Summit Station, Calif., 162
Sutro, Adolph, 204 (XVI, 5)
Sutro Tunnel, 204 (XVI, 5)
Sutter, John A., 163

Tamarack, Calif., 162
Tecoma, Utah, 112
Territorial Enterprise, 161
"Thousand Mile Tree," 92
Tides and Jessup, in Gold
Hill murder, 151, 204
(XVI, 3)
Tie Siding, Wyo., 77, 201
(IX, 2)
Toledo, Ohio, 18, *18*
Tracy, Neb., 61
Train, George Francis, 37,
200 (IV, 2)
Tramps and trains, 130–
131, *130–131*
Transcontinental railroad,
economic importance
of junction point, 203
(XII, 2)
gold spike ceremony at
Promontory, 96, 111,
202 (XI, 1)
Tremont House, Chicago,
22, 199 (II, 4)
Truckee, Calif., 162
Tunnels through Wasatch
Mountains, 93
Turin Mountains, 75
Turkey Leg, Cheyenne
chief, 56
Twelve-Mile Canyon, 115,
115

Uinta Mountains, 83–84
Union Pacific Railroad,
changing mails, 55

City of San Francisco,
35–36
depot at Cheyenne, *75*
Emigrant House, Omaha,
40
Ogden Junction, *97*
snow plows, *87*
Union Stockyards, Chicago,
199 (II, 5)
U.S. Army of the West,
90, 108, 202 (X, 2)
U.S. Mint, Carson City,
135, 203 (XV, 2)
Utah, 90–112. *See also*
Mormons; Young,
Brigham
defiance of Federal
authority, 90, 108,
202 (X, 2)
in 1967, 109–110
Utah Central Railroad, 96,
202 (XI, 2)
Ute Pass, 72–74

Virginia City, Nev., 136–
139, 143–159, 204
(XV, 5). *See also*
Mines, silver; Mining
silver
Virginia & Truckee
Railroad, 135–136, 203
(XV, 1)

Wagner, Webster, 199 (I, 1)
Wagner drawing room car,
199 (I, 1)
Wahsatch, Utah, 90, 202
(X, 1)
Wasatch Mountains, 90–93,
95
Washoe Indians, burial
customs, 203 (XII, 5)
Waterloo Station, Neb., 44–
45
Weber, John G., 202 (X, 4)
Weber Canyon, Devil's
Gate, *93*
Weber River, 90, 92–93,
202 (X, 4)
Wells, Daniel H., 90, 202
(X, 3)
Wells, Nev., 112, *113*
Wheaton College, 32, 200
(III, 4)
Wilcox Station train
robbery, 79, 202 (IX, 7)
Wilson's Ravine, 162
Wind River Mountains, 78,
80
Windmill manufacture at
Batavia, 33
Winnemucca, Nev., 117–
118, *118*
Winnemucca, Paiute chief,
117, 117–118
Woodbine, Iowa, 33–34
Woodward's Gardens, 174–
178, 205 (XVIII, 3)
Wyoming, 64–89
Indian raids, 79–80
mountain lions, 83

Yerba Buena, early name
for San Francisco, 204
(XVIII, 2)
Yerba Buena Island, 169,
204 (XVII, 5)
Young, Amelia, 98, *99,* 203
(XI, 13)
Young, Ann Eliza, 98, 202
(XI, 3)
Young, Brigham,
biographical sketch, 108
death of, 106, 108
interview with, 104–106,
106–107
residences of, *99*
wives and family, 98, *99,*
100, 105, 202–203
(XI, 3–5, 13)

Zion Cooperative
Mercantile Institution
(ZCMI), 93–94, 202
(X, 7)

This book was printed by the American Book — Stratford Press on white Shelley Lithobulk paper. The type faces are Craw Clarendon and Century Schoolbook, composition by Atherton's Typography. Designed by John Beyer.